Electronic Flashcards now available for your Palm device as well!

✔ Download the Flashcards to your Palm device, and go on the road. Now you can study anywhere, any time.

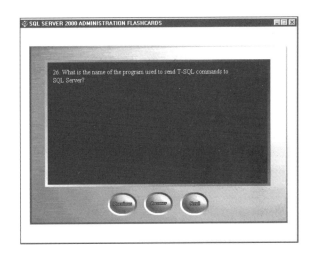

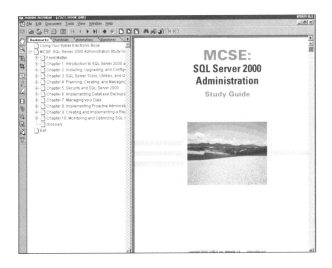

Search through the complete book in PDF.

✔ Access the entire *MCSE: SQL Server 2000 Administration Study Guide*, complete with figures and tables, in electronic format.

✔ Search the *MCSE: SQL Server 2000 Administration Study Guide* chapters to find information on any topic in seconds.

SYBEX

MCSE: SQL Server 2000 Administration Study Guide

Exam 70-288

SYBEX

Exam competencies are subject to change at any time without prior notice and at Lotus's sole discretion. Please visit the Lotus Certification Web site (http://www.lotus.com/home.nsf/welcome/certification) for the most current listing of exam competencies.

SYBEX

MCSE:
SQL Server 2000
Administration
Study Guide

MCSE:
SQL Server™ 2000
Administration
Study Guide

Lance Mortensen

Rick Sawtell

Joseph L. Jorden

San Francisco • Paris • Düsseldorf • Soest • London

SYBEX

Associate Publisher: Neil Edde
Contracts and Licensing Manager: Kristine O'Callaghan
Acquisitions and Developmental Editor: Jeff Kellum
Editors: Judy Flynn, Sally Engelfried
Production Editor: Liz Burke
Technical Editor: Gregory A. Beamer
Book Designer: Bill Gibson
Graphic Illustrator: Tony Jonnick
Electronic Publishing Specialist: Susie Hendrickson
Proofreaders: Yariv Rabinovitch, Laurie O'Connell, Andrea Fox, Amy Garber, Sarah Tannehill
Indexer: Nancy Guenther
CD Coordinator: Christine Harris
CD Technician: Kevin Ly
Cover Designer: Archer Design
Cover Photographer: The Image Bank

Library of Congress Control Number: 2001088051

ISBN: 0-7821-2921-8

SYBEX

To Our Valued Readers:

In recent years, Microsoft's MCSE program has established itself as the premier computer and networking industry certification. Nearly a quarter of a million IT professionals have attained MCSE status in the NT 4 track. Sybex is proud to have helped thousands of MCSE candidates prepare for their exams over these years, and we are excited about the opportunity to continue to provide people with the skills they'll need to succeed in the highly competitive IT industry.

For the Windows 2000 MCSE track, Microsoft has made it their mission to demand more of exam candidates. Exam developers have gone to great lengths to raise the bar in order to prevent a paper-certification syndrome, one in which individuals obtain a certification without a thorough understanding of the technology. Sybex welcomes this new philosophy as we have always advocated a comprehensive instructional approach to certification courseware. It has always been Sybex's mission to teach exam candidates how new technologies work in the real world, not to simply feed them answers to test questions. Sybex was founded on the premise of providing technical skills to IT professionals, and we have continued to build on that foundation, making significant improvements to our study guides based on feedback from readers, suggestions from instructors, and comments from industry leaders.

The depth and breadth of technical knowledge required to obtain Microsoft's new Windows 2000 MCSE is staggering. Sybex has assembled some of the most technically skilled instructors in the industry to write our study guides, and we're confident that our Windows 2000 MCSE study guides will meet and exceed the demanding standards both of Microsoft and you, the exam candidate.

Good luck in pursuit of your MCSE!

Neil Edde
Associate Publisher—Certification
Sybex, Inc.

SYBEX Inc. 1151 Marina Village Parkway, Alameda, CA 94501
Tel: 510/523-8233   Fax: 510/523-2373   HTTP://www.sybex.com

This book is dedicated to the many SQL students and study guide readers we've had over the years. We hope your new knowledge of SQL Server has helped you in your employment.

Lance Mortensen

For my wife Rachelle, for waiting on the shores while I went on yet another writing odyssey.

Joseph L. Jorden

Acknowledgments

I would like thank Joe for stepping in to help with the book.

Thanks also to my great family: Luann for putting up with me, Bryce for playing Mage Knight with me, Jessany for being my princess, Devin for playing MechWarrior with me, and Logan for taking naps with me. Life would be pretty boring without all of you.

Lance Mortensen

Thanks first to Rick Sawtell for his hard work that laid the foundation for my sections of this book. And to Lance Mortensen, it has been a privilege to author with you once again.

I also need to thank some friends and family. Mom, as always, I know these books couldn't happen without you. Jason and Jeanine Derr, thanks for helping me to see how bad I am at poker. Bob and Jeanette Haskett, we've had too much fun to recount, so thanks for all the good times. Grant Gipson, thanks for letting me tag along all of those early mornings. Special thanks to Randy Dugger and Jim Crutchfield, let's go make some money. Finally, and most importantly, thanks to my beloved wife Rachelle for being patient while I wrote yet another book.

Joseph L. Jorden

We both would like to thank everyone at Sybex once again for a job well done. Thanks to Neil for getting the project off the ground, Jeff overseeing it, Liz for making sure everything was in, and Judy and Sally for being great editors. Thanks also to Nancy Guenther for the indexing and Yariv Rabinovitch, Amy Garber, Andrea Fox, Laurie O'Connell, and Sarah Tannehill for proofreading, as well as Susie Hendrickson for the composition.

Contents at a Glance

Contents

Table of Exercises

Introduction

Microsoft's new Microsoft Certified Systems Engineer (MCSE) track for Windows 2000 is the premier certification for computer industry professionals. Covering the core technologies around which Microsoft's future will be built, the new MCSE certification is a powerful credential for career advancement.

This book has been developed to give you the critical skills and knowledge you need to prepare for one of the elective requirements of the new MCSE certification program for SQL Server 2000 Administration. You will find the information you need to acquire a solid understanding of SQL Server 2000, to prepare for Exam 70-228, Installing, Configuring, and Administering Microsoft® SQL Server™ 2000 Enterprise Edition, and to progress toward MCSE certification.

Why Become Certified in Windows 2000?

As the computer network industry grows in both size and complexity, the need for *proven* ability is increasing. Companies rely on certifications to verify the skills of prospective employees and contractors.

Whether you are just getting started or are ready to move ahead in the computer industry, the knowledge, skills, and credentials you have are your most valuable assets. Microsoft has developed its Microsoft Certified Professional (MCP) program to give you credentials that verify your ability to work with Microsoft products effectively and professionally. The MCP credential for professionals who work with Microsoft Windows 2000 networks is the new MCSE certification.

Over the next few years, companies around the world will deploy millions of copies of Windows 2000 as the central operating system for their mission-critical networks. This will generate an enormous need for qualified consultants and personnel to design, deploy, and support Windows 2000 networks.

Windows 2000 is a huge product that requires professional skills of its administrators. Consider that Windows NT 4 has about 12 million lines of code, while Windows 2000 has more than 35 million! Much of this code is needed to deal with the wide range of functionality that Windows 2000 offers.

Windows 2000 actually consists of several different versions:

Windows 2000 Professional The client edition of Windows 2000. It's comparable to Windows NT 4 Workstation 4, but also includes the best features of Windows 98 and many new features.

Windows 2000 Server/Windows 2000 Advanced Server A server edition of Windows 2000 for small to mid-sized deployments. Advanced Server supports more memory and processors than Server does.

Windows 2000 Datacenter Server A server edition of Windows 2000 for large, wide-scale deployments and computer clusters. Datacenter Server supports the most memory and processors of the three versions.

With such an expansive operating system, companies need to be certain that you are the right person for the job being offered. The MCSE is designed to help prove that you are.

 As part of its promotion of Windows 2000, Microsoft has announced that MCSEs who have passed the Windows NT 4 core exams must upgrade their certifications to the new Windows 2000 track by December 31, 2001, to remain certified. The Network Press MCSE Study Guide series, published by Sybex, covers the full range of exams required for either obtaining or upgrading your certification. For more information, see the "Exam Requirements" section later in this Introduction.

Is This Book for You?

If you want to acquire a solid foundation in SQL Server 2000, this book is for you. You'll find clear explanations of the fundamental concepts you need to grasp.

If you want to become certified as an MCSE, this book is definitely for you. However, if you just want to attempt to pass the exam without really understanding SQL Server 2000, this book is *not* for you. This book is written for those who want to acquire hands-on skills and in-depth knowledge of SQL Server 2000.

If your goal is to prepare for the exam by learning how to use and manage a great database system, this book is for you. It will help you to achieve the high level of professional competency you need to succeed in this field.

What Does This Book Cover?

This book contains detailed explanations, hands-on exercises, and review questions to test your knowledge.

Think of this book as your complete guide to SQL Server 2000. It begins by covering the most basic concepts, such as the features of the database engine and how to install and configure it. Next, you will learn how to perform important tasks, including:

- Upgrading and configuring SQL Server

- Using the SQL Server utilities to administer your system

- Creating and managing databases and users

- Setting up database security

- Backing up and restoring databases

- Automating maintenance tasks

- Managing, copying, and moving data

- Setting up replication

- Tuning SQL Server performance

- Troubleshooting SQL Server

Throughout the book, you will be guided through hands-on exercises, which give you practical experience for each exam objective. At the end of each chapter, you'll find a summary of the topics covered in the chapter and a list of the key terms used. The key terms represent not only the terminology that you should recognize, but also the underlying concepts that you should understand to pass the exam. All of the key terms are defined in the glossary at the back of the study guide.

Finally, each chapter concludes with 20 review questions that test your knowledge of the information covered. You'll find an entire practice exam, with 60 additional questions, in Appendix A. Many more questions (another complete practice test) are included on the CD that accompanies this book, as explained in "What's on the CD?" at the end of this introduction.

The topics covered in this book map directly to Microsoft's official exam objectives. Each exam objective is covered completely.

How Do You Become an MCSE?

Attaining MCSE certification has always been a challenge. However, in the past, individuals could acquire detailed exam information—even most of the exam questions—from online "brain dumps" and third-party "cram" books or software products. For the new MCSE exams, this simply will not be the case.

To avoid the "paper-MCSE syndrome" (a devaluation of the MCSE certification because unqualified individuals manage to pass the exams), Microsoft has taken strong steps to protect the security and integrity of the new MCSE track. Prospective MSCEs will need to complete a course of study that provides not only detailed knowledge of a wide range of topics, but true skills derived from working with Windows 2000 and related software products.

In the new MCSE program, Microsoft is heavily emphasizing hands-on skills. Microsoft has stated that "nearly half of the core required exams' content demands that the candidate have troubleshooting skills acquired through hands-on experience and working knowledge."

Fortunately, if you are willing to dedicate time and effort with Windows 2000, you can prepare for the exams by using the proper tools. If you work through this book and the other books in this series, you should successfully meet the exam requirements.

 This book is a part of a series of MCSE Study Guides, published by Sybex, that covers the five core requirements as well as the electives you need to complete your MCSE track.

Exam Requirements

Successful candidates must pass a minimum set of exams that measure technical proficiency and expertise:

- Candidates for MCSE certification must pass seven exams, including four core operating system exams, one design exam, and two electives.

- Candidates who have already passed three Windows NT 4 exams (70-067, 70-068, and 70-073) may opt to take an "accelerated" exam plus one core design exam and two electives.

 If you do not pass the accelerated exam after one attempt, you must pass the five core requirements and two electives.

The following tables show the exams a new certification candidate must pass. *All* of the exams in this first table are required:

Exam #	Title	Requirement Met
70-216	Implementing and Administering a Microsoft® Windows® 2000 Network Infrastructure	Core (Operating System)
70-210	Installing, Configuring, and Administering Microsoft® Windows® 2000 Professional	Core (Operating System)
70-215	Installing, Configuring, and Administering Microsoft® Windows® 2000 Server	Core (Operating System)
70-217	Implementing and Administering a Microsoft® Windows® 2000 Directory Services Infrastructure	Core (Operating System)

One of these exams is required:

Exam #	Title	Requirement Met
70-219	Designing a Microsoft® Windows® 2000 Directory Services Infrastructure	Core (Design)

70-220	Designing Security for a Microsoft® Windows® 2000 Network	Core (Design)
70-221	Designing a Microsoft® Windows® 2000 Network Infrastructure	Core (Design)

Two of these exams are required:

Exam #	Title	Requirement Met
70-219	Designing a Microsoft® Windows® 2000 Directory Services Infrastructure	Elective
70-220	Designing Security for a Microsoft® Windows® 2000 Network	Elective
70-221	Designing a Microsoft® Windows® 2000 Network Infrastructure	Elective
70-228	Installing, Configuring, and Administering Microsoft® SQL Server™ 2000 Enterprise Edition	Elective
Any current MCSE elective	Exams cover topics such as Exchange Server, SQL Server, Systems Management Server, Internet Explorer Administrators Kit, and Proxy Server (new exams are added regularly)	Elective

For a more detailed description of the Microsoft certification programs, including a list of current MCSE electives, check Microsoft's Training and Certification Web site at www.microsoft.com/trainingandservices.

The Installing, Configuring, and Administering Microsoft® SQL Server™ 2000 Enterprise Edition Exam

The System Administration for SQL Server 2000 Certification exam covers concepts and skills required for the support of SQL Server 2000. It emphasizes the following areas:

- SQL Server hardware and software requirements
- Installing SQL Server
- Configuring SQL Server
- Creating databases and their devices
- Creating and managing transaction logs
- Backing up databases
- Backing up transaction logs
- Creating SQL Server users
- Managing database security
- Tuning SQL Server
- Replicating data
- Troubleshooting

If we had to create a single sentence to describe the test, it would be as follows: The exam will test your knowledge of tuning, configuring, and creating databases on SQL Server 2000; backing up and restoring databases on SQL Server 2000; and managing security on SQL Server 2000. To pass the test, you need to fully understand these topics.

Microsoft provides exam objectives to give you a very general overview of possible areas of coverage of the Microsoft exams. For your convenience, we have added in-text objectives listings at the points in the text where specific Microsoft exam objectives are covered. However, exam objectives are subject to change at any time without prior notice and at Microsoft's sole discretion. Please visit Microsoft's Training and Certification Web site (www.microsoft.com/trainingandservices) for the most current exam objectives listing.

Types of Exam Questions

In the previous tracks, the formats of the MCSE exams were fairly straightforward, consisting almost entirely of multiple-choice questions appearing in a few different sets. Prior to taking an exam, you knew how many questions you would see and what type of questions would appear. If you had purchased the right third-party exam preparation products, you could even be quite familiar with the pool of questions you might be asked. As mentioned earlier, all of this is changing.

In an effort to both refine the testing process and protect the quality of its certifications, Microsoft has introduced adaptive testing, as well as some new exam elements. You will not know in advance which type of format you will see on your exam. These innovations make the exams more challenging, and they make it much more difficult for someone to pass an exam after simply "cramming" for it.

Microsoft will be accomplishing its goal of protecting the exams by regularly adding and removing exam questions, limiting the number of questions that any individual sees in a beta exam, limiting the number of questions delivered to an individual by using adaptive testing, and adding new exam elements.

Exam questions may be in multiple-choice, select-and-place, simulation, or case study–based formats. You may also find yourself taking an adaptive format exam. Let's take a look at the exam question types and adaptive testing, so you can be prepared for all of the possibilities.

Multiple-Choice Questions

Multiple-choice questions include two main types. One is a straightforward type that presents a question followed by several possible answers, of which one or more is correct.

You will see many multiple-choice questions in this study guide and on the accompanying CD, as well as on your exam.

Case Study–Based Questions

Case study–based questions first appeared in the Microsoft Certified Solution Developer program (Microsoft's certification program for software programmers). Case study–based questions present a scenario with a range of requirements. Based on the information provided, you need to answer a series of multiple-choice and ranking questions. The interface for case study–based questions has a number of tabs that each contains information about the scenario. Questions similar to this style appear on the SQL Server 2000 exam.

Exam Question Development

Microsoft follows an exam-development process consisting of eight mandatory phases. The process takes an average of seven months and involves more than 150 specific steps. The MCP exam development consists of the following phases:

Phase 1: Job Analysis Phase 1 is an analysis of all of the tasks that make up a specific job function, based on tasks performed by people who are currently performing that job function. This phase also identifies the knowledge, skills, and abilities that relate specifically to the performance area to be certified.

Phase 2: Objective Domain Definition The results of the job analysis provide the framework used to develop objectives. The development of objectives involves translating the job-function tasks into a comprehensive set of more specific and measurable knowledge, skills, and abilities. The resulting list of objectives—the *objective domain*—is the basis for the development of both the certification exams and the training materials.

Phase 3: Blueprint Survey The final objective domain is transformed into a blueprint survey in which contributors are asked to rate each objective. These contributors may be past MCP candidates, appropriately skilled exam development volunteers, or Microsoft employees. Based on the contributors' input, the objectives are prioritized and weighted. The actual exam items are written according to the prioritized objectives. Contributors are queried about how they spend their time on the job. If a contributor doesn't spend an adequate amount of time actually performing the specified job function, his or her data is eliminated from the analysis. The blueprint survey phase helps determine which objectives to measure, as well as the appropriate number and types of items to include on the exam.

Phase 4: Item Development   A pool of items is developed to measure the blueprinted objective domain. The number and types of items to be written are based on the results of the blueprint survey.

Phase 5: Alpha Review and Item Revision   During this phase, a panel of technical and job-function experts reviews each item for technical accuracy, then answers each item, reaching a consensus on all technical issues. Once the items have been verified as technically accurate, they are edited to ensure that they are expressed in the clearest language possible.

Phase 6: Beta Exam   The reviewed and edited items are collected into beta exams. Based on the responses of all beta participants, Microsoft performs a statistical analysis to verify the validity of the exam items and to determine which items will be used in the certification exam. Once the analysis has been completed, the items are distributed into multiple parallel forms, or *versions*, of the final certification exam.

Phase 7: Item Selection and Cut-Score Setting   The results of the beta exams are analyzed to determine which items should be included in the certification exam based on many factors, including item difficulty and relevance. During this phase, a panel of job-function experts determines the *cut score* (minimum passing score) for the exams. The cut score differs from exam to exam because it is based on an item-by-item determination of the percentage of candidates who answered the item correctly and who would be expected to answer the item correctly.

Phase 8: Live Exam   As the final phase, the exams are given to candidates. MCP exams are administered by Sylvan Prometric and Virtual University Enterprises (VUE).

Microsoft will regularly add and remove questions from the exams. This is called item seeding. It is part of the effort to make it more difficult for individuals to merely memorize exam questions passed along by previous test-takers.

Tips for Taking the SQL Server 2000 Administration Exam

Here are some general tips for taking the exam successfully:

- Arrive early at the exam center so you can relax and review your study materials. During your final review, you can look over tables and lists of exam-related information.

- Read the questions carefully. Don't be tempted to jump to an early conclusion. Make sure you know *exactly* what the question is asking.

- Answer all questions. Remember that the adaptive format will *not* allow you to return to a question. Be very careful before entering your answer. Because your exam may be shortened by correct answers (and lengthened by incorrect answers), there is no advantage to rushing through questions.

- On simulations, do not change settings that are not directly related to the question. Also, assume default settings if the question does not specify or imply which settings are used.

- Use a process of elimination to get rid of the obviously incorrect answers first on questions that you're not sure about. This method will improve your odds of selecting the correct answer if you need to make an educated guess.

Exam Registration

You may take the exams at any of more than 1,000 Authorized Prometric Testing Centers (APTCs) and VUE Testing Centers around the world. For the location of a testing center near you, call Sylvan Prometric at 800-755-EXAM (755-3926), or call VUE at 888-837-8616. Outside the United States and Canada, contact your local Sylvan Prometric or VUE registration center.

You should determine the number of the exam you want to take and then register with the Sylvan Prometric or VUE registration center nearest to you. At this point, you will be asked for advance payment for the exam. The exams are $100 each. Exams must be taken within one year of payment. You can schedule exams up to six weeks in advance or as late as one working day prior to the date of the exam. You can cancel or reschedule your exam if you contact the center at least two working days prior to the exam. Same-day registration is available in some locations, subject to space availability. Where same-day registration is available, you must register a minimum of two hours before test time.

You may also register for your exams online at www.sylvanprometric.com or www.vue.com.

When you schedule the exam, you will be provided with instructions regarding appointment and cancellation procedures, ID requirements, and information about the testing center location. In addition, you will receive a registration and payment confirmation letter from Sylvan Prometric or VUE.

Microsoft requires certification candidates to accept the terms of a non-disclosure agreement before taking certification exams.

What's on the CD?

With this new book in our best-selling MCSE study guide series, we are including quite an array of training resources. On the CD are numerous simulations, practice exams, and flashcards to help you study for the exam. Also included are the entire contents of the study guide. These resources are described in the following sections.

The Sybex Ebook for the SQL Server 2000 Administration Study Guide

Many people like the convenience of being able to carry their whole study guide on a CD. They also like being able to search the text to find specific information quickly and easily. For these reasons, we have included the entire contents of this study guide on a CD, in PDF format. We've also included Adobe Acrobat Reader, which provides the interface for the contents, as well as the search capabilities.

The Sybex MCSE Edge Tests

The Edge Tests are a collection of multiple-choice questions that can help you prepare for your exam. There are three sets of questions:

- Bonus questions specially prepared for this edition of the study guide, including 60 questions that appear only on the CD

- An adaptive test simulator that will give the feel for how adaptive testing works

- All of the questions from the study guide presented in a test engine for your review

A sample screen from the Sybex MCSE Edge Tests is shown below.

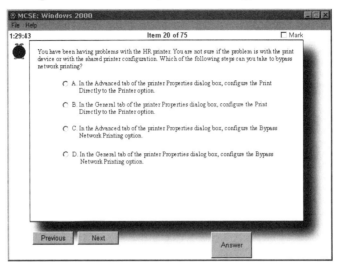

Sybex MCSE Flashcards for PCs and Palm Devices

The "flashcard" style of exam question offers an effective way to quickly and efficiently test your understanding of the fundamental concepts covered in the SQL Server 2000 Administration exam. The Sybex MCSE Flashcards set consists of 100 questions presented in a special engine developed specifically for this study guide series. The Sybex MCSE Flashcards interface is shown below.

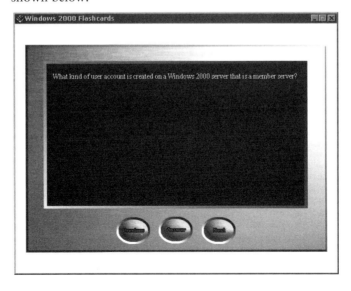

Because of the high demand for a product that will run on Palm devices, we have also developed, in conjunction with Land-J Technologies, a version of the flashcard questions that you can take with you on your Palm OS PDA (including the PalmPilot and Handspring's Visor).

How Do You Use This Book?

This book can provide a solid foundation for the serious effort of preparing for the SQL Server 2000 Administration exam. To best benefit from this book, you may wish to use the following study method:

1. Study each chapter carefully. Do your best to fully understand the information.

2. Complete all hands-on exercises in the chapter, referring back to the text as necessary so that you understand each step you take. Install the evaluation version of SQL Server and get some experience with the product.

3. Answer the review questions at the end of each chapter. If you would prefer to answer the questions in a timed and graded format, install the Edge Tests from the CD that accompanies this book and answer the chapter questions there instead of in the book.

4. Note which questions you did not understand and study the corresponding sections of the book again.

5. Make sure you complete the entire book.

6. Before taking the exam, go through the training resources included on the CD that accompanies this book. Try the adaptive version that is included with the Sybex MCSE Edge Test. Review and sharpen your knowledge with the MCSE Flashcards.

In order to install SQL Server 2000 to complete the exercises in this book, your hardware should meet the minimum hardware requirements for SQL Server 2000. See Chapter 2 for the minimum and recommended system requirements.

To learn all of the material covered in this book, you will need to study regularly and with discipline. Try to set aside the same time every day to study and select a comfortable and quiet place in which to do it. If you work hard, you will be surprised at how quickly you learn this material. Good luck!

Contacts and Resources

To find out more about Microsoft Education and Certification materials and programs, to register with Sylvan Prometric or VUE, or to get other useful information, check the following resources.

Microsoft Certification Development Team

www.microsoft.com/trainingandservices

Contact the Microsoft Certification Development Team through their Web site to volunteer for one or more exam development phases or to report a problem with an exam. The address for written correspondence is as follows:

Certification Development Team
Microsoft Education and Certification
One Microsoft Way
Redmond, WA 98052

Microsoft TechNet Technical Information Network

www.microsoft.com/technet/subscription/about.htm

(800) 344-2121

Use this Web site or number to contact support professionals and system administrators. Outside the United States and Canada, contact your local Microsoft subsidiary for information.

Microsoft Training and Certification Home Page

www.microsoft.com/trainingandservices

This Web site provides information about the MCP program and exams. You can also order the latest Microsoft Roadmap to Education and Certification.

PalmPilot Training Product Development: Land-J

www.land-j.com

(407) 359-2217

Land-J Technologies is a consulting and programming business currently specializing in application development for the 3Com PalmPilot Personal Digital Assistant. Land-J developed the Palm version of the Edge Tests, which is included on the CD that accompanies this study guide.

Sylvan Prometric

www.sylvanprometric.com

(800) 755-EXAM

Contact Sylvan Prometric to register to take an MCP exam at any of more than 800 Sylvan Prometric Testing Centers around the world.

Virtual University Enterprises (VUE)

www.vue.com

(888) 837-8616

Contact the VUE registration center to register to take an MCP exam at one of the VUE Testing Centers.

How to Contact the Authors

Lance Mortensen can be contacted at Lmortensen@teachresults-nv.com. Joseph L. Jorden can be contacted at JLJorden@pacbell.net.

Assessment Test

1. What is an acceptable sustained value for the % Processor Time counter?

   A. 70

   B. 75

   C. 80

   D. 85

2. You want to install SQL Server on a Windows 2000 cluster. Which of these versions could you use?

   A. Personal

   B. Developer

   C. Standard

   D. Enterprise

3. Linked servers are configured under which folder in Enterprise Manager?

   A. Servers

   B. Security

   C. Management

   D. Replication

4. If you want BCP to record an error file when performing imports or exports, which switch should you use?

   A. -E

   B. -e

   C. -err

   D. -ERR

5. You have a database that is acting weird when you run a set of queries. What command would you run to see if there was a problem?

   A. SELECT

   B. RESTORE

   C. DBCC CHECKDB

   D. DBCC TESTDB

6. Which of these recovery models allows you to recover your database up to the point of the last backup in the event of a crash:

   A. Simple

   B. Bulk-Logged

   C. Full

   D. Select Into/Bulk Copy

7. You install SQL Server Personal edition on your laptop running Windows 98. What security model can you run in?

   A. Integrated

   B. Standard

   C. Integrated or Standard

   D. Neither

8. You have Novell, Macintosh, and Windows clients on your network that all need access to SQL Server. Which authentication mode should you implement?

   A. Standard Authentication

   B. Mixed Mode

   C. Windows Authentication

9. Which of these can be installed as a named instance? (Select all that apply.)

   A. SQL Server 6.5

   B. SQL Server 7

   C. SQL Server 2000 Standard

   D. SQL Server 2000 Enterprise

10. Which command would you use to remove all free space from a data file and return it to the operating system?

    A. DBCC SHRINKDATABASE(*dbname*, notruncate)

    B. DBCC SHRINKDATABASE(*dbname*, truncateonly)

    C. DBCC SHRINKFILE(*dbname*, TRUNCATEONLY)

    D. DBCC SHRINKFILE(*dbname*, TRUNCATEONLY)

11. Which tool should be used to monitor SQL Server database engine activity on a regular basis?

    A. SQL Trace

    B. Query Analyzer

    C. Windows System Monitor

    D. Profiler

12. You install a default instance of SQL Server 2000. You have an application that must be isolated from other users. Resources are at a premium. What should you do?

    A. Install a new default instance in a different folder.

    B. Install a new default instance on a different server.

    C. Install a named instance in the same folder the default instance is in.

    D. Install a named instance in a different folder than the folder the default instance is in.

13. You are running SQL Server 6. You want to upgrade to SQL Server 2000. Which of these would not work?

    A. Do an in-place upgrade to SQL Server 2000.

    B. Do a side-by-side installation of SQL Server 2000 and then migrate the database.

    C. Upgrade to SQL Server 6.5 and then do an in-place upgrade to SQL Server 2000.

    D. Install SQL Server 2000 on a different computer and use DTS to copy the database.

14. What should you do if the Buffer Cache Hit Ratio counter is below 90?

    A. Nothing; this is acceptable.

    B. Add more RAM.

    C. Add another disk to the system.

    D. Purchase a faster processor.

15. Which of these commands will select all of the columns in the Authors table in the Pubs database? Your default database is Master, and you open a new query in Query Analyzer.

    A. SELECT * from pubs

    B. SELECT * from authors

    C. SELECT * from pubs.authors

    D. SELECT * from pubs..authors

16. You have a service set for the Local logon account. You set up e-mail and nothing happens. What do you need to do?

   A. Give the Local logon account the Logon as a Service right.

   B. Use a domain user account.

   C. Create an e-mail account for the Local logon account.

   D. Set a password on the Local logon account.

17. Which tools can you use to export data from a SQL Server table to a text file? (Select all that apply.)

   A. DTSRUNUI

   B. BCP

   C. BULK INSERT

   D. DTSRUN

18. John is a member of the accounting role, which has been granted SELECT permission on the accounting table. He is also a member of the sales role, which has been denied SELECT permission on the accounting table. The Public role has also been granted SELECT permission on the Accounting table. What happens when John tries to SELECT from the accounting table?

   A. He is allowed to select because he has been specifically granted the permission.

   B. He is not allowed to select because the sales role has been specifically denied the SELECT permission.

   C. He is allowed to select but he receives an error message warning him of the denied permission.

   D. He is allowed to select because the public role is granted the SELECT permission.

19. You manage 10 servers and you don't want to have to check each one of them. What feature should you use?

   A. MAPI operators

   B. Master and slave servers for jobs

   C. Event forwarding

   D. Alerts that check for severity 20 or higher

20. You regularly import data from text files into your inventory tables and you want to offload this task to one of your assistants. How can you do this?

    A. Add your assistant to the sysadmin fixed server role.

    B. Add your assistant to the bulkadmin fixed server role.

    C. Add your assistant to the db_owner fixed database role.

    D. Do nothing, the user already has permission to do this.

21. Microsoft SQL Server follows which standard?

    A. SQL Review

    B. ANSI SQL

    C. ISO SQL

    D. IEEE SQL

22. You just spent three days creating new indexes in your database. You are worried that you will need to re-create your work. How would you back up the indexes you just created?

    A. You don't—the indexes get re-created when you restore a backup.

    B. You don't—you have to manually rebuild the indexes after a backup.

    C. By performing a full backup.

    D. By performing a differential backup.

23. Which of the following replication servers contains the replicated data?

    A. Publisher

    B. Subscriber

    C. Distributor

    D. All of the above

24. What step(s) should you perform before switching a standby server to a production server? (Select all that apply.)

    A. Copy the syslogins to the standby server using DTS.

    B. Create the standby server with the Allow Database to Assume Primary Role option.

    C. Designate a folder for the transaction log directory on the standby server.

    D. Create a new transaction log backup on the production server.

25. Which database object would you use to force users to enter acceptable data in your tables?

 A. Trigger

 B. Index

 C. View

 D. Constraint

26. You have a database that tracks power usage at a substation. The same row gets updated every 5 seconds. You don't need to keep historical data. The database is online 24 hours a day and is in a single MDF file. You perform a full backup every weekend. What type of backup should you perform each night?

 A. Full

 B. Transactional

 C. Differential

 D. Filegroup

27. What is the name of the DLL that translates from XML to SQL in IIS?

 A. `Sqlisapi.dll`

 B. `Sqlxml.dll`

 C. `Iisxml.dll`

 D. `Sqliis.dll`

28. Which DTS object performs data transformation?

 A. Task

 B. Step

 C. Connection

 D. Data pump

29. When the distribution database transaction log fills up, what happens?

 A. Replication continues unabated.

 B. Replication continues but generates errors.

 C. Transactional and merge replication stop.

 D. All replication stops.

30. You have several servers that need to replicate data to one another using merge replication. Which replication model should you consider using?

A. Central subscriber/multiple publishers

B. Multiple publishers/multiple subscribers

C. Central publisher/central distributor

D. Central publisher/remote distributor

Answers to Assessment Test

1. A. The % Processor Time counter should be below 75 on a sustained basis.

2. D. Only the Enterprise version of SQL Server supports clusters. See Chapter 1 for more information.

3. B. Linked servers are created and configured under the Security folder of Enterprise Manager. There are no Servers and Replication folders, and the Management folder holds items such as the SQL Server Agent and backup information. See Chapter 3 for more information.

4. B. The -e err_file switch will cause BCP to record an error file that you can read if you run into problems with your BCP operation. See Chapter 7 for more information.

5. C. The DBCC CHECKDB command tests a database for errors. The SELECT command might show you weird results if there was a problem, but is not a reliable way to check for problems. You could restore the database, but you should check for actual problems first before you just restore it. There is no such command as DBCC TESTDB. See Chapter 3 for more information.

6. A. The simple recovery model in SQL Server 2000 is the equivalent of setting the Select Into/Bulk Copy option in previous versions of SQL Server. It bypasses the transaction log. See Chapter 4 for more information.

7. B. Windows 9*x*/Me cannot be run in integrated mode; they run in standard security mode. See Chapter 1 for more information.

8. B. There is no Standard mode in SQL Server 2000; you need Mixed Mode because there are a number of clients that do not have Windows accounts to be verified against. See Chapter 5 for more information.

9. C, D. All versions of SQL Server 2000 for servers support named instances. See Chapter 2 for more information.

10. B. The TRUNCATEONLY option is used to remove all free space from a database and return it to the operating system. See Chapter 4 for more information.

11. D. Profiler is used to monitor database engine activity.

12. D. To conserve resources, you can install a named instance on the same server the default instance is on. Named instances go in different folders than default instances. See Chapter 2 for more information.

13. A. If you have SQL Server 6, you have to upgrade to SQL Server 6.5 before you can do an in-place upgrade to SQL Server 2000. See Chapter 2 for more information.

14. B. When the Buffer Cache Hit Ratio counter falls below 90 on a sustained basis, it means that you need more RAM.

15. D. Because you are in the Master database, you need to specify both the database and table in the SELECT command. See Chapter 3 for more information.

16. B. In order to use e-mail, the SQL services must be assigned to a domain user account. See Chapter 8 for more information.

17. B. Of the tools listed, only BCP is capable of exporting from a table to a text file. See Chapter 7 for more information.

18. B. DENY takes precedence over any other permission state. Because John is a member of a group that has been denied SELECT permission, John loses the permission. See Chapter 5 for more information.

19. C. Event forwarding allows you to forward all unhandled events to a central server. See Chapter 8 for more information.

20. B. Adding the user to the sysadmin fixed server role would give the user permission to perform bulk inserts of data as well as a plethora of other unneeded permissions. Db_owner does not have permission to bulk insert, so you should add the user to the bulkadmin role. See Chapter 5 for more information.

21. B. SQL Server follows the ANSI standards for SQL relation servers. See Chapter 1 for more information.

22. C. When you perform a full backup, you get all of the indexes in a database. See Chapter 6 for more information.

23. B. The subscriber contains the replicated copy of the data. See Chapter 9 for more information.

24. A, B, C, D. All of these steps ensure that a standby server can successfully be switched to a production mode server. See Chapter 6 for more information.

25. D. Constraints are used to compare data that users try to input against a list of acceptable values. If the data from the user does not meet the confines of the constraint, it is rejected. See Chapter 4 for more information.

26. C. Differential backups would be great in this circumstance because you are only concerned with the current data, not historical, so you don't need individual transactions. See Chapter 6 for more information.

27. A. The Sqlisapi.dll program translates XML to SQL. See Chapter 8 for more information.

28. D. The data pump object performs data transformation as well as import and export of data. See Chapter 7 for more information.

29. D. All replication stops because all types of replication use the distribution database, even snapshot replication. See Chapter 9 for more information.

30. B. Answer B best fits the scenario because all of the servers will be publishers and subscribers. See Chapter 9 for more information.

Chapter

1

Introduction to SQL Server 2000 and Relational Databases

NOTE This chapter is here mostly for background material; no test objectives are directly addressed.

SQL Server 2000 is a client/server-based relational database management system that runs on Windows 2000 Professional, Server, and Advanced Server; Windows NT 4; Windows 9x/Millennium; or Windows CE. It's also included in Microsoft's BackOffice suite. In this chapter, we'll begin by defining a client/server environment, the types of databases involved, and what they contain. We'll then provide some background material on SQL Server and Windows 2000, including the new features of SQL Server 2000. In addition, we'll discuss the tasks of the SQL Server developer and those of the SQL Server administrator.

What Is Client/Server?

Microsoft's SQL Server is a client/server database engine. SQL Server is the server part of the equation.

Client/server can be defined as an application that is split into at least two parts: One part runs on a server, and the other part runs on client computers, or workstations. The server side of the application provides security, fault-tolerance, performance, concurrency, and reliable backups. The client side provides the user interface and may contain such items as empty reports, queries, and forms.

In older, non-client/server database systems, the work is not shared between the server and workstation machines. For example, suppose you have a 10MB database stored on your network server. When a client opens the database and runs a query, all 10MB are downloaded to the client and then the query is processed at the client computer (Figure 1.1).

FIGURE 1.1   In a non-client/server database system, the work is not shared between the server and the workstation computers.

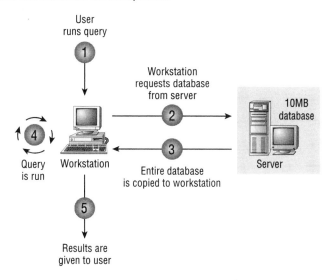

In contrast, when a query is run on a client/server system, the server searches the database and then sends back to the client just those rows that match the search conditions (Figure 1.2). This not only saves bandwidth on your network, it (if the server is a powerful enough machine) is often faster than having the workstations do all the work(although workstations still do some work even in client/server computing).

FIGURE 1.2   In a client/server application, the server and workstation share the work.

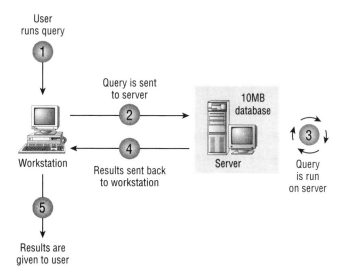

Types of Databases

A database can generally be thought of as a collection of related data that can be organized in various ways. The database can be designed to store historical data or changing data. In the following sections, we will take a look at the different types of databases.

Relational Databases vs. Flat-File Databases

In earlier database products, a database usually consisted of one file—something like `Payroll.dbf` for an employee file or `Patients.dbf` for use in a doctor's office. When all its information is stored in a single file, or *page,* and is accessed sequentially, the database resembles a spreadsheet and is considered a *flat-file database.* Many older database applications were flat-file databases. Although flat-file databases are relatively easy to set up, those that contain complex data are more difficult to maintain. A *relational database* is composed of tables that contain related data. The process of organizing data into tables (in a consistent and complete format) is referred to as *normalizing* the database.

Normalization of relational designs is a complex topic that will not be addressed in this book; it can be found in other books that are devoted to this topic. Before you implement your database design, however, you should start with a fully normalized view of the database.

In a relational database management system (RDBMS), such as SQL Server, while a database is held on one or more operating system files; it is more of a logical concept based on a collection of related *objects.* A database in SQL Server not only contains the raw data, it also contains the structure of the database, the security of the database, and any views or stored procedures related to that particular database.

A SQL Server database is composed of different types of objects (see Figure 1.3).

FIGURE 1.3   Common database objects

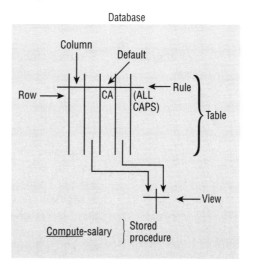

Table 1.1 lists some of the more common types of objects used in a database.

TABLE 1.1   Common Database Objects

Object	Description
Table	A table is the object that contains rows, columns, and the actual raw data.
Column	A column is a part of the table—the object that holds the data.
Row	A row is not a separate object, but rather a complete set of columns within a single table. Unlike the rest of the items discussed here, it is a logical construct, not a physically implemented object.
Datatype	There are various datatypes that can be used in columns, such as character, numeric, and date. A column can hold only data of a single datatype.

TABLE 1.1 Common Database Objects *(continued)*

Object	Description
Stored procedure	A stored procedure is a set of Transact-SQL (T-SQL) statements that are combined to perform a single task or set of tasks. This object is like a macro, in that SQL code can be written and stored under a name. By invoking the name, you actually run the code.
Trigger	A trigger is an object that is a stored procedure that activates when data is added to, edited, or deleted from a table. Triggers are used to implement business rules in the database. For example, an automobile dealer's database might contain a trigger that activates when a car is sold and credits the appropriate salesperson with a bonus depending of the profit from the sale.
Rule	A rule is an object that is assigned to a column so that data being entered conforms to standards you set. For example, rules can be used to make sure that the state in a person's address is entered in uppercase letters and that phone numbers contain only numbers.
Default	A default is an object that is assigned to a column so that, if no data is entered, the default value will be used. For example, you might set the state code to the state where most of your customers reside so the default can be accepted for most entries.
View	A view is much like a stored query. You don't need to rewrite the query every time you'd like to run it; you can use the view instead. A view appears very much like a table to most users. A view usually either excludes certain fields from a table or links two or more tables together.
Index	An index is a way of storing data or metadata about your data so that retrievals are much faster.

Data Warehousing vs. Transaction Processing

Databases fall into two general categories:

- Stored historical data that can be queried. This is often referred to as *data warehousing* or *decision support systems*. The main focus of data warehousing is the ability to quickly query existing data and perform complex analyses, usually looking for patterns or other relationships that are difficult to locate during the day-to-day operations of a company.

- Live, continually changing data. This type of database activity is referred to as an *OLTP (Online Transaction Processing)*. In this case, the flexibility to expand and edit the database is the main focus.

Although these types of databases may appear to be the same at first glance, they are basically opposites. Data warehousing emphasizes reading the historical database with long-running transactions; OLTP emphasizes writing to a live, production database with very quick transactions.

SQL Server makes a great server for both OLTP and data warehousing types of databases, but if your company uses both types, you may want to consider using two SQL Server machines—one for each function—in order to get optimal performance.

Another related (and rapidly growing) use of databases is to put the data into a Web page and publish it either internally on an intranet or to the public on the Internet. Again, the same basic types of databases are used: data warehousing if the data on the Web page is for historical reporting purposes or OLTP if the customer can order from the Web page. Currently, most of the data is historical, or static, but that will change as the security and tools for transaction processing across the Internet improve.

Some Background on SQL Server

The release of SQL Server 2000 for Windows 2000 (and Windows 9x/Millennium and CE) continues a strong tradition of easy-to-use relational database engines that are also very powerful. While earlier versions of SQL Server have allowed many companies to downsize from mainframes to networks based on personal computers, SQL Server 2000 adds many important new functions, including an interface that's vastly easier to use and many more automated tuning and optimization features. More than two million copies of Microsoft's SQL Server have been sold since it was first introduced, and it is installed in a significant percentage of the companies that use some kind of database server.

SQL Server is one of the cornerstones of Microsoft's strategy for its Back Office and soon to be .NET family of server applications (Microsoft's line of client/server support applications). Microsoft's other BackOffice (and .NET) software includes Windows 2000 Advanced Server, Exchange 2000 (the e-mail server), Internet Information Server (IIS, the WWW server), Systems Management Server 2, (the workstation management piece), ISA (Internet Security and Acceleration server), and Host Integration Server (the next generation SNA protocol connectivity server) as well as other software that runs on Windows NT.

Every company has data, and almost every program generates even more data. Data in the paperless office needs to be stored somewhere—usually in some kind of data server.

Before you work with SQL Server system administration, you need to understand its native language and history and how it works with Windows 2000 and Windows 9x, Millennium, and CE.

History of Structured Query Language (SQL)

During the 1970s, IBM invented a computer language designed specifically for database queries. This language was called SEQUEL, which stood for Structured English Query Language. IBM released SEQUEL into the public domain, where it soon became known as SQL (pronounced "S-Q-L" when you are referring to the language; when you're referring to the server or database, you can pronounce it "sequel)."

Over time, the language has been expanded so that it is not just a language for queries but can also be used to build databases and manage security of the database engine. Currently, there are various versions of SQL in use.

Microsoft SQL Server uses a version called T-SQL, or Transact-SQL (both stand for Transaction SQL).

T-SQL can be divided into two generic categories of commands:

- Database schema commands, also known as the Data Definition Language (DDL), are used to define the database, tables, and other objects that have are used for managing the structure of the database.

- Data management commands, also known as Data Manipulation Language (DML), are used much like the original SQL commands in that they manipulate, add to, or delete data in the database.

 Although T-SQL is the programming language used by SQL Server, in this book our emphasis is on installing, maintaining, and connecting to SQL Server. In some cases, however, using T-SQL is one way to accomplish some of these tasks, such as creating and modifying SQL Server logons. Many of the exercises will show you both graphical and syntax methods of doing things because you may be tested on both.

History of Microsoft's SQL Server and Windows 2000

Microsoft initially worked with Sybase Corporation on a version of a SQL server system for OS/2. When Microsoft abandoned OS/2 in favor of its new network operating system, Windows NT, it decided to enhance the SQL server engine from Sybase and help modify the code for Windows NT. The resulting product was Microsoft SQL Server 4 for Windows NT, stabilizing at 4.21.

Over time, Microsoft took over more and more responsibility for the development of SQL Server; by version 6, Microsoft was in complete control of the software. Sybase engineers continued developing their database engine to run on Windows NT (Sybase version 10), while Microsoft developers continued enhancing SQL Server 6 (which quickly turned into version 6.5). Sybase continues to develop its product for Windows NT and Windows 2000; Microsoft's current version of SQL Server (SQL Server 2000) was officially launched in the last quarter of 2000.

A Brief History of Windows 2000

Microsoft started developing Windows NT in 1990 when it became obvious that running a 16-bit version of Windows on top of MS-DOS could not provide the performance and security that businesses needed. Windows NT 4 came out in 1996, and Windows 2000 came out in early 2000.

Windows 2000 is a 32-bit operating system that has been designed with a familiar user interface (basically an upgraded look of the Windows 9*x* interface). One way to look at Windows 2000 is that it is much like a mainframe operating system under the hood, but the user interface is a friendly desktop. Windows 2000 has both server and client properties; that is, it can simultaneously function as a network server and as a client on the network. We'll talk more about client/server systems in the next section.

Windows 2000 comes in four versions:

- A Professional (Workstation) version that is primarily used on desktop and laptop computers but can act as a server for up to 10 simultaneous connections at a time.

- A Server version that is primarily used as a file/application server that can theoretically have thousands of simultaneous users connected to it.

- An Advanced Server version that contains all of the server functions plus clustering and support for more CPUs.

- A Datacenter version that is designed to be installed with SQL Server 2000 to provide the ultimate Microsoft database solution. Datacenter is OEM only—in other words, you cannot purchase it alone and install it yourself. It is designed to compete with the high-end Unix servers.

Windows 2000 is the ultimate general-purpose server. You can add functionality to the base server by installing services. SQL Server is implemented as a set of services on either Windows 2000 Professional or Windows 2000 Server and Advanced Server.

SQL Server 2000 Basics

Although SQL Server 2000 is similar to earlier editions in many respects, Microsoft has continued to modify and differentiate its several versions of SQL Server to meet the differing needs of various users.

SQL Server 2000 not only adds a lower-end version (the Personal version), it also adds support on the high end for various clustered Windows 2000 servers. SQL Server 2000 continues the tradition of strong client support by providing backward compatibility with older SQL clients while also adding new, enhanced client features.

Versions of SQL Server 2000

SQL Server comes in five basic versions:

- Windows CE
- Personal
- Developer
- Standard
- Enterprise

Windows CE Version

The Windows CE version of SQL Server 2000 is designed for use on Windows CE devices. This version can replicate data to and from Standard and Enterprise versions of SQL Server.

Personal Version

SQL Server 2000 can be run on the Windows 9*x*/2000 and Millennium operating systems. The Personal version of SQL Server is meant to be used for traveling applications that occasionally link back to the primary network and for ease of use in developing applications. The Personal version installs and operates very much like the Standard and Enterprise versions running on Windows 2000. If you purchase and license the Standard or Enterprise version of SQL Server, you can install the Personal version on any of your clients without having to purchase additional licenses.

Developer Version

The Developer version is designed to be used by developers on a single computer that no one connects to via the network. The major advantage of the Developer version is that it is much cheaper than the Standard version and it works just fine if all you are doing is developing applications and code on it. (The Developer version of SQL Server 2000 only runs on Windows NT and Windows 2000.)

Standard Version

The Standard version of SQL Server 2000 is designed to support workgroups and small departments. The Standard version comes with all of the core features of SQL Server 2000 but lacks features that allow it to scale out to a large number of servers.

Enterprise Version

The Enterprise version of SQL Server 2000 includes all of the features of SQL Server 2000 including clustering support, log shipping, parallel computing support, enhanced read-aheads, partitioning support, HTTP support, and very large database (VLDB) support.

For this book, we are assuming that you are using the Enterprise version of SQL Server 2000 on Windows 2000 Advanced Server. When the Personal and Standard versions differ greatly from the Enterprise version, it will be noted.

Clients Supported by SQL Server 2000

SQL Server 2000 supports the following clients directly:

- Windows 9x and Millennium
- Windows NT
- Windows 2000

Because SQL Server 2000 does not ship with 16-bit client support, you will have to use drivers from earlier versions of SQL Server.

When SQL Server 2000 is correctly linked to a WWW server, any client that can access the WWW server can also retrieve data from SQL Server 2000.

SQL Server 2000 Features

There are many features of SQL Server 2000 that make it a compelling platform for client/server computing. Although a number of these features were present in version 7, they have been enhanced in 2000. These features include the following:

- Support for both the Windows 9*x* and Windows 2000 operating systems
- Identical application programming interface (API) support for both the Windows 9*x* and Windows 2000 operating systems
- Integrated Online Analytical Processing (OLAP) server
- Integrated Simple Network Management Protocol (SNMP) support via Windows 2000
- Integrated user-account support via Windows 2000
- Automated task management
- Alert management
- Sophisticated replication support
- Query and index optimization wizards
- Database management wizards
- Full-text search capabilities
- Object Linking and Embedding DataBase (OLE-DB), Open Database Connectivity (ODBC), SQL Data Management Objects (SQL-DMO), and Database Library (DB-Library) API support
- Dynamic enlarging and shrinking of databases
- Full and differential database backups
- Graphical query tools
- Improved, graphical import and export capabilities
- Graphical management tools using Microsoft Management Console (MMC) snap-ins

Although SQL Server 2000 can run on both the Windows 9x (and Millennium) and Windows 2000 platforms, there are some differences between the two types of installations, as shown in Table 1.2.

TABLE 1.2 Differences between Windows 9x and Windows 2000 Installations of SQL Server

Difference	Windows 9x	Windows 2000 AS
SQL engine	Runs as an application	Runs as a service
Integrated security	No	Yes
Automated alerts	No	Yes
Maximum users (recommended)	Five	Limited by hardware
Performance Monitor	No	Yes

Tasks of a SQL Server Developer

A SQL Server developer is responsible for designing, programming, and populating the database. Because the focus of this book is the administration rather than the development of SQL Server, the duties of the developer are not covered in detail. The developer's responsibilities can be summarized as follows:

- Analyze the business situation to see what type of system is required. Is a new system or an upgrade needed? Is it a small company at one location or a big corporation with multiple locations?

- Design the database, tables, and all objects. In the design process, the developer identifies objects and relationships and how they all fit together as logical entities; the logical entities are then translated into physical tables (normalized). The developer must then plan for the application design, including reports and queries as well as other pieces, such as access to Web pages.

- Design the security for SQL Server and for individual databases. Implementing security is covered in Chapter 5.

- Design any data-replication scenarios. Replication, including scenarios and implementation, is covered in Chapter 9.

- Program the database, tables, and all objects. This involves working with T-SQL.

- Program the initial security of the database, possibly planning Windows 2000 groups to help ease ongoing SQL Server administration.

- Design the user interface, reports, and update screens. This is the front end of the system and will probably have the most impact on the users.

- Test the design, interface, reports, and update screens.

- Populate the database with live data from legacy systems and prepare the database to receive new data.

- Hand the project with appropriate documentation and training over to the administrator.

Tasks of a SQL Server Administrator

A SQL Server administrator is usually responsible for the day-to-day administration of the database. The administrator takes over where the programmer left off.

The tasks of the SQL Server administrator are the focus of this book. Microsoft has two separate SQL tests: one designed for the administrator (the test that is the focus of this book) and one designed for T-SQL programmers (the implementation test).

In many companies, the lines between administrator and developer may become quite blurred because the same person may be doing tasks related to both roles.

The administrator's duties can be summarized as the following:

- Install and configure SQL Server 2000 (see Chapter 2).

- Plan and create databases (see Chapter 4).

- Back up the databases (see Chapter 6).

- Restore the databases when necessary (see Chapter 6).

- Set up and manage users for SQL Server (see Chapter 5).

- Manage security for new users and existing users (see Chapter 5).

- Import and export data (see Chapter 7).

- Set up and manage tasks, alerts, and operators (see Chapter 8).

- Manage the replication environment (see Chapter 9).

- Tune the SQL Server system for the optimal performance (see Chapter 10).

- Troubleshoot any SQL Server problems (see Chapter 10).

Summary

This chapter served as an introduction to SQL Server and relational databases. Here are some of the key points covered:

- Microsoft's SQL Server is a client/server-based relational database management system (RDBMS) that uses T-SQL as its dialect of the SQL language. Its ever-increasing popularity makes learning SQL Server 2000 a wise career decision.

- A *client/server* database is an application that is divided into a part that runs on a server and a part that runs on workstations (clients). The server side provides security, fault-tolerance, performance, concurrency, and reliable backups. The client side provides the user interface.

- A *relational* database is composed of tables that contain related data. The process of breaking a database into related tables is called *normalization*.

- SQL Server developers are responsible for designing and implementing the databases. Designing a good database starts with understanding the client's requirements for the database. The data can then be grouped into related tables.

- SQL Server administrators are responsible for the day-to-day tasks of maintaining and managing the databases. SQL Server administration involves backing up databases and restoring them when necessary, setting up and managing users, managing database security, managing the replication environment, tuning the database system, and troubleshooting any problems that arise.

Key Terms

client/server	objects
data warehousing	OLTP (Online Transaction Processing)
decision support system	page
flat-file database	relational database
normalizing	

Review Questions

1. Which of the following is a database object? (Select all that apply.)

   A. Table

   B. Index

   C. Rule

   D. Default

2. You are the sales department manager. Your main application runs on SQL Server. Because your department has doubled in size the last year, you purchased a new computer to serve as your SQL Server computer. The network administrator, SQL administrator, and SQL programmer came in last weekend to move your application to the new server. You want to make sure the database is still getting backed up. Who would you ask first?

   A. The database administrator

   B. The database developer

   C. Database users

   D. The Windows 2000 administrator

3. You are the sales department manager. Your main application runs on SQL Server. You know the SQL programmer who designed and wrote the application. You hire a new user and need to grant them the proper permissions to use your application. Who would you talk to first?

   A. The database administrator

   B. The database developer

   C. The database users

   D. The Windows NT administrator

4. You are the sales department manager. Your main application runs on SQL Server. You know the SQL programmer who designed and wrote the application. You add 25 new users to the application and the server gets much slower. Who would you talk to first about getting the server to run faster?

   A. The database administrator

   B. The database developer

   C. Database users

   D. The Windows NT administrator

5. You have an Excel spreadsheet you want to convert to a SQL Server database. You want to search for any white papers that might help you design a relational database. What keyword best describes breaking related information into tables?

   A. Fragmentation

   B. Database design

   C. Normalization

   D. Tabulating the data

6. On your workstation, you are running an application that uses a SQL Server database. You are given 256MB of RAM. Queries take a long time to run and you want to speed them up. Where should you install the RAM?

   A. The client.

   B. The server.

   C. Both the client and the server.

   D. Neither; a "middleware" application runs the query.

7. SQL Server is an example of what kind of database system?

   A. Flat-file

   B. 3D

   C. RDBMS

   D. Hierarchical

8. You are going to design a database that will hold your customer and sales data. Customers tend to order more than once from you. You should design your database so that your customers and their sales are held in separate _____ .

    A. Fields

    B. Files

    C. Reports

    D. Tables

9. You have a sales force with various operating systems installed on their laptops. Your new sales force application requires that SQL Server 2000 Personal be installed on every laptop. You need to budget for new hardware if a laptop can't handle a new operating system and SQL Server. You won't need to upgrade the laptops with which operating systems? (Select all that apply.)

    A. Windows for Workgroups

    B. Windows 9x

    C. Windows 2000 Professional

    D. Windows Millennium

10. You are in a bookstore browsing through programming books. You want to buy one that helps you program SQL Server. Which topic best suits your needs?

    A. DBMS

    B. T-SQL

    C. PL-SQL

    D. QUERY

11. One of your users asks what a view is. Which answer would you give?

    A. Precompiled code that stores data

    B. A stored query that operates like a virtual table

    C. A method for organizing like data

    D. A way of entering default values

12. You have 50 users who telecommute from home and need access to your SQL Server computer. By corporate policy, they can use only Internet Explorer on the corporate network. Which version of SQL Server would you install for those users?

A. The Personal version on every user's computer

B. The Personal version on the server

C. The Standard version on the server

D. The Enterprise version on the server

13. Your programmers are getting ready to code an application for SQL Server 2000. You buy all of them the Developer version. Some of the programmers work from home and have older computers. Which operating system will you *not* need to upgrade to run the Developer version?

A. Windows 95

B. Windows 98

C. Windows Millennium

D. Windows 2000 Professional

14. You win a copy of the Enterprise version of SQL Server. Which operating system can be on your test computers in order to install it? (Select all that apply.)

A. Windows 98

B. Windows 2000 Professional

C. Windows 2000 Server

D. Windows 2000 Advanced Server

15. You read an article about tuning OLTP databases. You are not sure if you should implement any of the suggested changes. What type of database is typical for OLTP?

    A. Quick writes

    B. Quick reads

    C. Long writes

    D. Long reads

16. Your SQL programmer tells you that you have an OLAP-type application. Which of these best describes your database?

    A. Lots of new rows

    B. Lots of updates rows

    C. Lots of deleted rows

    D. Fewer, long-running queries

17. You create some new tables and populate them with copies of your production data. You run reports on your new tables but your queries take a lot longer than on the original tables. What should you create to help speed up reads in the database?

    A. Stored procedure

    B. Index

    C. Default

    D. Primary key

18. You have salespeople who are running Windows CE devices. They each need a local copy of the corporate database on their local device. What version of SQL Server would you install on their device?

    A. CE

    B. Personal

    C. Standard

    D. Enterprise

19. You need to obtain copies of SQL Server Personal for all of your sales-people. How can you acquire the Personal version of SQL Server?

    A. It can be purchased separately.

    B. It comes with Office 2000.

    C. It comes with Windows 2000.

    D. Purchase and license SQL Server 2000 (Standard or Enterprise).

20. You are creating a data entry application. You wish to lower the amount of time it takes for users to enter repetitive data. What type of database object would you use?

    A. Index

    B. View

    C. Default

    D. Rule

Answers to Review Questions

1. A, B, C, D. Tables, indexes, rules, and defaults are all database objects. Other database objects include stored procedures, triggers, and views.

2. A. The database administrator is usually in charge of database backups, so they would logically be the first person you would ask about current database backups.

3. A. Although the SQL programmer who wrote the initial database would generally have information about the application, the database administrator is usually in charge of ongoing database security, so they would be the one to talk to about a new user.

4. A. The database administrator is usually in charge of SQL Server optimization. Although it could be a programming or operating system problem as well, the database administrator is the best place to start.

5. C. Normalization is the process of designing relational tables and would be a good keyword for a search on designing relational databases.

6. B. When a query is run in client/server computing, the server executes the query, so upgrading the server will probably give you the best performance increase.

7. C. SQL Server is a relational database management system (RDBMS). In an RDBMS, a database is not necessarily tied to a file; it is more of a logical concept based on a collection of related objects.

8. D. Related data in a relational database is organized into tables, so you would have one table for customers and one for sales. Because relational columns cannot contain multiple values, you would duplicate customer data for every second order, third order, and so on if you only used one table.

9. B, C, D. SQL Server 2000 Personal can run on Windows 9x, Windows 2000 (Professional and Server), and Windows Millenium.

10. B. SQL Server 2000 uses Transact-SQL (T-SQL), which is a version of Structured Query Language (SQL). SQL is a language that was designed for database queries and that can be used to build databases and manage the security of the database engine.

11. B. A view is simply a stored query that operates like a virtual table.

12. D. The Enterprise version has HTTP support built into it so you can access your data via IIS and HTTP.

13. D. The Developer version of SQL 2000 only runs on Windows NT and Windows 2000.

14. C, D. SQL Server 2000 Enterprise edition requires Windows 2000 Server or Advanced Server.

15. A. OLTP stands for Online Transaction Processing, which emphasizes lots of quick writes to the database.

16. D. OLAP stands for Online Analytical Processing, which emphasizes reads over writes. OLAP databases tend to be report oriented, which requires long-running queries, usually from only a few users.

17. B. Indexes help ensure quick reads of the database. Indexes organize the database based on the specified columns. If a query uses an index, the query time is usually sped up dramatically.

18. A. Only the CE version of SQL Server 2000 will run on Windows CE.

19. D. The Personal version of SQL Server can be installed (for no additional charge) if you have purchased and licensed the Standard or Enterprise version of SQL Server.

20. C. A column default is an optional database object that can be used to enter default data so users won't have to when they add a new row to the database.

Chapter 2

Installing, Upgrading, and Configuring SQL Server 2000

MICROSOFT EXAM OBJECTIVES COVERED IN THIS CHAPTER:

✓ **Install SQL Server 2000. Considerations include clustering, default collation, file locations, number of instances, and service accounts.**

✓ **Upgrade to SQL Server 2000.**

  ▪ Perform a custom upgrade.

  ▪ Upgrade to SQL Server 2000 from SQL Server 6.5.

  ▪ Upgrade to SQL Server 2000 from SQL Server 7.0.

✓ **Configure network libraries.**

✓ **Troubleshoot failed installations.**

SQL Server installations usually go quite smoothly, especially when you are prepared with the knowledge this chapter will give you. Although Microsoft products are usually easy to install, there are several installation options that drastically change the way SQL Server operates, as well as a few "gotchas" when dealing with SQL Server installations.

In this chapter, we'll walk you through an actual installation of SQL Server 2000, paying attention to the various options along the way. We will look at the options available for upgrading from SQL Server 6.5 and SQL Server 7 as well as the options for automating the setup process.

Once the installation is complete, we will focus on configuring both the server and the clients.

For additional coverage of the objectives in this chapter, see Chapter 3.

Installing SQL Server 2000

Like most Microsoft applications, the setup routine for SQL Server is both powerful and relatively intuitive. There are several decisions that, once made, are rather difficult to change, however, so before starting the installation, look at the various options that are available to you and plan accordingly.

Microsoft
Exam
Objective

Install SQL Server 2000. Considerations include clustering, default collation, file locations, number of instances, and service accounts.

Before You Install

Although some of the SQL configurations can be changed after installation, several of the options cannot be changed. You need to consider the following items before doing an installation:

- Hardware requirements

- Software requirements

- License mode

- Collations

- Sort orders

- Unicode support

- Network libraries

- User accounts

- Default and named instances

- Installation path

- Upgrade versus side-by-side installation

- Which components to install

Hardware Requirements

The hardware that SQL Server needs to run depends on the operating system you are using. Windows 2000 should have at least 256MB of RAM, while Windows NT needs only 64MB of RAM as a minimum. SQL Server takes approximately 270MB of disk space for an installation, plus room for the user databases.

Software Requirements

SQL Server 2000 can run on Windows NT 4 as well as Windows 2000. The Personal version of SQL Server can also run on Windows 9x and Windows Millennium. There is also a CE version of SQL Server that runs only on Windows CE.

If you want SQL Server 2000 to support Windows 2000 clusters, remember that you must install the Enterprise version of SQL Server 2000 on Windows 2000 Advanced Server, or have the Datacenter versions installed. For more details, see Chapter 1.

License Mode

SQL Server supports per-processor and per-seat licensing; there are advantages to both types. Many companies prefer per-seat licensing because they are buying complete BackOffice licenses for each client, but per-processor licensing also has its advantages.

Per-processor licensing means that you pay for each processor the SQL Server computer has. You can then connect an unlimited number of users to the SQL Server computer.

Per-seat licensing means that you pay for every person in the company, whether or not they use SQL Server. The advantage here is that you can add additional SQL Server computers for just the cost of Windows 2000 and SQL Server itself.

Collation

A *collation* is set of rules that Windows uses to support characters and locations. Collations roughly correspond to *character sets* from previous versions of SQL Server. The collation of SQL_Latin1_General_CP1_CI_AS matches best with the SQL Server 7 default character set and should be chosen if your SQL Server 2000 server still needs to interact with SQL Server 7.

If you are running a pure SQL Server 2000 environment, choose to support collations rather than character sets and sort orders.

Although you cannot change the default collation of the server once the server is installed, you can set the collation for each database and even each column so that it's different than that of the server. This allows you to, for example, have different text fields designed to hold comments from people who speak different languages all in the same database. Collations were designed to get past the limits of default code pages and sort orders in SQL Server 7. SQL Server 2000 also supports *Unicode* characters; because Unicode characters take up no more than 2 bytes of data, you can support more that 256 characters for any given character set. Unicode support is discussed later.

Don't change the default collation or sort order unless you are matching an older server, using a language other than English, or supporting an application that tells you to.

Sort Order

The *sort order* determines how data is stored, compared, and returned during queries. The available sort-order selections will be determined by the character set chosen.

The following are the main sort orders:

Dictionary sort order, case insensitive   This is the default sort order and treats upper- and lowercase characters the same for comparison purposes.

Dictionary sort order, case sensitive   This sort order retains and enforces all cases in the database and when using SQL Server. For example, if the database is called Pubs (note the capital *P* and lowercase *ubs*), then a use pubs or use PUBS command would fail—only the use Pubs command would succeed.

Binary order   This sort order sorts everything by its binary representation of the data, not as a dictionary would sort characters.

If you choose a case-sensitive sort order, all SQL passwords are case sensitive. If you choose a case-insensitive sort order, passwords (and all other keywords) are also case insensitive.

Unicode Support

SQL Server 2000 supports Unicode character types. Unicode characters are represented by 2 bytes (rather than a single byte), enabling more than 64,000 possible characters for a given field.

The default Unicode support is for case-insensitive, width-insensitive, Kana (Japanese)–insensitive support. Use the default selection unless you have been specifically instructed to change it. If you need to support multiple languages but have to use the 850- or 437-character sets, you can choose the Unicode datatype when you create your columns.

Network Libraries

SQL Server doesn't automatically support every protocol that is installed on the computer—you need to configure SQL Server to support specific protocols, which themselves must first be installed and correctly configured.

SQL Server supports the following protocols and standards:

TCP/IP   Support for this industry-standard protocol is enabled by default. SQL Server uses port 1433 as its default TCP/IP port. Because SQL Server uses configurations set by the operating system, TCP/IP connections to the SQL Server computer that do not function properly may be the result of problems with the TCP/IP protocol and configurations and not with SQL Server.

IPX/SPX   Support for this protocol, used by NetWare servers and clients, is not enabled by default. If IPX/SPX is installed on the SQL Server computer, NetWare clients can connect even if they don't have a Microsoft client installed. If you enable support for IPX/SPX, you can also configure the name of the server that NetWare clients will see. To avoid confusion, you should use the same server name for both NetWare and Microsoft clients.

Named Pipes   Support for this networking standard is enabled by default. Named Pipes is a common method for connecting to a resource using a network. Note that Microsoft's NetBEUI, TCP/IP, and IPX/SPX support the Named Pipes specification natively. Named Pipes are not supported on Windows 9*x* and Millennium because trusted connections are not supported.

Multiprotocol   Support for this standard is not enabled by default. Multiprotocol support allows clients to connect via two or more methods, allowing encryption across TCP/IP and IPX/SPX.

AppleTalk   Support for this protocol is not enabled by default. AppleTalk is used by Macintosh clients.

DecNet   Support for this protocol is not enabled by default. DecNet is used by some older Digital clients.

User Accounts

As with any service that connects to other computers and services, SQL Server and SQL Server Agent need a service account assigned to them. The account needs the following settings:

- The advanced Logon as a Service right
- User Must Change Password at Next Logon cleared
- Password Never Expires checked

The Logon as a Service right is needed so that the account can be used by a service. Because a service cannot change a password, you must clear the User Must Change Password at Next Logon box, and in order to keep the password from expiring, you should select Password Never Expires.

The service and agent won't need an account assigned to them if the server and agent don't communicate with any other service on the SQL Server computer (such as Exchange) or with any other SQL Server computer (as with replication).

You can create the user with the Windows 2000 Active Directory Users and Computers utility (see Figure 2.1) before installing SQL Server. The SQL Server installation program will assign the Logon as a Service right, but you need to configure the others.

FIGURE 2.1   Creating a user account for SQL Server services

New Object - User		

Create in: LBM.com/Users

First name: SQLAdmin   Initials:

Last name: SQLAdmin

Full name: SQLAdmin

User logon name:

SQLAdmin   @LBM.COM

User logon name (pre-Windows 2000):

LBM\   SQLAdmin

< Back   Next >   Cancel

Default and Named Instances

An instance is a single installation of SQL Server. There are two types of SQL Server 2000 instances:

- Default instance
- Named instance

With a *default instance*, the name of the SQL Server instance is the same as the name of the computer. SQL Server 6.5 and 7 can be installed only as default instances, whereas SQL Server 2000 can be installed as a default or named instance. You can only have a single default instance running at any given time.

SQL Server 2000 can be installed multiple times (in different directories) on the same computer. In order to run multiple copies at the same time, a named instance is installed. With a *named instance*, the computer name and the name of the instance are used for the full name of the SQL Server instance. For example, if the server Sales has an instance called Training, the instance would be known by Sales\Training, and Sales\Training would be used to connect to the instance.

Older applications and drivers can see only default instances. It takes new drivers and applications to see named instances. SQL Server 2000 as well as Windows 2000 install the new drivers by default.

Installation Path

The default path is \Program Files\Microsoft SQL Server for both default and named instances. The default instance will be under the \MSSQL folder, and a named instance will be under the \MSSQL$NameOfInstance folder. Administration tools are installed to the \Program Files\80 folder. You may choose a different path for the program files and/or database files. If you install named instances, a different directory structure will exist for each named instance.

Upgrading vs. Side-by-Side Installation

If SQL Server 6.5 is already installed on the server, the SQL Server 2000 Setup program will attempt to upgrade the installation by default. SQL Server 6.5 requires Service Pack 5 or later to be successfully upgraded to SQL Server 2000. If you choose to install SQL Server 2000 in a different path, you can choose which version of SQL Server to start. You can also leave the old SQL Server 6.5 installation alone and install SQL Server 2000 in a different directory so you can run both versions at the same time. To convert the databases at a later time, simply run the Upgrade Wizard.

As with any upgrade, thoroughly back up all valuable databases in SQL Server 6.5 before attempting a live upgrade.

If SQL Server 7 is installed on the server, you can choose to upgrade the installation to SQL Server 2000 or install SQL Server 2000 in a different directory.

Selecting Components

A default SQL Server installation includes the MSSQLSERVER service (the actual database engine), the management software (Enterprise Manager and others), and the documentation. You can select any combination of software components by choosing a custom installation.

The SQL Server 2000 Installation

Although there are many steps to the installation, the process is fairly straightforward. Some general steps, such as installing the latest Windows NT service pack and version of Internet Explorer, should be taken first. The Install Prerequisites option from the main setup screen allows you to install the required prerequisites for both Windows 95 and Windows NT.

Once the prerequisites have been installed, restart the SQL Server Setup program and select Install Database Components. The different versions of SQL Server 2000 that can be installed will be listed.

The Personal version is designed for Windows 9*x*, whereas the Standard and Enterprise versions are designed for Windows 2000. Chapter 1 provides more information on the differences between the two products. For the discussions in this book, we are assuming that the Enterprise version is installed on Windows 2000 Advanced Server.

The Setup program allows you to install SQL Server to the local computer or, if you have administrative rights, to a remote computer. Normally, to save network use, you would run the installation routine on the computer you wish to be your SQL Server computer. Remote sites can easily be installed by choosing the remote installation option.

You will then see a screen prompting you to back up anything valuable on your system, in case the unexpected happens. After choosing Next, you will see the license agreement form, which you must accept before being able to proceed.

The installation program will prompt you to enter a user and company, after which you will be asked if you want to run the SQL 6.5 to SQL 7 Upgrade Wizard. If you don't run the wizard during the setup, you can run it at a later time (recommended if you don't have reliable recent backups of your 6.5 databases).

The next screen is one of the most important ones because it allows you to select a custom setup routine. With custom setup routines, you can change the sort order, character set, network support, and even whether the SQL Server engine or just the management tools will be installed. If you choose the custom setup, you will be taken to the Select Components screen, where you can choose exactly which parts of SQL Server will be installed. You will probably want to make sure Full-Text Search Engine is selected (the default) in case you want to set up any text indexes later. Of course, you can always rerun the Setup program and add components after the initial installation.

The next screen allows you to change your sort order, character set, and Unicode collection. Note that you should leave these at the default settings unless you have a very good reason to change them.

On the following screen, you can select which network protocols to support. Note that Named Pipes TCP/IP are selected by default. Select additional protocols as required.

You can assign a user account to the various SQL services at the next screen. You can choose to assign the same account to all three services (SQL Server, SQL Server Agent, and MS-DTC) or to create individual user accounts for the various services. This is the last screen to fill out before the installation begins.

The SQL installation program will let you know when SQL Server has been successfully installed.

The SQL Server 2000 Enterprise Evaluation version is included on the CD-ROM that accompanies this book.

In Exercise 2.1, you will install SQL Server 2000, paying attention to the various options available during the installation. Although you'll do a custom installation, you won't change any of the default settings (which is basically a typical installation).

EXERCISE 2.1

Installing SQL Server

1. Run the Setup program from the SQL Server 2000 CD-ROM.

2. Install the prerequisites (if not already installed) by choosing the SQL Server 2000 Prerequisites option from the main setup screen. Reboot after installing all prerequisites and rerun the Setup program.

3. Select SQL Server 2000 Components to start the install.

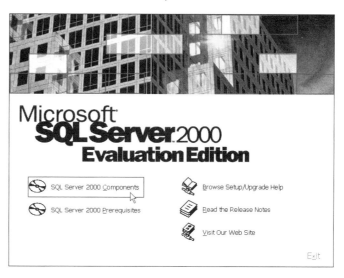

4. Select Install Database Server to install the main SQL Server service.

5. The Installation Wizard will start. Click Next to continue.

6. From the Computer Name screen, confirm that you want to do a local install (the default), or enter the name of the computer on which you wish to install SQL Server. Choose to do a local install for this exercise.

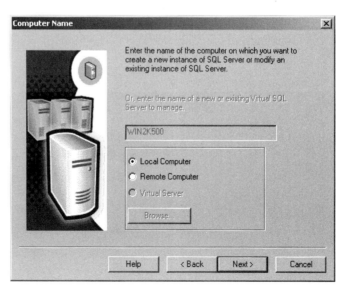

7. From the Installation Selection screen, you can choose to install a new instance of SQL Server (the default), delete an existing copy, or perform advanced management on a previously installed version. Choose to install a new instance and click Next to continue.

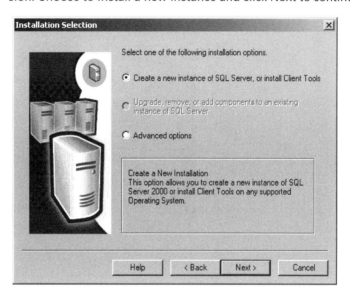

8. At the User Information screen, enter your username and company name. Click Next to continue.

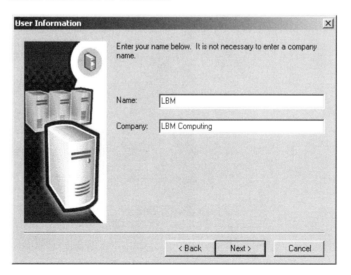

9. Select Yes on the license agreement screen.

10. At the Installation Definition screen, choose to install both the server and the client tools. (Note that, in a later exercise, you'll install just the client tools on an administration computer.) Click Next to continue.

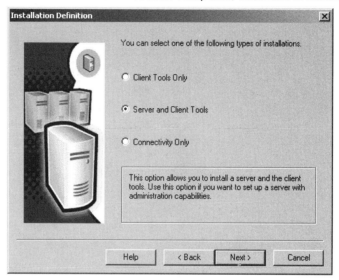

11. At the Instance Name screen, choose to install the default instance. You'll install an additional instance later in the chapter. Click Next to continue.

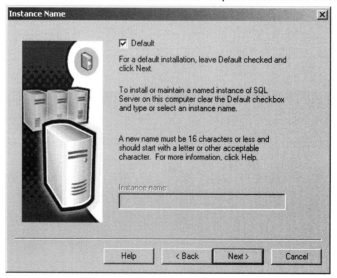

12. At the Setup Type screen, choose to do a custom installation. You can also choose the destination folders for the program and data files. Click Next to continue.

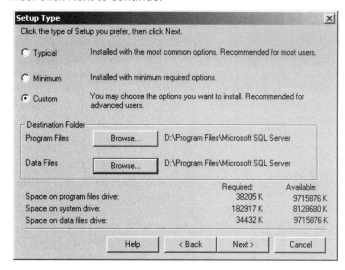

13. The Select Component screen appears because you chose to do a custom installation. Although you can change various components that will be installed, for this exercise, leave everything selected and click Next to continue. You might want to uncheck the Upgrade Tools check box if you do not have an instance to upgrade because the upgrade tools are useless in a new install.

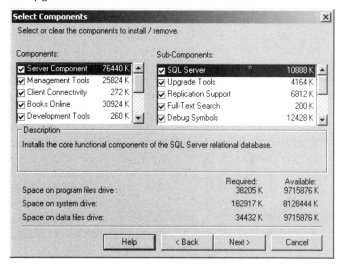

EXERCISE 2.1 *(continued)*

14. On the Services Accounts screen, you can assign user accounts to the SQL Server Agent and Server services. By default, the user account you used to log in will be assigned to the services. Enter the password for the account and click Next to continue.

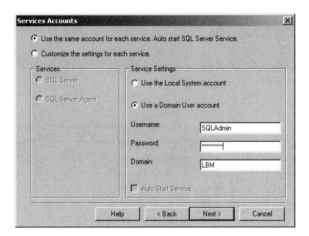

15. The Authentication Mode screen allows you to set either Windows Authentication mode (which means all users of SQL Server must first be authenticated by Windows) or Mixed mode (which means accounts can exist in SQL Server outside of Windows). Change the mode to Mixed, enter a password you can remember, and click Next to continue.

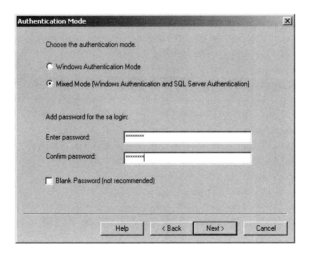

EXERCISE 2.1 *(continued)*

16. On the Collation Settings screen, you can choose a native SQL Server 2000 collation or choose a collation method compatible with previous versions of SQL Server. Leave the setting on the SQL Collations (for backward compatibility) and click Next to continue.

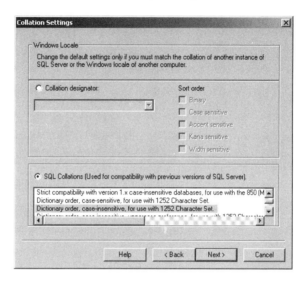

17. Use the Network Libraries screen to choose the protocols that SQL Server will use to listen to the network. Leave the default selections and click Next to continue.

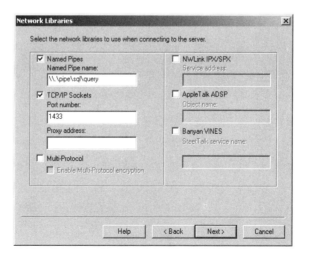

EXERCISE 2.1 *(continued)*

18. You will see a screen titled Start Copying Files. If you are happy with your selections, click Next to start the installation.

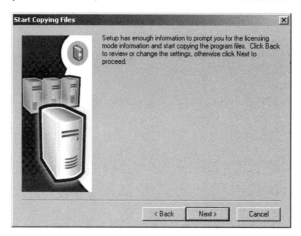

19. The Choose Licensing Mode screen will be the last one you see. Enter the appropriate licensing for your installation and click Next to continue.

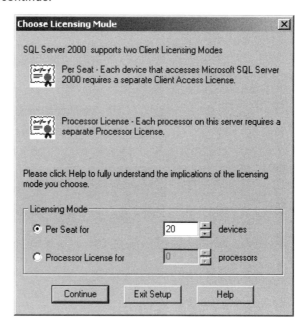

EXERCISE 2.1 *(continued)*

20. You may get a message stating that certain components are in use. Click OK to stop the components so that SQL Server 2000 can be installed. The installation should only take a few minutes.

21. When you're prompted that the installation has finished, click OK to restart your system.

Installing a Second Instance of SQL Server

SQL Server 2000 can have up to 16 simultaneous copies, or instances, running. If a default instance is used, the default instance acts just as SQL Server 7 and earlier versions would, with the name of the computer acting as the name of the SQL Server. When you install a second instance, the second instance is referred to by *Server/Instance*. Instances that use the new name can be seen only by SQL Server 2000 database clients. In other words, older client software such as ODBC connections will not be able to communicate with named instances. Although it's easier to isolate security for separate instances, having many separate instances is not as efficient with system resources as having one large instance is.

In Exercise 2.2, you'll install a named (second) instance to the server.

EXERCISE 2.2

Installing a Named Instance

1. Start the Setup program (just as you did in Exercise 2.1).

2. Select SQL Server 2000 Components to start the install.

3. Select Install Database Server to install the main SQL Server service.

4. The Installation Wizard will start. Click Next to continue.

5. From the Computer Name screen, confirm that you want to do a local install (the default), or enter the name of the computer on which you wish to install SQL Server.

EXERCISE 2.2 *(continued)*

6. From the Installation Selection screen, you can choose to install a new instance of SQL Server (the default), delete an existing copy, or perform advanced management on a previously installed version. Choose to install a new instance and click Next to continue.

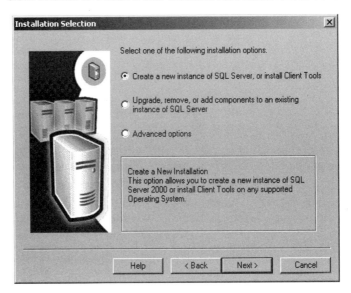

7. At the User Information screen, enter your username and company name. Click Next to continue.

8. Choose Yes at the license agreement screen.

9. At the Installation Definition screen, choose to install both the server and the client tools. (Note that in a later lab you will install just the client tools on an administration computer.) Click Next to continue.

10. Notice that you have to create a named instance because you already have a default instance. Enter **TRAINING** for the named instance. Click Next to continue.

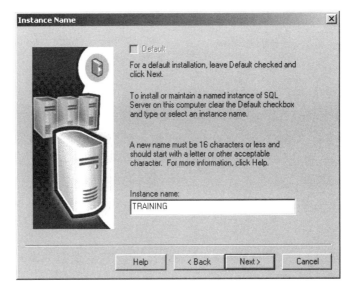

11. At the Setup Type screen, choose to do a custom installation. You can also choose the destination folders for the program and data files. Click Next to continue.

12. The Select Components screen appears because you chose to do a custom installation. Although you can change various components that will be installed, for this exercise leave everything selected and click Next to continue.

13. On the Service Accounts screen, you can assign user accounts to the SQL Server Agent and Server services. By default, the user account you used to log in as will be assigned to the services. Enter the password for the account and click Next to continue.

14. On the Authentication Mode screen, change the mode to Mixed, enter a password you can remember, and click Next to continue.

15. On the Collation Settings screen, leave the setting on the SQL Collations (the backward-compatible options) and click Next to continue.

EXERCISE 2.2 *(continued)*

16. The Network Libraries screen allows you to choose the protocols that SQL Server will use to listen to the network. Notice that the Named Pipes option includes the instance name and that the TCP/IP port has been changed to 0. Leave the default selections and click Next to continue.

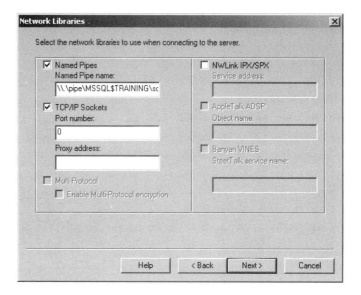

17. You will see a screen titled Start Copying Files. If you are happy with your selections, click Next to start the installation.

18. The Licensing Mode screen will be the last one you see. Enter the appropriate licensing for your installation and click Next to continue.

19. You may get a message stating that certain components are in use. Click OK to stop the components so that SQL Server 2000 can be installed. The installation should only take a few minutes.

20. When prompted that the installation has finished, click OK to restart your system.

Real World Scenario: Named Instances

Installing and running named instances has to be one of the greatest new features of SQL Server. After you use the feature, you will wonder how you got along without it.

There are several reasons for running more than one instance on the same computer. For example, you might want to copy the database for test or training purposes, or you could have separate applications residing in separate instances. With named instances, you can play with different settings and features without fear of damaging your production environment.

Unattended Installations

SQL Server can be installed without prompts by using various batch files and initialization files.

The SQL Server 2000 CD-ROM contains sample batch files and initialization files as shown in Table 2.1.

TABLE 2.1   Sample Batch and Initialization Files for SQL Server 2000

Batch File	Initialization File	Action
Sqlcli.bat	Sqlcli.iss	Installs SQL Server administration tools
Sqlins.bat	Sqlins.iss	Installs a typical version of SQL Server
Sqlcst.bat	Sqlcst.iss	Installs all components of SQL Server
Sqlrem.bat		Uninstalls SQL Server

You can edit the sample initialization files to fit your site. You can also look at the initialization file that was created during an installation (stored as Setup.iss in the \MSSQL7\Install folder) and edit the file as needed.

You can also run the SQL Setup program and choose the Advanced function, which will allow you to generate a setup script.

The default SQL Server services login account for an unattended install is the LocalSystem account.

Testing and Troubleshooting the Installation

Once SQL Server is installed, you can easily and quickly test the installation. If the installation did not install correctly, these tests may help you troubleshoot where the problem lies. You can also examine the Windows application log or the SQL logs to help troubleshoot a damaged installation.

Microsoft **Troubleshoot failed installations.**
Exam
Objective

Start SQL Enterprise Manager from the Microsoft SQL Server group and open the SQL Server group. You should see both the default instance and the named instance.

SQL Server 2000 Enterprise Manager automatically registers a connection to the SQL Server computer using an integrated server account or the SA login account. The SA login account is the only SQL login account installed by default. Both the default and named instances will be registered.

Your server should be listed on the screen. Open it by clicking the + sign and you should see folders for the various databases, security settings, and so on for your SQL Server computer (see Figure 2.2). If the server opens successfully in Enterprise Manager, it probably installed successfully.

FIGURE 2.2 Examining SQL Server in Enterprise Manager

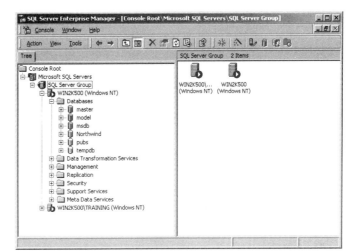

Another way to test the installation is by running a simple query in the Pubs sample database. To do so, start the Query Analyzer by choosing the Tools ➢ SQL Server ➢ Query Analyzer menu option in Enterprise Manager. You can also start the Query Analyzer separately by selecting its icon from the SQL Server group.

In Exercise 2.3, you'll test the SQL Server installation by doing a simple query.

EXERCISE 2.3

Running a Simple SQL Query to Test the SQL Installation

1. Start the Query Analyzer from the Tools menu of Enterprise Manager or by selecting the icon in the SQL Server 2000 group.

2. Enter the following command:

```
use pubs

select * from authors
```

EXERCISE 2.3 *(continued)*

3. Click the green arrow or press Ctrl+E to run the query. Your results should show 23 rows of authors.

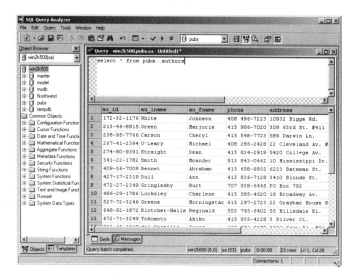

4. Close Query Analyzer. Click No when prompted to save the output of the query.

SQL Server Services

The SQL Server suite of applications is composed of four separate services—Distributed Transaction Coordinator (DTC), Microsoft Search, SQL Server, and SQL Server Agent—all of which install on a Windows 2000 computer. A SQL Server 2000 installation on a Windows 9*x* computer does not include Microsoft Search services.

Distributed Transaction Coordinator (DTC)

The Distributed Transaction Coordinator (DTC) service is an optional service designed to take care of transactions that span multiple servers. When a transaction is made across two or more servers, the DTC service ensures that the transaction is made on all servers; otherwise, the transaction is rolled back.

Microsoft Search

When you install full-text index support, you install the Microsoft Search service, which is, at its heart, basically the same service as the Microsoft's Index Server engine.

SQL Server (MSSQLSERVER)

The SQL Server service is the actual database engine. This service is required for any computer you wish to be a SQL Server computer.

To see whether the service has been installed, choose Computer Management (or Control Panel in NT) ➤ Services and look for it by its service name (MSSQLSERVER).

SQL Server Agent (SQLSERVERAGENT)

The SQL Server Agent (SQLSERVERAGENT) service is a helper service designed to take care of the automation involved in SQL Server. Although this service is not technically required, few, if any, sites run without it. You can check on its installation by choosing Computer Management (or Control Panel in NT) ➤ Services.

Registry Settings

SQL Server creates a key in the Hkey_Local_Machine/Software/Microsoft key as well as in the Hkey_Users key. Settings that apply to the SQL Server as a service are stored in the Hkey_Local_Machine/Software hive, while settings that apply to the management software configurations are stored (uniquely for each user) in the Hkey_Users key.

Installation Path

You can also check the installation path to see whether SQL Server has been installed correctly. There should be subdirectories under the \Program Files\Microsoft SQL Server folder.

Each instance will have a separate set of folders under \Program Files\Microsoft SQL Server. The default instance uses \MSSQL as its path, and named instances use \MSSQL$<NameOfInstance> as their path.

Subfolderss under the main folder are shown in Table 2.2.

TABLE 2.2 Subfolders and Their Contents

Folder Name	Content
Backup	Default folder for backup files
Binn	EXE and setup files
Data	Default and system databases
Install	Scripts used during installation
Jobs	Default folder for automated jobs
Log	Log files (including errors, version numbers, and FYI-type messages) created by various SQL Server services
Repldata	Working folder for replication
Upgrade	Scripts and output used during upgrades

Upgrading SQL Server 6.5 and 7 to 2000

SQL Server 2000 has a robust Upgrade Wizard that can easily convert a SQL Server 6.5 or 7 system to a SQL Server 2000 system. Because the upgrade is not reversible, there are several items to be aware of before you start.

Microsoft ✓ *Exam Objective*

Upgrade to SQL Server 2000.

- Perform a custom upgrade.
- Upgrade to SQL Server 2000 from SQL Server 6.5.
- Upgrade to SQL Server 2000 from SQL Server 7.0.

SQL Server 2000 allows you to upgrade databases and entire servers from SQL Server 6.5 and 7, but it does not support upgrades directly from earlier versions (6.0 or 4.21). SQL Server 2000 has many available options when you upgrade from earlier versions, each with its advantages and disadvantages. The various methods and requirements when upgrading are discussed in the following sections.

Before You Begin the Upgrade

There are several things you need to consider before upgrading:

- Whether to upgrade the old computer or upgrade just the databases to a new computer

- If upgrading the old computer, whether to upgrade the old installation or run the existing version and the new version side by side

- Whether you meet the prerequisites for upgrading the old computer

- How to upgrade databases successfully

If you are upgrading servers involved in replication, you must upgrade the distribution server first because SQL Server 2000 has support for SQL Server 6.5 and 7 replication tasks, but the reverse is not necessarily true.

One-Computer vs. Two-Computer Upgrades

One of the major considerations is whether to leave the old SQL Server installation in place and migrate the data to a new server or to upgrade the original 6.5 or 7 server to SQL Server 2000.

The main advantage to using a second box is that the original server is untouched during the upgrade and can quickly be brought back online if there is a problem with either the migration to SQL Server 2000 or the server itself. The major disadvantage here is that a second server at least as powerful as the original 6.5 or 7 server must be purchased or leased.

Upgrading vs. Side-by-Side Installation

If you decide to upgrade a SQL Server 6.5 or 7 server to SQL Server 2000, you have one more decision to make. You can choose to install SQL Server 2000 in the same folder that 6.5 or 7 occupied, or you can install SQL Server 2000 in a different folder.

The advantage to installing SQL Server 2000 in a different folder is that you can run SQL Server 2000 and 6.5 or 7 simultaneously and can thoroughly test the SQL Server 2000 installation before converting your databases from 6.5 or 7 to SQL Server 2000. In addition, the conversion process can be set to preserve the old databases. This allows you to use your 6.5 or 7 server in the event of a problem during conversion. The disadvantage to installing SQL Server 2000 in a new folder is that it will take significantly more hard drive space and you must manually convert your databases and settings. Running multiple copies of SQL Server will also significantly increase the RAM and processor requirements of the server to maintain the same performance you would get if you were running only a single instance.

Switching between SQL 6.5, 7, and 2000

SQL Server 6.5 and 7 allow only a single copy to run (the default instance) at any given time, whereas SQL Server 2000 allows you to run multiple copies or instances (as named instances). In other words, you can run SQL Server 6.5 as a default instance and SQL Server 2000 as a named instance or SQL Server 7 as a default instance and SQL Server 2000 as a named instance, but you can't run SQL Server 6.5 and SQL Server 7 at the same time.

SQL Server 7 and SQL Server 2000 come with a program (Switch to SQL 6.5/Switch to 7) that can be run to rename various services so you can start either older version of SQL Server if you have all three versions on the same server installed as default instances. Note that some functions (such as using Performance Monitor to check a 6.5 server) will not work if you are switching back and forth.

Upgrade Prerequisites

Several prerequisites must be met in order to upgrade SQL Server 6.5 to SQL Server 2000:

- Service Pack 4 for Windows NT 4 or Windows 2000.

- Internet Explorer 4.01 Service Pack 1 or higher.

- 256MB of RAM.

- 180MB of free hard drive space (for full installation), plus free space equal to about 1.5 times the size of the databases being upgraded.

- If upgrading SQL Server 6.5, Service Pack 5 (or higher) for SQL Server 6.5 is required.
- If upgrading SQL Server 6 or earlier, you must first upgrade to SQL Server 7.

Because upgrades—especially live, in-place upgrades—have a chance of failing, always do a full backup of your 6.5 or 7 SQL Server computer and databases first.

Upgrading Databases

You can use the Upgrade Wizard to upgrade databases. SQL Server 6.5 and 7 databases can be directly upgraded to SQL Server 2000 with the Upgrade Wizard. SQL Server 7 databases can also be copied to the SQL Server 2000 server using the new Database Copy Wizard. Note that SQL Server 2000 cannot load backups made from earlier versions of SQL Server. It must be able to read a live database in order to create a converted copy of it.

If you choose to have the Upgrade Wizard delete old SQL 6.5 devices and databases, it deletes *all* devices and databases, whether or not they were upgraded. For this reason, you should upgrade all user databases at the same time. Remember: Always back up before upgrading, regardless of the upgrade method used.

Upgrade Issues

When upgrading SQL Server computers and databases, there are some issues that you need to be aware of. One issue is that often objects in the old databases cannot be created in the new database. This happens for various reasons:

- The object has been renamed with the `sp_rename` stored procedure.
- The accompanying text in the syscomments table is missing.

- Stored procedures have been created within other stored procedures.

- The owner of an object's login ID is not created at the new server.

- The older server was using integrated security but the new server is using mixed security and the NT groups have not been created at the new server.

These are also some of the issues that you may encounter when upgrading servers and databases:

- The upgrade process will fail if @@SERVERNAME returns NULL.

- Stored procedures that reference or modify system tables will not be converted.

- Servers involved with replication should be upgraded in a certain order: The Distribution server must be upgraded first, and many SQL 2000 replication functions will not be enabled until all involved servers are upgraded.

Configuring SQL Server 2000

Although SQL Server follows the ANSI specifications for relational database engines, it also allows you to make changes to various internal settings to control the way it deals with issues such as the use of quotes or the use of the NULL character. You may want to make changes to the default settings to support legacy applications or for convenience when working with SQL Server.

ANSI settings are discussed later in this chapter. Configuring linked servers is covered in Chapter 3, while configuring SQL Mail is covered in detail in Chapter 8.

SQL Server Settings

SQL Server 2000 automatically configures the most common settings, including the memory and the number of connections used and the percentage of cache devoted to procedures instead of data.

You can manually configure the most common items using Enterprise Manager, but for those items not shown in Enterprise Manager, you will need to use the `sp_configure` stored procedure.

Configuring SQL Internal Settings

Configure SQL Server by highlighting the server and choosing Tools ➢ SQL Server Configuration Properties or by right-clicking and choosing Properties.

In Exercise 2.4, you'll look at the major configuration parameters of SQL Server.

EXERCISE 2.4

Configuring SQL Server

1. Start Enterprise Manager and connect to your SQL Server computer.

2. Highlight your server and choose Tools ➢ SQL Server Configuration Properties or right-click and choose Properties.

3. From the main property sheet (the General tab), you can choose the startup parameters and whether the services autostart.

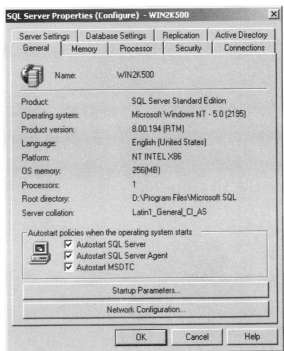

4. On the Memory tab, change the amount of RAM SQL Server uses. Note that SQL Server 2000 dynamically allocates RAM and that you should be careful when adjusting this default. You may want to lower the maximum amount available for SQL Server so that the operating system and other applications will have enough RAM to function efficiently. You might also consider raising the minimum RAM for cases in which SQL Server acts sluggish when it is first started.

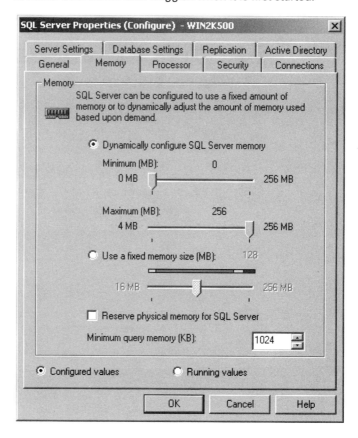

5. The number and priorities of the CPUs used by SQL Server can be controlled from the Processor tab. Note that Windows 9*x*/Me (and thus SQL Server running on Windows 9*x*/Me) does not support more than one CPU. Do not boost SQL Server's priority unless it is on a dedicated server; an increase will slow all other processes.

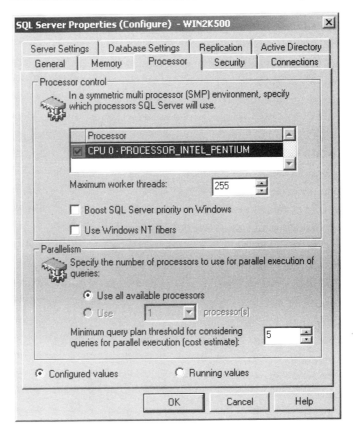

EXERCISE 2.4 *(continued)*

6. Click the Security tab. Here you can change SQL Server to use security that is integrated with NT. You can also assign a user account or change the account's password from this tab.

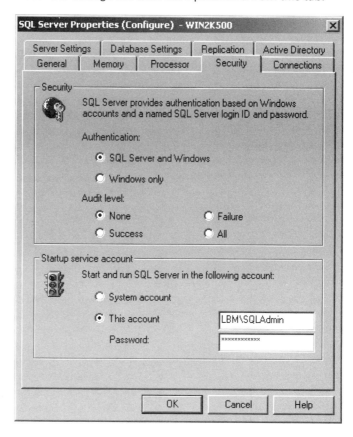

7. Click the Connections tab to configure the number of connections that SQL Server will support. Because SQL Server 2000 dynamically allocates connections as needed (0 is the default, which means that connections will be allocated as long as enough RAM exists), adjust the connections only if you want to limit them. Connections are not the same as users. For example, a user with Excel, Access (with three windows), and Crystal Reports open has five connections but only counts as one user. You need to license the number of users connected to SQL Server (except in per-CPU licensing, which is open), but the number of connections is a function of how many applications they have open at any given time and does not affect licensing. It will, however, affect the hardware that SQL Server runs on because, in order to maintain good response time with more connections, you'll need a higher level of hardware for SQL Server.

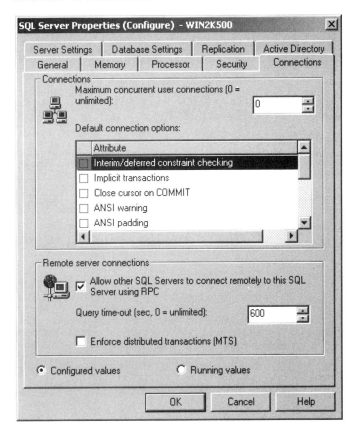

8. Go to the Server Settings tab. You can control the direct editing of system tables, allow nested triggers, and prevent runaway queries. You can also configure the SQL Mail session here.

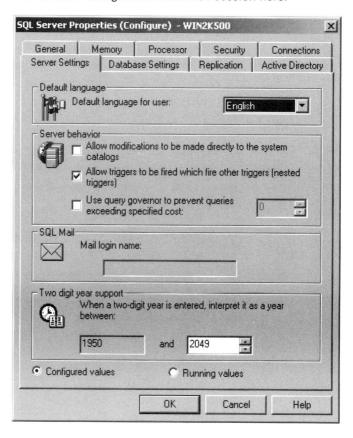

9. Choose the Database Settings tab. On this tab, you can set a default fill factor for indexes, a retry time for backups, and the recovery interval. Note that settings of 0 are automatically configured by SQL Server.

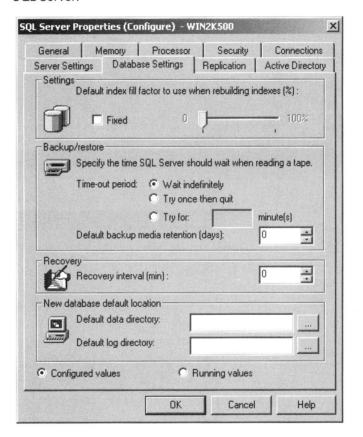

10. Click OK to save your changes or Cancel to leave the property sheet without saving them.

Configuring SQL Network Protocol Settings

SQL Server acts as a server separate from Windows 2000 and must be specifically configured to support the various protocols installed on Windows 2000.

Of course, protocols that are misconfigured (or not installed) in Windows 2000 will not work for SQL Server.

Microsoft
Exam
Objective

Configure network libraries.

The Network Configuration button on the General tab of the server's property sheet can also be used to set the protocols for the server.

In Exercise 2.5, you'll configure protocols for SQL Server using the Server Network utility from the SQL Server program group.

EXERCISE 2.5

Configuring Protocols Supported by SQL Server

1. Start the Server Network utility from the SQL Server program group. You will see a list of protocols and configurations that SQL Server currently supports (some are enabled and some aren't). Note that you can change the network protocols for a named instance by choosing it from the drop-down box.

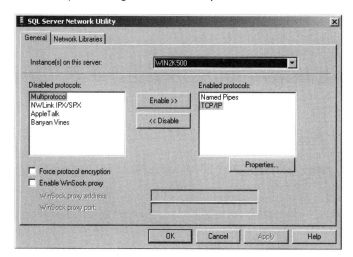

2. Add support for a new protocol by highlighting it and clicking Enable. Many protocols have configurations that can be changed, such as the port for TCP/IP or the server name for IPX/SPX. You will be prompted for any changes when you add the protocol.

3. Change the properties of existing protocols by highlighting the protocol (we show TCP/IP) and clicking Properties from the main protocol screen.

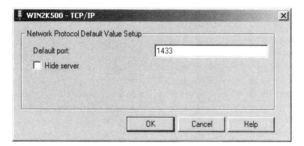

4. Click OK and then click OK in the main protocol screen to save your changes when you have finished.

Configuring ANSI Settings

SQL Server 2000 follows ANSI standards more closely than SQL Server 6.5 or 7 did. In SQL Server 6.5, for example, even though the ANSI standard is NULL, a column was considered NOT NULL unless you specified that the column should allow NULL data. SQL Server 2000, however, allows all columns to contain NULL data unless you specify otherwise.

Although most settings are global for SQL Server, some options are unique for each database. Database options are covered in detail in Chapter 4.

Real World Scenario: Why Set Different Database Options?

There are several cases in which it would be useful to configure databases differently from each other—to set them to different collations, for example. You may need to have one server that contains databases for both an American and Chinese application. You could combine the databases into one large database and change the collations on a per-column basis or leave them as separate databases. In that case, the Chinese database can be set for a different collation than the American database.

Another reason you may want to set different database options involves the transaction log and how you back up the database. For a historical database, you may wish to have the log autowrap, whereas you would not want the log for a database that tracks important information to autowrap; that way, it could be backed up consistently.

If you upgrade a database from SQL Server 6.5 and leave the columns at the default (NOT NULL), the columns will allow NULL data after being converted to SQL Server 2000. When creating columns and tables, you should always specifically state whether the column should allow NULL or NOT NULL. An upgrade to SQL Server 2000 would then have no effect on the columns.

In Exercise 2.6, you will configure different ANSI standards for SQL Server.

EXERCISE 2.6

Changing ANSI Settings for SQL Server

1. Set the properties of SQL Server by opening Enterprise Manager, highlighting the server, and choosing Tools ➢ Properties or by right-clicking and choosing Properties.

2. Go to the Connections option screen by clicking the Connections tab (see Exercise 2.4).

3. Set various options as desired. Click OK to save your settings.

4. Set the desired database options by highlighting a database, right-clicking, and choosing Properties.

5. Go to the Options tab.

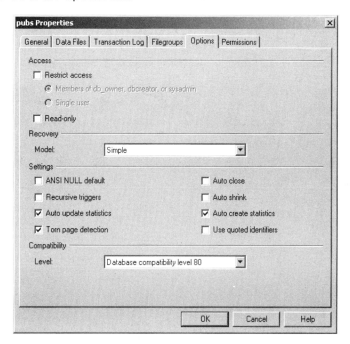

6. Set the various database options as desired. Click OK to save your settings.

Installing SQL Server Clients

SQL Server 2000 supports various network clients, including non-Microsoft clients, MS-DOS, Windows 3.*x*, Windows 9*x*, and Windows NT and 2000, although SQL Server only ships with Microsoft 32-bit client support. Once you install the desired connectivity software, you can configure connections by using the ODBC Administrator (for ODBC connections) or the Client Network utility (for DB-Library and OLE-DB connections).

Many applications, such as Office 95/97 and Internet Information Server (IIS), install ODBC drivers for SQL Server. If client computers already have ODBC and SQL drivers installed, all you will need to do is configure the ODBC connections via the ODBC Data Sources utility of the Control Panel or Administration Tools (see Figure 2.3).

FIGURE 2.3 The ODBC Data Sources utility of the Control Panel

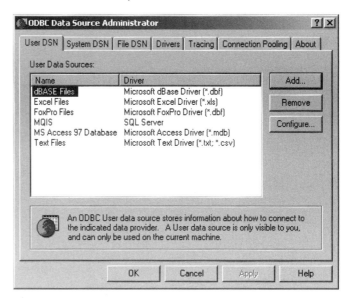

Once inside the ODBC program, you generally add one of two types of configurations:

- User DSN, which can be used only by the user who created it

- System DSN, which can be used by any user and application on the computer

 When you install a SQL Server client, you can install just the client piece (which allows the client to connect to SQL Server), or you can install the SQL Server management tools (Enterprise Manager, Query Analyzer, etc.). To install the client connectivity software and/or the management tools, choose a custom installation and leave only the management tools and/or the connectivity boxes selected.

In Exercise 2.7, you'll install the client connectivity software.

EXERCISE 2.7

Installing SQL Server Client Connectivity Software

1. Start the installation by running the Setup program from the SQL Server CD-ROM.

2. Go through the steps for a normal installation, making sure you choose to do a custom installation (see step 12 in Exercise 2.1).

3. From the Installation Definition screen, clear all of the boxes except Connectivity Only and click Next to install just the client components.

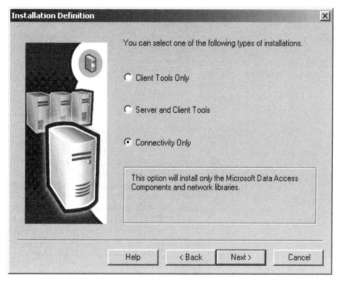

4. Click OK when the installation is complete. You may need to reboot the client if some sort of ODBC driver wasn't already installed.

In Exercise 2.8, you'll configure an ODBC connection.

EXERCISE 2.8

Configuring an ODBC Connection

1. Choose Administrative Tools ➤ Data Sources (ODBC) utility.

2. Create a new User DSN configuration by clicking Add (see Figure 2.3).

EXERCISE 2.8 *(continued)*

3. In the Create New Data Source dialog box, select the SQL Server driver. Click Finish to continue.

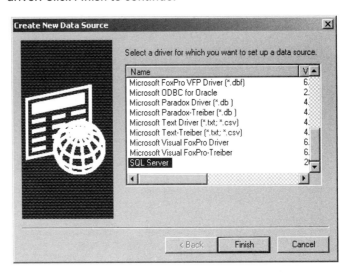

4. Enter a name and a description for the connection and choose the instance of SQL Server you wish to connect to. Click Next to continue.

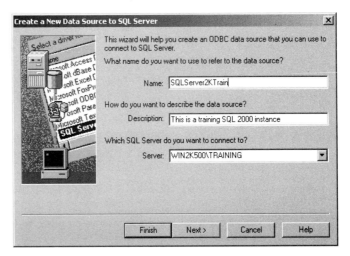

EXERCISE 2.8 *(continued)*

5. Enter the security information necessary to connect to the SQL Server computer. Click Next to continue.

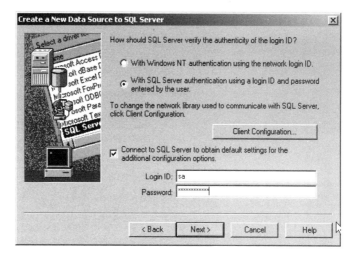

6. Select the database you wish to use. Click Next to continue.

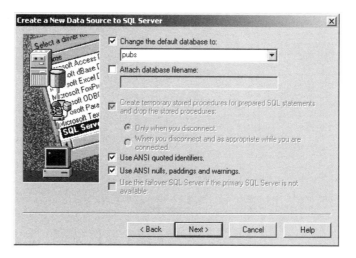

7. Click Finish to use the default language and logging options.

8. Select Test Data Source to test the configuration. A screen similar to the one shown should appear.

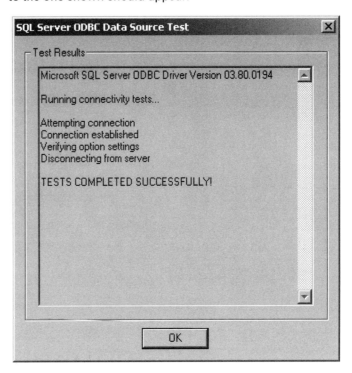

9. Click OK to close the test results screen, then click OK in the next two dialog boxes that appear to save the configuration and close the ODBC Data Source Administrator.

English Query Support

SQL Server 2000 comes with English Query, an additional component that allows users to ask a question in simple English, such as "How many red cars did we sell in December?" The English Query module will convert it to an SQL query, send the query to SQL Server, and show the results.

Real World Scenario: Setting Up ODBC

ODBC configurations are like a bridge between applications—they just provide the means for two applications to communicate. You should configure ODBC connections to point the user to the database they use for a particular application. If a user uses more than one server or database, you can define multiple ODBC connections—one for each server or database. However, ODBC is slower than OLE-DB and should be used for one of two reasons:

- When the level of programming experience is such that writing connection strings would be overbearing (such as those used for Visual InterDev data tools)

- When using a client that cannot connect with OLE-DB for one reason or another

---

To install English Query, simply choose Install English Query from the main SQL Server Setup screen. Configuring English Query is rather complex, however, and is beyond the scope of this book. For more information, refer to the demonstration files as well as the online documentation for English Query.

OLAP Server Support

SQL Server includes an OLAP (Online Analytical Processing) server component (called Analysis Services) that must be installed and configured separately. OLAP servers presummarize data to speed responses to queries running against a data warehouse. For example, an OLAP server can analyze and store sales totals based on salesperson, category of item, location of store, and day of week. Reports can easily be generated that look at data across three or more variables, such as "Show me the best salesperson for each store" or "Show me the lowest selling category for each month."

The OLAP server component is installed from the main SQL Server Setup screen by selecting Install Analysis Services. Configuring and using an OLAP server is beyond the scope of this book. Microsoft will have a separate test designed for data warehouse applications and the use of an OLAP server.

Neither English Query nor OLAP server is covered on the current Administration exam.

Summary

SQL Server 2000 is the latest generation of relational database servers from Microsoft and can be installed on Windows 9x/Millennium platforms, as well as on Windows NT and Windows 2000. Although the installations are similar, the functions that are limited to Windows NT and Windows 2000 servers (multiple CPU support, user accounts assigned to the SQL Server services, etc.) make the two installations different. In this chapter, you learned the following:

- How to install SQL Server 2000 and the necessary hardware and software

- How to install a second instance of SQL Server 2000

- How to upgrade from SQL Server 6.5 or 7 to SQL Server 2000

- How to configure SQL Server 2000

- How to install SQL Server 2000 clients

You also learned about the English Query component, which allows users to ask questions in simple English, and OLAP SQL Server support. Neither the English Query component nor OLAP SQL Server support will be covered on the exam; we mentioned them in this chapter to give you a basic understanding of SQL Server 2000.

Exam Essentials

Know how to install SQL Server 2000 You need to be able to install and connect to both default and named instances. Know when to use a named instance and the advantages and disadvantages a named instance gives you. Understand that named instances are not compatible with older applications and software.

Know how to upgrade from SQL Server 6.5 or 7   You need to be able to do live, side-by-side, and named instance upgrades. Know the advantages and disadvantages of the various upgrade possibilities. You also need to know in which of several given scenarios you can upgrade successfully to SQL Server 2000.

Be able to configure the server and a database   You need to be able to configure a server and database to support nonstandard settings. You also need to know how to configure basic items of a server, such as memory used.

Be able to install and configure a client   You need to be able to configure SQL client protocol options and ODBC connections. Pay close attention to User versus System ODBC configurations.

Key Terms

character set	named instance
collation	sort order
default instance	Unicode

Review Questions

1. Which batch file is used to do an unattended installation of the server?

   A. Sqlcli.bat

   B. Sqlful.bat

   C. Sqlcst.bat

   D. Sqlrem.bat

2. If you do an unattended installation and do not specify which user account to assign to the SQL Server services, which account will be chosen?

   A. You must always specify an account to use.

   B. The Administrator account.

   C. The SA account.

   D. The LocalSystem account.

3. Which is the folder for the database files of a default instance of SQL 2000 if Windows 2000 is installed on the C: drive?

   A. C:\Program Files\80\Data

   B. C:\MSSQL2000\Data

   C. C:\SQLServer\Data

   D. C:\Program Files\Microsoft SQL Server\MSSQL\Data

4. You just promoted Sue to backup database administrator. You need to make shortcuts for her for Enterprise Manager and the other tools. You have a default instance and an instance called Training on the C: drive. Select the path you would have to go to in order to build her shortcuts.

   A. C:\Program Files\Microsoft SQL Server\80

   B. C:\Program Files\Microsoft SQL Server\MSSQL

   C. C:\Program Files\Microsoft SQL Server\MSSQL$Training

   D. C:\Program Files\Microsoft SQL Server\Tools

5. In which Registry key will you find the majority of information on SQL Server 2000 services?

   A. Hkey_Local_Machine\Software\SQLServer

   B. Hkey_Local_Machine\Software\Microsoft\MSSQLServer

   C. Hkey_Current_Config\Software\Microsoft\SQLServer

   D. Hkey_Current_User\Software\Microsoft\SQLServer

6. You have turned auditing on inside SQL Server. What folder would you look in to find out who is attempting to connect to SQL Server?

   A. \Errors

   B. \Audit

   C. \Status

   D. \Log

7. You install SQL Server with Windows Authentication mode selected. Sue is a member of the local Administrators group, and Katie is a member of the local Server Operators group. Which of these Windows accounts will be able to connect to SQL Server?

   A. Both Sue and Katie

   B. Sue

   C. Katie

   D. SA

8. How do you change the configurations for SQL Server from within Enterprise Manager? (Select all that apply.)

   A. Highlight the server, right-click, and choose Settings.

   B. Highlight the server, right-click, and choose Properties.

   C. Highlight the server and choose Tools ➤ Settings.

   D. Highlight the server and choose Tools ➤ SQL Server Configuration Properties.

9. What is the default port for TCP/IP and SQL Server?

   A. 433

   B. 520

   C. 1020

   D. 1433

10. How many simultaneous instances can you run on SQL Server 2000 as supported by Microsoft?

    A. 1

    B. 4

    C. 16

    D. 32

11. You have a SQL Server 7 computer. You are going to upgrade to SQL Server 2000 and want to have no impact on the clients. You are worried about your applications running under SQL Server 2000. You want to be able to convert to SQL Server 2000 but be able to go back to SQL Server 7 if needed. Which of these solutions would work?

    A. Install SQL Server 2000 in the same folder as SQL Server 7.

    B. Install SQL Server 2000 in a different folder than SQL Server 7 and as a named instance.

    C. Install SQL Server 2000 in a different folder than SQL Server 7 and as a default instance.

    D. Install SQL Server 2000 on a different server than SQL Server 7 and move the databases using the Database Copy Wizard.

12. An administrator in a branch office wants a copy of the settings you used when you installed SQL Server so he can use the same settings for his installation. What file can you send him?

    A. Setup.iss

    B. Sql.iss

    C. Sqlsettings.iss

    D. Auto.iss

13. You are configuring clients for SQL Server 2000. Which of these can you select? (Select all that apply.)

   A. XML

   B. ODBC

   C. OLE-DB

   D. SQL-DB

14. What utility is used to configure ODBC connections in Windows 2000?

   A. Data Sources (ODBC)

   B. ODBC Setup

   C. ODBC Client Config utility

   D. SQL Client Config utility

15. You want to set your SQL Server computer to a nonstandard port. What would you use to configure the server to use a custom port? (Select all that apply.)

   A. Network Configuration button on the server's property sheet in Enterprise Manager

   B. Server Network utility

   C. Network Configuration button on the database's property sheet in Enterprise Manager

   D. Query Analyzer

16. You have a SQL Server 6.5 server with Service Pack 2. You also have 4GB of user databases on a Windows NT 3.51 server with Service Pack 5 and 256MB of RAM. You have 4GB of free space. You wish to upgrade the computer in place to SQL Server 2000. Which of the following will happen when you attempt to upgrade?

   A. The upgrade will work correctly.

   B. The upgrade will not work because of a single problem.

   C. The upgrade will not work because of two problems.

   D. The upgrade will not work because of three problems.

17. You have a server called SQL1. You install a default instance. How do you refer to the instance in your client applications?

A. SQL1

B. SQL1\Default

C. SQL1\MSSQLServer

D. SQL1\Instance1

18. You have a server called SQL1. You install an instance called training. How do you refer to the instance in your client applications?

A. SQL1

B. SQL1\training

C. SQL1\instance1

D. SQL1\instance0

19. You install SQL Server but get a "Service cannot start" failure message when you attempt to start SQL Server. You installed a default instance. What could be the problem?

A. You assigned the service to the Local account.

B. The account you used needs the Logon as a Service right.

C. The account you used needs to be a member of the Domain Admins group.

D. The account you used needs to have the password set to Change on Logon.

20. You install SQL Server. Whenever you reboot your server, you have to start SQL Server before anyone can connect. How can you fix this?

A. Set the SQL Server Agent to autostart when the OS starts.

B. Set the SQL Server service to autostart when the OS starts.

C. Set the user account assigned to the service to log on locally.

D. Set the user account assigned to the Agent to log on locally.

Answers to Review Questions

1. C. The batch file that Microsoft has written to help automate unattended installations is `Sqlcst.bat`.

2. D. If you don't specify in your ISS file which account (and corresponding password) to use, the Local System account will be used.

3. D. SQL Server installs the default databases to the `Program Files\Microsoft SQL Server\MSSQL\Data` folder for the default instance. Named instances would replace the `MSSQL` folder with `MSSQL$NameOfInstance` for the path.

4. A. The folder for administration tools is `\ProgramFiles\Microsoft SQL Server\80`. Note that this folder is created on the system drive no matter where SQL Server was installed.

5. B. Information for SQL Server services is held in the Hkey_Local_Machine\Software\Microsoft\MSSQLServer key.

6. D. The default folder for log files is the `\Log` folder. On a default instance, the `\Log` folder will be under `\Program Files\Microsoft SQL Server \MSSQL`, while logs for a named instance would be under `\Program Files\Microsoft SQL Server\MSSQL$NameOfInstance`.

7. B. The default logins for SQL Server are SA (which only works in mixed mode) and Builtin\Administrators, which is the local Administrators group. In this case, only Sue can access SQL Server because only she is a member of the local Administrators group. There is no Windows user called SA—the SA account only exists on the SQL Server side.

8. B, D. There is no Settings option. All settings are changed from the property sheets. You get to the properties of an object by right-clicking the object and choosing Properties or by choosing Tools ➢ SQL Server Configuration Properties for properties of the server.

9. D. The default port for TCP/IP and SQL Server is 1433. If you change the port on the server, you have to change the port on every client because the clients assume you are using the default port.

10. C. You can run 16 supported instances at the same time (if you have enough resources). In real life, you may actually be able to run more, but Microsoft only officially supports up to 16.

11. C. If you install SQL Server 2000 in the same folder SQL Server 7 is in, you can't switch between the two, and if you install it as a named instance, you have to configure every client to use the named instance instead of the default instance. Option D would have worked except that, by moving the database (instead of copying it) to the new SQL Server 2000 server, you can't go back to the SQL Server 7 server if you have to. You would also have to point the clients to the new server if you kept the old one in place. If you install SQL Server 2000 in a different folder than SQL Server 7 (option C), you can switch between the two default instances as needed.

12. A. The Setup program keeps track of all of your settings in a file called Setup.iss in case you want to use the same configuration again later (on your computer or an entirely different computer).

13. A, B, C. There is no such thing as SQL-DB. SQL Server 2000 supports XML-, ODBC-, and OLE-DB-based clients.

14. A. The Data Sources (ODBC) utility of the Administrative Tools is used to configure ODBC connections. Administrative Tools can be found in Control Panel as well as the main Start ➤ Programs menu. ODBC Setup would install the ODBC drivers, the ODBC Client Config utility is not called by that name, and the SQL Client Config utility only specifies which protocols to use—not the actual ODBC settings.

15. A, B. The Network Configuration button on the server's property sheet and the Server Network utility are used to configure the protocols and ports on which the server listens.

16. C. There are two reasons the upgrade will not work. First, you must be using Service Pack 5 for SQL Server 6.5 to upgrade SQL Server 6.5 to SQL Server 2000. Second, you must use NT 4 Service Pack 4 instead of NT 3.51 Server with Service Pack 5 to upgrade to SQL Server 2000.

17. A. To refer to a default instance, just use the server name (in this case, SQL1).

18. B. To refer to a named instance, use the name of the instance after the server name (in this case, SQL1\training).

19. B. Accounts assigned to services need the Logon as a Service right. Although they may require other rights as well (such as local Administrator rights in the case of SQL Server), they must have the Logon as a Service right. If you assigned an account, you are not using the Local account. If the account is set to Change on Logon, the service will not be able to use the account because a service cannot change a password.

20. B. In order for SQL Server to automatically start, it needs to be set to start when the OS starts. Of course, you would probably also set the agent to start automatically.

Chapter

3

SQL Server Tools, Utilities, and Queries

MICROSOFT EXAM OBJECTIVES COVERED IN THIS CHAPTER:

- ✓ Create a linked server.
- ✓ Configure network libraries.
- ✓ Perform integrity checks. Methods include configuring the Database Maintenance Plan Wizard and using the Database Consistency Checker (DBCC).

In this chapter, we'll examine some of the utilities that come packaged with SQL Server. Because we've already looked at a few, and because later chapters cover the tools in more detail, this chapter should serve as more of an introduction to the tools and Structured Query Language (SQL). We'll also explore the SQL Enterprise Manager in more detail. The *Enterprise Manager* is so large and flexible that the different aspects of its management capabilities must be presented in more than one chapter. In this chapter, we'll focus on creating and managing multiple servers and server groups. You'll learn how to modify server options, configure SQL clients, and use the OSQL and Query Analyzer utilities.

This chapter also presents an overview of SQL and Query Analyzer. We'll discuss the SQL Profiler utility that allows you to track connections and disconnections from your SQL Server computer and determine which SQL scripts were run. In addition, we'll look at running local queries, as well as linking to a remote server.

Although most of the utilities covered in this chapter are not listed specifically in the objectives for the test, you will need to know what each does and when to use it. The test may contain questions that require you to choose the best utility to use for a given situation, and many of the situations involve some form of troubleshooting. You also need to know how to perform basic queries using Query Analyzer and OSQL.EXE, which will be discussed in this chapter.

For additional coverage of the objectives in this chapter, see also Chapters 2 and 6.

Managing the Server with Enterprise Manager

Before you can manage SQL Server computers in your enterprise, you must register the servers in the SQL Enterprise Manager. In this section, you will create server groups and then register SQL Server computers to place into them.

Once you register your server, your registration is held encrypted in the Registry under your Windows user account. If you need to change your registration (to change accounts or passwords, for example), you can easily edit it in Enterprise Manager. Another reason to edit the registration properties would be to hide or show system databases and objects.

Server groups are used to provide logical groupings for administrative purposes. Exercise 3.1 will take you through the steps for creating a new server group (for the Sales SQL Server computers). You will then register a new SQL Server computer in the group.

Because Windows 9x does not support the server Named Pipes net library, you must make sure your client is configured to use a different protocol (such as TCP/IP) so that Enterprise Manager will connect to the server. Note that because of the lack of support for Named Pipes, you cannot connect to servers running on Windows 9x by using the browser window—you will need to enter the name of the server manually. Windows 9x clients making connections to a local (running on that computer) SQL Server computer use a "shared memory" net library so they can browse and see the server by name.

There are a few rules that you should be aware of before creating your servers and groups:

- Server groups can be created at the local server only. If you want the SQL Enterprise Manager running on other machines to have the same logical groups, you must go to each of those machines and repeat the steps you took to create groups on the first server. You can get by this restriction by copying settings from the Registry of a computer that has registered servers.

- Group names must be unique at each server.

- SQL Server computer names can be only letters, numbers, and these characters: _, #, $. Avoid using punctuation symbols because they have special meaning in the SQL Server environment.

EXERCISE 3.1

Using Enterprise Manager to Create Server Groups and Register to SQL Server

1. Start Enterprise Manager by choosing Start ➤ Programs ➤ Microsoft SQL Server ➤ Enterprise Manager.

2. Click the plus sign next to Microsoft SQL Servers to open the default SQL Server groups.

3. Click the plus sign next to SQL Server Group to open the group and get a list of the servers currently in the group. If you are running Enterprise Manager from your SQL Server computer, the server will automatically be a member of the group.

4. Create a new group called Sales Servers by right-clicking the Microsoft SQL Servers item and choosing New SQL Server Group (you can also choose the Action ➤ New SQL Server Group menu item).

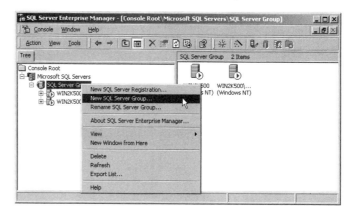

5. Enter a name for the group (call it Sales Servers) and click OK to save the group.

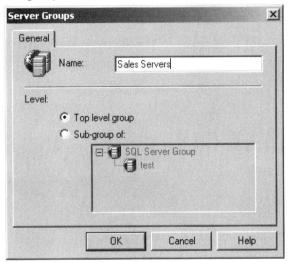

6. Register a server in the Sales Servers group by highlighting the group, right-clicking, and selecting New SQL Server Registration or by choosing Action ➢ New SQL Server Registration.

7. Select the From Now On, I Want to Perform This Task without Using a Wizard check box and click Next.

8. Enter the name of an existing server that is not currently registered (you can register a server only once in Enterprise Manager) or use a made-up name such as TEMP. Leave Use Windows Authentication checked (if your Windows user has sufficient rights assigned in SQL Server) or select Use SQL Server Authentication and enter the name and password of the account you wish to use (such as the SA account).

9. You may want to select Show System Databases and System Objects, which lets you see and manipulate the system objects using Enterprise Manager. Although this option is currently enabled by default, you should check this option when system databases and tables disappear.

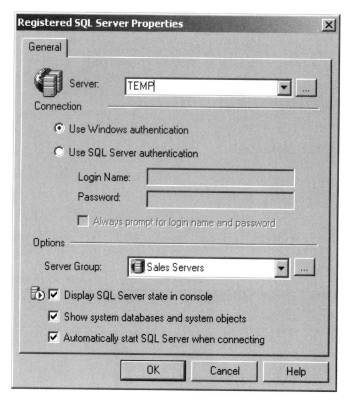

10. Click OK, and if your information is correct, the server will now be registered.

Before you can manage a server, you will need to register it. To register it, you need a SQL Server user account and password, or your current Windows user account needs to have been granted rights in SQL Server. Normal users will probably never need to run Enterprise Manager.

The Enterprise Manager Wizards

Once the server is registered, SQL Server provides various wizards for common tasks (see Figure 3.1).

FIGURE 3.1 The Enterprise Manager wizards

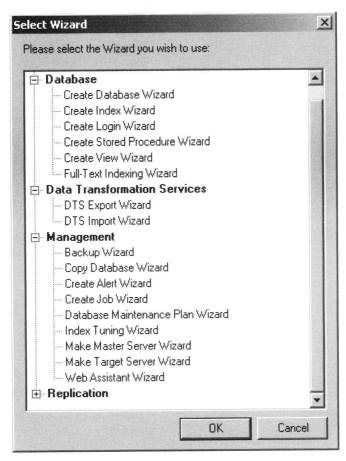

Many people do not like to use wizards. Microsoft has obliged the more experienced user by making all functions available with a right-click in the SQL Server folders (discussed later).

In the Select Wizard dialog box, the wizards are listed by category:

Database   Wizards for tasks such as creating databases, indexes, and stored procedures; restoring databases; and performing queries.

Data Transformation Services   Wizards for tasks such as importing and exporting data using the Data Transformation Services (DTS).

Management   Contains backup and restoration wizards as well as copy, maintenance, and tuning wizards.

Replication   Wizards for tasks such as creating and managing push or pull publications and removing replication from a server.

The SQL Server Folders

Enterprise Manager allows you to "drill down" into SQL Server in order to quickly get to the function you want to manage. By opening the subfolders listed under your server, you can view and manage databases, Data Transformation Services, the SQL Server Agent, backups and maintenance plans, security, and support services settings (Figure 3.2).

FIGURE 3.2   Managing SQL Server from its various folders

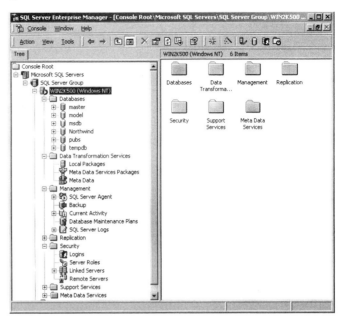

The various functions of Enterprise Manager will be covered in their respective chapters. For example, the Security folder and managing SQL Server security issues will be covered in detail in Chapter 5.

The Action Menu

The Action menu is context sensitive; the options correspond to the highlighted server or folder. For example, if you highlight the Databases folder, you can choose to create, back up, or restore a database, as well as import or export data to or from a database.

The Action menu items can also be called up by highlighting the desired folder and right-clicking.

The Tools Menu

The Tools menu allows you to quickly start many of the wizards and applications associated with SQL Server. For example, you can start the *Query Analyzer* from the Tools menu no matter where you are in Enterprise Manager.

> Don't be afraid of using the wizards in real life. When we go out consulting, we show our clients how to use the wizards so they don't have to call us back for the mundane stuff.

SQL Server Queries

If you can't get the data out of the server, there is no sense in putting it in. SQL Server was designed to allow you to easily retrieve your data. In this section, we will look at local and remote queries, and then we will look at some tools you can use to run queries. We will then go into details on the *SELECT command* and how to use it.

Local Queries

A local query is a query that is run against a server you are directly connected to. Local queries are by far the most common type of queries. To run a local query, you must first connect to the server and then run some type of program that allows you to run queries.

Therefore, to run a local query, you need some sort of application that can connect to SQL Server. Many great utilities come with SQL Server and are installed to the server by default. We'll look at these in the following sections.

Transact-SQL and the SQL Utilities

You use the Structured Query Language (SQL) to manipulate information stored in your database. These queries can be created and run from the *OSQL*, Query Analyzer, or *MS Query* utilities or from program code in such external programs as Microsoft Access or Microsoft Visual Basic.

Running Queries with OSQL

The OSQL (ODBC SQL) utility, which is accessed from the command prompt, allows you to establish a connection to the SQL Server so that you can execute T-SQL statements. OSQL is command-line driven, making it very useful for automating execution of scheduled statements; however, it is less friendly to use than a graphical interface. (Query Analyzer is a graphical front-end tool with functionality that is very similar to OSQL.)

Earlier versions of SQL Server included a similar utility called ISQL (Interactive SQL). ISQL uses DB-Library to connect to SQL Server and is thus more efficient than OSQL. If performance is an issue, ISQL is recommended over OSQL for clients that can use it. Support for DB-Library, and thus ISQL, may be dropped in future versions of SQL Server, however.

For a quick overview of the OSQL utility, follow the steps outlined in Exercise 3.2.

EXERCISE 3.2

The OSQL Utility

1. Go to a command prompt by choosing Start ➢ Programs ➢ Accessories ➢ Command Prompt (in Windows 9*x*, choose Start ➢ Programs ➢ MS-DOS).

2. From the command prompt, you must log in to a SQL Server computer. The command syntax is osql /U<user id> /P<password> / S<server name>. If you do not supply a server name, you will be logged in to the local server. Remember that passwords are always case sensitive. For our server, we would type (make sure you change this to match your password and server) the following:

   osql /Usa /P /Swin2k500

3. You should now see a command prompt similar to this: 1>

4. To run a query, type it at the prompt and then execute the batch by adding the word "GO" on a line all by itself. For example, if you wanted to find out the name of your SQL Server, you would type this:

   SELECT @@version

   GO

EXERCISE 3.2 *(continued)*

5. Your results will be similar to the following:

```
Microsoft SQL Server  2000 - 8.00.194 (Intel X86)

      Aug  6 2000 00:57:48

      Copyright (c) 1988-2000 Microsoft Corporation

      /Enterprise Evaluation Edition on Windows NT 5.0
(Build 2195: )
```

6. You can also run this next set of simple SELECT statements. You will quickly notice one of the major limitations of using the OSQL utility. Type in the following:

USE pubs

Go

SELECT *

FROM authors

GO

7. Although you retrieved all the information from the Authors table in the Pubs database, it scrolled past the top of your screen and word-wrapped in such a way that it made it difficult to read. For this reason, you will find the Query Analyzer utility to be much more useful.

8. To exit the OSQL utility and return to a command prompt, type this:

`Exit`

9. To exit the command prompt, type in again:

`Exit`

Running Queries with Query Analyzer

You can run all the same queries in the Query Analyzer interface as you can in OSQL. The Query Analyzer interface has the advantage of being a multiple-document interface (MDI).

Query Analyzer has changed dramatically from SQL Server 7. What was a very good program is now an excellent tool for viewing data and developing for SQL Server.

MDI allows you to run multiple queries in separate windows and then view the results at the bottom of your query window. The results window is especially helpful because it presents all results in a single window. This allows you to scroll through the results and use the cut, copy, and paste features as desired. Another of the many features of the Query Analyzer interface is that it gives you the ability to retrieve and store SQL scripts.

Because Windows 9x does not support the server Named Pipes net library, you must make sure your client is configured to use a different protocol (such as TCP/IP) so that Query Analyzer will connect to the remote SQL Server computers. If you are connecting to a local server, this is not an issue.

There are two ways to open up the Query Analyzer utility. The first method is to start it as a stand-alone utility. This is done by choosing Start ≻ Programs ≻ Microsoft SQL Server ≻ Query Analyzer. Using this method, you will be asked to provide a server name, login ID, and password (see Figure 3.3).

FIGURE 3.3   The Query Analyzer login screen

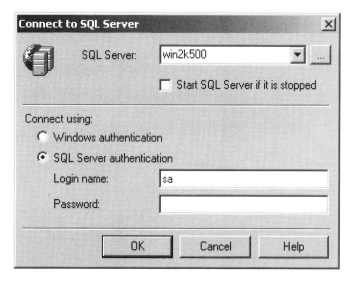

The second method is to enter through the SQL Enterprise Manager and choose the SQL Query Analyzer from the Tools menu. When you enter this way, there is no login screen: You are already logged in to a SQL Server computer. You can type your SQL statements directly into the query window or use the folders on the left side of the screen to graphically build SQL statements (see the first graphic in Exercise 3.3).

The Create New Query button allows you to create a new query. It will open a new window for the query and a new connection to the SQL Server.

Let's take a look at the different options available in the Query Analyzer utility. Exercise 3.3 will walk you through some of the most common ways to use the utility.

EXERCISE 3.3

The Query Analyzer Utility

1. Start the Query Analyzer tool either by choosing Start ➢ Programs ➢ Microsoft SQL Server ➢ Query Analyzer (and log in) or by choosing Tools ➢ SQL Query Analyzer from within SQL Enterprise Manager.

2. In the query window, enter the following:

   SELECT * FROM pubs..authors

3. Click the green arrow or press Ctrl+E or F5.

4. The query will execute and should give you results that look something like this.

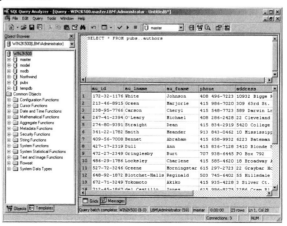

5. You could have run this query differently. Open a new query window.

6. From the Current Database listbox, select the Pubs database.

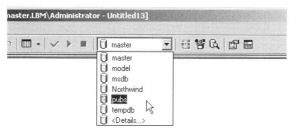

7. Run the following query:

   SELECT * FROM authors

8. You will get the same result set.

9. Here is yet another way to do the same query. From the left pane, open the Pubs database.

10. Highlight the Authors table, right-click, and choose Script Object to New Window As ➢ Select.

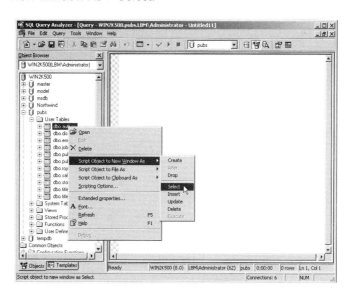

EXERCISE 3.3 *(continued)*

11. You should see that a new window was opened, with a SELECT command followed by a list of all of the columns in the Authors table.

12. Go ahead and run the query. You should get the same results you got in step 4.

13. Go to the Query menu and select Show Execution Plan. Run the query again.

14. You should have a new tab labeled Execution Plan at the bottom of the screen. This is a graphical representation of how the query was performed. In complex, multiple-table queries, the execution plan is invaluable.

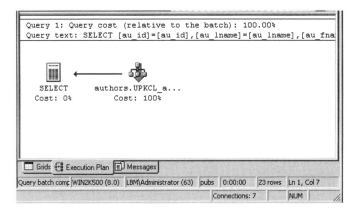

15. To open a previously saved script, click the Open Query button from the main Query Analyzer screen (or choose File ➢ Open). The Open Query button looks just like the Open button in other Microsoft products such as Word. The Open Query button allows you to browse for SQL scripts that you have saved. These are generally stored as ASCII text files with an .sql extension. There are many prebuilt SQL scripts that are used by the SQL Server installation process. These are stored in the \Microsoft SQL Server\Install folder. Browse to the \Install folder.

EXERCISE 3.3 *(continued)*

If you would like to review the results or even rerun an earlier query, simply select that query from the Window menu. You can look at the saved result set by clicking the result window, or you can reexecute the query and view the new results (which in this case will be the same as before).

The Save button allows you to save the current query as an ASCII text file with the .sql default extension. You can delete a query from the Current Query listbox by clicking the Delete Query button. The Query Options button will allow you to modify the query options. These options are beyond the scope of this book; for more information, see the SQL Server Books Online.

16. When you are finished, close the SQL Query Analyzer.

Running Queries with MSQuery

You can also use the MSQuery tool, which comes with Office 97 and Office 2000 and many other Microsoft applications, to create queries. One of the nice features of the MSQuery tool is that you can visually create your queries and then cut and paste the SQL statements into your programs or into Query Analyzer. You simply add the tables you wish to work with and then drag and drop the fields you want into the lower panel. You can also paste the results into applications such as Word or Excel. Exercise 3.4 will give you a general overview of how the MSQuery tool works.

To use MSQuery, you must already have an ODBC source set up. See Chapter 2 for more details on configuring ODBC.

EXERCISE 3.4

Using the MSQuery Tool

1. Start Excel and choose Data ➢ Get External Data ➢ Create New Query. If you don't see this menu option, run the Office Setup program and make sure you install the database connectors, (including those for Excell) and the MSQuery tool.

EXERCISE 3.4 *(continued)*

2. Highlight <New Data Source> and then click OK.

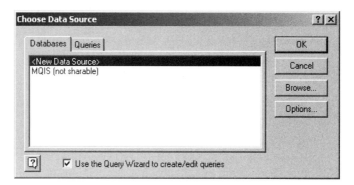

3. Enter a name for your server (on line 1) and choose the SQL Server driver (on line 2).

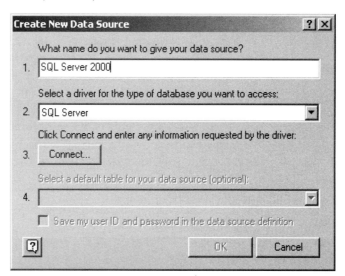

4. Click the Connect button.

5. In the SQL Server Login dialog box, choose your server from the drop-down list.

6. Leave Use Trusted Connection checked if your Windows account has enough rights in SQL Server.

7. Go to the Options section.

8. In the database listbox, switch from Master to Pubs. You will now be in the Pubs database by default when you use this configuration. Click OK to save your settings.

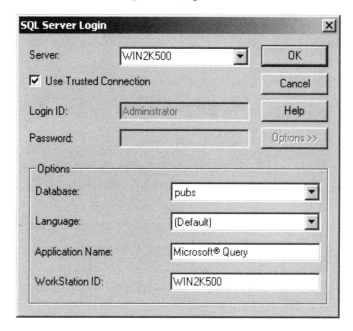

9. Click OK to save your connection. In the dialog box that appears, click OK to use your new connection.

10. Select the Authors table and then click the Add (right arrow) button. This will add the table to the top panel for use in this query.

11. Add the Titleauthor and Titles tables.

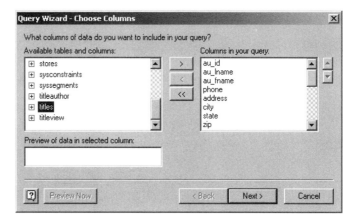

12. Click the Next button.

13. At the Filter Data screen, you can create a filter so that only certain rows will show in the result set. For this exercise, leave the fields blank and click Next.

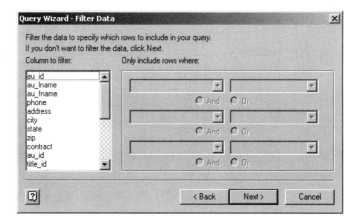

14. Choose to sort by the authors' last name and then the title. Click Next to continue.

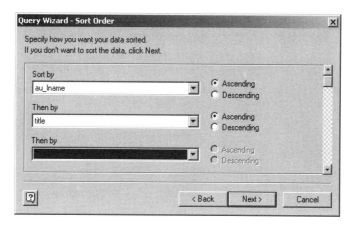

15. Leave Return Data to Microsoft Excel selected and click Finish.

16. When prompted for a location, leave the default location of A1 and click OK. The results of your query appears. Close Excel.

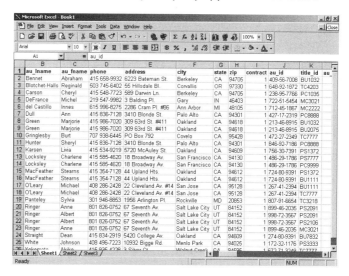

Although this was a relatively simple query, you can build extremely complex queries using the MSQuery tool.

Remote Queries

One of the great features of SQL Server 2000 is its ability to use distributed queries. A *distributed query* allows you to gather and manipulate data from multiple databases that may or may not be hosted by Microsoft SQL Server. To accomplish this task, you use *linked servers*. By definition, the SQL Server computer to which the user is connected is considered the local server, while all other servers, whether they are SQL Server computers or not, are considered remote servers. If you are connecting to these remote servers through the OLE-DB providers in SQL Server, then these remote servers are referred to as linked servers.

The first part of this section provides you with a general understanding of linked servers. You will be introduced to a few definitions and you will learn the fundamentals needed to create and maintain your linked servers.

The use of linked servers will be demonstrated in this section through the use of a distributed query example. Even though this section will not cover every aspect of a distributed query, it will give you a conceptual understanding of what your clients can do through a linked server.

You will learn the procedures necessary to establish a link to a variety of database systems, such as Oracle and Access, as well as to other SQL Server computers using both the Enterprise Manager and the Query Analyzer. We will also show you the procedures needed to designate your security credentials when your clients access a linked server. You will see how to set up security using both the Enterprise Manager and the Query Analyzer.

What Is a Linked Server?

Although SQL Server 6.5 could be set up to allow users to pull or manipulate data on remote servers, these remote servers had to be SQL Server computers. Another drawback was that users could execute only stored procedures on the remote servers. Of course, these stored procedures had to be created in advance and had to reside on the remote server.

If the user wanted to pull data from a remote server, a stored procedure had to be created on the remote server to perform the SELECT statement. If the user wanted to manipulate data on the remote server, another stored procedure had to be created on the remote server to perform the INSERT, UPDATE, or DELETE statement. The user was not able to connect or use the JOIN statement to connect tables that resided on separate physical servers.

SQL Server 2000 allows linking of remote servers that are not Microsoft SQL Server computers. These linked servers are accessed via an OLE-DB provider from the local SQL Server computer. As a result, your users can create SELECT statements that join two or more tables residing on separate servers. The fact that these tables are not on the local server is transparent to the user—you just specify the entire name of the table in the statement. For example, after you complete Exercise 3.6 (where the training instance is set up as a linked server), the following command would work: `Select * from WIN2K500\TRAINING.pubs..authors`.

Generically, an OLE-DB provider (from the viewpoint of SQL Server) is a registered Component Object Model (COM) object, which can establish a connection to a specific type of database. This COM object can translate statements issued from the local server into statements understood by the remote server.

For backward compatibility, SQL Server 2000 can still be configured to use remote servers that allow only the execution of remote stored procedures. You can upgrade a SQL Server 6.5 computer that is using remote servers to SQL Server 2000 and still maintain compatibility. Once this upgrade has been performed, you can then upgrade the remote servers to linked servers.

What Is a Distributed Query?

Suppose one of your users needs information from a couple of databases that do not reside on their SQL Server computer. If the other database servers have been linked, the user could create and run a distributed query. Take a look at this example.

Assume that XYZ Corporation has three databases with the following characteristics (Figure 3.4):

- A SEATTLE_MKTG database residing on the MARKETING server and hosted by SQL Server 2000. The SEATTLE_MKTG database contains customer sales information.

- A WAREHOUSE database hosted by Oracle 9i and containing in-stock information.

- An INVENTORY database hosted by Microsoft Access and containing parts information.

FIGURE 3.4 Linked servers

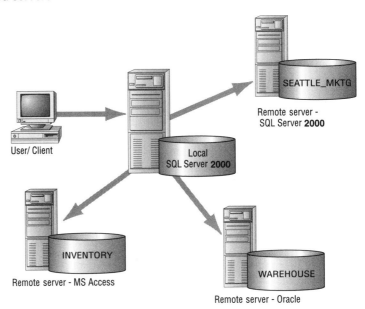

As long as the user is connected to the local SQL Server computer that has been linked to the remote database servers, they could execute a query that would pull information from some or all of the databases. The user could produce a report that would list each item contained in the corporate inventory database from the INVENTORY database on the Access server. The report could include each item's total sales from the SEATTLE_MKTG database on the SQL Server 2000 computer and the number of parts that were still in stock from the WAREHOUSE database running on Oracle. That report might look similar to Table 3.1.

TABLE 3.1 Sample Report

Part Name	Total in Stock	Total Sold
Chrome bumper, front	200	1250
Chrome bumper, rear	300	1000
Driver-side back door	15	50

TABLE 3.1 Sample Report *(continued)*

Part Name	Total in Stock	Total Sold
Driver-side front door	15	60
Left-side mirror	1000	3000
Left-side quarter–panel	50	250
Passenger-side back door	15	50
Passenger-side front door	15	60
Rear-view mirror (3-1/2 x 5)	3000	3000
Rear-view mirror (5-1/2 x 7)	1500	500
Right-side mirror	750	2000
Right-side quarter-panel	50	250
Window: back windshield	750	3500
Window: driver-side back door	50	300
Window: driver-side front door	60	400
Window: front windshield	500	2500
Window: passenger-side back door	50	300
Window: passenger-side front door	60	400

The following SELECT statement could produce such a report:

```
SELECT part_name AS [PART NAME],
sum(part_in_stock) AS [TOTAL IN STOCK],
sum(part_quantity_sold) AS [TOTAL SOLD]
FROM INVENTORY...ITEMS ITEMS
INNER JOIN WAREHOUSE..system.INSTOCK INS
```

```
ON ITEMS.part_number = INS.part_number

INNER JOIN MARKETING.SEATTLE_MKTG.dbo.SALES SALES
ON ITEMS.part_number = SALES.part_number

GROUP BY part_name
ORDER BY part_name
```

In order to reference a table residing on a linked server, you must use a fully qualified name, such as *LinkedServerName.Database.Owner.Table*. If you're using a third-party OLE-DB provider, the accompanying documentation supplied by the vendor should give you a more detailed explanation on which parts of the fully qualified name are required. You also have to use aliases when referring to the tables, as shown in the following examples.

Keep the following in mind when you are using fully qualified names and trying to link to another server:

SQL Server   Use the fully qualified naming convention *LinkedServerName.Database.Owner.Table*. Here is an example: MARKETING.SEATTLE_MKTG.dbo.SALES.

Oracle   Use the convention *LinkedServerName Owner.Table*. Here is an example: WAREHOUSE system.INSTOCK.

Access   Use the convention *LinkedServerName...Table*. Here is an example: INVENTORY PARTS.

When you're executing a SQL statement in SQL Server 2000, the local server is also considered the default server. If your SQL statement does not specify a server name, SQL Server 2000 will default to the local default server.

In our example, the SEATTLE_MKTG database is on the MARKETING server. If your user is connected to the MARKETING server, the MARKETING server is considered the local default server. The user does not need to specify MARKETING in the SQL statement if the statement references a table in the SEATTLE_MKTG database.

Continuing with our example, the SELECT statement can be altered in the way it accesses the SALES table by removing the server name MARKETING.

The following example illustrates what the SELECT statement would look like if your clients were connected to the MARKETING server:

```
SELECT part_name AS [PART NAME],
sum(part_in_stock) AS [TOTAL IN STOCK],
sum(part_quantity_sold) AS [TOTAL SOLD]
FROM INVENTORY...ITEMS ITEMS
INNER JOIN WAREHOUSE..system.INSTOCK INS
ON ITEMS.part_number = INS.part_number
INNER JOIN SEATTLE_MKTG.dbo.SALES SALES
ON ITEMS.part_number = SALES.part_number
GROUP BY part_name
ORDER BY part_name
```

Installing and Configuring Linked Servers

Creating and configuring linked servers involves two main steps:

1. Configure the link from the local server to the remote servers.

2. Configure logon security on the linked server(s) for the user(s).

Microsoft
Exam
Objective

Create a linked server.

Only SQL Server administrators (SA, or members of the SysAdmin fixed server role) can set up linked servers, and they must be set up from the SQL Server 2000 computer you wish to designate as the local server. Most of the users who will be using distributed queries will log on to this server.

When you create a link to a remote server, you have to provide several pieces of information:

Server Name   This is the mandatory name your users will use to reference the linked server.

Product Name   This is the name of the database software hosting the remote database. This parameter defaults to SQL Server if the provider name supplied is SQLOLEDB.

OLE-DB Provider Name   This is the name of the OLE-DB COM object as it is registered with the local server; it is mandatory if the product name is not SQL Server.

Data Source   This is the remote database name/alias or remote database filename, depending on which OLE-DB provider is used.

Location   This is the physical location of the remote database and depends on which OLE-DB provider is used.

Provider String   This is the setup string passed to the remote server to establish the connection or link. It can contain a remote login, remote password, remote database name, and so on, depending on which OLE-DB provider is used.

Catalog Name   This is the remote catalog or database name and also depends on which OLE-DB provider is used.

When you purchase and install a new OLE-DB provider, you should also receive documentation from the vendor specifying the required parameters and what type of information you should supply for them.

There are only two parameters that are mandatory for all providers: server name and provider name. The remaining parameters may be required, may have defaults, or may not be used at all, depending on the OLE-DB provider you choose.

As this book is being written, only a few OLE-DB providers have been tested for use with SQL Server: SQL Server 6.5, 7, and 2000; Oracle; Access; and ODBC-compliant OLE-DB providers.

There are two ways to create a linked server: through the Enterprise Manager or by executing system stored procedures. The setup procedures that follow will demonstrate both ways of creating a linked server.

When you are using the Query Analyzer, you will be using the `sp_addlinkedserver` and `sp_addlinkedsrvlogin` stored procedures. The `sp_addlinkedserver` system stored procedure tells your local server which OLE-DB provider to use and how to establish a connection through the provider. The `sp_addlinkedsrvlogin` system stored procedure tells your local server which login ID and password combinations to use to log on to the linked server.

Creating Links

Now that you have seen what parameters to use, let's see how to set up your linked servers. In the next section, you will see the procedures required to create links to SQL Server 2000, SQL Server 6.5, Access, and Oracle.

Linking to a Remote SQL Server 2000 Database Server

Linking to a remote SQL Server 2000 database is the most straightforward type of linking to configure. There are only two parameters you have to supply: the server name of the remote SQL Server 2000 computer and the product name, SQL Server.

The server name should be the actual server name (the name you would use to register the remote SQL Server 2000 computer in Enterprise Manager). If you decide to use a server name other than the actual name, you will have to specify the actual name of the remote server for the data source parameter.

It is better to use the actual name of the remote SQL Server 2000 computer for the server name parameter because most of the setup between the two databases will occur when you establish the link. If you specify the actual name in the data source parameter instead, the connection and setup will occur with the first distributed query run. Because of the setup time involved, this query may receive a time-out error and will have to be run again.

Follow the steps in Exercise 3.5 to use Enterprise Manager to link to a SQL Server 2000 server named instance called (in our case) WIN2K500\TRAINING.

EXERCISE 3.5

Establishing a Linked Server from within Enterprise Manager for a Remote SQL Server 2000 Named Instance

1. Open Enterprise Manager and connect to the computer you wish to use as the local server.

2. Right-click the Linked Servers icon and choose New Linked Server from the context menu.

EXERCISE 3.5 *(continued)*

3. Type in a named instance such as WIN2K500\TRAINING for the Linked Server option.

4. Select SQL Server as the server type. When you are finished, you should see something similar to what is shown here.

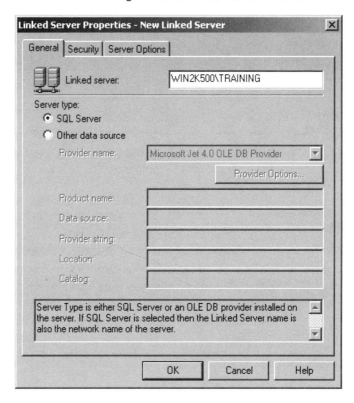

5. Click the OK button to complete the link. You may get prompted to confirm the linked server. Click Yes to finish the creation. (You will see how to use the Security tab later in this chapter.)

You can accomplish the same thing using the Query Analyzer:

1. Open the Query Analyzer.

2. In the Login screen's SQL Server option, specify the name of the server you wish to be the local server.

3. Specify your security type by checking Use Windows NT Authentication or Use SQL Server Authentication. Type in your login name and password if required and click OK.

4. Make sure that you are in the Master database.

5. Enter the following to add the WIN2K500\TRAINING server as a new linked server:

   ```
   EXEC sp_addlinkedserver Win2k500\training, N'SQL
   Server'
   ```

6. If the statement ran correctly, then your results should be as follows:

   ```
   1 row(s) affected
   ```

7. Close the Query Analyzer.

Linking to a Remote SQL Server 6.5 Database Server

Linking to a SQL Server 6.5 database is almost as straightforward as creating a link to a remote SQL Server 2000 computer. Before you can create a link to the remote SQL Server 6.5 computer, however, you will need to prepare the remote server by executing a SQL script using the SA account or an account with SQL Server administrative privileges on it. You must run `Instcat.sql` query on the SQL Server 6.5 computer. This file can be found on your SQL Server 2000 CD-ROM under the `\Install` directory or in the `\Install` directory on your local SQL Server computer. Once you have done that, the rest of the installation is almost identical to the SQL Server 2000 linked server installation.

Here are the steps needed to install and configure your SQL Server 6.5 computer for use as a linked server:

1. Copy the `Instcat.sql` file from the `\Install` directory on the CD or the SQL Server computer to a directory on the SQL Server 6.5 machine.

2. Start the ISQLW utility on the SQL 6.5 computer. Select Start ➢ Programs ➢ Microsoft SQL Server 6.5 ➢ ISQL_W.

3. Supply the security credentials necessary to log in to SQL Server.

4. Load the `Instcat.sql` file by choosing File ➢ Open and then navigating to the file.

5. Click Open. The query will be loaded into the ISQLW window.

6. Execute the script by clicking the green triangle in the upper-right corner of the query window or by pressing Ctrl+E.

7. This script will take a couple of minutes to run and will have a great deal of output. As you scroll down the results screen, you will see several messages that instruct you to ignore the errors.

Follow these steps to create a link through Enterprise Manager:

1. Run Enterprise Manager on your SQL Server 2000 computer and connect to your local server.

2. Right-click the Linked Servers icon and choose New Linked Server from the context menu.

3. Type in the name of the SQL Server 6.5 computer (such as Marketing) for the Linked Server option, and choose SQL Server as the server type.

4. Click OK when you are finished.

To use the Query Analyzer, use the same code for linking a SQL Server 6.5 computer you used when you linked the SQL Server 2000 database earlier:

```
EXEC sp_addlinkedserver 'MARKETING', 'SQL Server'
```

Linking to an Access Database

Linking to an Access database can be a bit tricky. There is a new parameter introduced called the data source that requires you to specify the complete path to the Access database. If the database is on a remote server, you may need to map a drive letter or use the universal naming convention (UNC).

Look at this scenario:

- The Access database is on a machine named ATLANTA.

- The directory in which the Access database is located is shared as INVENTORY.

- The database filename is Invdb.mdb.

You would need to specify the following data source parameter:

```
\\Atlanta\Inventory\InvDB.MDB
```

If you have Microsoft Access installed in the default folder, Exercise 3.6 will run normally. If you do not, you will need to locate an Access database. In the exercise, the Access database (INVENTORY) is on the local computer.

EXERCISE 3.6

Establishing a Linked Server to an Access Database Named INVENTORY

1. Start Enterprise Manager and connect to your local server.

2. Right-click the Linked Servers icon and choose New Linked Server from the context menu.

3. Type in **INVENTORY** for the Linked Server option.

4. Select Other Data Source as the server type.

5. Select Microsoft.Jet 4.0 OLE DB Provider from the Provider Name drop-down menu.

6. For the data source, type in the full path of the Access database file:

   `C:\INVENTORY\INVDB.MDB`

7. When you are finished, you should see something similar to what is shown here.

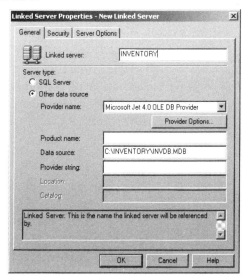

8. Click OK to complete the link.

Exercise 3.7 walks you through this same process using the Query Analyzer. If you implement SQL scripts, you can save the scripts for later use in rebuilding and reconnecting your linked server.

EXERCISE 3.7

Using T-SQL to Link to an Access Database

1. Start the Query Analyzer.

2. Log on to the local server and supply your security credentials.

3. Ensure that you are working in the Master database.

4. Run the following query to link to the Access INVENTORY database:

```
EXEC sp_addlinkedserver 'INVENTORY', 'Access',

     'Microsoft.Jet.OLEDB4.0', 'C:\INVENTORY\INVDB.MDB'
```

5. If the statement ran correctly, then the last line in the lower half of the query window should read as follows:

```
1 row(s) affected
```

Linking to Access

SQL Server's ability to create a link to Access is great stuff. Most companies have data scattered all over the place. Microsoft's philosophy is that no matter where your data is, you should be able to get to it. By being able to link to existing Access databases, you can slowly convert to a SQL Server–centric application instead of having to convert the data and application at once.

 You can use the same Microsoft.Jet 4.0 OLE DB driver to link to an Excel spreadsheet.

Linking to an Oracle Database Server

When setting up a link to an Oracle database, you will have to install two pieces of software onto your local server: Oracle client software and Oracle's SQL*Net software. The version you will need depends on your OLE-DB provider.

If you use the supplied Microsoft OLE-DB provider for Oracle, you will have to install Oracle's client software support file, version 7.3.3.0.4 or later, and SQL*Net, version 2.3.3.0.4 or later.

Oracle implements databases in a fundamentally different way than SQL Server does. To access a database on Oracle from SQL Server 2000, you will have to set up an *alias* to the Oracle database using Oracle's SQL*Net software. SQL*Net is the networking software used by a database system (including other Oracle servers) to talk to a remote Oracle server over a network.

The documentation accompanying the SQL*Net software details how to set up a SQL*Net alias to an Oracle database.

If you were to look at how these software packages work together, you would see that SQL Server talks to the OLE-DB layer, which talks to the Oracle client software layer, which talks to the SQL*Net layer, which in turn talks to the TCP/IP stack—which then sends the data onto the wire. Figure 3.5 illustrates this.

FIGURE 3.5 Communicating with an Oracle server

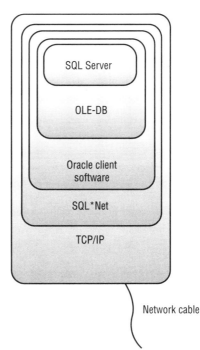

Because most of us don't have a copy of Oracle to play with, we will provide you with the steps necessary to connect to an Oracle server rather than take you through a full-blown exercise.

For those who want to play with new toys, anyone can freely download a developer version of all Oracle products at technet.oracle.com.

In the following examples, you will see how to connect using both Enterprise Manager and the Query Analyzer. The example uses the WHAlias through the SQL*Net software.

To use Enterprise Manager to connect to an Oracle server, follow these steps:

1. Open Enterprise Manager and connect to your SQL Server computer.

2. Right-click the Linked Servers icon and choose New Linked Server from the context menu.

3. Type in **Warehouse** for the Linked Server option.

4. Select Other Data Source as the server type.

5. Select MSDAORA for the Provider Name option.

6. For the Data Source option, type in the SQL*Net alias name for the Warehouse database: **WHAlias**. When you are finished, you should see something similar to Figure 3.6.

FIGURE 3.6 Connecting to Oracle through the SQL*Net alias

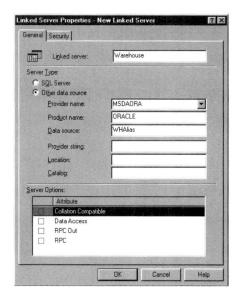

7. Click OK to complete the link.

Using Query Analyzer, you would do the following:

1. Open the Query Analyzer and connect to your local server. Be sure to provide sysadmin-level security credentials.

2. Be sure that you are using the Master database.

3. Run the following query:

```
EXEC sp_addlinkedserver
     'WAREHOUSE', 'Oracle', 'MSDAORA', 'WHAlias'
```

4. If the statement ran correctly, then the last line in the lower half of the query window should read as follows:

```
1 row(s) affected
```

Establishing Security for Linked Servers

Once you have created a link to a remote server, you have to set up the security to the linked server. Because security mechanisms differ from system to system, you need to specify what login ID and password you want the local SQL Server 2000 computer to use on the remote system on behalf of your individual local clients or group of local clients.

Say that you have a client who is logging on to the local SQL Server 2000 computer as JohnD. You need to tell SQL Server 2000 which login ID and password to use to log in to the remote database server when JohnD tries to gain access to the remote database. If everyone on your local server is to use a different login ID and password on the remote database system, you will have to tell SQL Server 2000 about each of them. To make things easier, you can designate a login ID and password on the remote database system for a group of local logins.

If you are using a Windows local or global group as the login account, you can map this Windows group to a remote database login ID and password.

You can map a local login ID or group to a remote login ID and password through Enterprise Manager or through T-SQL using the `sp_addlinkedsrv-login` stored procedure (in this case, you will have to know the local login ID in advance). You can save time by mapping a Windows local or global group to a remote login ID. Because you are creating one mapping to one remote login ID for a group of clients, you will eliminate the administrative annoyances of creating and maintaining several individual mappings.

Figure 3.7 shows the Security tab of the Linked Server property sheet. As you can see, you can use any SQL Server login ID to map to a remote database.

FIGURE 3.7 The Security tab of the Linked Server property sheet

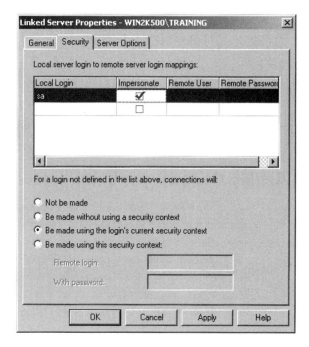

When you are setting up security to a remote database server, you will have to provide several pieces of information:

Local Login This is mandatory. The login ID on the local server that you wish to map to a remote login ID can be an NT login ID, an NT group login ID, or the login ID the client uses to log on to SQL Server.

Impersonate This option allows local clients to retain their username and password when accessing a remote server. Only use this option if you are sure the username and passwords are the same on both servers.

Remote User This is the login ID to use on the remote server. Your local login ID will map to the remote login ID.

Remote Password This is the password to use on the remote server with the remote login ID.

With security account delegation, users authenticated by Windows to access the local SQL Server computer would have their Windows credentials sent to the remote SQL Server computer to access the remote database.

Mapping Login IDs Using Enterprise Manager

In this section, we'll discuss the procedures required to configure the security for different types of local logins. Here you will use Enterprise Manager to accomplish this task. In the next section, you will see the equivalent procedures using Query Analyzer.

The following steps outline the process of mapping an ID in SQL Server to a remote server using Enterprise Manager. You'll be mapping the SA local login ID to the linked named instance WIN2K500\TRAINING server. The WIN2K500\TRAINING server has an account set up as SA with a password of passwd:

1. Open Enterprise Manager and connect to your SQL Server computer.

2. Expand the Linked Servers icon and then right-click the Win2k500\training icon. Select Properties.

3. You will now see the property sheet. Click the Security tab to view the security information for this linked server.

4. In the Local Login column, click in an unused box.

5. From the drop-down list, you can choose the local login ID that you wish to map. Choose SA.

6. Because the SA account on both servers has the same password, select the Impersonate check box (refer back to Figure 3.7).

7. Repeat steps 4 through 6 for each local login ID to be mapped.

8. When you are finished, click OK.

Configuring Security for an Access Database

If you are mapping to an unsecured Access database, you must use the remote login ID Admin and no password. In addition, when you set up your connections through Enterprise Manager, you need to specify which users will connect via the Admin account. If you want only specific users to access the Access database, choose the option Not Be Made, which will apply to any accounts that have not been specifically assigned to the Admin account.

If you are accessing a secured Access database, you will have to make a change to your Registry. Configure the Registry to use the correct Workgroup

Information file used by Access. You must enter the full pathname of the Workgroup Information file used by Access to this Registry entry:

HKEY_LOCAL_
MACHINE\SOFTWARE\Microsoft\JET\4.0\Engines\SystemDB

Once you have made the necessary changes to the Registry, you can map your SQL Server accounts to the secured Access database.

Here are the steps necessary to connect to an unsecured Access database through Enterprise Manager. In this example, we will use the Admin ID with no password for the SA account to use. The Admin account is the default security in an Access database:

1. Open Enterprise Manager and connect to your local server.

2. Expand the Linked Server, right-click the Inventory server, and choose Properties.

3. Click the Security tab.

4. Specify Admin and no password for the SA account. Then be sure to select Not Be Made (under "For a login not defined in the list above, connections will," as shown in Figure 3.8).

5. Click OK when you are finished.

FIGURE 3.8 Security for an unsecured Access database

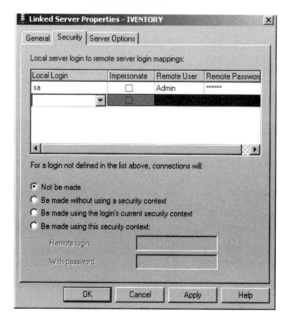

Mapping Login IDs Using the Query Analyzer

Follow these steps to map your login IDs using the Query Analyzer and the sp_addlinkedsrvlogin stored procedure:

1. Open the Query Analyzer and connect to your local SQL Server database.

2. Make sure that you are in the Master database.

3. Run the following query to map the SQL Server login ID JohnD to the linked Warehouse server. You will be mapping in as D_JOHN with a password of passwd:

```
sp_addlinkedsrvlogin 'Win2k500\training',
    'false','JOHND','D_JOHN','passwd'
```

4. If the stored procedure was successful, you will see one of the following in the lower half of the window:

```
(0 row(s) affected)
(0 row(s) affected)
(0 row(s) affected)
(1 row(s) affected)
```

or

```
(1 row(s) affected)
(0 row(s) affected)
(0 row(s) affected)
(1 row(s) affected)
```

5. Close the Query Analyzer when you are finished.

If you are mapping a SQL Server login ID that is using NT Authentication, you must specify the domain name as well as the login ID. For example, WIN2K500\TRAINING would be the login ID to be mapped to D_JOHN in step 3.

Working with Access Databases

For an unsecured database, all you need to do is specify Admin for the mapped login ID and NULL for the password. Here is an example:

```
sp_addlinkedsrvlogin 'INVENTORY', FALSE, 'JOHND', 'Admin',
NULL
```

For a secured Access database, be sure that you make the necessary changes to the Registry key. Once you have done that, you can access the database using the `sp_addlinkedsrvlogin` stored procedure with the normal parameters. For example, if your Access database (Inventory) has a login ID of D_JOHN with a password of passwd, you would run the following:

```
sp_addlinkedsrvlogin 'INVENTORY', FALSE, 'JOHND',
  'D_JOHN', 'passwd'
```

The *SELECT* Command

Although the SELECT command is not directly tested on the MCSE exam, being able to read simple SELECT statements and understand their functions will be helpful not only as you take the exam, but in your work as an administrator as well.

The SELECT statement can be used to retrieve specific rows and columns of information from one or more tables in one or more databases. There are three basic components to every SELECT statement: SELECT, FROM, and WHERE. Although the T-SQL utility is not case sensitive when you are using SQL statements, we will present the SQL keywords here in uppercase.

The syntax for a simple SELECT statement is as follows:

```
SELECT <column_list>
FROM <table(s)>
WHERE <search_criteria>
```

One of the simplest SELECT statements is the one that selects all columns from a single table. You use the * operator to do this, as in the following example:

```
SELECT *
FROM pubs..authors
```

You can specify the database in your table names (such as PUBS..AUTHORS) or you can move to the Pubs database using the USE PUBS command, or you can choose the Pubs database from the drop-down box in Query Analyzer. For all of the examples in the rest of this chapter, we'll assume you are in the Pubs database.

This statement will select all columns and all rows from the authors table in the Pubs database; the result set would look like this:

```
au_id          au_lname     au_fname     phone
172-32-1176    White        Johnson      408 496-7223
213-46-8915    Green        Marjorie     415 986-7020
238-95-7766    Carson       Cheryl       415 548-7723
267-41-2394    O'Leary      Michael      408 286-2428
274-80-9391    Straight     Dean         415 834-2919
341-22-1782    Smith        Meander      913 843-0462
409-56-7008    Bennet       Abraham      415 658-9932
427-17-2319    Dull         Ann          415 836-7128
472-27-2349    Gringlesby   Burt         707 938-6445
486-29-1786    Locksley     Charlene     415 585-4620
527-72-3246    Greene       Morningstar  615 297-2723
648-92-1872    Blotchet     Reginald     503 745-6402
672-71-3249    Yokomoto     Akiko        415 935-4228
712-45-1867    delCastillo  Innes        615 996-8275
722-51-5454    DeFrance     Michel       219 547-9982
724-08-9931    Stringer     Dirk         415 843-2991
724-80-9391    MacFeather   Stearns      415 354-7128
756-30-7391    Karsen       Livia        415 534-9219
807-91-6654    Panteley     Sylvia       301 946-8853
846-92-7186    Hunter       Sheryl       415 836-7128
893-72-1158    McBadden     Heather      707 448-4982
899-46-2035    Ringer       Anne         801 826-0752
998-72-3567    Ringer       Albert       801 826-0752
(23 row(s) affected)
```

You can specify individual columns in the column list parameter. This is sometimes called *vertical partitioning* because you are selecting only certain columns. For example, if you wanted to get only the authors' last names and first names, you could run this query:

```
SELECT au_lname, au_fname
FROM authors
```

The result set would look like this:

```
au_lname            au_fname
----------------    ---------------
White               Johnson
Green               Marjorie
Carson              Cheryl
O'Leary             Michael
...                 ...
3Panteley           Sylvia
Hunter              Sheryl
McBadden            Heather
Ringer              Anne
Ringer              Albert
(23 row(s) affected)
```

The *WHERE* clause

You can also specify search criteria by using the WHERE clause. The WHERE clause is used to discriminate between rows of information. This is also known as *horizontal partitioning* because you are selecting only certain rows of information. For example, if you wanted to get information on all authors whose last names begin with the letter *M*, you could run this query:

```
SELECT *
FROM authors
WHERE au_lname LIKE 'M%'
```

You would get this result:

```
au_id           au_lname        au_fname        phone
-----------     ------------    -------------   -----------
724-80-9391     MacFeather      Stearns         415 354-7128
```

893-72-1158   McBadden   Heather   707 448-4982
(2 row(s) affected)

 Indexes can help you only if the SELECT statement has a WHERE clause.

Joining Tables

Relational databases function by splitting related data into separate tables. You will usually need to recombine the data from two or more tables before you can retrieve the data you're interested in from relational databases. This is done by joining tables. There are several ways to join tables, including the following:

- Inner joins or equijoins
- Outer joins
- Cross joins or a Cartisian product

 If the type of join is not specified, an inner join will be performed (inner joins are performed the majority of the time). Another term for inner join is *equijoin*. The technical definition of an equijoin is joining two or more tables using values they have in common (equal); a non-equijoin is joining tables using nonequal values (which usually produces nonsensical data).

Note that if the same table is used, a self join is created. Inner and self joins can consist of multiple tables, whereas outer and cross joins only join two tables.

Inner Joins (Equijoins)

Inner joins only show results where rows from both tables have matching data. A graphical representation of an inner join is shown in Figure 3.9.

FIGURE 3.9   Inner joins (equijoins) between tables

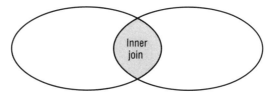

For more complex queries, you can join information from three or more tables at the same time. For example, to find out which authors publish which titles, you would need to join the Authors table, Titleauthor table, and Titles table and then display results based on a matching title_id between the Authors and Titles table on a join table called Titleauthor. Here is an example statement:

```
SELECT authors.au_lname, authors.au_fname, titles.title
FROM authors, titleauthor, titles
WHERE titleauthor.au_id = authors.au_id
AND titles.title_id = titleauthor.title_id
```

Your results would look like the following:

```
au_lname          au_fname          title
-----------       -----------       --------------------
Green             Marjorie          The Busy Executive's
    Database Guide
Bennet            Abraham           The Busy Executive's
    Database Guide
O'Leary           Michael           Cooking with Computers:
    Surreptitious Balance Sheets
MacFeather        Stearns           Cooking with Computers:
    Surreptitious Balance Sheets
Green             Marjorie          You Can Combat Computer
    Stress!
Straight          Dean              Straight Talk About
    Computers
Del Castillo      Innes             Silicon Valley
Gastronomic
    Treats
DeFrance          Michel            The Gourmet Microwave
Ringer            Anne              The Gourmet Microwave

O'Leary           Michael           Sushi, Anyone?
Gringlesby        Burt              Sushi, Anyone?
Yokomoto          Akiko             Sushi, Anyone?
(25 row(s) affected)
```

Outer Joins

Outer joins are useful for showing all of the rows from one table with any matching rows of a second table. A graphical representation of an outer join is shown in Figure 3.10.

FIGURE 3.10   Outer joins between tables

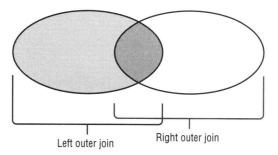

Left outer join   Right outer join

For example, you may have a customers table and a sales_order table. An inner join would show you all the customers that placed orders. An outer join would show you all customers, regardless of whether they placed orders or not. Any orders placed would be shown for the customers that placed them, and for the customers without orders, NULL would be generated for the order columns.

There are two types of outer joins: left outer joins and right outer joins. In a left outer join, the results will show all of the rows from the leftmost table in the statement but only matched rows from the rightmost table. In a right outer join, the results will show all of the rows from the rightmost table in the statement but only matched rows from the leftmost table. If you reverse the order of the tables in the statement, a left outer join would become a right outer join and vice versa.

Cross Joins (Cartesian Products)

In a *cross join*, every row of one table is listed against every row of another table. A cross join is sometimes referred to as a Cartesian product because every possible result is computed. A graphical representation of a cross join is shown in Figure 3.11.

FIGURE 3.11   Outer joins between tables

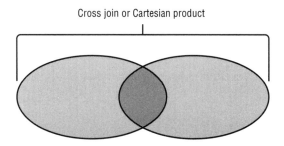

Cross join or Cartesian product

For example, if there are 50 customers and 100 orders, a cross join would produce a result set of 5,000 rows, which would be meaningless. Cross joins are used to create lots of dummy data for testing performance, but they aren't useful for any business situation.

Cross joins are performed when the WHERE clause is left out of a JOIN statement. If you are attempting to run a join but it is taking an extraordinary amount of time, you may have triggered a cross join.

Ordering Results

You can also order your result sets in either ascending (default) or descending order. For ascending, you can use ASC or just leave it out because it is the default. For descending results, use DESC after the ORDER BY statement. For example, if you wanted to list some author information in descending order by last name, you could run this query:

```
SELECT au_fname, au_lname
FROM authors
ORDER BY au_lname DESC
```

Your results would look like this table:

au_fname	au_lname
Akiko	Yokomoto
Johnson	White
Dirk	Stringer
Dean	Straight

```
...                        ...
Cheryl                     Carson
Reginald                   Blotchet-Halls
Abraham                    Bennet
(23 row(s) affected)
```

Configuration Utilities

SQL Server comes with several configuration utilities that can change the way SQL Server runs. The main configuration programs are SQL Setup, the Client Network utility, the Server Network utility, and Enterprise Manager.

The Server Network utility was discussed in Chapter 2, and Enterprise Manager was covered both in Chapter 2 and earlier in this chapter.

SQL Setup Program

The SQL Setup program can be used to upgrade your SQL Server computer or to add additional components; you will need the original CD-ROM to do either. Choose to do a custom installation, and then choose to upgrade, remove, or add components to an existing installation of SQL Server. Check the additional components you wish to add (see Figure 3.12).

FIGURE 3.12 The SQL Server Select Components dialog box

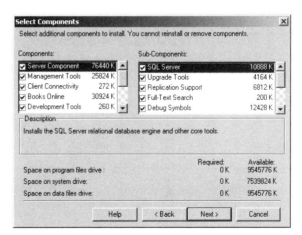

Many of the functions you had to do manually with the previous version of the Setup utility, such as changing the supported network protocols and security mode, are now done with new utility programs (such as the Server Network utility) or from within Enterprise Manager.

SQL Client Network Utility

The Client Network utility is used to change the protocols and ports the client uses to communicate with the server. If you are using default settings, you shouldn't have to run the utility, but if you have changed protocols or ports on the server, you may need to go to every workstation and change the configurations for the clients to match the (non-default) configurations of the server.

Microsoft
Exam
Objective

Configure network libraries.

The utility, shown in Figure 3.13, looks a lot like the Server Network utility and is pretty self-explanatory.

FIGURE 3.13   The Client Network utility

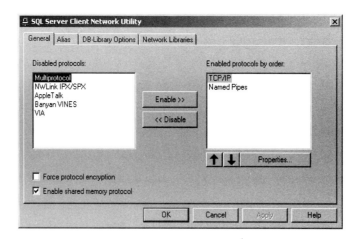

Remember, you may also need to configure ODBC connections in order to allow clients to connect to SQL Server. ODBC connections can be user based, which work for the user that created them, or system based, which work for all users and applications on the system. (Local) is a shortcut for the server you can use when you're at the server itself. ODBC connections were covered in Chapter 2.

Troubleshooting Tools and Commands

SQL Server comes with many tools you can use to help troubleshoot problems. Tools include Profiler, Performance Monitor, Windows Event Viewer, *database consistency checker (DBCC)* commands, and Enterprise Manager. The SQL Profiler and System Monitor (Performance Monitor in NT 4) will be discussed in Chapter 10. The other common tools are discussed in the following sections.

The Windows Event Viewer

The Windows Event Viewer can be used to track SQL Server events and errors by viewing the Windows application log. For SQL Server administrators, the disadvantage of using the Event Viewer is that it logs not only SQL Server events but also events from other applications running in Windows.

Each event is labeled with the level of its severity: informational, warning, or error. You can use the time stamp, severity, and source of the error to help determine whether it might have had an impact on your SQL Server computer. In Exercise 3.8, you'll use the Windows Event Viewer to troubleshoot SQL Server.

EXERCISE 3.8

Troubleshooting SQL Server with the Windows Event Viewer

1. Choose Start ➤ Programs ➤ Administrative Tools ➤ Event Viewer to open the Event Viewer.

EXERCISE 3.8 *(continued)*

2. When the Event Viewer opens, the default log is the system log. Click Application Log in the left pane to view the application log.

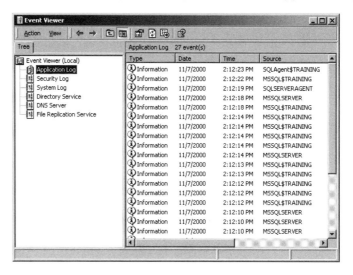

3. If you see any red stop signs with SQLAgent or MSSQLServer in the Source column, double-click them for more information.

DBCC Commands

Database consistency checker (DBCC) commands are used to check the logical and physical consistency of your databases but are generally not used to fix the problems. Use stored procedures and SQL statements to resolve the problems reported.

Microsoft ✓ *Exam* *Objective*

Perform integrity checks. Methods include configuring the Database Maintenance Plan Wizard and using the Database Consistency Checker (DBCC).

As an administrator, you should become familiar with the DBCC commands, especially the following:

DBCC CHECKCATALOG   Checks for consistency between system tables.

DBCC CHECKDB   Checks all tables in a database to see that index pages are correctly linked to their data pages. Also makes sure that the indexes are in sorted order and that the information on each page is reasonable.

DBCC CHECKALLOC   Ensures that all pages in a database are correctly allocated and used.

DBCC SQLPERF(LOGSPACE)   Reports on the currently used amount of transaction log space, expressed as a percentage.

DBCC SQLPERF(LRUSTATS)   Reports on how your procedure and data caches are being used.

DBCC CHECKFILEGROUP   Check all the tables held on a specific file group for damage.

Reading through and practicing the DBCC commands will allow you to diagnose problems with SQL Server more quickly and efficiently and to optimize the system.

Makepipe and Readpipe

Each client can run the Client Network utility to change the type of network connections used to connect to SQL Server. Two other utilities, Makepipe and Readpipe, can be used for checking network connections.

The Makepipe and Readpipe utilities are not installed by the Setup program. They can be found in the x:\x86\Binn directory on the SQL Server compact disc. You can run the utilities from the CD-ROM or copy them to the server and client.

Makepipe and Readpipe are almost always used together and are especially useful for tracking down network or security problems. The Makepipe utility is used at the server to make a temporary pipe, or network slot, and the Readpipe utility is used at the client end to attempt to connect to the server. If the connection is successful, the network and the associated protocols are OK. Note that neither Windows NT nor SQL Server security is used by the utilities, which is helpful when diagnosing security-related problems.

SQL Server uses Named Pipes, which is one method of communication between computers across a network.

If Named Pipes comes up successfully but you still cannot connect, you probably have a DB-Library problem. You should verify that you have the same network library and DB-Library on both the server and the client computer. This can be done with the Setup program or with the Client Network utility as shown earlier.

Other Utilities on the Server

There are several other utilities for SQL Server that will be covered later in the book in their respective chapters. Some of the utilities you might see installed are explained here:

SQLServer   This is the actual EXE file. You can use special options to start SQL Server from the command line in troubleshooting mode. Note that the actual service is named MSSQLSERVER for the default instance and MSSQL$NameOfInstance for named instances.

SQLAgent   This is the SQL Agent, which is in charge of automation and scheduling in SQL Server. Note that the service itself is named SQLSERVERAGENT for the default instance, and SQLAgent$<Instance Name> for a named instance.

SQLMaint   This utility can be used to create tasks that will take care of day-to-day administration of your SQL Server computer. This includes automating backups, updating statistics, and rebuilding indexes. Information generated here can be sent out in a report locally or to an e-mail operator.

SQL Service Manager   This utility can be used to start, stop, and pause SQL Server, SQL Agent, and the Distributed Transaction Coordinator on the local as well as remote servers.

SQLDiag   You can use this utility to check versions and diagnose problems with SQL Server.

VSWITCH   This utility lets you switch between different versions of SQL Server if you have different versions (6.5, 7, 2000) on the same computer.

Other Utilities on the Management Client

There are several additional utilities on the client that you may use as you do various operations in SQL Server. One great thing about Microsoft SQL Server is that the online documentation, including the Books Online, are excellent, and should be one of the first places you go for additional information on topics or utilities you need to know more about. Remember also that `www.microsoft.com/sql/` has the latest on SQL Server 2000.

bcp   The Bulk Copy program is a command-line utility used for transferring information into and out of SQL Server. Bcp will be covered in Chapter 7.

SQL Client Network utility   This utility is used to configure SQL Server clients' network libraries. It also reports on the network libraries that are in use for a particular client as well as the versions of the libraries.

Books Online   An electronic version of the SQL Server manuals, this contains a fully cross-referenced search engine.

Profiler   This utility can be used to monitor what is being run on your SQL Server computer and by whom. Profiler will be covered in Chapter 10.

DTSWIZ   With this utility, you can create Data Transformation Services (DTS) packages for import and export. DTS is covered in Chapter 7.

DTSRUN   You can use this command-line utility to run DTS packages you have created previously.

DTSRUNUI   This stand-alone graphical utility lets you run DTS packages that you have previously created.

Summary

In this chapter, we explored many of the utilities used for administering SQL Server and offered an overview of the T-SQL language. Here are some of the important points covered in this chapter:

- You can implement and manage multiple SQL Server computers by creating different server groups. You learned how to register new servers in the enterprise.

- The SQL Setup utility can be used to add new components to SQL Server and to upgrade an earlier version of SQL Server.

- Linked servers are used to run both remote stored procedures and distributed queries.

- You can use Enterprise Manager or Query Analyzer to successfully create and configure your linked servers.

- There are many ways to view and manipulate data in tables, including using the SELECT statement, partitioning tables vertically and horizontally, sorting the result set in either an ascending or descending fashion, and performing a simple query with multiple tables.

- The DBCC commands check databases and database objects for damage and generally comment on the database itself rather than making any changes to the database.

Exam Essentials

Know how to use Enterprise Manager   Enterprise Manager is the main configuration tool for SQL Server. Use it, play with it, and understand it. Although not as heavily tested as in the past, Enterprise Manager is still the most-used utility in SQL Server.

Know how to run queries with Query Analyzer   Query Analyzer is the main programming tool that comes with SQL Server. Among its many features, the Query Analyzer interface is a multiple-document interface (MDI), and it gives you the ability to retrieve and store SQL scripts.

Know the basic SELECT syntax   The SELECT command is the basic command. Do some queries and try different options. Know how to use the WHERE clause as well as the ORDER BY clause and how to sort in ascending and descending orders.

Know the basic JOIN syntax   Most of the time, a SELECT command will be used to gather data from two or more tables. The JOIN syntax allows the SELECT command to get data from two or more tables. You need to know the syntax for doing joins and specifying the columns and operators that make the join work.

Key Terms

cross join	MS Query
database consistency checker (DBCC)	OSQL
distributed query	outer join
Enterprise Manager	Query Analyzer
inner join	SELECT command
linked server	

Review Questions

1. When you execute the stored procedure sp_addlinkedserver, it ends successfully, but when you click over to Enterprise Manager (which has also been open), you do not see the new linked server. Which of the following will correct the problem?

   A. Exit and reenter Enterprise Manager.

   B. Reexecute the stored procedure.

   C. Execute the stored procedure sp_addlinkedsrvlogin.

   D. In Enterprise Manager, click Linked Servers with the right mouse button and refresh the list.

2. The SQL Client Network utility can be used to do which of the following?

   A. Configure network libraries on the client.

   B. Add database libraries to the server.

   C. Configure languages on the server.

   D. Rebuild the Master database.

3. Which of the following will start the OSQL command-line utility and log you in using the SA account and no password?

   A. osql /Login sa /Pwd *****

   B. osql /Lsa /S

   C. osql /Usa /P

   D. sqlservr /OSQL /Usa /P

4. You can specify the database you wish to work with in the Query Analyzer utility in which of the following ways? (Select all that apply.)

   A. Use the USE *<databasename>* command in your SQL script.

   B. Click the databases listbox and select your database.

   C. Just run the command; it will know which database you want to use.

   D. Use the full name of the object, such as Server1.pubs.dbo.authors.

5. What does this T-SQL script do?
```
SELECT Employee.FirstName, Employee.LastName,
WorkInfo.YearsExp FROM Employees, WorkInfo WHERE
Employee.EmpID = WorkInfo.EmpID.
```

   A. Displays all information in an employee record and all associated work information.

   B. Displays first name and last name in an employee record; if they have work experience, it will display that too.

   C. Displays all employees' first names and last names and their work experience where there are records that have a matching employee ID in the WorkInfo table.

   D. Displays all employees' first names and last names and their work experience whether or not they have a matching employee ID in the WorkInfo table.

6. You have successfully established a link to a remote server and have mapped a few local SQL Server login IDs to their respective remote login IDs. When you run the sp_addlinkedsrvlogin stored procedure to map the local SQL Server login ID JOHND to the remote login ID JOHND, you receive the following error message: "'JOHND' is not a local user. Remote login denied." When you installed the local server, you used the default settings. Which of the following will prevent you from receiving this error message?

   A. Add JOHND to the remote server.

   B. Add JOHND to the local server.

   C. Add JOHND as an NT login ID.

   D. Use all lowercase letters (johnd) when executing the stored procedure.

7. When you execute the `sp_addlinkedserver` stored procedure to link a remote SQL Server 6.5 computer, you receive an error message stating that there are missing system tables. Which of the following solutions should you perform?

   A. Reinstall SQL Server 6.5 on the remote server.

   B. Apply SQL Server 6.5 Service Pack 5 on the remote server.

   C. Execute the `Instcat.sql` script on the local SQL Server computer.

   D. Execute the `Instcat.sql` script on the remote SQL Server computer.

8. You run this query that shows all of your customers:
   `Select fname, lname, address from customers`
   What index could you create to speed up the query?

   A. Index on fname (first name).

   B. Index on lname (last name).

   C. Index on both first name and last name.

   D. Indexing won't help.

9. SQL Server error messages can be viewed in the SQL error log and which Windows application?

   A. Performance Monitor

   B. Control Panel's Network program

   C. Network Monitor

   D. Event Viewer

10. You have a database called Sales with a table called SalesTD. Which of these commands will perform a query on the table no matter which database you run it from?

    A. `Select all from SalesTD`

    B. `Select * from SalesTD`

    C. `Select * from Sales (SalesTD)`

    D. `Select * from Sales..SalesTD`

11. You register your server and want to check on some system stored procedures but the Master database does not show up in the database folder. Why is that happening?

   A. You are looking at SQL Server 2000 running on Windows $9x$.

   B. You need to edit your registration properties to display system data.

   C. You need to edit your registration properties to connect with SA rights.

   D. The Master database is not listed with other databases—it is listed in the `Configuration` folder.

12. Which of the following database servers are supported as linked servers? (Select all that apply.)

   A. SQL Server 6.5

   B. SQL Server 7

   C. Oracle

   D. Microsoft Access

13. Your boss has an Excel spreadsheet in which he keeps salesperson bonus amounts. He wants to keep control of the spreadsheet. The payroll database is in a SQL Server database. You need to print a report that shows what each salesperson should receive for the year. What is the easiest way to do this?

   A. Use DTS to copy the spreadsheet to SQL Server. Use a `JOIN` statement.

   B. Create a linked server to the Excel spreadsheet. Use a `JOIN` statement.

   C. Use DTS to copy the payroll data to Excel.

   D. Import the spreadsheet using Bulk Copy.

14. You have created two groups called Production and Testing for your registered servers. How can you move your production servers to the Production group and the testing servers to the Testing group?

    A. Drag and drop them.

    B. Use the property sheets of the servers.

    C. Reregister them in the new groups

    D. Open the property sheet of the group and add them.

15. You are a programmer who has DBO rights in the Training instance. You register a server using Windows Authentication. Later, you get promoted and get the SA password. You try to make a new login for the instance, but you can't. What do you need to do?

    A. Disconnect from the server and supply the SA password when you reconnect.

    B. Edit the registration properties so that system objects are viewable.

    C. Edit the server so it is running in Windows Authentication mode.

    D. Edit the registration properties so that you connect with the SA SQL login.

16. You are going to fill in for the DBA for a week and have been given the SA password. You need to back up the Master database tonight. You open Enterprise Manager but the Master database isn't there. What do you need to do?

    A. Disconnect from the server and supply the SA password when you reconnect.

    B. Edit the registration properties so that system objects are viewable.

    C. Edit the server so it is running in Windows Authentication mode.

    D. Edit the registration properties so that you connect with the SA SQL login.

17. Which driver would you use to access Access for a SQL linked server?

   A. SQL Server

   B. Generic Data Driver

   C. OR-DBL

   D. Microsoft Jet

18. What button do you use to test an ODBC connection?

   A. Test Data Source

   B. Check Data Source

   C. Confirm Data Source

   D. Verify Data Source

19. What type of ODBC connection would you create to allow any application to use the configuration?

   A. User DSN

   B. System DSN

   C. Computer DSN

   D. Global DSN

20. You need to build an ODBC connection to a SQL Server computer called SQL1. You are at the SQL Server computer itself. What should you specify for the SQL Server name? (Select all that apply.)

   A. (local)

   B. SQL1

   C. SQL1\SQL

   D. SQL1\local

Answers to Review Questions

1. D. You often need to refresh the view in Enterprise Manager to see anything you have done with Query Analyzer while Enterprise Manager was open. While disconcerting at first, always remember, When in doubt, refresh.

2. A. The Client Network utility only manages items on the client. The client utility only affects the client, not anything on the server, such as database libraries, languages, or rebuilding the Master database.

3. C. The `/U` option allows you to specify the user, and OSQL will start the utility.

4. A, B, D. You need to have a USE command, select the database from the drop-down list, or use the full path to the object. If you name just an object in your statement, SQL Server will look only in the current database for the object and may not be able to find the it—or worse, create it in the wrong database.

5. C. The `WHERE` clause indicates that they need a matching record in the employee and WorkInfo tables. Option A is wrong because not all records will be shown. Option B is wrong because there has to be work information or the employee information won't be shown. Option D is wrong because there has to be a match in the WorkInfo table.

6. B. JOHND has to exist on the local server before you can map him to a remote account.

7. D. The `Instcal.sql` script needs to be run on the remote SQL Server 6.5 server. Reinstalling or reapplying service packs will not ensure that the correct script will be run.

8. D. Because there is no `WHERE` clause, indexing won't help this query. This is a trick question, but it illustrates an important distinction as to how indexes help queries.

9. D. The Event Viewer is used to look at Windows logs (including the application log, which will contain SQL events).

10. D. If you use the full path (`db..object`), the statement will run from any database.

11. B. You can choose to hide system databases and tables from the registration screen. Because the Master database is a system database, if you choose to hide system items, the Master database will be hidden as well.

12. A, B, C, D. All of these are supported as linked servers. SQL Server lets you build a permanent link to earlier SQL Server versions as well as any ODBC- or OLE-DB–compliant databases such as Access or Oracle.

13. B. By creating a linked server, you can get to the Excel data and use it in statements such as a `JOIN` command. If you imported the data, you would have an obsolete copy very quickly, but by linking to the original spreadsheet, your `JOIN` statement is up-to-date when you reexecute it.

14. C. In order to put a server in a group, you have to reregister it, which means you need to delete it and then read it. Drag and drop doesn't work when moving servers around between groups.

15. D. If your Windows account doesn't have SysAdmin privileges but you have the SA account, you need to register the server with the SA account and password.

16. B. You need to edit the registration properties to show system objects. When you hide system objects, it doesn't matter what user you log in as— even the SA can have the objects hidden.

17. D. To get to Access, you need to use the Microsoft Jet driver. The database engine for Access is known as the Jet engine, which is why you need the Jet driver.

18. A. The Test Data Source button allows you to test an ODBC connection. The Check Data Source, Confirm Data Source, and Verify Data Source buttons do not exist.

19. B. A system DSN allows any application on the computer to use the ODBC configuration. User DSNs only apply for the user that created them, and there are no such things as Computer or Global DSNs.

20. A, B. When registering the server at the server itself, you have two options: You can use the name (local), or you can use the name of the SQL Server computer.

Chapter 4

Planning, Creating, and Managing a Database in SQL Server 2000

MICROSOFT EXAM OBJECTIVES COVERED IN THIS CHAPTER:

- ✓ Configure database options for performance. Considerations include capacity, network connectivity, physical drive configurations, and storage locations.

- ✓ Attach and detach databases.

- ✓ Create and alter databases.

  - Add filegroups.
  - Configure filegroup usage.
  - Expand and shrink a database.
  - Set database options by using ALTER DATABASE or CREATE DATABASE statements.
  - Size and place the transaction log.

- ✓ Create and manage objects. Objects include constraints, indexes, stored procedures, triggers, and views.

- ✓ Modify the database schema.

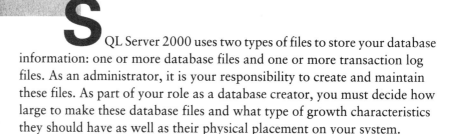

SQL Server 2000 uses two types of files to store your database information: one or more database files and one or more transaction log files. As an administrator, it is your responsibility to create and maintain these files. As part of your role as a database creator, you must decide how large to make these database files and what type of growth characteristics they should have as well as their physical placement on your system.

This chapter will examine these topics in more detail, first covering some planning issues, then looking at how to create a database and transaction log. We will then learn how to manage these database objects by altering their various configuration options and by removing them from the SQL Server. The chapter also discusses database filegroups, which are used for optimizing file access and backups.

Database Planning Considerations

Database planning requires you to consider both the size and the physical location of your database files. To make an informed decision about these items, it is helpful to understand how memory is allocated in SQL Server. In this section, we will talk about how your database is created, where you should place the database, and the different internal memory management structures.

Database Files

In SQL Server 2000, a new user database is really a copy of the Model database. Everything in the Model database will show up in your newly created database. Once the copy of the database has been made, it is expanded to the requested size. When you create a database in SQL Server 2000, you must specify at least one file to store the data and hold your system tables and another file to hold the transaction log.

Microsoft **Configure database options for performance. Considerations**
Exam **include capacity, network connectivity, physical drive**
Objective **configurations, and storage locations.**

Data files have a default extension of MDF. The *transaction log* is stored in one or more files, with a default LDF extension. If you create a database that spans multiple database files, the additional database files have a default filename extension of NDF. Additional transaction log files, however, don't change their extensions. There are several important things to remember about your data and log files:

- All data and log files that a particular SQL Server manages must reside on that SQL Server machine.

- Only one database is allowed per data file, but a single database can span multiple data files.

- Transaction logs must reside on their own file; they can also span multiple log files.

- Database files fill up their available space by *striping* across all data files in the filegroup. In this manner, you can eliminate hot spots and reduce contention in high-volume OLTP (Online Transaction Processing) environments.

- Transaction log files do not use striping but fill each log file to capacity before continuing on to the next log file.

- When you create a database and don't specify a transaction log size, the transaction log will be resized to 25 percent of the size of your data files.

It is suggested that you place your transaction logs on separate physical hard drives. In this manner, you can recover your data up to the second in the event of a media failure.

When you create a database, you are allocating hard-disk space for both the data and the transaction log. Your data files can be stored in a variety of methods, depending on your hardware and software.

Database File Placement

Placing database files in the appropriate location is highly dependent on the available hardware and software. There are very few hard-and-fast rules when it comes to databases. In fact, the only definite rule is that of design. The more thoroughly you plan and design your system, the less work it will be later, which is why it is so important to develop a good capacity plan.

There are several issues to keep in mind when you are attempting to decide where to place your database files. This includes planning for growth, communication, fault-tolerance, reliability, and speed.

Among the several measures you can take to ensure the reliability and consistency of your database—each with its own features and drawbacks—are the different levels of *RAID* (Redundant Array of Inexpensive Disks).

RAID 0

RAID 0 uses disk striping; that is, it writes data across multiple hard-disk partitions in what is called a *stripe set*. This can greatly improve speed as multiple hard disks are working at the same time. RAID 0 can be implemented through the use of Windows NT software or third-party hardware. While RAID 0 gives you the best speed, it does not provide any fault-tolerance. If one of the hard disks in the stripe set is damaged, you lose all of your data.

RAID 1

RAID 1 uses disk mirroring. Disk mirroring actually writes your information to disk twice—once to the primary file, and once to the mirror. This gives you excellent fault-tolerance, but it is fairly slow, as you must write to disk twice. Windows NT includes the ability to mirror your hard disks. RAID 1 requires only a single hard-disk controller.

RAID 5

RAID 5—*striping with parity*—writes data to hard disk in stripe sets. Parity checksums will be written across all disks in the stripe set. This gives you excellent fault-tolerance as well as excellent speed with a reasonable amount of overhead. The parity checksums can be used to recreate information lost if a single disk in the stripe set fails. If more than one disk in the stripe set fails, however, you will lose all your data. Although Windows NT supports RAID 5 in a software implementation, a hardware implementation is faster and more reliable, and we suggest that you use it if you can afford it.

RAID 10

RAID 10 (sometimes referred to as RAID 0+1) is the big daddy. This level of RAID should be used in mission-critical systems that require 24 hours a day, 7 days a week uptime and the fastest possible access. RAID 10 implements striping with parity as in RAID 5 and then mirrors the stripe sets. You still have excellent speed and excellent fault-tolerance, but you also have the added expense of using more than twice the disk space of RAID 1. Then again, we are talking about a situation that can afford no SQL Server downtime.

The other issue you need to keep in mind when working with databases is communication. SQL Server can only have database files on what it deems a local hard disk. Your local hard disks can be on your local machine or on a hardware device that is connected directly to the SQL Server machine (such as a hardware RAID array). Although you have this limitation with your active database files, this rule does not apply to your backups. Backups can be placed anywhere in your enterprise, including a named pipe, local hard disks, networked hard disks, and tape.

Microsoft suggests a combination of RAID 5 and RAID 1. In their scenario, you place your data files on the RAID 5 array for speed and redundancy. You place your transaction log files on the RAID 1 drives so that they can be mirrored.

Real World Scenario: File Placement

Many companies have a substantial budget for the IT department and can there-fore afford more expensive hardware. If this is the case where you work, you may want to budget for a hardware-based RAID solution. This gives a number of benefits, most noticeably, hardware-based RAID off-loads processing from the CPU to the RAID controller, speeding up your system. Another benefit of the hardware-based RAID system is that this is the only way to get RAID 10, which offers a great deal more fault-tolerance than the other types of RAID discussed in this chapter. The drawback to using a separate RAID controller is that you must *not* use a caching controller unless it is specifically designed for a database server. Such a controller will have a battery backup so that in the event of a crash or power spike, data is not lost.

Quite often, though, in the real world you are faced with the fact that money is tight and there is just no budget for lots of hardware. That is when you need to decide where to put your files using the RAID capabilities that are built into Windows. The options are the same in Windows NT and Windows 2000: RAID 0, 1, and 5.

RAID 0 gives no fault-tolerance and therefore is not a good choice for data protection. RAID 1 is a mirror, two disks that are duplicates of each other. This type of RAID protection is great for transaction logs because they require fast sequential writes (writes placed in sequence on the disk). RAID 5 is a stripe set with parity and does not offer fast sequential writes, but it is very fast at reading. This makes RAID 5 perfect for data files because SQL Server uses lazy writes to write to the database. That means that SQL Server will write to the database when it gets the chance. You need to be able to read from it as fast as you can, though, to service user needs.

If you are faced with the choice, you should use one mirror for operating system and binary files, another mirror for transaction logs, and a RAID 5 array for data files. Because of the expense involved, however, you may not be able to afford this configuration. In that case, you can place the binary files, OS, and T-logs on the same mirror and the data files on a RAID 5 array.

Data Storage Structures

There are two main types of storage structures in SQL Server 2000: extents and pages.

Extents

An *extent* is a block of eight pages totaling 64KB in size. Because the extent is the basic unit of allocation for tables and indexes and all objects are saved in a table of some kind, all objects are stored in extents. There are two types of extents in SQL Server:

Uniform   In uniform extents, all eight pages are used by the same object.

Mixed   Mixed extents are used by objects that are too small to take up eight pages, so more than one object is stored in the extent.

When a table or an index needs additional storage space, another extent is allocated to that object. A new extent will generally not be allocated for a table or index until all pages on that extent have been used. This process of allocating extents rather than individual pages to objects serves two useful purposes.

First, the time-consuming process of allocation is done in one batch rather than forcing each allocation to occur whenever a new page is needed. Second, it forces the pages allocated to an object to be at least somewhat contiguous. If pages were allocated directly, on an as-needed basis, the likelihood is quite high that pages allocated to different objects would be next to each other in physical order. This arrangement would have a significant negative impact on performance. When pages for a single object are contiguous, reads and writes can occur much more quickly.

Pages

At the most fundamental level, everything in SQL Server is stored on an 8KB *page*. The page is the one common denominator for all objects in SQL Server. There are many different types of pages, but every page has some factors in common. Pages are always 8KB in size and always have a header, leaving about 8060 bytes of usable space on every page.

There are six primary types of pages in SQL Server:

Data pages   Data pages hold the actual database records. The data page is 8192 bytes, but only 8060 of those bytes are available for data storage because there is a header at the beginning of each data page that contains information about the page itself. Records are not allowed to span more than one page (limiting their size to 8060 bytes), but a page can contain several records.

Index pages   Index pages store the index keys and levels making up the entire index tree. Unlike data pages, there is no limit to the total number of entries that can be made on an index page.

Text/image pages   Text and image pages hold the actual data associated with text, ntext, and image datatypes. When a text field is saved, the record will contain a 16-byte pointer to a linked list of text pages that hold the actual text data. Only the 16-byte pointer inside the record is counted against the 8060-byte record-size limit.

Global Allocation Map   The Global Allocation Map (GAM) page type is used to keep track of which extents in a data file are allocated and which are still available.

Index Allocation Map   Index Allocation Map (IAM) pages are used to keep track of what an extent is being used for—specifically, to which table or index the extent has been allocated.

Page Free Space   This is not an empty page; rather, it is a special type of page used to keep track of free space on all of the other pages in the database. Each Page Free Space page can keep track of the amount of free space of up to 8000 other pages.

The page is the smallest unit of I/O in SQL Server. Every time data is either read from or written to a database, this occurs in page units. Most of the time this reading and writing is actually going back and forth between data cache and disk. Data cache is divided into 8KB buffers, intended solely for the purpose of holding 8KB pages. This is an important part of database capacity planning.

Estimating Storage Requirements

All storage space in SQL Server is preallocated. Databases can be both expanded and contracted. This used to pose an interesting dilemma for database administrators. How large should your databases be? They need to be large enough to accommodate your data needs without having to expand shortly after being created, but making them too large will waste space. When estimating storage requirements, we must go to the basic level of data storage: the table and the index. Let's look at how storage space can be estimated by using these objects.

Estimating Table Storage Requirements

Tables are really nothing more than templates specifying how data is to be stored. All data stored in a table must adhere to a datatype. You can follow a specific process to estimate the space required by a table:

1. Calculate the space used by a single row of the table.

2. Calculate the number of rows that will fit on one page.

3. Estimate the number of rows the table will hold.

4. Calculate the total number of pages that will be required to hold these rows.

Calculating Row Size

Datatypes are of various shapes and sizes and allow you incredible control over how your data is stored. Table 4.1 lists some of the most common datatypes.

TABLE 4.1 Datatypes and Sizes

Datatype Name	Description	Size
TinyInt	Integer from 0 to 255	1 byte
SmallInt	Integer from -32,768 to 32,767	2 bytes
Int	Integer from -2,147,483,648 to 2,147,483,647	4 bytes
Real	1- to7-digit precision, floating-point	4 bytes

TABLE 4.1 Datatypes and Sizes *(continued)*

Datatype Name	Description	Size
Float	8- to15-digit precision, floating-point	8 bytes
Small-datetime	1/1/1900 to 6/6/2079 with accuracy to the minute	4 bytes
Datetime	1/1/100 to 12/31/9999 with accuracy to 3.33 milliseconds	8 bytes
Smallmoney	4-byte integer with 4-digit scale	4 bytes
Money	8-byte integer with 4-digit scale	8 bytes
Char	Character data	1 byte per character

When calculating storage requirements for a table, you simply add the storage requirements for each datatype in the table plus an additional two bytes per row of overhead. This will give you the total space that is occupied by a single row. For example, if a table in a database has three fields defined as Char(10), Int, and Money, the storage space required for each row could be calculated as follows:

- Char(10) = 10 bytes

- Int = 4 bytes

- Money = 8 bytes

- Overhead = 2 bytes

- Total = 24 bytes

A row is limited to two bytes of overhead only when no variable-length datatypes (varchar, nvarchar, and varbinary) have been used and when no columns allow nulls. If variable-length columns are used or nulls are allowed, additional overhead must be added. The amount will then depend on the datatype and number of columns.

Calculating Rows per Page

Once you have a number indicating the total bytes used per row, you can easily calculate the number of rows that will fit on a single page. Because every page is 8KB in size and has a header, about 8060 bytes are free for storing data. The total number of rows per page can be calculated as 8060 ÷ RowSize. The resulting value is truncated to an integer.

In our example, each row requires 24 bytes of space to store. You can calculate the rows per page as follows: 8060 ÷ 24 = 335.

In our example, we rounded down the result to the nearest whole number.

Special Considerations

When calculating rows per page, there are some additional factors that you will need to consider. Remember that rows can never cross pages. If there is not enough space on a page to complete the row, the entire row will be placed on the next page. This is why we had to truncate the result of our calculation.

In addition, the number of rows that can fit on one page may also be dependent on a *fill factor* that is used for the clustered index. Fill factor is a way of keeping the page from becoming 100 percent full when the index is created. Using a fill factor may reduce the amount of space used on a page when the index is built, but since fill factor is not maintained, the space will be eventually used.

As an example, if a clustered index were built on our example table with a fill factor of 75 percent, the data would be reorganized such that the data pages would be only 75 percent full. This means that instead of 8060 bytes free on each page, you could use only 6045 bytes.

Estimating the Number of Rows for the Table

There is no magic secret to estimating the number of rows used in your table. You have to know your data to estimate how many rows your table will eventually hold. When you make this estimate, try to consider as well as possible how large you expect your table to grow. If you do not allow for this growth in your estimates, the database will need to be expanded. That would make this exercise in projecting storage requirements a somewhat wasted effort.

Calculating the Number of Pages Needed

Calculating the number of pages needed is another simple calculation, as long as you have reliable figures on the number of rows per page and the number of rows you expect the table to hold. The calculation is the number of rows in the table divided by the number of rows per page. Here, the result will be rounded up to the nearest whole number.

In the example you saw that 335 rows would fit in a single page of the table. If you expected this table to eventually hold 1,000,000 records, the calculation would be as follows:

1. $1,000,000 \div 335 = 2985.07$

2. Round the value up to 2986 pages

Now you can extend your calculation to determine the number of extents that must be allocated to this table to hold this data. Since all space is allocated in extents, you again need to round up to the nearest integer when calculating extents. Remember that there are eight 8KB pages per extent. Your calculation would be as follows:

- $2986 \div 8 = 374$

Since a megabyte can store 16 extents, this table would take about 23.2MB of space to store. Add a little bit of extra space "just in case," and you are ready to proceed to the next table.

Estimating Index Storage Requirements

Indexes in SQL Server are stored in a B-Tree format; that is, you can think of an index as a large tree. You can also think of an index as a table with a pyramid on top of it. The ultimate concept here is that for every index, there is a single entry point: the root of the tree or the apex of the pyramid.

When estimating storage requirements, the base of this pyramid can be thought of as a table. You go through the same process in estimating the "leaf" level of an index as you would in estimating the storage requirements of a table. Although the process is very similar, there are a few issues that are important to consider:

- You are adding the datatypes of the index keys, not the data rows.

- Clustered indexes use the data page as the leaf level. There is no need to add additional storage requirements for a clustered-index leaf level.

The toughest part of estimating the size of an index is estimating the size and number of levels you will have in your index. While there is a fairly long and complex series of calculations to determine this exactly, we usually find it sufficient to add an additional 35 percent of the leaf-level space estimated for the other levels of the index.

Creating and Managing Databases

In this section, we will look at creating, expanding, shrinking, and dropping databases. The approaches demonstrated will use both Enterprise Manager and Transact-SQL (referred to as T-SQL in the remainder of this chapter).

Microsoft
✓ *Exam*
Objective

Attach and detach databases.

Create and alter databases.

- **Expand and shrink a database.**

- Set database options by using the ALTER DATABASE or CREATE DATABASE statements.

- Size and place the transaction log.

Creating a Database Using T-SQL

Let's start with the more difficult way of creating a database: using T-SQL. When you create a database, you should specify the logical name of the database, the physical filename where the database file will reside, and the size of the database file. Optional parameters include the maximum size to which the database is allowed to grow and the growth characteristics. You can also specify the logical and physical filenames of the transaction log as well as its maximum size and growth characteristics. Here is the basic syntax of the CREATE DATABASE statement:

```
CREATE DATABASE db_name
[ON { [PRIMARY]
(NAME = logical name,
```

```
FILENAME = 'physical filename',
[SIZE = initial size,]
[MAXSIZE = maxsize,]
[FILEGROWTH = [filegrowth MB | %])} [ n]]
[LOG ON
{(NAME = logical name,
 FILENAME = 'physical filename',
 [SIZE = initial size],
 [MAXSIZE = maxsize],
 [FILEGROWTH = filegrowth MB | %])} [ n]]
 [COLLATE collation_name]
 [FOR LOAD | FOR ATTACH]
```

The following explains the uses of the listed parameters:

db_name   This is the name that you are going to give this database. It must follow the rules for SQL Server identifiers.

PRIMARY   This parameter, the name of the filegroup, defaults to PRIMARY. (Filegroups are an advanced topic that we will cover later in this chapter.) In short, filegroups allow you to place individual database objects in separate files. For example, you might place a large table on one filegroup and the table's index on another filegroup. In this manner, writes to the table do not interfere with writes to the index. These are used with the ALTER DATABASE statement, not the CREATE DATABASE statement.

logical name   This is the logical name of the database file, which you will use to reference this particular database file while in SQL Server.

'physical filename'   This is the complete path and filename of the file you are creating. Note that it is surrounded by single quotation marks.

initial size   This is the initial size of the database expressed in either kilobytes or megabytes. Keep in mind that this will allocate hard-disk space.

maxsize   This is the maximum size to which the database can grow. This is useful when you specify FILEGROWTH options. This parameter is specified in kilobytes or megabytes.

filegrowth   This option specifies the size of the increments by which a given database file should grow. It can be expressed in either kilobytes or megabytes or as a percentage. If not specified, and the MAXSIZE parameter is specified, then the default file growth will be 1MB. If neither

FILEGROWTH nor MAXSIZE are specified, then the database will not automatically grow.

COLLATE   A collation determines the physical bit patterns that SQL Server uses to store characters on disk. This option can be used to specify which collation is used. If this option is left out, then the default collation for the particular instance of SQL Server is used.

FOR LOAD   This option marks the database for DBO (Database Owner) use only and is used for backward compatibility with SQL Server 6.5. This means that the database is not marked online but is waiting for data to be loaded into it through a select into/bulk copy operation or through the restoration of a backup.

FOR ATTACH   This option reattaches the files that make up a database. It essentially recreates entries in the system tables regarding this database file. This should be used only when you must specify more than 16 files to be reattached. Otherwise, use the sp_attachdb stored procedure (discussed later in this chapter).

Let's take a look at a few examples of using the CREATE DATABASE statement. In this first example, you will create a very simple database with no growth characteristics.

```
CREATE DATABASE Simple
ON PRIMARY
(NAME = 'Simple_Data',
 FILENAME = 'C:\MICROSOFT SQL SERVER\MSSQL\Data\Simple_
Data.mdf',
 SIZE = 5MB)
LOG ON
(NAME = 'Simple_Log',
 FILENAME = 'C:\MICROSOFT SQL SERVER\MSSQL\DATA\Simple_
Log.ldf',
 SIZE = 2MB)
```

The size of this database is 7MB, with 5MB being used to store the data and system tables and 2MB being used to store the transaction log. The file does not have any FILEGROWTH parameters and therefore will not grow automatically.

You can use the ALTER DATABASE statement to specify new database growth parameters. This simplifies altering the MAXSIZE and FILEGROWTH properties.

Now let's look at a more complex database. In this example, you will create a database that has data spanning two files and a transaction log. You will also set the FILEGROWTH and MAXSIZE parameters. Here is the example:

```
CREATE DATABASE Complex
ON PRIMARY
(NAME = Complex_Data1,
 FILENAME = 'C:\MICROSOFT SQL SERVER\MSSQL\Data\Complex_
Data1.mdf',
 SIZE = 5MB,
 MAXSIZE = 10MB,
 FILEGROWTH = 1MB),
(NAME = Complex_Data2,
 FILENAME = 'C:\MICROSOFT SQL SERVER\MSSQL\Data\Complex_
Data2.ndf',
 SIZE = 2MB,
 MAXSIZE = 10MB,
 FILEGROWTH = 2MB),
LOG ON
(NAME = Complex_Log1,
 FILENAME = 'D:\Logs\Complex_Log1.ldf',
 SIZE = 2MB,
 MAXSIZE = 8MB,
 FILEGROWTH = 1MB)
```

This creates a database with an initial size of 9MB—5MB for the first file, 2MB for the second file, and 2MB for the log. The database has a maximum size of 28MB.

You should always specify a maximum size for data and transaction log files for which the FILEGROWTH option is specified. If you do not, it is possible for the file to fill the entire hard-disk partition. If this happens, Windows will no longer allow you to use that partition. If the partition also has the Windows system files on it, you will no longer be able to use Windows until the situation is remedied.

Follow the steps outlined in Exercise 4.1 to create a new database named Sample with an initial database size of 4MB and a transaction log of 1MB. You will also set the maximum size of the database to 10MB and the maximum size of the log to 4MB. Both will have a FILEGROWTH of 10 percent.

EXERCISE 4.1

Create a Database Using T-SQL

1. Open the SQL Server Query Analyzer. Do this through the SQL Enterprise Manager by selecting Tools ➢ SQL Query Analyzer or by choosing Start ➢ Programs ➢ Microsoft SQL Server 2000 ➢ SQL Query Analyzer.

2. Enter the following query:

```
CREATE DATABASE Sample

ON PRIMARY

(NAME = 'SampleData',

 FILENAME = 'C:\Microsoft SQL Server\
 MSSQL\Data\SampleData.MDF',

 SIZE = 4,

 MAXSIZE = 10,

 FILEGROWTH = 10%)

LOG ON

(NAME = 'SampleLog',

 FILENAME = 'C:\Microsoft SQL Server\
 MSSQL\Data\SampleLog.LDF',

 SIZE = 1,
```

EXERCISE 4.1 *(continued)*

```
MAXSIZE = 4,

FILEGROWTH = 10%)
```

3. Execute the query. You should receive notification that the query successfully completed and that the two new database files were created. It should look something like this:

```
The CREATE DATABASE process is allocating 4.00 MB on disk
'SampleData'. The CREATE DATABASE process is allocating
1.00 MB on disk 'SampleLog'.
```

Creating a Database Using Enterprise Manager

Now that you have created a database using T-SQL, let's do it with Enterprise Manager. Follow the steps outlined in Exercise 4.2 to create a database named Sybex. There will be two data files, each 2MB in size, with a FILEGROWTH of 1MB and a maximum size of 20MB. You will also create a transaction log with a size of 1MB, a FILEGROWTH of 1MB, and no maximum size.

EXERCISE 4.2

Creating a Database Using Enterprise Manager

1. Start Enterprise Manager by selecting Start ➤ Programs ➤ Microsoft SQL Server ➤ Enterprise Manager.

2. Connect to your SQL Server.

3. Expand your Databases folder as shown here:

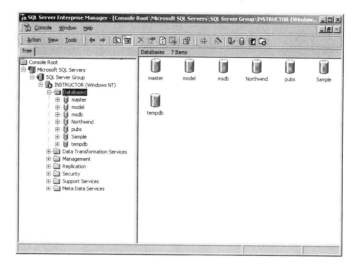

4. Right-click either the Databases folder in the console tree, or the white space in the right pane, and choose New Database from the context menu.

5. You should now see the General tab of the Database properties sheet. Type in the database name **Sybex**.

6. Click the Data Files tab and fill in the other boxes as shown here. Set the File Name field to **Sybex_Data2**. Use the default value for the Location field. For both the Sybex_Data file and the Sybex_ Data2 file, set the Initial Size field to 2MB. Set the Automatically Grow File option to true (checked) and set the File Growth increment to 1MB. Set the Restrict File Growth option to 20MB.

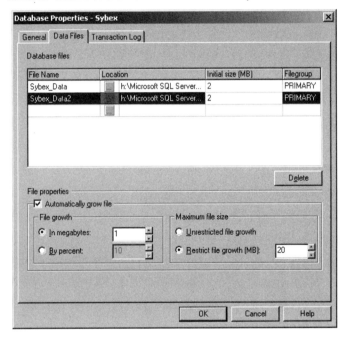

7. Now click the Transaction Log tab. Set the options as shown here. The file name should be **Sybex_Log**. Use the default value for the Location field and set the Initial Size to 1MB. Set the Automatically Grow File option to true (checked) and set the File Growth parameter to 1MB. Set the Maximum File Size to Unrestricted File Growth.

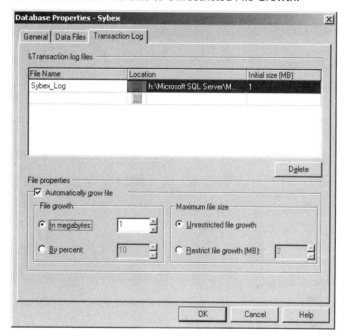

8. Click OK when you are finished. You should now have a new Sybex database.

Gathering Information about Your Database

Now that you have successfully created a couple of databases, it is time to learn how to gather more information about them. There are two ways to gather information about your database: you can use Enterprise Manager or the Query Analyzer.

Let's start with the graphical tool first. Using Enterprise Manager, you can gather a wealth of information about your database. This includes the size of the database, its current capacity, any options that are currently set, and so on.

By right-clicking a database in Enterprise Manager and selecting Properties, you will see the database information dialog box as shown in Figure 4.1.

FIGURE 4.1   The database information pane

You can also use system stored procedures to gather information about your database. The sp_helpdb stored procedure used by itself will give you information about all databases in your SQL Server. You can gather information about a particular database by using the database name as a parameter. Figure 4.2 shows the sp_helpdb stored procedure and its result set.

FIGURE 4.2 The sp_helpdb stored procedure

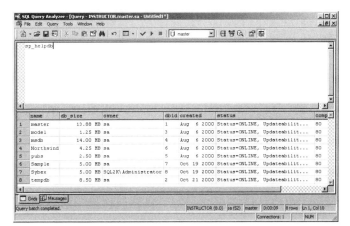

Notice that both the Sample and the Sybex databases are 5MB in size. The status parameter describes which database options have been set. For example, the Master database has the Truncate Log on Checkpoint database option enabled. We'll talk about the database options later in this chapter.

If you switch to the Sybex database and run the sp_helpfile stored procedure, you can gather information about the data and log files that are used for the Sybex database (see Figure 4.3).

FIGURE 4.3 The sp_helpfile stored procedure

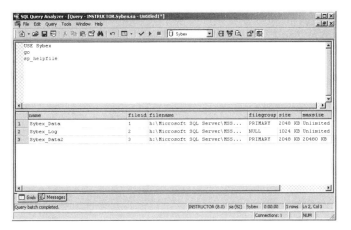

As you can see from Figure 4.3, you can gather information about file sizes and locations, the filegroup they are a member of, and the database file use (either data or log).

Managing Your Database

In this section, you will learn more about the various methods used to manage your database. This includes database options and their effects, altering the database by adding additional database files, attaching and detaching databases, and removing a database from your system.

Working with Database Options

Database options allow you to specify how your database will behave in given situations. You can view and modify database options using Enterprise Manager or the sp_dboption stored procedure. The sp_dboption stored procedure includes database options that are not available through the GUI.

Let's take a look at the database options currently set on your Sybex database that you created earlier. Start Enterprise Manager and move down through the console tree until you see your database. Right-click your database and choose Properties. From the Database properties sheet, click the Options tab as shown in Figure 4.4.

FIGURE 4.4 The Database Options tab

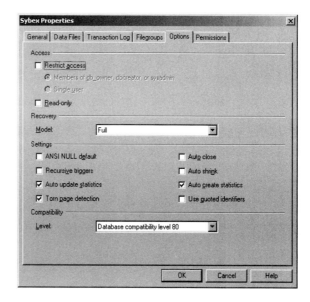

The database options are broken into separate categories for Access, Recovery, and Settings. This is what the different settings mean:

Members of db_owner, dbcreator, or sysadmin   Only members of one of these three security roles have access to this database when this option is selected. This option is frequently used when performing a restoration or other task where you do not want to allow nonowners in the database.

Single User   Only one user at a time can access the database and with only a single connection. Make sure no one is using the database when you set this option.

Read-Only   This option marks the database as read-only. No changes to the database will be allowed.

Recovery   There are three recovery models to choose from:

Simple   This is the default option, which allows the database to be recovered to the point of the last backup (not up to the minute of a crash). This is the equivalent of setting the Truncate Log on Checkpoint option in previous versions of SQL Server. This option is especially useful for development databases where an active transaction log is not required.

Bulk-Logged   This allows you to recover most of the data in the event of a crash. The only data that may be lost are bulk operations such as SELECT INTO, BCP, BULK INSERT, CREATE INDEX, and text and ntext operations. This is the equivalent of setting the SELECT INTO/BULK COPY option in previous versions of SQL Server. Note that you should back up your database immediately after performing bulk operations if this option is selected.

Full   This allows every operation against a database to be backed up so that the database can be recovered up to the minute of a crash.

ANSI NULL Default   This option specifies that new columns created or added to tables have a default value of NULL. Although this is a default setting for the entire database, you can override this value by specifying either NULL or NOT NULL when you create your columns.

Recursive Triggers   This option allows recursive triggers to fire. Recursive triggers occur when one trigger fires a trigger on another table, which in turn fires another trigger on the originating table.

Auto Update Statistics   This option works with the Auto-Create Statistics option. As you make changes to the data in your database, the statistics will be less and less accurate. This option periodically updates those statistics.

Torn Page Detection The smallest unit of data the SQL Server works with is 8K, but the smallest unit of data that is written to disk is 512 bytes. This means that parts of a page may not be written to disk, a condition known as a torn page. This option allows SQL Server to detect when this problem occurs. Because this is a form of data corruption that should be avoided, we suggest you enable this option.

Auto Close This option safely closes your database when the last user has exited from it. This can be a useful option for optimization on databases that are infrequently accessed because it decreases the amount of resources that SQL Server needs to consume in order to maintain user information and locks. This should not be set on databases that are accessed on a frequent basis because the overhead of opening the database can outweigh the benefits of closing the database in the first place.

Auto Shrink This option will automatically shrink both data and log files. Log files will be shrunk after a backup of the log has been made. Data files will be shrunk when a periodic check of the database finds that the database has more than 25 percent of its assigned space free. Your database will then be shrunk to a size that leaves 25 percent free.

Auto Create Statistics This option will automatically generate statistics on the distribution of values found in your columns. The SQL Server Query optimizer uses these statistics to determine the best method to run a particular query.

Use Quoted Identifiers This option allows you to use double quotation marks as part of a SQL Server identifier (object name). This can be useful in situations in which you have identifiers that are also SQL Server reserved words.

Compatibility Level This option will change the way a database behaves so that it is compatible with previous versions of SQL Server. The four levels of compatibility are 60, 65, 70, and 80 (the latter corresponds to SQL Server 2000).

When you have made your selections, click OK to apply them and continue using SQL Server. You can also use the sp_dboption stored procedure to accomplish these same tasks. For example, to mark the Sybex database as read-only, you could enter this code:

```
use master
go
```

```
exec sp_dboption sybex, 'Single User', true
```
When you run this command, you should get the following data back:
```
The command(s) completed successfully.
```

To verify, you could run the sp_helpdb system stored procedure and check the status of the database. You can also review the database in Enterprise Manager. In Enterprise Manager, you should now see a face icon superimposed on your database in the console tree, as shown in Figure 4.5. If the icon is missing, right-click your Databases folder and choose Refresh. You may also find that changes you make in the Query Analyzer do not show up in Enterprise Manager. Here too, right-click the object you are viewing and choose Refresh. This will refresh the information displayed.

FIGURE 4.5 The Single-User Database option has been set on the Sybex database.

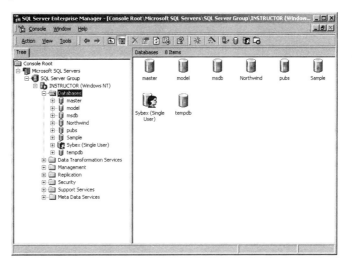

The sp_dboption stored procedure includes the following additional database options that are not available through Enterprise Manager:

Concat Null Yields Null   This option specifies that anything you concatenate to a null value will return a null value.

Cursor Close on Commit   This option automatically closes any open cursors when the transaction that created the cursor completes. (Cursors are the results from a query.)

Default to Local Cursor This option creates cursors that are local in nature and available only to the local batch, trigger, or stored procedure that generated the trigger. This option can be overridden by using the GLOBAL keyword when creating the cursor.

Merge Publish This option allows a database to be a publisher as part of merge replication.

Offline This option takes a database offline and shuts it down. When a database has been taken offline, it can be placed on removable media such as CD-ROM.

Published This option specifies that the database is allowed to publish data for use in replication.

Subscribed This option specifies that the database can participate in the subscriber side of replication.

Select Into/Bulk Copy This option is the same as the simple recovery option in that it bypasses the transaction log. It is especially useful for importing large amounts of data into a database.

Numeric_roundabort When this is on, a loss of precision will generate an error message. When it is off, a message will not be generated.

Arithabort When this is set to on, a divide-by-zero error will cause a query to terminate. If this is off, the query will continue but a message is displayed.

Altering Databases

There may be times that you wish to make changes to your database or the database files. These include expanding your data files or adding more data files, shrinking the database, or even removing the database from your system. This section discusses all these topics. Let's start with the ALTER DATABASE statement itself; then we'll cover expanding, shrinking, and removing databases and data files.

Here is the basic syntax of the ALTER DATABASE statement:

```
ALTER DATABASE database
{ ADD FILE < filespec > [ ,...n ] [ TO FILEGROUP
filegroup_name ]
| ADD LOG FILE < filespec > [ ,...n ]
| REMOVE FILE logical_file_name
| ADD FILEGROUP filegroup_name
```

```
| REMOVE FILEGROUP filegroup_name
| MODIFY FILE < filespec >
| MODIFY NAME = new_dbname
| MODIFY FILEGROUP filegroup_name {filegroup_property |
NAME = new_filegroup_name }
| SET < optionspec > [ ,...n ] [ WITH < termination > ]
| COLLATE < collation_name >
}
```

The `file_spec` option includes the following syntax, which you saw earlier in the CREATE DATABASE statements:

```
(NAME = logical name,
 FILENAME = 'physical filename',
 [SIZE = initial size,]
 [MAXSIZE = maxsize,]
 [FILEGROWTH = [filegrowth MB | %])} [ n]]
```

With the ALTER DATABASE statement, you can add or expand data and log files. You can also add or modify filegroups and remove data files, log files, and filegroups.

Expanding Databases

You can expand databases in SQL Server by using the SQL Enterprise Manager or the ALTER DATABASE statement. When you expand a database, you can make the current database files larger, or you can add additional database files. This is a relatively straightforward task when using the Enterprise Manager—it's a little more tricky when using ALTER DATABASE statements in T-SQL. First, let's look at expanding databases using Enterprise Manager.

Expanding Databases Using Enterprise Manager

In Exercise 4.3, you will expand the Sample database by increasing the size of the data files and the log files by 2MB. You will also increase the maximum size of the data files by 10MB.

EXERCISE 4.3

Expanding a Database Using Enterprise Manager

1. Start Enterprise Manager.

2. Drill down through the console tree to the Sample database.

EXERCISE 4.3 *(continued)*

3. Right-click the Sample database and choose Properties.

4. Switch to the Data Files tab and change the space allocated from 4MB to 6MB.

5. Increase the maximum file size from 10MB to 20MB, as shown here.

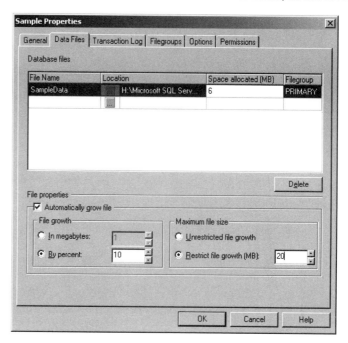

6. Now switch to the Transaction Log tab and increase its initial size from 1MB to 3MB and increase the Restrict File Growth Parameter from 4MB to 14MB.

7. Click OK when you are finished.

8. If you now right-click your database in the console tree and choose Properties, you will see that your database has increased in size from its old 5MB to a new size of 9MB, as shown here.

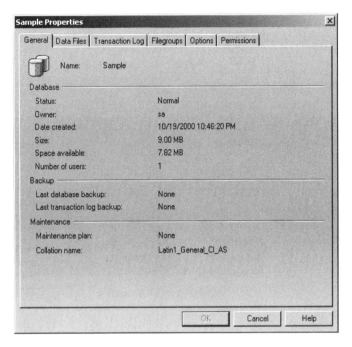

You can add additional data files as well as log files from the Database properties sheet. Simply click in a new box and fill in the new logical name, physical location, initial size, and other properties.

Expanding Databases Using T-SQL

Now let's do some modifications using the ALTER DATABASE statements. In this example, you will add a new log file to the Sample database. The log file will have the following characteristics:

Option	Value
Name	Sample_Log2
Physical Name	C:\MICROSOFT SQL SERVER\MSSQL\Data\Sample_Log2.ldf
Size	4MB
Maxsize	10MB
Filegrowth	2MB

Follow the steps outlined in Exercise 4.4 to complete this example.

EXERCISE 4.4

Expanding a Database Using T-SQL

1. Open the SQL Server Query Analyzer.

2. Enter the following code to alter the Sample database:

```
ALTER DATABASE Sample

ADD LOG FILE

(NAME = Sample_Log2,

  FILENAME = 'C:\Microsoft SQL Server\MSSQL\Data\Sample_
Log2.ldf',

  SIZE = 4MB,

  MAXSIZE = 10MB,

  FILEGROWTH = 2MB)
```

3. When you have completed the command, you should get something similar to the following information:

`Extending database by 4.00 MB on disk 'Sample_Log2'.`

4. Run the `sp_helpdb` and the `sp_helpfile` stored procedures discussed earlier in this chapter to verify that the new log file has been created.

There are certain advantages and disadvantages to having multiple database files as opposed to just enlarging your current database files. The main disadvantage of multiple database files is administration. You need to be aware of these different files, their locations, and their use. There are advantages, however. For example, you can place these files on separate physical hard disks (if you are not using striping), avoiding the creation of "hot spots" and thereby improving performance. When you use database files, you can back up individual database files rather than the whole database in one session. If you also take advantage of filegroups, you can improve performance by explicitly placing tables on one filegroup and the indexes for those tables on a separate filegroup. A filegroup is a logical grouping of database files used for performance and to improve administration on VLDBs. We will discuss filegroups later in this chapter.

Shrinking Databases

When you wish to shrink your database, you can choose to shrink individual files within the database or all files in the database. There are three methods you can use to shrink your database: the DBCC SHRINKDATABASE or DBCC SHRINKFILE commands, Enterprise Manager, and the Autoshrink Database option.

To understand what is really happening in your database when it is being shrunk, let's first take a look at the database consistency checker (or DBCC) statements.

Shrinking Databases Using T-SQL

To shrink a database using T-SQL, you can use the DBCC SHRINKDATABASE command, which will attempt to shrink all files in the database, or the DBCC

SHRINKFILE command, which will attempt to shrink a specific database file. Here is the syntax of the SHRINKDATABASE command:

```
DBCC SHRINKDATABASE {
(db_name,
[target_percent],
[{NOTRUNCATE | TRUNCATEONLY}])}
```

The following lists the arguments and their meanings:

db_name   The logical name of the database that you wish to shrink.

target_percent   The percentage of free space left in the database after it has been shrunk.

NOTRUNCATE   Does not release the free space back to the operating system.

TRUNCATEONLY   Releases all free space back to the operating system. Note that when you use TRUNCATEONLY, the target_percent parameter is ignored.

Understanding how the SHRINKDATABASE statements work is very tricky (search for SHRINKDATABASE in Books Online). When you use the SHRINKDATABASE statement, it attempts to shrink all data files in the database to a new size. When you run DBCC SHRINKDATBASE (db_name) by itself, it will tell you how much your database can be shrunk.

The target percentage parameter is used to specify how much free space you wish to have in your database after it is shrunk. Let's say that you have a 100MB database and you're currently using 50MB for data storage, with the other 50MB as free space. To shrink the database and leave yourself with 10MB of free space, you must determine what percentage of 100MB (the current size of the database) is 10MB (the desired amount of free space). The answer in this case is 10 percent. This is your target percentage. Run the following command:

```
DBCC SHRINKDATABASE (Foo, 10%)
```

You should end up with a database that is 60MB in size: 50MB for the used data pages and 10MB of free space. You should be aware of some additional issues with this statement. For example, you cannot set the target percentage to a value that is larger than the current database: using your 100MB database with 50MB free and 50MB used, if you set the target percentage to 60 percent, you'd get the following numbers: 60 percent of 100MB is 60MB. The current data size is 50MB, which is 50 percent of the database. Since 50 percent plus 60 percent is more than 100 percent, this cannot be done.

This example is fairly straightforward, but what happens if you have a 817MB database with 709MB used, and you want to shrink it and leave 30 percent free space as your target percentage? This would not work, because 30 percent of 817 is roughly 245MB. Adding 245MB to the existing 709MB gives you 954MB, which is more than 817MB. The maximum percentage you could set would be considerably less: 817MB – 709MB = 108MB. Dividing 108MB by 817MB gives you 13 percent. While this would not shrink the database at all, the statement would complete successfully.

When using a SHRINKDATABASE or SHRINKFILE statement, it is important to understand the functions of the TRUNCATEONLY and NOTRUNCATE options as well as what is happening to the data within the database files.

The SHRINKDATABASE and SHRINKFILE statements work in a fashion similar to the disk defragmenter. Keep in mind that data is striped across multiple data files automatically. When you issue one of the shrink commands, the data in the stripes is consolidated; the free space that was between the data in the stripe sets is also consolidated and moved to the bottom of the stripe set.

- The TRUNCATEONLY clause will ignore the target_percentage parameter and shrink the database to the size of data. It will also release all of the freed-up disk space back to the operating system.

- The NOTRUNCATE option just consolidates the data into one area and the free space into another area without releasing any free space back to the operating system. For obvious reasons, the NOTRUNCATE ignores the target_percentage parameter also.

Figure 4.6 shows a before-and-after representation of a SHRINKDATABASE command with the NOTRUNCATE option. As you can see, all of the data (the shaded blocks) was consolidated, and the free space was moved to the end of the files.

FIGURE 4.6 Effects of the SHRINKDATABASE command with NOTRUNCATE

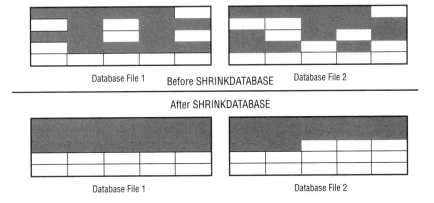

Database File 1   Before SHRINKDATABASE   Database File 2

After SHRINKDATABASE

Database File 1   Database File 2

The SHRINKFILE command allows you to shrink a single database file. Here is the syntax:

```
DBCC SHRINKFILE {
(filename | file_id}
[, target_percentage]
[, {EMPTYFILE | NOTRUNCATE | TRUNCATEONLY}])}
```

The *filename* and *file_id* parameters are used to specify the individual database file you wish to shrink. The *file_id* can be found by first running the sp_helpdb stored procedure. The other parameter is the EMPTYFILE option, which is used in conjunction with a filegroup. You can use this option to move all data stored on a particular file to other files in the file-group. EMPTYFILE will then mark the file as empty. Once a file has been marked empty, you can remove it from the filegroup using the ALTER DATABASE command with the REMOVE FILE parameter.

The following is an example of what you would see if you used the SHRINKFILE command and then the REMOVE FILE commands. In this example, we will assume you have a filegroup with three files in it. The files are named fgTest_Data1 through fgTest_Data3. The database is named Test. You will first empty the fgTest_Data3 file and then remove it.

```
USE Test
GO
DBCC SHRINKFILE (fgTest_Data3, EMPTYFILE)
GO
```

This is what your output might look like:

DbId	FileID	CurrentSize	MinimumSize	UsedPages	EstimatedPages
12	7	56	256	0	0

```
(1 row(s) affected)
```

Now you can drop the file, as it has been emptied and marked as empty:

```
ALTER DATABASE Test
REMOVE FILE fgTest_Data3
```

Your output should be similar to this:

```
DBCC execution completed. If DBCC printed error messages,
contact your system administrator.
The file 'fgTest_Data3' has been removed.
```

If you now run sp_helpdb on the Test database, you will see that the file has successfully been removed. However, there is an easier way to achieve the same results.

Shrinking Databases Using the Enterprise Manager

You can also use Enterprise Manager to shrink your databases. Another nice feature of Enterprise Manager is the ability to have the database shrink automatically over time. We'll take a look at that in a minute, but first let's see how to shrink a database once.

Shrinking a database using Enterprise Manager is not particularly intuitive. Right-clicking your way to the properties sheet and entering a smaller value for the Initial Space option will not shrink the database: it will actually run either the CREATE DATABASE command or the ALTER DATABASE command. Enterprise Manager works it a little differently. Follow the steps outlined in Exercise 4.5 to shrink the Sample database.

EXERCISE 4.5

Shrinking a Database Using Enterprise Manager

1. Open Enterprise Manager.

2. Drill down to the Database folder, right-click the Sample database, and select Properties. You should now see some general information about your Sample database, as shown below.

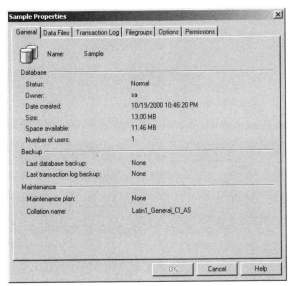

3. Notice that the current size of the Sample database is 13MB and that there is about 11MB of free space. You will attempt to shrink the database down to 7MB or so. To do this, click Cancel, then right-click the Sample database in the console tree and choose All Tasks Shrink Database.

4. You should now see something similar to the graphic shown here. Since you want to shrink the 13MB of database to about 7MB, click Shrink Database by % and change the value to 50. Click OK when you are finished.

5. You should get a confirmation message that tells you that the database has been successfully shrunk.

EXERCISE 4.5 *(continued)*

6. There are two other important options. Move Pages to the Beginning of the File Before Shrinking will defragment the database as it shrinks it. This slows the shrinking process, but it can improve database performance.

7. The other option allows you to set up your database to shrink itself automatically over time. When this option is enabled, the scheduler will create a job that will check the database. Whenever it find that the database has more than 25 percent of its space free, it will automatically shrink the database to reflect a database with 25 percent free space.

Renaming a Database

During your tenure as a SQL Server administrator you may find it necessary to change the name of a database because of a departmental shift, because you're turning a development database into a production database, or for any other reason.

To rename a database in SQL Server 2000 is as simple as running the sp_ renamedb stored procedure. However, there are several restrictions that you should be aware of when you do this:

- The database must be set to single-user.

- You must be in the master database to run the sp_renamedb stored procedure.

- You must be a member of the sysadmin fixed server role.

- Data files and filegroups are not affected.

- Fully qualified database object names may be affected. A fully qualified object name is in the form servername.databasename.owner.object, for example: HomePC.Sample.dbo.Table1.

 You can also change the name of a database with the ALTER DATABASE statement using the MODIFY NAME parameter.

Follow the steps outlined in Exercise 4.6 to rename the Sample database to NewSample. Keep in mind that you are changing just the logical name of the database, nothing else.

EXERCISE 4.6

Renaming a Database Using T-SQL

1. Open the SQL Server Query Analyzer.

2. In the query window, enter the following:

```
USE master

GO

EXEC sp_dboption 'Sample', 'Single User', True

EXEC sp_renamedb 'Sample', 'NewSample'

EXEC sp_dboption 'NewSample', 'Single User', False

GO
```

3. When you have completed the command, you should get something similar to the following:

```
The database name 'NewSample' has been set.
```

4. You can now run the sp_helpdb stored procedure to see the new NewSample database in the output.

5. Close the Query Analyzer when you are finished.

Attaching and Detaching Databases

If the disk that your database is on becomes full or you need to move the database to another server, you can detach the database and then reattach it to another server—or even the same server it was detached from. Detaching a database leaves the database intact and allows it to be moved to a new location. Attaching a database allows users to start using the database again. In

Exercise 4.7, you will see how to detach and then reattach a database using Enterprise Manager.

EXERCISE 4.7

Detaching and Attaching a Database with Enterprise Manager

1. Open Enterprise Manager and drill down to and expand Databases.

2. Right-click Northwind, point to All Tasks, and select Detach Database.

3. Verify that there are no connections to the database and click OK.

4. To reattach the database, right-click Databases, point to All Tasks and select Attach Database.

5. In the MDF file of database to attach box type `C:\Microsoft SQL Server\MSSQL\Data\northwnd.mdf`.

6. Notice that the remainder of the files needed by the database are filled in for you from data stored in the primary data file. Click OK to reattach the database.

Another way to accomplish this same task is by using the T-SQL equivalent commands `sp_detach_db` and `sp_attach_db`. They look like this:

```
sp_detach_db 'database'
sp_attach_db 'database', 'file1', 'file2',…'file16'
```

The `sp_attach_db` command is extremely useful when there are multiple files to be reattached and the file location has changed for more than one of them. You will see how to use them in Exercise 4.8.

EXERCISE 4.8

Detaching and Attaching a Database with T-SQL

1. Open Query Analyzer and execute the following command to detach the NewSample database:

```
exec sp_detach_db 'NewSample'
```

2. Execute the following command to reattach the NewSample database (this is wrapped for readability):

```
exec sp_attach_db 'NewSample', 'c:\Microsoft SQL
Server\MSSQL\Data\SampleData.mdf',

'c:\Microsoft SQL Server\MSSQL\Data\SampleLog.ldf',
'c:\Microsoft SQL Server\MSSQL\Data\Sample_log2.ldf'
```

3. Close Query Analyzer.

Dropping Databases

When you no longer need a database, it can be dropped from your server, freeing up disk space for other database files. Only the owner of a database has the authority to drop a database. Dropping a database is a very simple task, with both Enterprise Manager and T-SQL. Although the process is easy, remember that dropping a database is permanent. If you need to recover your database later, you will need to restore it from a backup.

When using Enterprise Manager to drop databases, simply locate the desired database in the console tree and press the Delete key on your keyboard, or right-click and choose Delete. You will be asked to confirm the deletion, after which the database will be dropped.

With T-SQL, databases are dropped using the DROP DATABASE statement. The syntax is as follows:

```
DROP DATABASE database_name [, database_name...]
```

Notice that multiple databases can be dropped at once using this statement. Just separate the database names with commas.

There are three databases that cannot be dropped: the Master, Model, and Tempdb databases. However, although you can drop the Msdb database, doing so will render the SQL Server Agent service and replication completely unusable. It will also cause errors to be reported whenever you do a backup or restore, as the system will attempt to write information to the detail and history tables in the Msdb database. You are free to drop the Pubs and the Northwind databases if you wish.

Working with Filegroups

A final feature of database management is the *filegroup*. In this section, you will learn more about filegroups, how they are created and modified, and how they affect your overall database strategy.

Microsoft
Exam
Objective

Create and alter databases.

- Add filegroups.

- Configure filegroup usage.

When you use filegroups, you can explicitly place database objects onto a particular set of database files. For example, you can separate tables and their nonclustered indexes onto separate filegroups. This can improve performance, as modifications to the table can be written to both the table and the index at the same time. This can be especially useful if you are not using striping with parity (RAID 5). Another advantage of filegroups is the ability to back up only a single filegroup at a time. This can be extremely useful for a VLDB, as the sheer size of the database could make backing up an extremely time-consuming process. Yet another advantage is the ability to mark the filegroup and all data on the files that are part of it as either READ-ONLY or READWRITE. There are really only two disadvantages to using filegroups. The first is the administration that is involved in keeping track of the files in the filegroup and the database objects that are placed in them. The other is that if you are working with a smaller database and have RAID 5 implemented, you may not be improving performance.

The two basic filegroups in SQL Server 2000 are the primary, or default, filegroup that is created with every database, and the user-defined filegroups created for a particular database. The primary filegroup will always contain the primary data file and any other files that are not specifically created on a user-defined filegroup. You can create additional filegroups using the ALTER DATABASE command or Enterprise Manager.

Filegroups have several rules that you should follow when you are working with them:

- The first (or primary) data file must reside on the primary filegroup.

- All system files must be placed on the primary filegroup.

- A file cannot be a member of more than one filegroup at a time.

- Filegroups can be allocated indexes, tables, text, ntext, and image data.

- New data pages are not automatically allocated to user-defined filegroups if the primary filegroup runs out of space.

If you place tables in one filegroup and their corresponding indexes in a different filegroup, the two file groups must be backed up as a single unit—they cannot be backed up separately.

Creating Filegroups with Enterprise Manager

Creating new filegroups and adding data files to them is a relatively straightforward task when using Enterprise Manager. You can create the filegroups when you create a new database or when you alter an existing database. Follow the steps in Exercise 4.9 to create a new filegroup and add two new database files to it. You will be using the NewSample database (formerly the Sample database) to do this.

EXERCISE 4.9

Creating a Filegroup with Enterprise Manager

1. Open Enterprise Manager.

2. Drill down in the console tree to the NewSample database.

3. Right-click the NewSample database and choose Properties from the context menu. You are now looking at the NewSample database properties sheet.

4. Switch to the Data Files tab and add a new data file called fgTable_Data1, with a filename of C:\Microsoft SQL Server\MSSQL\Data\ fgTable_Data1.dat that's 5MB in size, and then set the File Group box to Table.

EXERCISE 4.9 *(continued)*

5. Add another new data file called fgIndex_Data1, with a filename of C:\Microsoft SQL Server\MSSQL\Data\fgIndex_Data1.dat that's 2MB in size, and then set the File Group box to Index.

6. Click OK when you are finished. Your database properties sheet should look similar to the graphic shown here.

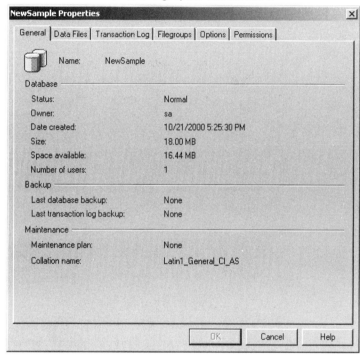

Creating Filegroups with T-SQL

As might be expected, using T-SQL to create a filegroup is a bit trickier. To add a filegroup and then to add data files to the filegroup, you need to use the ALTER DATABASE statement that we covered earlier in this chapter.

In this example, you will create a new filegroup called Testing on the Dummy database. (You will also see the results of the query.)

```
ALTER DATABASE Dummy
ADD FILEGROUP Testing
GO
The command(s) completed successfully
```

You can verify your filegroups by running the sp_helpfilegroup stored procedure. For example, you could run the following command on the NewSample database:

```
USE NewSample
GO
EXEC sp_helpfilegroup
```

Your results might look like this:

```
Groupname      Groupid      filecount
----------     --------     ----------
Index          3            1
PRIMARY        1            1
Table          2            1
```

Now let's add another data file to the Table filegroup on the NewSample database. Follow the steps outlined in Exercise 4.10. You will be creating a new table called fgTable_Data2, which will be 2MB in size and be a part of the Table filegroup. You will then verify the table using the sp_helpfilegroup stored procedure.

EXERCISE 4.10

Adding a Data File to a Filegroup Using T-SQL

1. Open the Query Analyzer.

2. Run the following query. Note the square brackets around the Table filegroup. This was done to ensure that SQL Server doesn't confuse the Table keyword with the filegroup of the same name.

```
USE NewSample

GO

ALTER DATABASE NewSample

ADD FILE

(NAME = fgTable_Data2,

 FILENAME = 'C:\MICROSOFT SQL SERVER\MSSQL\Data\fgTable_
Data2.ndf',

 SIZE = 2MB)
```

```
TO FILEGROUP [Table]

GO
```

You should get the following result:

```
Extending database by 2.00 MB on disk 'fgTable_Data2'.
```

3. You can verify your new file by running the sp_helpfilegroup stored procedure.

```
USE NewSample

GO

EXEC sp_helpfilegroup
```

4. You should get the following results:

Groupname	Groupid	filecount
PRIMARY	1	1
Table	2	2
Index	3	1

Removing a Filegroup

To remove a filegroup, you must first ensure that all the files that make up the filegroup have been removed. You cannot move a data file from one filegroup to another. Keep in mind that files can be resized or deleted.

Once the files have been removed, you can remove the filegroup using the ALTER DATABASE statement. Follow the steps in Exercise 4.11 to remove the table data files and the table filegroup as well as the index filegroup from the NewSample database.

EXERCISE 4.11

Removing Files and Filegroups

1. Open the Query Analyzer.

2. Run the following query, which will remove the files and then the filegroup:

   USE NewSample

   GO

   ALTER DATABASE NewSample

   REMOVE FILE fgTable_Data1

   GO

   ALTER DATABASE NewSample

   REMOVE FILE fgTable_Data2

   GO

   ALTER DATABASE NewSample

   REMOVE FILE fgIndex_Data1

   GO

You should get the following result:

   The file 'fgTable_Data1' has been removed.

   The file 'fgTable_Data2' has been removed.

   The file 'fgIndex_Data1' has been removed.

3. Now that the data files have been removed, you can remove the filegroups themselves. Run the following query:

   USE NewSample

   GO

   ALTER DATABASE NewSample

   REMOVE FILEGROUP [Table]

EXERCISE 4.11 *(continued)*

GO

ALTER DATABASE NewSample

REMOVE FILEGROUP [Index]

GO

You should get the following result:

The filegroup 'Table' has been removed.

The filegroup 'Index' has been removed.

4. To verify that the filegroups have been removed, you can run either sp_helpfile or the sp_helpfilegroup stored procedure, or you can look at the database properties in Enterprise Manager. To use Enterprise Manager, drill down in the console tree to your database. Right-click the database and choose Refresh. Once the database properties have been refreshed, take a look at them.

5. Right-click the NewSample database and choose Properties, then switch to the Data Files tab. You should now see something similar to graphic shown here:

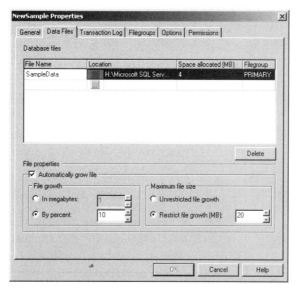

We have given you a broad overview of the uses and simple implementation of database filegroups (filegroups are very similar to segments in SQL Server 6.5). While this database structure can be a key component of your database optimization tasks, it is beyond the scope of this book. For further information on filegroups, see the SQL Server Books Online, or pick up a book on performance tuning and optimization in SQL Server such as *Mastering SQL Server 2000* (Sybex, 2000).

Creating Objects in Your Database

Now that you know how to create and alter databases, you can start filling them with objects. In this section, we will look at creating and managing objects.

Microsoft Exam Objective

Create and manage objects. Objects include constraints, indexes, stored procedures, triggers, and views.

Modify the database schema.

Think of a database as an empty storage box: without it, you have no place to store your data, but it is useless when empty. As a database administrator, you will not often find the need to create these objects—database developers usually take care of this task as part of the development cycle—but it is certainly good to know what is in your database when the time comes to repair or restore it. To that end, we're going to create tables, constraints, indexes, stored procedures, triggers, and views. Adding, deleting, or changing objects such as these is known as modifying the shema, or structure, of the database.

Tables

Tables are the objects in the database that actually store the data. You must have tables in place before you can create any other object in the database. The data stored in tables is organized further into fields and rows.

A *field* (or column) can be thought of as a vertical element in the table and contains information of the same type, such as last name or zip code. Each of the fields in a table can contain only one type of data, such as character or numeric data. This aspect of the field is referred to as the column's datatype.

A *record* (or row) can be thought of as a horizontal element and contains information that spans all of the fields in the table. One record in an employee database, for example, might contain the last name, first name, address, social security number, and hire date of a single employee.

There are two ways to create a table: T-SQL and Enterprise Manager. In Exercise 4.12, you will see how to use Enterprise Manager and the CREATE TABLE statement to create a table in the NewSample database.

EXERCISE 4.12

Creating Tables with Enterprise Manager and T-SQL

1. Open Enterprise Manager, drill down to the NewSample database, and expand it.

2. Right-click Tables and select New Table.

3. In the first row, under column name, type `Column1`, select char as the datatype, make the length 10, and leave Allow Nulls checked.

4. In the second row, under column name, type `Column2`, select int as the datatype, do not change the length, and leave Allow Nulls checked.

5. Click the Save button at the far left of the toolbar (it looks like a floppy disk). When asked for a name for the table, leave it as Table1 and click OK.

6. Close the Table Designer and open Query Analyzer.

7. To create a table using T-SQL code, execute the following query in Query Analyzer:

   ```
   CREATE TABLE Table2

   ( column1 char(10) NULL,

      column2 int NULL)
   ```

8. Close Query Analyzer and return to Enterprise Manager.

9. Drill down to Tables under NewSample. You should now see Table1 and Table2.

Constraints

There are many occasions when a datatype is just not restrictive enough to protect your data. For instance, what if you have a field designed to store the state in which someone lives? This field would be a character-type field limited to storing two characters; this would work fine except for one small problem: SQL accepts XZ as a value, even though it is not a valid abbreviation. To avoid something like this, you can put a *constraint* in place, which would instruct SQL to verify all of the data inserted in a particular field against a list of acceptable values. That way, a value that is not in the constraint list will be rejected. Exercise 4.13 will show you how to create a constraint through Enterprise Manager.

EXERCISE 4.13

Creating Constraints Using Enterprise Manager

1. Open Enterprise Manager and drill down to Tables under NewSample.

2. In the right pane, right-click Table1 and select Design Table.

3. Right-click Column2 and select Check Constraints.

4. Click the New button and in the Constraint Expression dialog box type:

   Column2 BETWEEN 0 and 100

5. Click OK to create the constraint.

Exercise 4.14 will use the CREATE TABLE statement to create a constraint.

EXERCISE 4.14

Creating Constraints Using T-SQL

1. Open Query Analyzer and execute the following command:

   CREATE TABLE Table3

   (

   Column1intNULL,

   Column2char(10)Null,

   CONSTRAINT chk_id CHECK (Column1 BETWEEN 0 and 100)

)

2. Close Query Analyzer.

Indexes

When you first create a table and start inserting data, there is no organization to the table whatsoever—information is inserted on a first come, first served basis. When you want to find a specific record later, SQL Server will have to look through every record in the table to find the record you need. That is called a table scan, and it can slow the database server down considerably. Because you need fast access to your data, you need to add organization to the tables that contain that data, much as this book is organized with chapters, page numbers, and indexes. There are two types of indexes available to you in SQL: clustered and nonclustered.

A *clustered index* is much like a dictionary in that the data contained therein is physically arranged to meet the constraints of the index. For example, if you wanted to find *triggers* in a dictionary, you would just turn to the *T* section and find your way from there.

A *nonclustered index* is more like the index at the back of a book. If you wanted to find *triggers* in this book, you couldn't just turn to the *T* section and look for *triggers* because there is no *T* section as there is in a dictionary. Instead, you turn to the back of the book and refer to the index, which does have a *T* section. Once you locate *triggers* in the index, you simply turn to the page number listed to find the information you need.

Of course, you can create indexes graphically or through T-SQL commands. Exercise 4.15 will show you how to create clustered and nonclustered indexes.

Creating an Index with Enterprise Manager

1. Open Enterprise Manager and drill down to Tables under the NewSample database.

2. In the right pane, right-click Table1, point to All Tasks and select Manage Indexes.

3. Click the New button at the bottom of the dialog box to create a new index for Table1.

4. In the Name box, enter **Table1_Clustered**.

5. Check the box next to Column1 to index that column.

6. Under Index options check Clustered Index.

7. Click OK to create the index, then click close.

Exercise 4.16 will show you how to create an index with T-SQL.

Creating an Index with T-SQL

1. Open Query Analyzer.

2. Execute the following query to create a nonclustered index using T-SQL code:

   ```
   USE NewSample

   CREATE INDEX Table1_Non

   ON Table1(column2)
   ```

3. Note that the command for creating this as a clustered index would be as follows:

   ```
   CREATE CLUSTERED INDEX Table1_Non ON Table1(column2)
   ```

4. Close Query Analyzer.

Stored Procedures

You already know that data is stored in tables and that you need to execute queries to read the data in the tables. But where should those queries be stored? There are two places to keep them: the client machines or the server. Storing queries on the client machines can cause performance problems because the entire query must be sent over the network to the server for processing, and once the query arrives at the server it must be parsed and compiled. Compiling a query in SQL Server just means that it must compare the query against the available indexes to see which one will return results fastest. If the queries are stored on the server as *stored procedures*, the performance problems are done away with. Stored procedures are precompiled, and the only code to send over the network is EXEC *stored_procedure*. In Exercise 4.17, you'll see how to create stored procedures using Enterprise Manager (note that the code you will see in Enterprise Manager is also the T-SQL code that would be used in Query Analyzer).

EXERCISE 4.17

Creating Stored Procedures in Enterprise Manager

1. Open Enterprise Manager and drill down to the NewSample database.

2. Right-click NewSample, point to New, and select Stored Procedure.

3. Change the code to this:

```
CREATE PROCEDURE [DBO].[PRINT] AS

PRINT 'This is a stored procedure'
```

4. Click OK to create the stored procedure

5. Open Query Analyzer and execute the following code to test the new stored procedure:

```
USE NewSample

EXEC Print
```

6. Close Query Analyzer

In Exercise 4.18 you'll see how to create a stored procedure using T-SQL.

EXERCISE 4.18

Creating Stored Procedures using T-SQL

1. Open Query Analyzer.

2. Execute the following code to create a stored procedure:

```
Use NewSample

CREATE PROCEDURE [DBO].[PRINT2] AS
```

EXERCISE 4.18 *(continued)*

```
PRINT 'This is the second stored procedure'
```

3. Execute the following code to test the new stored procedure:

```
USE NewSample
```

```
EXEC Print2
```

4. Close Query Analyzer.

Triggers

A *trigger* is a collection of SQL statements that looks and acts a great deal like a stored procedure. The only real difference between the two is that a trigger cannot be called with the EXEC (short for execute) command; triggers are activated (or fired) when a user tries to insert, update, or delete data. For example, you could define an INSERT trigger on a sales information table that could update an inventory table every time a sale is made to decrement the inventory and keep your records up to date. Or you could define a DELETE trigger to make sure that no customer reps delete a customer that has outstanding orders. There are a variety of uses for triggers. In Exercise 4.19, you'll see how to create them using Enterprise Manager.

EXERCISE 4.19

Creating Triggers

1. Open Enterprise Manager and drill down to Tables under the NewSample database.

2. In the right pane, right-click Table1, point to All Tasks, and select Manage Triggers.

3. Change the code to this:

```
CREATE TRIGGER [Table1_Insert] ON [dbo].[Table1]

FOR INSERT

AS

Print 'You have inserted a record'
```

4. Click OK to create the stored procedure.

5. Open Query Analyzer and execute the following code to test the new trigger:

```
USE NewSample

INSERT Table1 VALUES('Value', 1)
```

6. You should see a line informing you that you have inserted a record.

7. Close Query Analyzer.

In Exercise 4.20, you'll see how to accomplish this task with T-SQL.

EXERCISE 4.20

Creating Triggers Using T-SQL

1. Open Query Analyzer and execute the following code to create a trigger on the NewSample Database:

```
USE NewSample

GO

CREATE TRIGGER [Table1_Update] ON [dbo].[Table1]

FOR UPDATE

AS

Print 'You have updated a record'
```

2. Execute the following code to test the new trigger:

```
USE NewSample

UPDATE Table1 SET Column2 = 2 where Column2 = 1
```

3. You should see a line informing you that you have updated a record.

4. Close Query Analyzer.

Views

Views are used to provide a different perspective of data that is stored in your tables. They do not contain any data themselves, they just display the data stored in tables in a different light. For example, suppose that you have a human resources database that contains employee names, addresses, phone numbers, social security numbers, and pay rates. The names, addresses, and phone numbers are usually public information, but the social security numbers and pay rates are not meant for the general populace. One way to secure this data so that only authorized people can see it is by creating a view that does not contain the latter two columns and setting permissions on the table and view. This way, only people with the proper authority can read from the table itself, and everyone else can read from the view.

Views are also useful for combining data from two or more separate tables into one easy-to-read format. For instance, suppose that you have two tables, one that contains customer information such as name, address, and so on, and another that contains information about what those customers have ordered from you. If you want to see your customers' names, addresses, and details about what they have ordered, you can create a view that combines the two tables and presents the data all at once, rather than executing two separate queries to get the data. In Exercise 4.21, you'll create and test a view.

EXERCISE 4.21

Creating Views in Enterprise Manager

1. Open Enterprise Manager and drill down to the NewSample database.

2. Right-click NewSample, point to New, and select View.

3. Click the Add Table button (at the far right of the toolbar) and select Table1.

4. Check the box next to Column2.

5. Click the Save button (at the far left of the toolbar).

6. Name the view View1.

7. Close the View Designer and open Query Analyzer.

8. Execute the following query to test your new view. You should only receive data from Column2 (the only column placed in the view definition):

```
USE NewSample

SELECT * FROM View1
```

9. Close Query Analyzer.

Now we'll show you how to create a view using T-SQL in Exercise 4.22.

Creating Views Using T-SQL

1. Open Query Analyzer and execute the following code to create a trigger on the NewSample Database:

```
USE NewSample

GO

CREATE VIEW [Veiw2] ON [dbo].[Table1]

AS

SELECT Column1 FROM Table1
```

2. Execute the following code to test the new view:

```
USE NewSample

SELECT * FROM View2
```

3. Close Query Analyzer.

Summary

There is much more to data storage in SQL Server than meets the eye. The SQL Server data storage structure is more than just a file or a collection of files. It is an entire internal architecture designed for one purpose alone: to extract and modify your data as quickly and efficiently as possible. In this chapter, we covered many aspects of data storage.

- We defined databases and the files they are made of, including:
  - The primary data file has an MDF extension and is used to hold data.
  - Secondary data files have an NDF extension and are used to hold data.
  - Log files have an LDF extension and are used to store transactions before they are written to the database so that it can be recovered in the event of an emergency.
- We looked at the various RAID levels that you can use for fault tolerance and performance:
  - RAID 1 is used primarily for transaction logs.
  - RAID 5 should be used for your databases.
  - RAID 10 (also called RAID/ 0+1 can be used for either data or logs but it is more expensive.
- You learned how to estimate the size of a data file before creating it.
- You learned how to create databases using Enterprise Manager and T-SQL.
- You learned several ways to alter your databases:
  - Renaming databases.
  - Expanding and shrinking databases.
  - Attaching and detaching databases.
- You learned how to use filegroups to improve performance by placing objects in different files, perhaps to separate read activity from write activity or to make a VLDB easier to manage.
- You learned what many of the objects in the database are used for and how to create them.

Exam Essentials

Know how to create databases. It is essential to know how to create databases because that is what SQL Server is all about: storing data in databases.

Know how to alter databases. You should be familiar with all of the methods of altering a database: expanding, shrinking, renaming, and adding and removing files.

Understand filegroups. You need to know what filegroups are for and how to work with them.

Remember how to attach and detach databases. You need to know how to do this in both Enterprise Manager and T-SQL. Don't forget that you cannot detach a system database.

Know your objects. You should be familiar with the objects in the database that we discussed in this chapter. You need to know what they are for and how to create them.

Know your options. You need to know what the database options are for and when to set them.

Key Terms

clustered index	RAID
constraint	record
data files	stored procedures
extent	stripe set
field	striping with parity
filegroup	tables
fill factor	transaction log
nonclustered index	trigger
page	views

Review Questions

1. When considering where to place your data files, you realize that you need fault tolerance as well as speed. Which of the following RAID implementations has the least fault-tolerance?

   A. RAID 0

   B. RAID 1

   C. RAID 5

   D. RAID 10

2. You need to create a table in which each record will be 100 bytes long. How much disk space will this table require with 100,000 rows?

   A. 9MB

   B. 10MB

   C. 11MB

   D. 15MB

3. You are working on a development database and do not want to keep an active transaction log. You are not concerned with backing up the log. Which recovery option should you set for the database?

   A. Simple

   B. Full

   C. Bulk-Logged

   D. None of the above

4. When creating a new database, you execute the following command:

```
CREATE DATABASE acctg
ON PRIMARY
(NAME = Acctg_Data1,
 FILENAME = 'C:\MICROSOFT SQL SERVER\MSSQL\Data\Acctg_
Data1.mdf',
 SIZE = 200MB,
 MAXSIZE = 250MB,
 FILEGROWTH = 5MB)
```

How big will your transaction log be?

A. 20MB

B. 35MB

C. 40MB

D. 50MB

5. You're concerned that your hard disk controller may not be functioning properly. What option can you set to ensure that SQL Server double-checks the data written to disk to make sure it is all there?

A. Torn Extent Detection

B. Auto Update Statistics

C. Torn Page Detection

D. AutoClose

6. When you insert a new record into your Sales table, you receive a message stating that a record cannot be inserted into the Sales table unless there is a corresponding record in the Customers table. What database object gave you this message?

A. Constraint

B. View

C. Index

D. Trigger

7. You are about to bring a new server online, and you want the most efficient disk configuration possible for your new system. Select the proper RAID array to place your files on optimum performance and fault tolerance. Choose from RAID 1, RAID 2, RAID 0, RAID 5:

[ ]	RAID 0
[ ]	RAID 1
[ ]	RAID 2
[ ]	RAID 5

OS/Binaries
Data files
Transaction

8. What is the most granular unit of storage in SQL Server 2000?

   A. Column

   B. Extent

   C. Page

   D. File

9. How many pages make up an extent?

   A. 2

   B. 4

   C. 6

   D. 8

   E. 10

10. You have set the Recovery option on one of your databases to Simple. If it crashes, how much data can you recover?

A. You can recover all data up to the minute of the crash.

B. You can recover all data except bulk operations such as BULK INSERT operations.

C. You can recover up to the last good backup because the transaction log is unavailable.

D. You cannot recover the database because backup functionality has been disabled.

11. You need to configure your system for optimum accesses to a 1.5TB database. Approximately half of the tables are used primarily for writing; the rest are used primarily for reading and generating reports. How can you optimize this database for the fastest access?

A. Place the log file and data file on the same disk so that the system only has to work from one disk.

B. Create two log files and place each on a separate disk while leaving the data file on a single disk array.

C. Place the files that are used for reading in one filegroup and the files that are used primarily for writing in a second filegroup on another disk array.

D. Limit the number of users that can access the database at once.

12. You have just brought a new system online and you need to move one of your databases to the new system. Place the following steps in order to move the database to the new system.

A. Attach the database to the new system with sp_attach.

B. Detach the database from the old system with sp_detach.

C. Copy the database to the new system over the network.

D. Point client software to the new system to access the database.

13. You have just issued the command DBCC SHRINKDATABASE (Main, 10%) on a 640MB database that contains 560MB of data. How big will your database be after the command completes?

    A. 624MB

    B. 616MB

    C. 576MB

    D. The statement will fail because the target percentage is too small.

14. Which database object can be used to prevent users from entering invalid data in a column?

    A. View

    B. Record

    C. Constraint

    D. Index

15. You have just deleted a database with the DROP DATABASE command, but it was the wrong database. How do you get it back?

    A. Use the DBCC REGENERATE(db_name) statement.

    B. Restore from your last backup.

    C. Reattach the database with sp_attachdb.

    D. Create a new database with the same name as the deleted database and restart the system to initiate auto-recovery.

16. When your customer service reps make a sale to a customer, you want to automatically update the inventory table to decrement the quantity in stock. What database object should you use for this?

    A. Trigger

    B. Stored procedure

    C. Index

    D. Constraint

17. You try to remove a filegroup with the ALTER DATABASE command and it fails. Why?

   A. There are no data files in the filegroup.

   B. There are still data files in the filegroup.

   C. There are system files in the filegroup.

   D. The filegroup still contains files from another database.

18. You are using the command DBCC SHRINKDATABASE (MyDB, 20%, TRUNCATEONLY) against a 780MB database with 590MB of data. How big will the database be when you are done?

   A. 746MB

   B. 649MB

   C. 590MB

   D. 780MB

19. Which statement about placing tables and indexes on filegroups is true?

   A. Tables and their corresponding indexes must be placed on the same filegroup.

   B. Tables and their corresponding indexes must be placed on separate filegroups.

   C. Tables and indexes that are placed on separate filegroups must be backed up together.

   D. Tables and indexes that are placed on separate filegroups cannot be backed up together.

20. Why does the following command fail?

```
USE Main
EXEC sp_dboption 'Main', 'Single User', True
EXEC sp_renamedb 'Main', 'Acctg'
EXEC sp_dboption 'Acctg', 'Single User', False
```

A. The database cannot be in single user mode when it is renamed.

B. You must be in the master database when renaming a database.

C. The database can only be renamed by the SA user.

D. Databases cannot be renamed if they contain multiple files.

Answers to Review Questions

1. A. RAID 0 offers no fault-tolerance at all; it simply stripes data across all of the drives in the array.

2. B. When you do the math presented earlier in the chapter you realize that the table will take approximately 10MB.

3. A. The simple recovery model is equivalent to shutting off the transaction log. Because it is empty all of the time, it will not take up much space and it does not need to be backed up.

4. D. When you do not specify the size of the transaction log in the CREATE DATABASE statement, SQL Server automatically creates a transaction log that is 25 percent of the size of the data files.

5. C. When the Torn Page Detection option is turned on, SQL Server writes a bit to each page when it has completed writing it to disk. If this bit is in the wrong state, SQL Server knows that it has been damaged.

6. D. Triggers are like data watchdogs. They are designed to fire off on an INSERT, UPDATE, or DELETE action and perform whatever tasks you've programmed them to do. In this example, the trigger is designed to look at the customers table for a corresponding record on an INSERT event.

7. OS and Binaries should be on a mirror. Transaction logs should be on a mirror because they need the sequential write speed that a mirror provides. Data files should be on a stripe set with parity for the read speed that it provides.

☐	RAID 0
OS/Binaries	
	RAID 1
Transaction	
☐	RAID 2
Data files	RAID 5

> OS/Binaries
> Data files
> Transaction

8. C. The smallest unit of storage that SQL Server recognizes is the 8092-byte page.

9. D. There are eight pages in an extent.

10. C. The simple recovery model does not log transactions in the transaction log and therefore cannot be used to recover missing data. You can only recover data up to the last good backup.

11. C. In order to specify which disk you want to place an object on, you must create a filegroup and then specify which filegroup to place the object in at the time it is created.

12. B, C, A, D. First, detach the database from the existing system, then you can copy the files over the network to the new system. Once the files have been copied, they need to be attached to the new system. Finally, you need to point the clients to the new system to access the database in its new location.

13. A. When you run this command, you are actually telling SQL Server to take the size of the data (560MB) and add 10 percent of the current size of the data files (10 percent of 640 is 64); 560 + 64 is 624MB.

14. C. Use constraints to verify data that is entered into a column. If the data fits that constraint parameter, it is allowed. If not, it is disallowed.

15. B. Once you delete a database in SQL Server 2000, it is completely removed from the system. You must restore to get it back.

16. A. You can use a trigger to watch for INSERT events on a table and then decrement the inventory table every time a sales is made.

17. B. You cannot delete a filegroup that still contains data files.

18. C. The TRUNCATEONLY option tells SQL Server to remove all free space in the database. The free space percentage is ignored.

19. C. Tables and indexes can be placed on separate filegroups, but if you do that they must be backed up as a unit.

20. B. Because each database has a record in the sysdatabases table in the master database, you must be in the master database to change the name of the database.

Chapter

5

Security and SQL Server 2000

MICROSOFT EXAM OBJECTIVES COVERED IN THIS CHAPTER:

✓ **Manage linked servers.**

- Configure security mapping.

✓ **Configure mixed security modes or Windows Authentication. Considerations include client connectivity, client operating system, and security infrastructure.**

✓ **Create and manage logins.**

✓ **Create and manage database users.**

✓ **Create and manage security roles. Roles include application, database, and server.**

- Add and remove users from roles.
- Create roles in order to manage database security.

✓ **Enforce and manage security by using stored procedures, triggers, views, and user-defined functions.**

✓ **Set permissions in a database. Considerations include object permissions, object ownership, and statement permissions.**

✓ **Manage security auditing. Methods include SQL Profiler, SQL Trace, and C2 auditing.**

Protecting information, guarding access to an organization's data, is much like protecting a physical structure. For example, imagine that you own a business and the building that houses it. You do not want the general public to gain access to your building—only your employees should be able to. Even here, however, you need restrictions on the areas to which your employees have access. Because only accountants should have access to the accounting department, and almost no one should have access to your office, you must put various security systems in place to ensure this.

Protecting SQL Server (your "building") holds true to this concept: no one gets in unless granted access, and once inside, various security systems keep prying eyes out of sensitive areas. In this chapter we will discuss the methods used to apply security to SQL Server.

Understanding Security Modes

To continue our analogy, in order for your employees to gain access to the building, they will need some sort of key, whether a metal key or an electronic access card. In order for your users to gain access to SQL Server, you will need to give them a key as well. The type of key you give them largely depends on the type of lock—*authentication mode*—you use.

Microsoft *Exam* *Objective*	**Configure mixed security modes or Windows Authentication.** **Considerations include client connectivity, client operating** **system, and security infrastructure.**

An authentication mode is how SQL processes usernames and passwords. There are two such modes in SQL Server 2000: Windows Authentication mode and Mixed Mode.

Windows Authentication Mode

In *Windows Authentication mode*, a user can simply sit down at their computer, log on to the Windows domain and gain access to SQL Server. Here's how it works:

1. The user logs on to a Windows domain; the username and password are verified by Windows.

2. The user then opens a *trusted connection* (see Figure 5.1) with SQL Server.

3. SQL will then try to match the username or group membership to an entry in the Sysxlogins table.

4. Since this is a trusted connection, SQL does not need to verify the user password; that is, SQL trusts Windows to perform that function.

FIGURE 5.1 Trusted connection to SQL Server

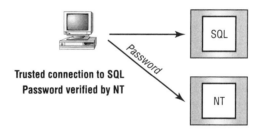

Trusted connection to SQL
Password verified by NT

The main advantage to Windows Authentication mode is that users do not have to remember multiple usernames and passwords. That will vastly increase security since there is less danger of users writing their passwords down and storing them in an unsafe place (like a sticky note on their monitor). This mode also gives you tighter reign over security since you can apply Windows password policies that will do such things as expire passwords, require a minimum length for passwords, keep a history of passwords, and so on.

One of the disadvantages is that only users with a Windows account can open a trusted connection to SQL Server. That means that someone like a Novell client running the IPX net library cannot use Windows Authentication mode. If it turns out that you have such clients, you will need to implement Mixed Mode.

Mixed Mode

Mixed Mode allows both Windows Authentication and SQL Authentication. In SQL Authentication:

1. The user logs on to their network, Windows or otherwise.

2. Next, the user opens a *nontrusted connection* (see Figure 5.2) to SQL Server using a separate username and password.

3. SQL then matches the username and password entered by the user to an entry in the Sysxlogins table.

FIGURE 5.2   Nontrusted connection to SQL Server

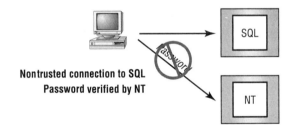

The primary advantage here is that anyone can gain access to SQL using Mixed Mode, regardless of the net library used. This means that Mac users, Novell users, Banyan Vines users, and the like can gain access. You could also consider this to be a second layer of security, since hacking into the network in Mixed Mode does not mean that someone has automatically hacked into SQL at the same time.

Multiple passwords can be a problem as well as an advantage. Consider that users will have one username and password to log on to the network and a completely separate username and password to gain access to SQL. When users have multiple sets of credentials, they tend to write them down and thus breach the security system you have worked so hard to set up.

Setting the Authentication Mode

As an administrator you will probably set the authentication mode no more than once, at installation time. The only other time you might need to change the authentication mode would be if changes were made to your network. For example, if you had set your SQL Server to Windows Authentication mode and needed to include Macintosh clients, you would need to change to Mixed Mode.

It is interesting to note that although most things in SQL can be done through either Enterprise Manager or Transact-SQL (T-SQL), setting the authentication mode is one of the rare things that can be done only through Enterprise Manager. Exercise 5.1 takes you through the steps of setting the authentication mode.

EXERCISE 5.1

Setting the Authentication Mode

1. Open Enterprise Manager, right-click your server (either your server name or Local), and select Properties.

2. Select the Security tab.

3. In the Authentication section, select SQL Server and Widows. This will set you to Mixed Mode for the rest of the exercises.

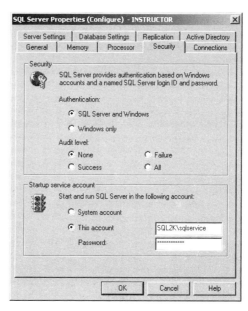

4. Click the OK button to close the property sheet.

Now that you have set the proper authentication mode, it is time to move forward and give your users a key to your building with SQL Server logins.

SQL Server Logins

Once you have decided what type of "lock" (authentication mode) to use on your "building," you can start handing out "keys" so that your employees can gain access. A real key will give your employees access to the building as a whole but to none of the resources (like filing cabinets) inside. In the same way, a SQL Server key, a *login*, will give your users access to SQL Server as a whole but not to the resources (like databases) inside. If you are a member of the sysadmin or securityadmin *fixed server roles* (discussed later), you will be able to create one of two types of logins: standard logins (like the metal key in our analogy) and Windows logins (like the newer electronic access cards).

Microsoft Exam Objective	**Create and manage logins.**

Standard Logins

You learned earlier that only clients with a Windows account can make trusted connections to SQL (SQL trusts Windows to validate the user's password). If the user (such as a Macintosh or Novell client) for whom you are creating a login cannot make a trusted connection, you must create a standard login for them (as discussed in Exercises 5.2 and 5.3).

While you can create standard logins in Windows Authentication mode, you won't be able to use them. If you try, SQL will ignore you and use your Windows credentials instead.

EXERCISE 5.2

Creating and Testing a Standard Login Using Enterprise Manager

1. Open Enterprise Manager and expand your server by clicking the + sign next to the icon named after your server.

2. Expand Security and then click Logins.

3. Click the Action menu and select New Login.

4. In the Name box, type **SmithB**.

5. In the Authentication section, select SQL Server Authentication.

6. In the Password text box, type **password**.

7. Under Defaults, select Pubs as the default database.

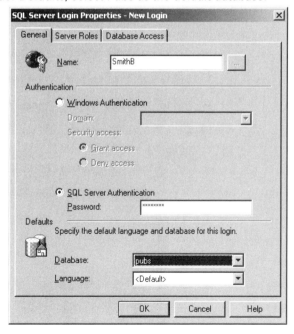

8. Click the OK button.

9. In the Confirm New Password text box, type **password**.

EXERCISE 5.2 *(continued)*

10. Click OK and notice your new Standard Type login in the contents pane.

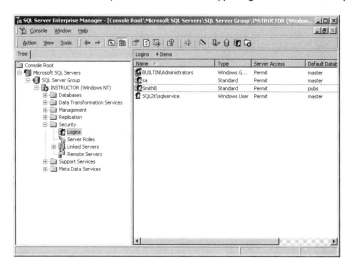

11. To test the new login, open Query Analyzer.

12. Under Connection Information, select Use SQL Server Authentication.

13. In the Login Name box, type **SmithB**.

14. In the Password box, type **password**.

15. Click OK and notice the title bar. It should read "*sqlserver*.pubs.SmithB."

EXERCISE 5.3

Creating and Testing a Standard Login Using T-SQL

1. Open Query Analyzer and log in using Windows Authentication.

2. Execute the following query to create a standard login for GibsonH:

   `sp_addlogin @loginame='GibsonH', @passwd='password', @defdb='pubs'`

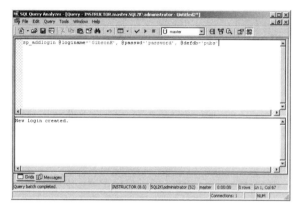

3. On the File menu, select Disconnect and do not save your changes.

4. On the File menu, select Connect.

5. Log in using SQL Authentication with a username of GibsonH and a password of password. You are able to log in because you successfully created GibsonH.

6. For further verification, close Query Analyzer and open Enterprise Manager.

7. Select Logins and notice the new Standard Type user GibsonH.

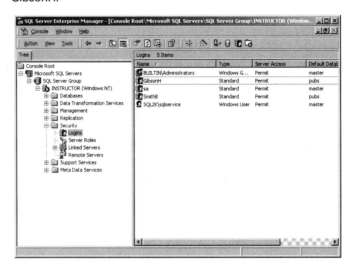

Windows Logins

Creating Windows logins (as described in Exercise 5.4) is not much different from creating standard logins. While standard logins may be applied to only one user, however, a Windows login can be mapped to one of the following:

- A single user
- A Windows group an administrator has created
- A Windows *builtin* group (e.g., Administrators)

Before you create a Windows login, you must decide which of these three you want to map it to. Generally, you will want to map to a group that you have created. This will help you a great deal in later administration. For example, suppose you have an Accounting database to which all 50 of your accountants require access. You could create a separate login for each of them, which would require you to manage 50 SQL logins. On the other hand, if you create a Windows group for these 50 accountants and map your SQL login to this group, you will have only one SQL login to manage.

To simplify the writing process when creating or modifying user accounts in this chapter, we will use Windows 2000 with Active Directory. Bear in mind though that SQL Server 2000 will recognize Windows NT 4 accounts as well.

EXERCISE 5.4

Creating Windows-to-SQL Logins in Windows 2000 Using Enterprise Manager

1. Open Active Directory Users and Computers.

2. Create six new users with the criteria from the following table:

User Logon Name/Full Name	Password	Must Change	Never Expires
MorrisL	Password	Uncheck	Check
ThompsonA	Password	Uncheck	Check
JohnsonK	Password	Uncheck	Check
JonesB	Password	Uncheck	Check
ChenJ	Password	Uncheck	Check
SamuelsR	Password	Uncheck	Check

3. Now right-click each user and change the description to match the criteria in the following table:

User Logon Name/Full Name	Description
MorrisL	IT
ThompsonA	Administration
JohnsonK	Accounting
JonesB	Accounting
ChenJ	Sales

SamuelsR Sales

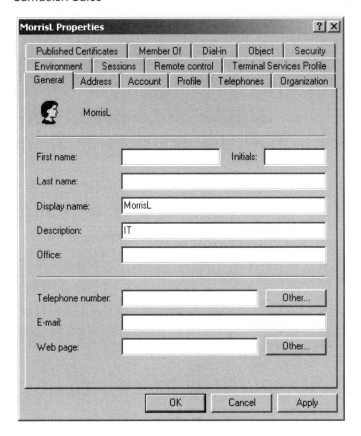

4. While in Active Directory Users and Computers, create a Domain
Local Security group called Accounting.

5. Add the new users you just created with a description of Accounting.

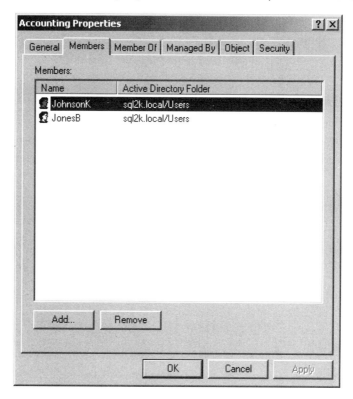

6. While still in Active Directory Users and Computers, create a Domain Local Security group named Sales.

7. Add all the users with a description of Sales.

8. Close Active Directory Users and Computers and open Domain Controller Security Policy from the Administrative Tools menu.

9. Expand Security Settings, then expand Local Policy and then select User Rights Assignment.

10. In the right pane, double-click the Log on Locally right and add Everyone to the list.

11. Click OK and close Domain Controller Security Policy.

12. Open Enterprise Manager, expand your server, then expand Security, and click the Logins folder.

13. On the Actions menu, select New Login.

14. In the Name box, type **Accounting** (the name of the Local group created earlier).

15. Select Windows Authentication and select your domain from the drop-down list next to Domain.

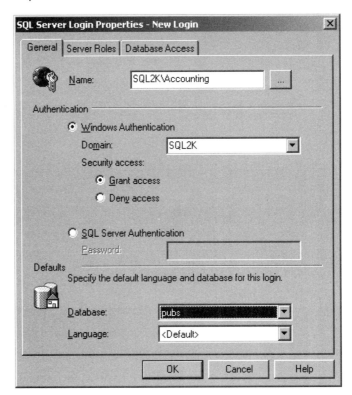

16. Click OK and notice the Accounting Login of Type NT group.

17. Go back into the New User dialog box by selecting New User from the Action menu.

18. Fill in the Name field with **ThompsonA**.

19. Select Windows Authentication and select your domain from the list.

20. Under Defaults, select Pubs as the default database.

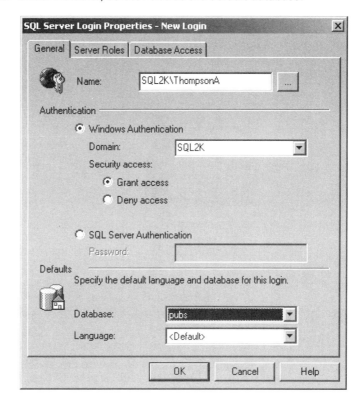

21. Click OK and notice the new login for ThompsonA of Type NT user.

22. To test your new logins, log off Windows and log back on as JonesB.

23. Open Query Analyzer and select Use Windows Authentication. Notice the title bar displays "sqlserver.pubs.sqldomain\accounting." This is because JonesB is a member of the Windows Accounting group.

24. Close Query Analyzer, log off Windows, and log back on as ThompsonA.

25. Open Query Analyzer and select Use Windows Authentication. The title bar displays "*sqlserver*.pubs.sqldomain\ThompsonA" because you created an account specifically for ThompsonA rather than making him a member of the Accounting group.

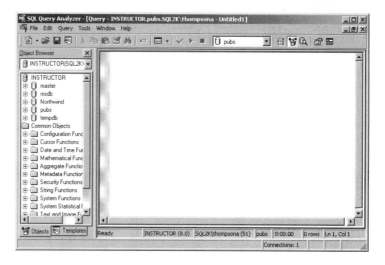

Exercise 5.5 shows you how to create Windows logins using T-SQL.

Creating Windows-to-SQL Logins Using T-SQL

1. Open Query Analyzer and log in using Windows Authentication.

2. Execute the following query to create a Windows login for the Sales group (note that the command is different from that used in creating a standard login):

sp_grantlogin @loginame='*domainname*\sales'

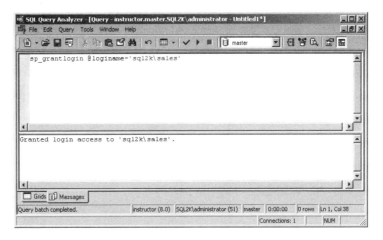

3. On the Edit menu, select Clear Window.

4. Execute the following query to create a Windows Login for MorrisL:

sp_grantlogin @loginame='*domainname*\MorrisL'

5. Close Query Analyzer and open Enterprise Manager.

EXERCISE 5.5 *(continued)*

6. Expand your server by clicking the + sign next to the server name.

7. Select Logins under Security and notice the two new logins for Sales and MorrisL.

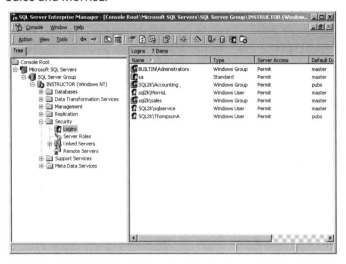

Items Common to All Logins

You may have noticed that some things are common to all the logins that you created.

The first is the default database. When a user first logs in to SQL they will connect to the default database. This is just a starting point, since users can't use the default database without a database user account: all they can do is connect to it. If you do not set the default database, it will be Master—which is not the best place for your users to get started. You will want to change that to a different database, for example, an Accounting database if you are working with an accounting user. You can also set a default language, which will not need frequent changing since the default is the server's language. A different language can be set here for users who require it.

In all types of logins, you can grant database access at create time. On the Database Access tab in the Enterprise Manager New Login dialog box, all you need to do is check the database to which this login will require access; this automatically creates a database user account. Although you didn't do that in the exercises, as an administrator, you will want to grant access to databases at create time.

If you create a Windows login using sp_grantlogin, you cannot set the default database or language.

In addition, you can add users to a fixed server role at the time you create them; this is done on the Server Roles tab in Enterprise Manager. Fixed server roles—limitations on access—are discussed next.

Fixed Server Roles

Back to our analogy: as the owner, when you walk into your building, you are allowed to do whatever you want (after all, you do own it). When members of the accounting department walk in, however, they are limited in what they can do. For example, they are not allowed to take keys away from other workers, but they may be allowed to do other administrative tasks like signing checks.

Microsoft ✓ *Exam* *Objective*

Create and manage security roles. Roles include application, database, and server.

- Add and remove users from roles.
- Create roles in order to manage database security.

That is what fixed server roles are used for, to limit the amount of administrative access that a user has once they're logged in to SQL Server. Some users may be allowed to do whatever they want, whereas other users may only be able to manage security. There are eight server roles to which you can assign users. The following list starts at the highest level and describes the administrative access granted:

sysadmin Members of the sysadmin role can do whatever they want in SQL Server. Be careful whom you assign to this role; people who are unfamiliar with SQL can accidentally create serious problems. This role is only for the database administrators (DBAs).

Builtin\Administrators is automatically made a member of the sysadmin server role, giving SQL administrative rights to all of your Windows administrators. Since not all of your Windows administrators should have these rights, you may want to create a SQLAdmins group and add your SQL Administrators and your SQLAgent service account to that group. Afterward, you should remove Builtin\ Administrators from the sysadmin role.

serveradmin   These users can set server-wide configuration options, like how much memory SQL can use or how much information to send over the network in a single frame. If you make your assistant DBAs members of this role, you can relieve yourself of some of the administrative burden.

setupadmin   Members of setupadmin can manage linked servers.

securityadmin   These users manage security issues such as creating and deleting logins, reading the audit logs, and granting users permission to create databases. This too is a good role for assistant DBAs.

processadmin   A member of the processadmin group can end (called *kill* in SQL) a process. This is another good role for assistant DBAs and developers. Developers especially need to be able to kill processes that may have been triggered by an improperly designed query or stored procedure.

SQL is capable of multitasking; that is, it can do more than one thing at a time by executing multiple processes. For instance, SQL might spawn one process for writing to cache and another for reading from cache.

dbcreator   These users can create and make changes to databases and restore backups. This may be a good role for assistant DBAs as well as developers (who should be warned against creating unnecessary databases and wasting server space).

diskadmin   These users manage files on disk. They do things like mirroring databases and adding backup devices. Assistant DBAs should be members of this role.

bulkadmin Members of this role can execute the BULK INSERT statement, which is used to insert large amounts of data into a database at high speed. Assistant DBAs should be in this role.

If you do not want users to have any administrative authority, do not assign them to a server role. This will limit them to being just normal users.

Exercises 5.6 and 5.7 show you how to assign users to a fixed server role with Enterprise Manager and T-SQL, respectively.

EXERCISE 5.6

Assigning a User to a Fixed Server Role Using Enterprise Manager

1. Open Enterprise Manager and select Server Roles under Security.

2. Double-click System Administrators to open the Sysadmin Server Role property sheet.

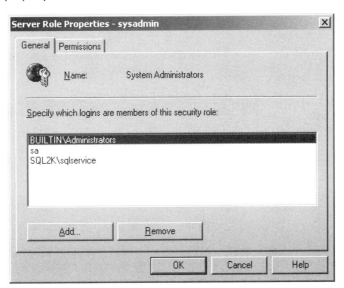

3. Click Add, select MorrisL, and click OK.

EXERCISE 5.6 *(continued)*

4. Click the Permissions tab and notice the extensive list of permissions granted to this role.

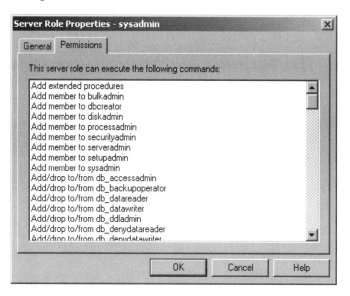

5. Click OK to exit the Server Role Properties dialog box.

EXERCISE 5.7

Assigning a User to a Fixed Server Role Using T-SQL

1. Open Query Analyzer and log in using Windows Authentication.

2. Execute the following query to add a member to the serveradmin fixed server role:

```
sp_addsrvrolemember @loginame='GibsonH',
@rolename='serveradmin'
```

3. Close Query Analyzer, open Enterprise Manager, expand your server, and select Logins.

4. Double-click GibsonH and notice that it has been added to the serveradmin fixed database role.

Creating Database User Accounts

Now that your employees have access to your building as well as the proper administrative access once they are inside, they will need access to other resources to do their work. For example, if you want to give your accounting department access to the accounting files, you need to give them a new key—one to the file cabinet. Your employees now have two keys, one for the front door and one for the file cabinet.

Microsoft Exam Objective

Create and manage database users.

In much the same way, you need to give users access to databases once they have logged in to SQL. This is accomplished by creating database user accounts and then assigning permissions to those user accounts (permissions are discussed later). Once complete, your SQL users will also have more than one key, one for the front door (the login) and one for each file cabinet (database) to which they need access. Exercises 5.8 and 5.9 describe how to create database user accounts.

EXERCISE 5.8

Creating Database User Accounts Using Enterprise Manager

1. Open Enterprise Manager and expand your server.
2. Expand Databases by clicking the plus sign next to the icon.
3. Expand the Pubs database.
4. Click the Users icon.
5. From the Action menu, select New Database User.

EXERCISE 5.8 *(continued)*

6. In the Login Name box, view all the available names; note that only logins that you have already created are available.

7. Select *domainname*\accounting.

8. In the Login Name box, leave *domainname*\accounting.

9. Click OK. You now have a new user named *domainname*\accounting.

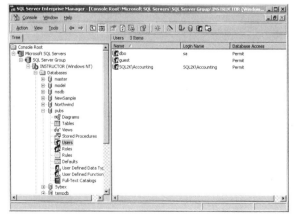

10. Repeat steps 5 through 9 for Sales, ThompsonA, MorrisL, and SmithB.

EXERCISE 5.9

Creating Database User Accounts Using Transact SQL

1. Open Query Analyzer and log in using Windows Authentication.

2. In the Database drop-down list at the top right of the query window, select the Pubs database. This sets Pubs as the active database.

3. Execute the following query to create a new user account:

   `sp_grantdbaccess @loginame='GibsonH'`

4. On the Query menu, select Clear Window and do not save the changes.

5. Execute the following query to create a database user account for the Sales group; the database username will be different from the login name:

   `sp_grantdbaccess @loginame='`*domainname*`\Sales', @name_in_db='SalesUsers'`

6. Close Query Analyzer, open Enterprise Manager and expand your server, then expand Databases.

7. Select Users; you have two new users: GibsonH and SalesUsers.

You may have noticed that one user account already exists in your database: DBO. Members of the sysadmin fixed server role automatically become the DBO (database owner) user in every database on the system. In this way they can perform all the necessary administrative functions in the databases, such as adding users and creating tables. *Guest user* is a catch-all term used for people who have a SQL login but not a user account in the database. These users can log in to SQL as themselves and access any database for which they do not have a user account. The guest account should be limited in function since anybody with a SQL login can make use of it.

When a member of the sysadmin fixed server role creates an object (like a table), it is not owned by that login. It is owned by the DBO. If MorrisL created a table, it would not be referred to as MorrisL.table, but as dbo.table instead.

Now that you have created user accounts for everyone, you need to restrict what they are capable of doing with the database. This is done by assigning permissions directly to the users or by adding the users to a database role with a predefined set of permissions.

Understanding Permissions

To continue our business analogy, it would be unthinkable for the sales department to go over to the accounting department and start writing themselves large checks. In most businesses today, the sales department does not have permission to use the checkbook. Even further, not all the people in the accounting department have full access to the checkbook; some only have permission to read from it, while others have permission to write checks from it.

Microsoft ✓ Exam Objective

Set permissions in a database. Considerations include object permissions, object ownership, and statement permissions.

We see the same situation in SQL Server. Not all your users should be able to access the Accounting or Human Resources databases, since they contain sensitive information. Even users who are allowed in should not necessarily be given full access. To enforce these restrictions you need to grant permissions.

Statement Permissions

In your building, do you allow the contractors who constructed it to come in and use your files and copiers and various other resources? No, you gave them permission to construct the building initially and to make renovations over time—but not to use the files and other such resources inside.

In SQL, this restriction would be akin to granting the contractors *statement permissions*. Statement permissions have nothing to do with the actual data; they allow users to create the structure that holds the data. It is important not to grant these permissions haphazardly because it can lead to such problems as *broken ownership chains* (discussed later) and wasted server resources. It is best to restrict these permissions to DBAs, assistant DBAs, and developers. The following are the statement permissions (Exercises 5.10 and 5.11 show how to apply them):

- Create Database
- Create Function
- Create Table
- Create View
- Create Procedure
- Create Rule
- Create Default
- Backup Database
- Backup Log

 The Create Database permission can be granted only on the master database.

EXERCISE 5.10

Granting Statement Permissions Using Enterprise Manager

1. To prepare SQL for the following exercises, you need to remove permissions from the public role. Open Query Analyzer and execute the following query:

   ```
   use pubs

   REVOKE all FROM public
   ```

2. Close Query Analyzer and do not save the changes.

3. Open Enterprise Manager and expand your server, then expand Databases.

4. Right-click the Pubs database and select Properties.

5. In the property sheet, select the Permissions tab.

6. Grant ThompsonA the Create Table permission by clicking the check box under Create Table until a green check appears.

EXERCISE 5.10 *(continued)*

7. Grant Accounting the permission to Backup DB and Backup Log.

8. If the guest user has any permissions granted, remove them by clicking each check box until it is cleared.

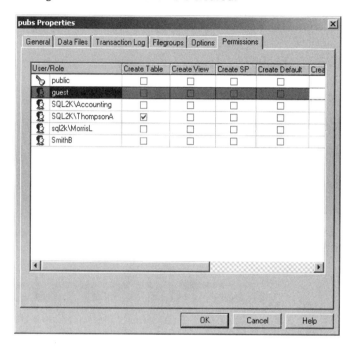

9. Log off Windows and log back on as JonesB.

10. Open Query Analyzer, log in using Windows Authentication, and type the following query:

```
Use pubs

Create table Statement1

(column1 varchar(5) not null,

column2 varchar(10) not null)
```

11. On the Query pull-down menu, select Execute Query and notice that the query is unsuccessful because JonesB (a member of the Accounting group) does not have permission to create a table.

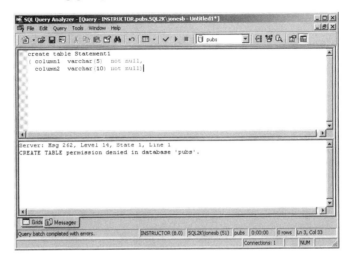

12. Close Query Analyzer, log off Windows, and log back on as ThompsonA.

13. Repeat step 10 and execute the query. This time it is successful since ThompsonA has permission to create tables.

EXERCISE 5.11

Granting Statement Permissions Using T-SQL

1. Open Query Analyzer and log in using Windows Authentication.

2. Execute the following query to grant GibsonH permission to create tables:

use pubs

GRANT create table to GibsonH

3. On the File menu, select Disconnect.

---

4. On the File menu, select Connect and log in using SQL Authentication. Enter **GibsonH** as the username and **password** as the password.

5. Execute the following query to verify that GibsonH has the Create Table permission:

```
Use pubs

Create table Statement2

(column1 varchar(5) not null,

column2 varchar(10) not null)
```

6. For further verification, close Query Analyzer and open Enterprise Manager.

7. Right-click the Pubs database icon and select Properties.

8. Select the Permissions tab and notice that GibsonH has been granted the Create Database permission.

Object Permissions

Once the structure exists to hold the data, you need to give users permission to start working with the data in the databases by granting your users *object permissions*. Using object permissions, you can control who is allowed to read from, write to, or otherwise manipulate your data. Exercises 5.12 and 5.13 will instruct you in the ways of setting the following object permissions:

SELECT Allows users to read data from the table or view. When granted at the column level, this will allow users to read from a single column.

INSERT Allows users to insert new rows into a table.

UPDATE Allows users to modify existing data in a table. When granted on a column, users will be able to modify data in that single column.

DELETE Allows users to remove rows from a table.

REFERENCES (or DRI [Declarative Referential Integrity])   When two tables are linked with a foreign key, this allows the user to select data from the primary table without having SELECT permission on the referenced table.

EXECUTE   This allows users to execute the stored procedure where the permission is applied.

EXERCISE 5.12

Assigning Object Permissions Using Enterprise Manager

1. Open Enterprise Manager, expand your server, then Databases, and select Pubs.

2. Select Tables in the right pane, right-click Authors, and select Properties.

3. Click the Permissions button.

4. Grant SalesUsers SELECT permission by clicking the check box under SELECT until a green check appears.

5. If the guest user has any permissions granted, remove them by clicking each one until all check boxes are clear.

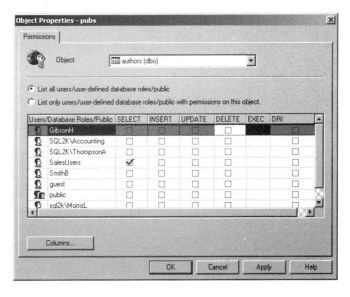

6. Click OK twice and close Enterprise Manager.

EXERCISE 5.12 *(continued)*

7. Log off Windows and log back on as JonesB.

8. Open Query Analyzer and select Windows Authentication.

9. Execute the following query:

   ```
   USE pubs
   ```

   ```
   SELECT * FROM authors
   ```

   It fails since Accounting does not have SELECT permission.

10. Close Query Analyzer and repeat steps 7 through 9 for ChenJ. The query succeeds this time since Sales (of which ChenJ is a member) has SELECT permission.

11. Log off Windows and log back in as Administrator.

EXERCISE 5.13

Assigning Object Permissions Using T-SQL

1. Open Query Analyzer and log in using Windows Authentication.

2. Execute the following query to grant SELECT permission to SmithB:

   ```
   USE pubs
   ```

   ```
   GRANT SELECT on authors to SmithB
   ```

3. On the File menu, select Disconnect.

4. On the File menu, select Connect and log in as SmithB using SQL Authentication.

5. Verify that SmithB has SELECT permission on the Authors table to execute the following query:

   ```
   USE pubs
   ```

   ```
   SELECT * FROM authors
   ```

6. Close Query Analyzer.

Although granting permissions to single users will be useful from time to time, it is better, faster, and easier to apply permissions en masse. This requires understanding database roles.

Database Roles

Continuing our business analogy, your accountants need to write corporate checks. You could give them permission to do so in one of two ways. First, you could give each of the accountants their own checkbook drawn from a single account with permission to write checks from it. That would be an accounting nightmare—trying to keep track of all the checks that were written during the month. The better way to accomplish this is to get one corporate account with one checkbook and give the accountants as a group permission to write checks from that one book.

Microsoft
Exam
Objective

Create and manage security roles. Roles include application, database, and server.

- Add and remove users from roles.
- Create roles in order to manage database security.

In SQL when several users need permission to access to a database, it is much easier to give them all permissions as a group rather than trying to manage each user separately. That is what database roles are for: granting permissions to groups of database users, rather than granting them to each database user separately. There are three types of database roles to consider: fixed, custom, and application.

Fixed Database Roles

Fixed database roles have permissions already applied; that is, all you have to do is add users to these roles and they inherit the associated permissions. (That is different from custom database roles, as you will see later.) There are several fixed database roles in SQL Server that can be used to grant permissions (Exercises 5.14 and 5.15 show how to assign users to these roles):

db_owner   Members of this role can do everything the members of the other roles can do as well as some administrative functions.

db_accessadmin   These users have the authority to say who gets access to the database by adding or removing users.

db_datareader   Members here can read data from any table in the database.

db_datawriter   These users can add, change, and delete data from all the tables in the database.

db_ddladmin   Data Definition Language administrators can issue all DDL commands; this allows them to create, modify, or change database objects without viewing the data inside.

db_securityadmin   Members here can add and remove users from database roles and manage statement and object permissions.

db_backupoperator   These users can back up the database.

db_denydatareader   Members cannot read the data in the database.

db_denydatawriter   These users cannot make changes to the data in the database.

Public   The purpose of this group is to grant users a default set of permissions in the database. All database users automatically join this group and cannot be removed.

EXERCISE 5.14

Assigning Users to Fixed Database Roles Using Enterprise Manager

1. Open Enterprise Manager, expand your server and Databases, then select Pubs.

EXERCISE 5.14 *(continued)*

2. Click Roles.

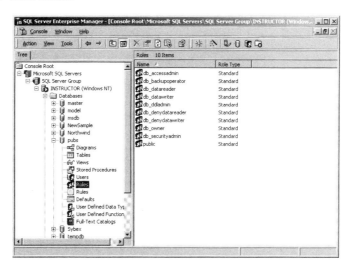

3. In the contents pane, double-click db_denydatawriter.

4. Click the Add button.

5. Select SmithB and click OK.

6. Click OK again to go back to Enterprise Manager.

7. Open Query Analyzer and select Use SQL Server Authentication.

8. In the User Name box, type **SmithB**; in the Password box, type **password**.

9. In the following query you will try to update information in the Authors table; it fails since SmithB is a member of the db_denydatawriter role:

```
UPDATE authors

Set authors.au_fname='Mike'

Where au_fname='Michael'
```

10. Close Query Analyzer.

EXERCISE 5.15

Assigning Users to Fixed Database Roles Using T-SQL

1. Open Query Analyzer and log in using Windows Authentication.

2. Execute the following query to add GibsonH to the db_denydata-reader role:

use pubs

exec sp_addrolemember @rolename='db_denydatareader', @membername='GibsonH'

3. On the File menu, select Disconnect.

4. On the File menu, select Connect and log in using Windows Authentication.

5. Execute the following query to verify that GibsonH does not have the permission to read data because of his membership in the db_denydatareader role:

use pubs

SELECT * FROM authors

6. Close Query Analyzer.

If you use the sp_addrolemember stored procedure to add a user to a database role, you do not need to create the user account first. SQL will create it for you.

Custom Database Roles

There will, of course, be times when the fixed database roles do not meet your security needs. You might have several users who need SELECT, UPDATE, and EXECUTE permissions in your database and nothing more. Because none of the fixed database roles will give you that set of permissions, you can create a *custom database role*. When you create this new role, you assign permissions to it and then assign users to the role; then the users will inherit whatever permissions you assign to the role. That is different from the fixed database roles where you do not need to assign permissions but just add users. Exercises 5.16 and 5.17 explain how to create a database role.

You can make your custom database roles members of other database roles. This is referred to as *nesting roles*.

EXERCISE 5.16

Creating Custom Database Roles Using Enterprise Manager

1. Open Enterprise Manager and expand your server, expand Databases, and select Pubs.

2. Click Roles.

3. On the Action menu, select New Database Role.

4. In the Name box, type **SelectOnly**.

5. Under Database Role Type, select Standard Role and click Add.

6. Select ThompsonA and click OK.

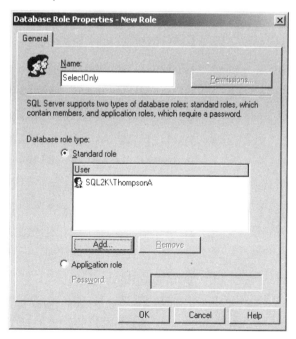

7. Click OK to go back to Enterprise Manager and notice the new role in the contents pane.

8. Double-click the role and then click the Permissions button.

9. Locate the Tables entry and check the corresponding SELECT check box to grant SELECT access to the Authors table.

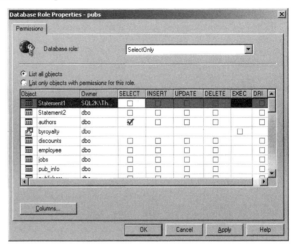

10. Click OK to go back to the previous dialog box.

11. Click OK once more to go back to Enterprise Manager.

12. Close all programs, log off Windows, and log back on as ThompsonA.

13. Open Query Analyzer and use Windows Authentication.

14. Notice that the following query succeeds since ThompsonA is a member of the new SelectOnly role:

```
use pubs
SELECT * FROM authors
```

15. Now notice the failure of the next query since ThompsonA is a member of a role that is allowed to SELECT only.

```
UPDATE authors
SET authors.au_fname='Mike'
WHERE au_fname='Michael'
```

16. Close all programs, log off Windows, and log back on as Administrator.

EXERCISE 5.17

Creating Custom Database Roles Using T-SQL

1. Open Query Analyzer and log in using Windows Authentication.

2. Execute the following query to create the UpdateOnly database role in the Pubs database:

   USE pubs

   EXEC sp_addrole @rolename='UpdateOnly'

3. On the Edit menu, select Clear Window.

4. Execute the following query to grant UPDATE permission to the new role:

   GRANT UPDATE on authors to updateonly

5. On the Query menu, select Clear Window and do not save the changes.

6. Execute the following query to add Sales to the UpdateOnly database role:

   EXEC sp_addrolemember @rolename='UpdateOnly',
   @membername='SalesUsers'

7. Close Query Analyzer, log off Windows, and log back in as ChenJ (a member of the Sales group).

8. Open Query Analyzer and log in using Windows Authentication.

9. Execute the following query and note its success since the Sales group's membership in the UpdateOnly role provides UPDATE permission:

   USE pubs

   UPDATE authors

   SET authors.au_fname='Mike'

   WHERE au_fname='Michael'

10. On the Edit menu, select Clear Window.

EXERCISE 5.17 *(continued)*

11. Execute the following query and note its failure since the Sales group does not have any permissions other than UPDATE:

SELECT * FROM authors

12. Close Query Analyzer, log off Windows, and log back in as Administrator.

Application Roles

Suppose that your human resources department uses a custom program to access their database, and you don't want them using any other program for fear of damaging the data. You can set this level of security by using an *application role*. With this special role, your users will not be able to access data using just their SQL login and database account; they will have to use the proper application.

Once you've created the application role described in Exercises 5.18 and 5.19, the user logs on to SQL, is authenticated, and opens the approved application. The application executes the sp_setapprole stored procedure to enable the application role. Once the application role is enabled, SQL no longer sees users as themselves; it sees users as the application and grants them application role permissions.

EXERCISE 5.18

Creating Application Roles Using Enterprise Manager

1. Open Enterprise Manager and select Roles in the Pubs database.

2. On the Action menu, select New Database Role.

3. In the Name box, type **EntAppRole**.

4. Under Database Role Type, select Application Role.

5. In the Password box, type **password**.

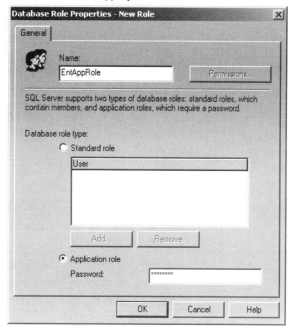

6. Click OK to get back to Enterprise Manager.

7. Double-click EntAppRole and click the Permissions button.

8. Grant SELECT permissions on Authors by clicking the SELECT check box next to the Authors line until a green checkmark appears.

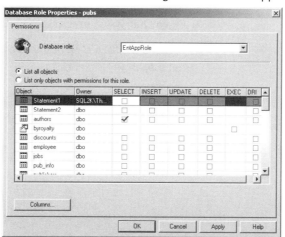

EXERCISE 5.18 *(continued)*

9. Click OK to get back to the previous dialog box and click OK again to return to Enterprise Manager.

10. Close Enterprise Manager and open Query Analyzer.

11. Use SQL Authentication and log on as GibsonH.

12. Notice that the following query fails since GibsonH has been denied SELECT permission because of membership in the db_denydatareader database role:

```
USE pubs

SELECT * FROM authors
```

13. To activate the application role, execute the following query:

```
exec sp_setapprole @rolename='EntAppRole',
@password='password'
```

14. Clear the query window and do not save the changes; repeat step 12 without opening a new query, and notice that the query is successful this time. This is because SQL now sees you as EntAppRole, which has SELECT permission.

15. Close Query Analyzer.

EXERCISE 5.19

Creating Application Roles Using T-SQL

1. Open Query Analyzer and log in using Windows Authentication.

2. Execute the following query to add an application role to the Pubs database:

```
EXEC sp_addapprole @rolename='TsqlAppRole',
@password='password'
```

3. Close Query Analyzer, open Enterprise Manager, and select Database Roles in the Pubs database. Note the new application role that was just added.

GRANT, REVOKE, and DENY

Permissions can be granted, revoked, or denied. Exercises 5.20 and 5.21 give you hands-on experience with these three states of permission:

GRANT   Granting allows users to use a specific permission. For instance, if you grant SmithB SELECT permission on a table, he can read the data within. A granted permission is signified by a black checkmark on the Permissions tab.

REVOKE   In this state, while users are not explicitly allowed to use a revoked permission, if they are a member of a role that is allowed they will inherit the permission. That is, if you revoke the SELECT permission from SmithB, he cannot use it. If he is a member of a role that has been granted SELECT permission, SmithB can read the data just as if he had the SELECT permission. Revocation is signified by a blank check box on the Permissions tab.

DENY   If you deny a permission, the user does not get the permission—no matter what. If you deny SmithB SELECT permission on a table then, even if he is a member of a role with SELECT permission, he cannot read the data. Denial is signified by a red X on the Permissions tab (Figure 5.3).

FIGURE 5.3   States of permissions in Enterprise Manager

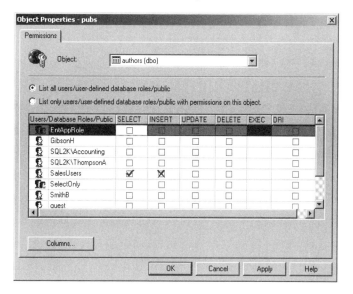

EXERCISE 5.20

Granting, Revoking, and Denying Permissions Using Enterprise Manager

1. Open Enterprise Manager, expand your server and Databases, then select the Pubs database.

2. Select Users, double-click SmithB, and click the Permissions button.

3. Grant SmithB SELECT permission on the Authors table by clicking the check box in the SELECT column on the Authors line until a green check box appears (this may already be completed from a previous exercise).

4. Click OK to go back to the previous dialog box and click OK again to return to Enterprise Manager.

5. Open Query Analyzer and log in as SmithB using SQL Authentication.

6. Execute the following query; it is successful since SmithB has SELECT permission on the Authors table:

use pubs

SELECT * FROM authors

7. Leave Query Analyzer open and return to Enterprise Manager.

8. Double-click the SmithB user in the Pubs database and click the Permissions button.

9. Revoke the SELECT permission on the Authors table by clicking the check box in the SELECT column next to Authors until the check box is blank.

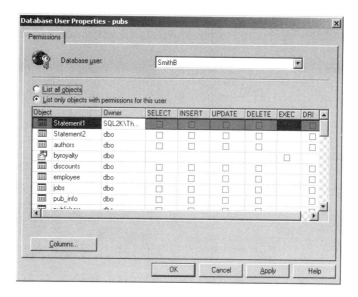

10. Return to Query Analyzer and execute the query in step 6. It fails because SmithB does not have explicit SELECT permission.

11. Leave Query Analyzer open and return to Enterprise Manager.

12. Double-click user SmithB in the Pubs database again and this time add him to the db_datareader role by clicking the check box next to db_datareader until a checkmark appears.

13. Return to Query Analyzer and rerun the same query. Now it is successful. This is because SmithB has inherited the SELECT permission from the Db_datareader role and does not need to have it explicitly applied.

14. Leave Query Analyzer open and return to Enterprise Manager.

15. Select Tables under the Pubs database and double-click the Authors table in the contents pane.

16. Click the Permissions button.

17. Deny SmithB SELECT permission by clicking the check box in the SELECT column next to SmithB until a red X appears.

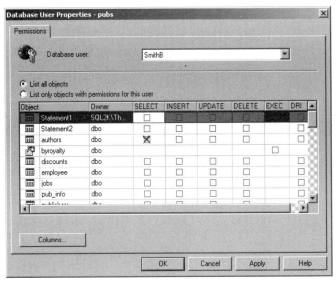

18. Click OK and then OK again to return to Enterprise Manager.

19. Return to Query Analyzer and again run the query from step 6. It fails this time because you have specifically denied SmithB access and therefore he can no longer inherit the SELECT permission from the db_datareader role.

20. Close Query Analyzer and return to Enterprise Manager.

21. Select Tables under the Pubs database and double-click the Authors table in the contents pane.

22. Click the Permissions button.

23. Return the SELECT permission for SmithB to the revoked state by clicking the check box in the SELECT column next to SmithB until it becomes blank.

24. Click OK, then OK again to return to Enterprise Manager.

25. Double-click user SmithB in the Pubs database and remove him from the db_datareader role by clicking the check box next to db_ datareader until it is blank.

26. Click OK to return to Enterprise Manager.

EXERCISE 5.21

Granting, Revoking, and Denying Permissions Using T-SQL

1. Open Query Analyzer and log in using Windows NT Authentication.

2. Execute the following query to grant SmithB SELECT permission on the Authors table:

   USE pubs

   GRANT SELECT on authors to SmithB

3. On the File menu, select Disconnect.

4. On the File menu, select Connect and log in as SmithB using SQL Authentication.

5. Execute the following query and note its success since SmithB has been granted SELECT permission:

   USE pubs

   SELECT * from authors

6. On the File menu, select Disconnect, then select Connect and log in using Windows NT Authentication.

7. Execute the following query to revoke the SELECT permission from SmithB:

   USE pubs

   REVOKE SELECT on authors from SmithB

8. On the Query menu, select Clear Window and do not save the changes.

EXERCISE 5.21 *(continued)*

9. Execute the following query to add SmithB to the db_datareader database role:

   USE pubs

   exec sp_addrolemember @rolename='db_datareader', @membername='SmithB'

10. On the File menu, select Disconnect.

11. On the File menu, select Connect and log in as SmithB using SQL Authentication.

12. Execute the following query and note its success. SmithB is a member of the db_datareader database role and therefore inherits the SELECT permission from that role.

    USE pubs

    SELECT * from authors

13. On the File menu, select Disconnect.

14. On the File menu, select Connect and log in using Windows NT Authentication.

15. Execute the following query to deny SELECT permission to SmithB:

    USE pubs

    DENY SELECT on authors to SmithB

16. On the File menu, select Disconnect.

17. On the File menu, select Connect and log in as SmithB using SQL Authentication.

18. Execute the following query and notice that it fails. This is because SmithB has now been explicitly denied permission and cannot inherit permission from the db_datareader role.

    USE pubs

    SELECT * from authors

19. Close Query Analyzer.

With a better understanding of how and where permissions are applied, we can look into one of the problems generated when permissions are applied improperly: the broken ownership chain.

Ownership Chains

In the physical world, people own objects—things—that they can do with as they please, including lending or giving them to others. SQL understands this concept of ownership. When a user creates an object, they own that object and can do whatever they want with it. For example, if ThompsonA creates a table, he can assign permissions as he chooses, granting access only to those users he deems worthy. That is a good thing until you consider what is known as an ownership chain.

An object that is on loan still belongs to the owner; the person who has borrowed it must ask the owner for permission before allowing another person to use it. Acting without such permission would be much like a broken *ownership chain.*

Suppose that ThompsonA creates a table and grants permissions on that table to Accounting (see Figure 5.4). Then one of the members of Accounting creates a view based on that table and grants SELECT permission to SmithB. Can SmithB select the data from that view? No, because the ownership chain has broken. SQL will check permissions on an underlying object (in this case, the table) only when the owner changes. Therefore, if ThompsonA had created both the table and the view there would be no problem since SQL would check only the permissions on the view. Because the owner changed from Accounting (who owned the view) to ThompsonA (who owned the table), SQL needed to check the permissions on both the view and the table.

FIGURE 5.4   Example of a broken ownership chain

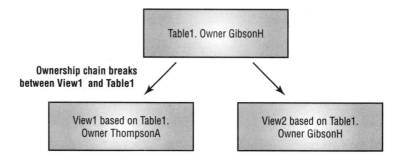

How can you avoid broken ownership chains? The first way is to make everyone who needs to create objects a member of the sysadmin fixed server role; then everything they create will be owned by the DBO user rather than by the login. For example, since MorrisL is a member of the sysadmin fixed server role, everything he creates in any database will be owned by the DBO, not MorrisL. While this is technically possible, it is a poor method since it grants a great deal of administrative privilege over the server to people who do not need it.

A much better way to avoid broken ownership chains is to make all the users who need to create objects members of either the db_owner or db_ddladmin fixed database roles. Then if they need to create objects, they can specify the owner as DBO (i.e., `create table dbo.table_name`). This way the DBO would own all objects in the database, and since the ownership would never change, SQL would never need to check any underlying permissions.

An added bonus to this method is that you can use it to allow people to work with the data in your tables while not actually having permission to do so. The secret lies in the ownership of the objects. For example, suppose that you need ThompsonA to be able to change salary values in the Human Resources database by percentage (i.e., Bob gets 15 percent more salary), but you do not want him to be able to read directly from the table to see what values are actually stored inside. This can be accomplished by creating the table with DBO as the user and then creating a stored procedure with DBO as the owner that is designed to modify the salary data. Next, grant ThompsonA execute permission on the stored procedure but do not grant him permission directly on the table. Now when ThompsonA tries to execute the stored procedure it will succeed because SQL Server does not need to check permissions at the table level because the table and stored procedure are both owned by DBO. This holds true for user-defined functions and views as well.

A db_owner or db_ddladmin member can create objects as any other database user, not just the DBO.

Now that you know how to implement security on your server, you need to know how to monitor your security. Let's see how to do that now.

N-Tier Security

Microsoft Exam Objective

Manage linked servers.

- Configure security mapping.

Let's return to our business analogy: Your business is prospering, and you have had to expand into two buildings. This means that your employees will need access to resources in both buildings, which in turn means you will need to give your users a key to the new place so they can gain access.

You have the same concerns when your resources are spread across multiple SQL servers: your users may need access to resources on multiple, or *n*, servers. This is especially true of something called a *distributed query* (see Figure 5.5), which returns result sets from databases on multiple servers. Although you might wonder why you would want to perform distributed queries when you could just replicate the data between servers, there are practical reasons for doing the former. Don't forget that because SQL Server is designed to store terabytes of data, some of your databases may grow to several hundred megabytes in size—and you really don't want to replicate several hundred megabytes under normal circumstances.

FIGURE 5.5 Distributed queries

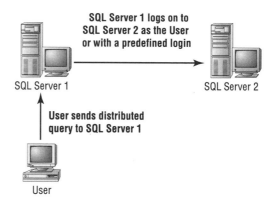

The first step is to inform SQL that it will be talking to other database servers by running the sp_addlinkedserver stored procedure. The procedure to link to a server named AccountingSQL looks something like this: sp_addlinkedserver @server='AccountingSQL', @provider='SQL Server'.

Your users can then run distributed queries by simply specifying two different servers in the query. The query: SELECT * from SQLServer.pubs.dbo.authors, AccountingSQL.pubs.dbo.employees would access data from both the SQLServer (the server the user is logged in to, or sending server) and AccountingSQL server (the remote server) in the same result set.

The security issue here is that the sending server must log in to the remote server on behalf of the user to gain access to the data. SQL can use one of two methods to send this security information: security account delegation or linked server login mapping. If your users have logged in using Windows Authentication and all of the servers in the query are capable of understanding Windows domain security, you can use account delegation. Here's how it works:

1. If the servers are in different domains, you must make certain that the appropriate Windows trust relationships are in place. The remote server's domain must trust the sending server's domain.

2. Add a Windows login to the sending server for the user to log in with.

3. Add the same account to the remote server.

4. Create a user account for the login in the remote server's database and assign permissions.

5. When the user executes the distributed query, SQL will send the user's Windows security credentials to the remote server, allowing access.

If you have users who access SQL with standard logins, or if some of the servers do not participate in Windows domain security, you will need to add a linked login. Here's how to do it:

1. On the remote server, create a standard login and assign the necessary permissions.

2. On the sending server, map a local login to the remote login using the `sp_addlinkedsrvlogin` stored procedure. To map all local logins to the remote login RemUser, type:
   ```
   sp_addlinkedsrvlogin @rmtsrvname='AccountingSQL',
   @useself=FALSE, @locallogin=NULL, @rmtuser='RemUser',
   @rmtpassword='password'
   ```

3. When a user executes a distributed query, the sending server will log in to the AccountingSQL (remote) server as RemUser with a password of password.

It is essential to monitor your office to be sure that no one is trying to bypass security; this can be done with the SQL Profiler.

Monitoring Security

Microsoft *Exam* *Objective*	**Manage security auditing. Methods include SQL Profiler, SQL Trace, and C2 auditing.**

Most people have at one time or another had to pass through a security checkpoint. At that checkpoint sat a security guard watching monitors and searching packages. Why was this guard there? Because you can have the most advanced security system in the world, but without someone keeping watch it will eventually fail. A thief would simply need to probe the system systematically for weak spots and, once they were found, take advantage of them to break in. With the guard watching, this becomes a great deal more difficult.

The same is true for SQL. You cannot simply put a security system in place and then leave it. You must keep watch, just like the security guard, to make certain no one is probing for weak spots and attempting to break in. This task of keeping watch has been delegated to Profiler.

Profiler is discussed in more detail in Chapter 10, "Monitoring and Optimizing SQL Server 2000."

Profiler is used to track and record activity on the SQL Server, which is done by performing a *trace* (as seen in Exercise 5.22). A trace is a record of the data captured about events, which can be a stored in a database table; a trace log file that can be opened and read in Profiler; or both.

The actions that are monitored on the server are known as *events* and those events are logically grouped together in *event classes*. Not all of these events have to do with security; in fact, most of them have to do with optimization and troubleshooting. The next section lists the classes and events that are important from a security standpoint.

Event Class Security Audit

Audit Add DB User Event   This can be used to audit the addition and removal of database user accounts.

Audit Add Login to Server Role Event   This records the modification of fixed server role membership.

Audit Add Member to DB Role Event   This records the modification of fixed or user-defined database role membership.

Audit Add Role Event   This is used to record the addition or removal of database roles.

Audit Addlogin Event   This is used to monitor the addition or deletion of SQL Server logins.

Audit App Role Change Password Event   This is used to monitor changes to the password of an application role.

Audit Backup/Restore Event   This can be used to track database backups and restores.

Audit Change Audit Event   This is used to monitor changes to your audit policy.

Audit DBCC Event   This event can be used to track any Database Consistency Checker command that is executed.

Audit Login Event   This is used to audit successful logins to SQL Server.

Audit Login Change Password Event   This is used to monitor when users change their password for a SQL Server login account (not a Windows account).

Audit Login Change Property Event   This is used to track changes to a login's default database or default language properties.

Audit Login Failed Event   This will tell you if someone has tried to log in unsuccessfully. If you notice someone repeatedly failing to log in, it means either the user forgot their password or someone is trying to hack in using that account.

Audit Login GDR Event   Windows accounts on SQL Server can be granted, denied, or revoked (GDR) access to SQL Server. This event is used to monitor changes in the accounts access status.

Audit Logout Event   This event is used to track when users disconnect from SQL Server.

Audit Object Derived Permission Event   This tracks CREATE, ALTER, and DROP commands for specific objects.

Audit Object GDR Event   This tracks changes for GRANT, DENY, and REVOKE permissions for specific objects.

Audit Object Permission Event   This records the use of object permissions whether successful or unsuccessful.

Audit Server Starts and Stops Event   This is used to track start, pause, and stop events for the SQL Server services.

Audit Statement GDR Event   This is used to track permission events for GRANT, DENY, and REVOKE statements.

Audit Statement Permission Event   This is used to record the use of statement permissions whether successful or not.

SQL Server 6.5 came with a utility called SQL Trace, which was the precursor to Profiler. SQL Trace is now the part of the database engine that returns data to Profiler. As a user, you will not see SQL Trace.

EXERCISE 5.22

Monitoring Login Failures with Profiler

1. Open Profiler in the SQL Server 2000 Program group.

2. On the File menu, select New, then Trace.

3. Connect to your server with Windows Authentication.

4. In the Trace Name box, type **Security**.

5. Leave the template as SQLProfilerStandard.

6. Click the check box next to Save to File and click Save to select the default filename. Leave the Enable File Rollover and SQL Server Processes Trace Data check boxes as the default settings.

7. Click the check box next to Capture to Table, connect using Windows Authentication, and use the following criteria to fill in the subsequent dialog box:

   Database: **Pubs**

   Table: **Security**

8. Click OK to return to the previous dialog box.

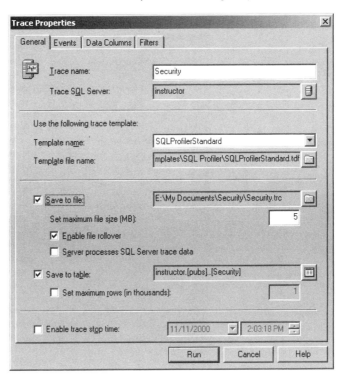

9. Select the Events tab.

10. Under Selected Event Classes, select Sessions and click Remove.

11. Under Selected Event Classes, select T-SQL and click Remove.

12. Under Selected Event Classes, select Stored Procedures and click Remove.

13. Under Selected Event Classes, select Security Audit and click Remove.

14. Under Available Event Classes, expand Security Audit and click Audit Login Failed.

15. Click Add to move Audit Login Failed to the Selected Event Classes column.

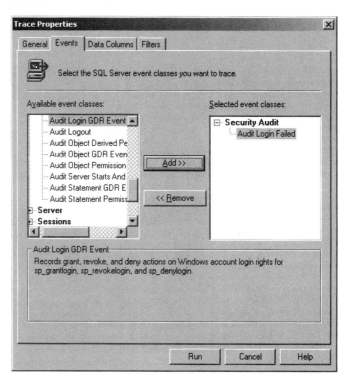

16. Click Run to start the trace.

17. To test the trace, leave Profiler open and open Query Analyzer.

18. Log in using SQL Authentication with the username SmithB and with a password of coconut. This will fail since you have supplied the wrong password.

19. Return to Profiler and notice that a login failure has been recorded for user SmithB.

20. Go back to Query Analyzer and log in as SmithB with a password of password. This will succeed since you have entered the correct password.

EXERCISE 5.22 *(continued)*

21. Close Query Analyzer and return to Profiler. Notice that there is no successful login record for SmithB since we are only monitoring failed logins.

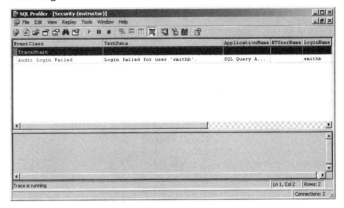

22. On the File menu, select Close and Yes.

23. On the File menu, select Open and then Trace File.

24. Open the Security.trc file and notice that all the events just recorded have been saved for later viewing.

25. Close Profiler, open Query Analyzer, and log in using Windows Authentication.

26. Execute the following query to view the newly created Security table:

USE pubs

SELECT * from security

27. Close Query Analyzer and do not save any changes.

Profiler can also be used to read files generated by C2 security auditing. C2 security is a government standard that states that properly configured computer systems have a high level of resistance to attack. Once you have configured your Windows system and your SQL Server system so that they are C2-compliant, you can configure C2 auditing so that you can verify that no one is trying to hack into your C2-compliant systems. Exercise 5.23 shows you how to enable and monitor C2 auditing.

For information on how to configure your Windows and SQL Server installations to meet C2 standards, consult the Microsoft Web site at www.microsoft.com.

EXERCISE 5.23

Enabling C2 Auditing

1. Open Query Analyzer and execute the following query to show advanced options and set C2 audit mode:

```
USE master

exec sp_configure 'show advanced options', '1'

go

exec sp_configure 'c2 audit mode', '1'

go
```

2. Stop and restart the SQL Server service.

SQL Server System Accounts

Before SQL Server can interact with outside applications, a user account must be assigned to the various SQL Server services.

Although creating SQL Server service accounts was covered in Chapter 2, "Installing, Upgrading, and Configuring SQL Server 2000," this section will cover why and how to create the accounts.

As a security precaution, the service needs a user account assigned to it whenever a service attempts to gain network access. This is to prevent hackers from writing a program that could compromise your network. Microsoft assumes that you are managing and controlling your user accounts carefully so that any unauthorized accounts would be detected and locked out. Accounts that are created primarily for services to use are called *service accounts*. Most services need at least one service account created for them, such as Systems Management Server and Exchange. SQL Server also benefits from having a service account assigned to it, as SQL Server can interact with

Exchange servers (or other MAPI-compatible e-mail servers) and can connect to other SQL Servers for replication or job-management purposes.

When you create a service account for SQL Server, you can create a single account for all SQL Server services to use or you can create separate accounts for the individual services.

While the service account assigned to the SQL Server Agent needs administrative rights, the account assigned to the other SQL Server services doesn't. You may want to create and assign separate accounts to limit the rights of the accounts assigned to the MSSQLSERVER service and also to help in auditing security issues.

Any account you create needs rights to the \MSSQL2000 folder and user rights on the domain and must be a domain user.

Real World Scenario: Creating a Security Plan

Suppose that you have just been hired as database administrator for Also Rann, Inc., a small company that relies heavily on their SQL Server. A great deal of the data on the SQL Server is proprietary and therefore must be secured. You realize, however, that jumping right in and randomly applying permissions to databases is going to result in a mess—if not a disaster—so you take a more logical approach: you develop a security plan.

A good security plan is always the first step in applying security to any type of system. Here are a few things that you will need to consider in your plan:

Type of Users   If all your users support trusted connections, you can use Windows accounts. If you have the authority to create groups in NT, you may be able to create Windows groups and then create logins for those groups rather than individual accounts. If not all your users support trusted connections (like Novell or Macintosh), then you will need to use Mixed Mode authentication and create some standard logins.

Fixed Server Roles   Once you have given users access to SQL, how much administrative power, if any, should they be given? If your users need administrative authority, you will add them to one of the fixed server roles; if not, there is no need to add them.

Database Access   Once logged in, to which databases will your users have access? It is highly unlikely that every user will need a user account in every database.

Type of Access Once the user has a database user account, how much authority will they have in the database? For example, can all users read and write, or is there a subset of users who are only allowed to read?

Group Permissions It is usually best to apply permissions to database roles and then add users to those roles. There are some exceptions in every system, though, and you may need to apply some permissions directly to users, especially those who need to be denied access to a resource.

Creating Figure out who needs the authority to create objects, such as tables and views, and group them together in either the db_owner or db_ddladmin role. Doing this will allow users to create objects as the DBO instead of themselves. In this way you can avoid broken ownership chains.

Public Access Remember that all database user accounts are members of the public role and cannot be removed. Whatever permission the public role has will be given to your users. Limit the permissions on the Public group.

Guest Access Do you want users with no database user account to be able to access databases through a guest account? For some databases, like a catalog, this may be acceptable. In general, however, this can be considered a security risk and should not be used on all databases.

Table 5.1 shows the employees of AlsoRann, Inc. and their security needs. The first thing you may notice is that there are two Novell network users. This means you need to create at least two standard logins, and it means you need to implement Mixed Mode authentication.

The next thing you may notice is that some of the users—specifically Accounting and Sales—are already grouped together in Windows. Rather than creating accounts for each individual member of these departments, you can instead add a Windows Group login for the whole lot of them. Because ThompsonA and MorrisL are not members of a Windows group, they will need Windows User logins.

Next, look at the administrative rights that each user will need over the system. Since GibsonH needs to be able to configure server settings like memory use, he should be added to the serveradmin fixed server role. And since MorrisL needs full administrative access to the entire system, she should be added to the sys-admin fixed server role.

To make the processes of writing a bit simpler, AlsoRann has only one database. Look at the permissions that everyone needs on that database. As a customer service rep, SmithB needs permission to read the data but not to write any data; the db_denydatawriter fixed database role will fit those needs well.

As a developer, GibsonH needs permission to create objects in the database, but he should not be able to read the data. Make GibsonH a member of the db_ddladmin role so that he can create objects as DBO and avoid broken ownership chains. You could have made him a member of the db_owner group and achieved the same effect, but then he would be able to do whatever he wanted in the database, including reading the data.

ThompsonA needs to be able to SELECT, INSERT, and UPDATE data, but he should not be able to delete any data. There is no fixed database role that grants these three permissions together. You could apply all of these permissions directly to ThompsonA, but what if you hire more people that need the same permissions? It might be a better idea to create a custom database role, grant that role the SELECT, INSERT, and UPDATE permissions, and make ThompsonA a member of that role. The same is true of the Sales group, which needs permission to read and update; they will require a custom role.

For Accounting, it will be easiest to add them to the db_datareader and db_datawriter roles; that way, they receive permissions to read and write to the database. MorrisL will not need to be a member of any role; since she is a member of the sysadmin fixed server role, she is automatically considered the DBO in every database on the server.

In the real world, of course, a security plan is not going to be nearly this simple. There will be hundreds, if not thousands, of users to deal with from a variety of networks, each needing different permissions. To sum up, although developing a security plan is probably more work than the actual implementation, you cannot do without it.

TABLE 5.1   The Employees of AlsoRann, Inc.

Name	NT Group	Department	Network	Admin	Permissions
SmithB	N/A	Service	Novell	None	Read, no Write
GibsonH	N/A	Development	Novell	Server Configuration	Write, Create, no Read
Thomp-sonA	None	Administration	NT	None	SELECT, INSERT, UPDATE
MorrisL	None	IT	NT	All	All
JohnsonK	Accounting	Accounting	NT	None	Read, Write
JonesB	Accounting	Accounting	NT	None	Read, Write
ChenJ	Sales	Sales	NT	None	Read, UPDATE
SamuelsR	Sales	Sales	NT	None	Read, UPDATE

Summary

SQL Server 2000 has a sophisticated security system that allows you to carefully implement your security plan, which we examined in this chapter.

- SQL Server can operate in Mixed Mode, which means that Windows users and groups can be given access directly into SQL Server, or separate, unique accounts can be created that reside only in SQL Server. If SQL Server is running in Windows Authentication mode, every user must first connect with a preauthorized Windows account.

- This chapter examined the processes of creating and managing logins, groups, and users. You learned how to create a standard login and a Windows user or group login using Enterprise Manager or T-SQL and when each type is appropriate. If you have a well-designed security plan that incorporates growth, managing your user base can be a painless task.

- To limit administrative access to SQL at the server level, you learned that you can add users to a fixed server role. For limiting access in a specific database, you can add users to a database role, and if one of the fixed database roles is not to your liking, you can create your own. You can even go so far as to limit access to specific applications by creating an application role.

- Each database in SQL Server 2000 has its own independent permissions. You looked at the two types of user permissions, statement permissions, which are used to create or change the data structure; and object permissions, which manipulate data. Remember that statement permissions cannot be granted to others.

- The next section described the database hierarchy. You looked at the permissions available to the most powerful user—the DBO—down through the lower-level database users.

- You then learned about chains of ownership. These are created when you grant permissions to others on objects you own. Adding more users who create dependent objects creates broken ownership chains, which can become complex and tricky to work with. You learned how to predict the permissions available to users at different locations within these ownership chains. You also learned that to avoid the broken ownership chains, you can add your users to either the db_owner or db_ddladmin database role and have them create objects as the DBO.

- Permissions can be granted to database users as well as database roles. When a user is added to a role they inherit the permissions of the role, including the public role of which everyone is a member. The only exception is when the user has been denied permission, since DENY takes precedence over any other right, no matter the level at which the permission was granted.

- We then looked at remote and linked servers and at how security needs to be set up to make remote queries work. We finished with a look at *n*-tier security and applications.

Exam Essentials

Know your T-SQL.   You need to know how to use T-SQL for security purposes because it can be a much faster solution in the real world.

Know the differences in authentication modes.   You need to know when to use Mixed Mode versus Windows Authentication mode on the exam.

Know your roles.   You need to be familiar with the various fixed server and database roles and what they can be used for in the real world.

Know your permissions.   You need to know what the permissions are and what they are for as well as how to assign them through T-SQL and Enterprise Manager.

Key Terms

application role	nesting roles
authentication mode	nontrusted connection
distributed query	object permissions
event classes	ownership chain
events	service accounts
fixed database roles	statement permissions
guest user	trace
login	trusted connection
Mixed Mode	Windows Authentication mode

Review Questions

1. Jason is a member of a Windows group named Sales that has been granted access to SQL Server via a group account in SQL Server. Jason should not have access to SQL Server, but he needs the permissions afforded the Sales group on other servers. How can you remedy this?

   A. Create a new Windows group named SQL_Sales and add everyone but Jason to the group. Next, grant access to the SQL_Sales group by creating a group account in SQL Server and then remove the Sales group account from SQL Server.

   B. Create a login on the SQL Server specifically for Jason and deny the account access.

   C. Delete the Sales group login and create separate accounts for everyone except Jason.

   D. Remove Jason from the Sales group in Windows and grant him all of the necessary permissions separately on all other servers on the network.

2. One of your users has created a table (John.table1) and granted Samantha SELECT permission on the table. Samantha, however, does not need to see all of the data in the table so she creates a view (Samantha.view1). Thomas now wants access to Samantha's view so Samantha grants Thomas SELECT permission on the view. What happens when Thomas tries to SELECT from the view?

   A. Thomas can select from the view because he has been granted permissions on the view directly.

   B. Thomas cannot select from the view because he does not have permission on the underlying table and the ownership chain is broken.

   C. Thomas can select from the view because Samantha granted him permission on the view and she has permission on the underlying table.

   D. Thomas can select, but he receives an error message stating that he does not have permission on the underlying table.

3. You enabled C2 auditing on your SQL Server some time ago but there are no logs for you to read. Why not?

   A. The SQL Server Agent must be stopped and restarted.

   B. The MSDTC service must be stopped and restarted.

   C. The SQL Server service must be stopped and restarted.

   D. The computer must be rebooted.

4. You execute the following command, but C2 auditing is not started. What do you need to do?

   ```
   USE master
   go
   exec sp_configure 'c2 audit mode', '1'
   go
   ```

   A. You need to enable advanced options with the command `exec sp_configure 'show advanced options', '1'` before configuring C2 audit mode.

   B. You need to enable advanced options with the command `exec sp_configure 'show advanced options', '0'` before configuring C2 audit mode.

   C. The SQL Server service must be stopped and restarted.

   D. You cannot be in the master database when configuring C2 auditing.

5. Andrea is a member of the sales and marketing roles in your database. She needs SELECT, INSERT, and UPDATE permissions on your table. With security configured as shown below, how can you grant her the necessary permissions?

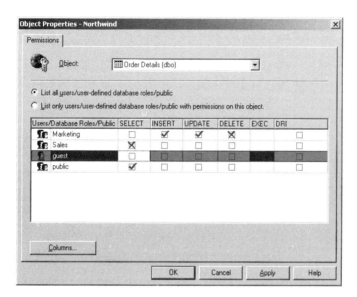

A. Add an account for Andrea and grant it the necessary permissions.

B. Grant SELECT permission to the marketing role.

C. Grant INSERT and UPDATE permissions to the public role.

D. Remove Andrea from the sales role.

6. What is the best way to avoid broken ownership chains and still maintain strict security?

A. Add all of the users that need to create objects to the db_owner fixed database role and instruct them to create objects as DBO.

B. Add all of the users that need to create objects to the db_ddladmin fixed database role and instruct them to create objects as DBO.

C. Add all of the users that need to create objects to the db_creator fixed server role and instruct them to create objects as DBO.

D. Grant users the permission to create objects in the database separately and instruct them to create objects as DBO.

7. You need to grant Robert permission to modify employee phone numbers in the employees table but you do not want him to be able to modify any other data in the table. What is the best way to accomplish this?

A. Grant Robert UPDATE permission on the phone number column of the table and do not grant him permissions on any other column.

B. Create a view that contains only the phone number column and grant Robert UPDATE permission on the view.

C. Create a stored procedure to change the phone number and grant Robert EXECUTE permission on the stored procedure.

D. Create triggers on the table that reject any updates from Robert on columns other than the phone number column.

8. You have spent a great deal of money and effort to create a custom accounting program in Visual Basic that is designed to meet some very specific needs of your company. You find that some of your users are still accessing your database through other methods such as Excel and Query Analyzer, and this is causing problems with the integrity of your database. How can you fix this problem?

   A. Create a filter in Profiler that will reject access by all programs except your custom program.

   B. Create an account for your new application and have all of your users log in to SQL using that account. Then remove permissions from any remaining user accounts in the database.

   C. Create an application role for the account and grant it the necessary permissions. Then add all of the users in the database to the application role.

   D. Create an application role and grant it the necessary permissions in the database. Then remove any permissions for your users in the database and hard code the `sp_activateapprole` stored procedure into your application to activate the role.

9. You have just created a new Windows account (Domain\BobH) for a new employee. You create a new SQL login for BobH using the command `sp_addlogin 'domain\BobH', 'password', 'accounting'`, but Bob is now complaining that he cannot access SQL Server when he logs in with his Windows account. Why not?

   A. You need to configure the SQL Server to allow trusted accounts by using the command `sp_configure 'allow trusted connections', '1'`.

   B. The `sp_addlogin` command is used to create standard login accounts, not mapped login accounts. You need to map Bob's account to a SQL login with the `sp_grantlogin` stored procedure.

   C. Bob is not using the right network library to log in with a trusted account. Set the network library to named pipes, Multiprotocol, or TCP/IP.

   D. Bob's SQL Server account password does not match his Windows account password. Change one of the two so that they match.

10. In order to maintain strict security on your database, you realize that you need to remove the default permissions that users have when they are first created in the database. What is the best way to do this?

    A. Remove users from the public role and add them back on an as-needed basis.

    B. In Enterprise Manager, remove all of the permissions from the public role by clicking each box until it is cleared.

    C. Execute the REVOKE ALL FROM PUBLIC command in Query Analyzer while using your database.

    D. Do nothing; there are no default permissions granted to users when they are first created.

11. You have the authority to create both Windows accounts and SQL logins and roles on your network. Ten of your users will be working on a short-term project together that requires them to access the same database resources on the SQL Server but not the same resources on the Windows servers. What is the best way to grant these users access to the database resources?

    A. Add all of the users to a Windows group and map a SQL Server login to the new group. Then grant permissions to the group login.

    B. Create separate Windows logins for each user and add them to a custom database role. Then assign permissions to the database role.

    C. Create a separate Windows login for each user and grant permissions on the database to each user login.

    D. Create one login for all of the users to log in with and grant that user account permissions on the database.

12. You have several SQL Servers in your organization that participate in linked server queries. On one of the servers some of your users are complaining that the linked server queries are not working. Why are some of the users not able to use linked server queries?

   A. The server was not added as a linked server with the `sp_addlinkedserver` stored procedure.

   B. The remote server has not been configured to accept incoming queries from other servers. You must configure it by setting the ALLOW LINKED QUERIES option to 1 using the `sp_configure` stored procedure.

   C. The users that cannot access the linked server use standard logins so you need to map a linked server login by executing `sp_addlinkedsrvlogin` on the destination server.

   D. The users that cannot access the linked server use standard logins so you need to map a linked server login by executing `sp_addlinkedsrvlogin` on the local server.

13. Many of your Windows administrators are capable in their field but they are unfamiliar with SQL Server. How can you keep them from accidentally damaging your SQL Server implementation?

   A. Remove the BUILTIN\Administrators account from SQL Server. Then create a SQLAdmins group in Windows and add all of the SQL Administrators to the new group. Finally, create a login mapped to the SQLAdmins group and add it to the sysadmins role.

   B. Create a separate login for each of your Windows administrators and deny access for each of their logins.

   C. Remove BUILTIN\Administrators from the sysadmins role and create separate logins for each of the SQL Administrators. Then add each separate login to the sysadmins role.

   D. Do nothing; the Windows administrators do not have administrative access in SQL Server by default.

14. You are setting up a kiosk in a library that hundreds of people will access every month. You realize that it would be impossible to grant security access to each individual that uses the system. What can you do to grant each user access without adding them individually?

A. Create a Windows account named Kiosk and map a SQL login to that account. Then create a database user account for Kiosk and grant it permissions on the database. Finally, have all of the library patrons log in to the computer system as Kiosk.

B. Enable the guest account in Windows and map a SQL login to it. Then create a guest database user account and grant it the proper permissions.

C. Enable the guest user account in Windows. No guest login or database accounts need to be created in SQL Server because they already exist.

D. Enable the guest user account in Windows and map it to a SQL login. No database user account named guest will need to be created because it already exists in each database.

15. You want to be able to use e-mail, replication, and other interserver services with SQL Server. When you install SQL Server, what type of account should you use?

A. The local server account

B. A local account

C. A domain account with administrative privileges

D. A domain account with no administrative access

16. You need to create a new login account for one of your UNIX users named WoodsJ. What command would you use to do this?

A. sp_addlogin 'WoodsJ', 'password', 'pubs'

B. sp_grantlogin 'WoodsJ', 'password', 'pubs'

C. sp_createlogin 'WoodsJ', 'password', 'pubs'

D. sp_makelogin 'WoodsJ', 'password', 'pubs'

17. You have a human resources database that all users will be allowed to read from to obtain information but only the human resources department should be able to read from and update the data in the database. What is the easiest and most secure way for you to ensure this?

A. Add all of the users that are not in the HR department to the db_datareader database role and add all of the users from the HR department to a custom database role that allows them all modification and selection permissions.

B. Add all of the users who are not in the HR department to the db_datareader and db_denydatawriter database roles and add all of the users from the HR department to the db_datareader and db_datawriter database roles.

C. Add all of the users that are not in the HR department to the db_datareader and db_denydatawriter database roles and add all of the users from the HR department to db_datamodifier database role.

D. Add all of the users that are not in the HR department to the db_datareader and db_denydatawriter database roles and add all of the users from the HR department to the db_owner database role.

18. You have a number of users in your customer service department that need SELECT, INSERT, and UPDATE permissions but they should not be able to delete—only managers should have the permission to delete data. How can you ensure that only managers can delete data and users can only perform the tasks listed?

A. Add the users to the db_datareader and db_datawriter roles and add the managers to the db_datadeleter role.

B. Add the users to the db_datareader role and the managers to the db_datawriter role.

C. Add the users to a custom role that allows only SELECT, INSERT, and UPDATE permissions and the managers to a custom role that allows them to read and modify data.

D. Add the users to a custom role that allows only SELECT, INSERT, and UPDATE permissions and the managers to the db_datareader and db_datawriter roles.

19. All of your developers need to be able to create databases and objects inside the databases, such as tables, views, etc. Which roles should they be added to at the server and database levels to accommodate these needs?

A. Sysadmins at the server level and db_owner at the database level

B. Sysadmins at the server level and db_ddladmins at the database level

C. Db_creator at the server level and db_ddladmin at the database level

D. Db_creator at the server level and db_owner at the database level

20. How can you offload the authority to create user accounts to one of your assistant DBAs?

A. Add them to the db_accessadmin role

B. Add them to the sysadmin role

C. Add them to the db_securityadmin role

D. Add them to the db_owner role

Answers to Review Questions

1. B. The best way to accomplish this is to create a separate SQL login for Jason and deny it access.

2. B. Because the ownership chain is broken Thomas cannot SELECT from the view unless he is granted SELECT permission on the underlying table (John.table1).

3. C. To start C2 auditing after it has been configured you must stop and restart the SQL Server service.

4. A. C2 auditing is an advanced option and advanced options are not available by default. Therefore, you must show advanced options by setting them to 1 before you can set C2 auditing mode.

5. D. Removing Andrea from the sales role will give her the permissions she needs. She will inherit the SELECT permission from the public role and the INSERT and UPDATE permissions from the marketing role. None of the other options would work because as long as Andrea is a member of Sales she would be denied the SELECT permission because Sales has been denied the permission.

6. B. Adding users to the db_ddladmin role is the most secure way to accomplish this goal. Adding them to the db_owner role would grant them too much authority over the database and would not maintain strict security.

7. C. Column-level permissions are possible in SQL Server 2000, but they are hard to maintain and rarely the answer to security problems. You could use a view, but it is not usually best to create a view for just a single column. Creating a stored procedure and granting Robert EXECUTE permission is the best way to fix this issue.

8. D. In this case, you need to create an application role and activate it through your Visual Basic code. This will cause SQL Server to see all of your users as the application role and grant them all of the rights and permissions therewith.

9. B. You must use `sp_grantlogin` to map a SQL Server login to a Windows login. `Sp_addlogin` is used to create standard logins.

10. C. Users cannot be removed from the public role, which has every permission granted by default. The easiest way to remove these permissions is with the REVOKE ALL FROM PUBLIC command.

11. B. Because the users do not need access to the same resources on the Windows servers, there is no reason to create a Windows group for them. Because there are so few users here, it is easiest to create user accounts for each user and add them to a custom database role.

12. D. In order for users that use standard logins to access a linked server you need to map a local login to a login on the remote server using the sp_addlinkedsrvlogin command.

13. A. The most secure and easiest way to accomplish this task is to remove the Windows Administrators group from the SQL Server and add a new group of your own creation in its place. You do not actually have to remove the login entirely, but because there is no use for it afterwards there is no sense in keeping it around.

14. D. Creating a user account especially for this application is possible but hard to manage, especially when a database user account already exists for each database. Therefore, creating a user login for the guest account is the easiest way to allow access to the kiosk.

15. C. If you want to perform replication, your SQL Server Agent service needs to log in with administrative access. All other interserver services (like e-mail) need at least a domain account with access to the requested services.

16. A. Because this is a UNIX user, you know that they do not have a Windows account against which to be verified. You must use sp_addlogin as opposed to sp_grantlogin, which is only used for mapping to Windows accounts. The other two stored procedures do not even exist.

17. B. Users can be members of more than one group so it is easiest to add the members of HR to the db_datareader and db_datawriter roles and add everyone else to the db_datareader role to grant the permission to read data and the dn_denydatawriter role to deny them the permission to modify data.

18. D. There is no fixed database role that allows the permissions that the users need, but the managers need the permissions that are allowed by the db_datareader and db_datawriter roles. Therefore, you need to use fixed roles for the managers and custom roles for the users.

19. C. The db_creator membership will give the developers just enough permission to create databases at the server level and db_ddladmins will give them just enough permission to create objects in the databases they create. The sysadmin and db_owner roles will give them too much permission and therefore allow for lax security.

20. A. The most secure method of granting your assistants the authority to create user accounts is to add them to the db_accessadmin role.

Implementing Database Backups and Restorations

MICROSOFT EXAM OBJECTIVES COVERED IN THIS CHAPTER:

✓ **Perform disaster recovery operations.**

   ▪ Perform backups.

   ▪ Recover the system state and restore data.

   ▪ Configure, maintain, and troubleshoot log shipping.

✓ **Perform integrity checks. Methods include configuring the Database Maintenance Plan Wizard and using the Database Consistency Checker (DBCC).**

In this chapter, we'll look at various options for protecting your data, an area of crucial importance. We'll discuss the reasons for backing up data and how to plan and choose appropriate backup strategies. We'll also show you how to perform various types of backups and how to restore databases when necessary.

Please also see Chapter 3 for complete coverage of the objectives in this chapter.

Before You Back Up

There are several questions you need to ask yourself before you perform the first backup. Because backups should be tailored for a particular environment, you need to understand your server, your data, and your organizational environment in order to configure the best backup scenario.

Why Back Up?

Having fault-tolerant disk drives doesn't mean you don't have to do backups. Data can be corrupted by a variety of problems:

- Failure of the hard disk drive
- Failure of the hard disk controller
- Motherboard failure

- Power outage or spike

- Virus attack

- Accidental change or deletion of data

- Malicious change or deletion of data

Creating (and testing) regular backups is an integral part of any good administrator's maintenance plan. You never, ever want to hear someone say, "The hard drive is dead and the backups are bad."

Developing a Backup Plan

As an administrator, you will probably be the one in charge of scheduling and verifying backups. You must consider the following issues before a backup plan can be designed and properly implemented:

- How often will the backups occur?

- To what medium will the backups be made?

- Who will be responsible for the backups?

- How will the backups be verified?

- What will the policies be for backing up nonlogged operations?

- Does a standby server make sense for the installation?

- Will Window 2000's capabilities (such as clustering, drive mirroring, or RAID 5) be used to help protect data?

How Often Will the Backups Occur?

A backup is much like a spare tire—you may never need it, but it is a lifesaver when you do. How often you back up your data is directly related to how much data you will lose if the system suffers a major catastrophe. If you back up only once a week on the weekends, any crash suffered late in the week could mean many days of data will be lost. Conversely, if you back up the transaction log every hour, the most data you will lose will be an hour's worth.

The following recommendations are general ones—feel free to customize them for your situation:

Master database Schedule it for weekly backups and perform a manual backup after major modifications to your databases, devices, or users.

Msdb database Schedule it for weekly backups and perform a manual backup after major changes to jobs, events, operators, or alerts.

Tempdb database Don't bother backing it up because it is automatically cleared every time SQL Server is stopped and started.

Model database You should make a baseline backup of the Model database and then manually back it up whenever it changes (which won't be very often).

Pubs database Don't bother backing it up because it is simply a sample database that gives you live data to practice with. The only reason for backing it up would be to test your scheduling or to restore procedures.

User databases Schedule these so that changed data is backed up at least every night. One option is to do an entire database backup every night. Another option is to do an entire database backup on the weekends and back up just the log on weeknights. Although you can schedule the log to be backed up during the day (in case of failure), backing up the entire database during production hours may cause a slowdown on a heavily used server, and it will be harder for you to track and restore from the backup.

To What Medium Will the Backups Be Made?

SQL Server can back up databases to tape or to a dump device (a file). If a tape drive is used, it must be on the Windows HCL (Hardware Compatibility List) and installed in the computer running SQL Server.

SQL Server 2000 and Windows 2000 now use compatible file formats for tape backups. You can use the same tape drive and tape to perform both SQL Server and Windows backups.

Who Will Be Responsible for the Backups?

The scariest thing in the world is when two coadministrators both think the other one took care of the backups. Have a plan in place for the person in charge, and detail what is to happen on that person's day off.

How Will the Backups Be Verified?

Trusting the backups you've made without verifying them is like trusting your spare tire to be in good condition—it *probably* is, but…. The purpose of a backup is not simply to have a backup copy of something but to be able to restore it in a reasonable manner.

One of the best ways to verify that your backups are working is to restore them to a separate computer. Not only does this verify the integrity of your backups, it helps prepare you in case you have to bring up a spare server quickly.

What Will the Policies Be for Backing Up Nonlogged Operations?

Most transactions are logged by SQL Server in the transaction log. There are some transactions that are not logged, which means that if a database had to be restored, any and all of the nonlogged operations that happened since the last backup would be lost.

Nonlogged operations include the following:

- Fast bulk copies when Simple or Bulk Copy recovery modes are enabled
- SELECT INTO commands when Simple/Bulk Copy recovery mode is enabled

Bulk copies and the SELECT INTO command are covered in Chapter 7.

Back up the database before starting a nonlogged operation in case you need to restore the database to its previous state quickly.

Using Windows and Hardware to Protect SQL Server

The ultimate goal of designing and implementing a disaster recovery plan is to plan for, and protect the data in case of, a major catastrophe. Windows has several options you can use to protect data in case of hard drive failure, effectively keeping SQL Server from knowing that there has been a problem. Most hardware controllers also have options for various RAID levels.

Computer Management (using the Storage folder) is the Windows 2000 program used to create mirrored, duplexed, striped, and striped-with-parity drives (RAID 5). For more information, see *MCSE: Windows 2000 Server Study Guide* (Sybex, 2000).

RAID Drives

RAID (Redundant Array of Inexpensive Disks) drive arrays allow multiple disk drives to work as a single unit, providing increased speed and fault-tolerance. There are several ways to set up RAID drives, and the main methods are discussed in the following sections.

Disk Mirroring (RAID 1)

One protective option is to mirror the hard drive partitions so that all data writes are made to two separate physical hard drives (*RAID 1*; see Figure 6.1). In case of a hard drive failure, Windows 2000 simply uses the remaining hard drive until you replace the broken hard drive and remirror the system again. Disk mirroring is transparent to SQL Server—you set up disk mirroring through Windows and then install SQL Server normally.

FIGURE 6.1 Disk mirroring (RAID 1)

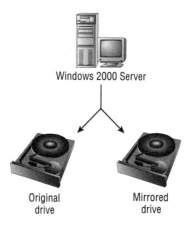

Windows 2000 Server

Original drive   Mirrored drive

Disk Duplexing (RAID 1)

Disk mirroring eliminates the hard drive as a single point of failure, but it still uses only one hard disk controller card. If the controller happens to fail, both the original and mirrored hard drives will contain corrupt data. Disk duplexing attempts to solve this potential problem by using two controller cards (see Figure 6.2).

FIGURE 6.2 Disk duplexing (RAID 1)

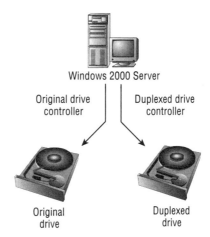

Disk duplexing is basically a fancier (and more reliable) way of doing disk mirroring. Simply install disk duplexing with Windows and then install SQL Server normally on the duplexed drives. In case of either a controller or hard disk failure, Windows will use the remaining controller and drive until a replacement can be made.

Make sure you use SCSI and not IDE or EIDE drives when you do your mirroring or duplexing. SCSI drives are independent, and a failure of one will not affect the others, whereas IDE and EIDE drives are linked in a master/slave relationship, where failure of one drive will probably keep the remaining drive from working.

Disk Striping (RAID 0)

Windows supports the creation of a stripe set (*RAID 0*) drive array, which is the fastest way you can set up your drives. Stripe sets run vertically across two or more physical drives so that more than one hard drive participates in writing and reading data (see Figure 6.3).

FIGURE 6.3 Disk striping (RAID 0)

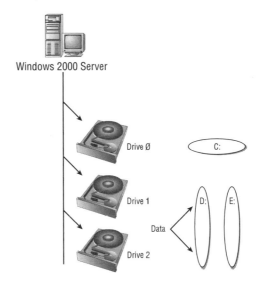

Stripe sets write in 64KB blocks of data and then move to the next drive for the next block of data. To use a striped drive array with SQL Server, create the striped drive array first with Windows and then install SQL Server normally.

Stripe sets have no redundancy built into them. If a hard drive that is part of a stripe set fails, none of the data in the stripe set (even on hard drives that are still good) will be usable. For data protection (at a cost of some speed), use striped-with-parity drive arrays (RAID 5 arrays).

Disk Striping with Parity (RAID 5)

Windows supports striped-with-parity drive arrays, commonly referred to as *RAID 5*, or just RAID, drives. When creating a striped-with-parity drive array, Windows will compute and store a parity or check bit that can be used to recover the data in case one of the hard drives in the array fails. RAID 5 drive arrays require at least three physical drives.

Figure 6.4 shows a striped-with-parity drive array with all the hard drives working. Figure 6.5 shows the same array but hard drive 2 has failed. Windows can reconstruct hard drive 2 in memory by using the parity bits spread across the remaining drives in the array (see Figure 6.6).

F I G U R E   6 . 4   Striped-with-parity (RAID 5) drive

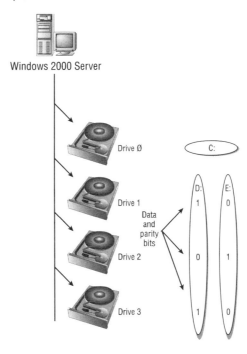

F I G U R E   6 . 5   Single hard drive failure on a striped-with-parity drive

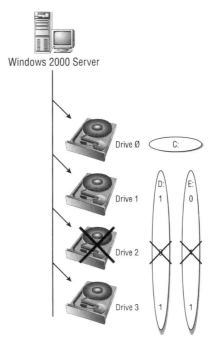

FIGURE 6.6 Reconstructing the lost drive

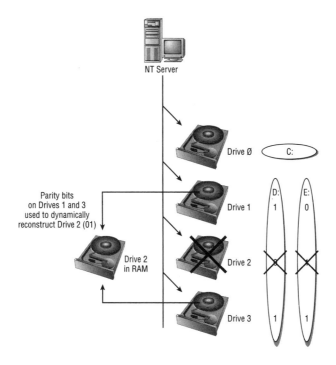

 Although striped-with-parity drives (RAID 5) aren't as fast as a plain striped drive (RAID 0), they do provide redundancy in case of hard disk failure.

To use striped-with-parity drives with SQL Server, simply create them using Windows and then install SQL Server normally.

 Most high-end servers support hardware-level RAID and may even provide a hot-backup hard drive (a spare hard drive already installed and connected) in case of failure. Hardware RAID, although faster than the software RAID that Windows NT supplies, is more expensive; it may also be proprietary, but it's highly recommended over software RAID (such as the software RAID that Windows supplies).

Mirroring a Striped Drive Array (RAID 0+1)

The major disadvantage of a striped drive (RAID 0) is its lack of fault-tolerance. If speed and fault-tolerance are both critical, you can create a striped drive array and then mirror it to provide fault-tolerance. This is called *RAID 0+1*. Although expensive, RAID 0+1 drives provide the fastest fault-tolerant solution.

Windows Clustering

Windows 2000 Advanced Server has a component that allows you to have a drive array shared between two file servers. The advantage of a Windows cluster is twofold. First, you have fault-tolerance in case of a physical problem with the server; second, you have increased performance if the bottleneck is not caused by the hard drive array.

A Windows cluster is made up of two servers that share the same hard drive array. There is an active/active cluster, where both servers are live and service requests, or an active/passive cluster, where the second server comes online only when the first server fails.

Windows clusters are designed to provide fault-tolerance for the operating system and the server hardware.

Standby Servers

A standby server consists of two servers: the production server and the standby server. The production server backs up the database on a regular basis (such as every 15 minutes) and the standby server restores those backups, so it is never more than 15 minutes behind. If the primary server goes down, the standby server can be renamed as the primary server and rebooted; it will then look and act like the primary server. Making a standby server work correctly involves a few steps:

1. Create the primary server as usual.

2. Create the secondary server with a unique name.

3. Do periodic full backups of the databases on the primary server.

4. Restore the backup files to the standby server.

5. Do frequent backups of the transaction log on the primary server.

6. Restore the backups of the transaction log to the standby server using the STANDBY switch (if you wish to make the standby database read-only) or the NO RECOVERY switch.

7. If you have the time to prepare to switch servers, perform a transaction log backup of the primary server and a restoration on the standby server and take the primary server offline.

8. Set the databases on the standby server for production use by using the RECOVERY switch.

9. Rename the standby server as the primary server and reboot the standby server.

10. Use the standby server normally until the primary server is ready to come back online; then simply follow steps 1 through 9 again.

Log Shipping

Log shipping is a way to automate the standby server process. Log shipping is only supported in SQL Server 2000 Enterprise Edition. It requires that you have a second server available with enough room for a copy of the database from the main server. Log shipping is configured by running the Database Maintenance Plan Wizard and choosing the Log Shipping option.

Microsoft
✓ *Exam*
Objective

Perform disaster recovery operations.

- Perform backups.

- Recover the system state and restore data.

- Configure, maintain, and troubleshoot log shipping.

For Exercise 6.1, we have two instances of SQL Server 2000 Enterprise Edition running: Win2k500\Production and Win2k500\Standby.

In Exercise 6.1, you'll use the Database Maintenance Plan Wizard to set up log shipping to configure a standby server.

Using Log Shipping to Configure a Standby Server

1. Create a directory on the production server in which to store the logs, such as `D:\Program Files\Microsoft SQL Server\MSSQL$Production\Logshipping`, and share the folder as `Logshipping`.

2. Create a directory for the standby server for the incoming logs, such as `D:\Program Files\Microsoft SQL Server\MSSQL$Standby\Logreceiving`, and share the folder as `Logreceiving`.

3. Start Enterprise Manager and make sure both servers are registered.

4. Go to the Options tab on the property sheet of the Pubs database of the Production instance and set the recovery option to Bulk-Logged. Click OK to save your change.

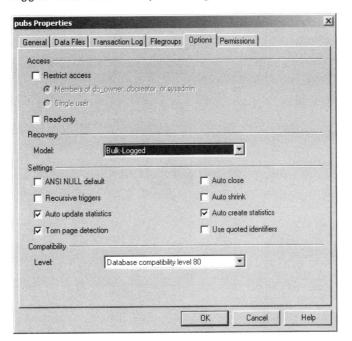

5. Highlight the Production instance and start the Database Maintenance Plan Wizard from the Tools menu.

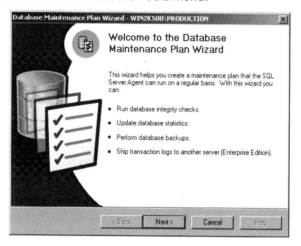

6. On the first screen, click Next to continue.

7. Check the bottom box, Ship the Transaction Logs…. Make sure the Pubs database is checked and click Next to continue.

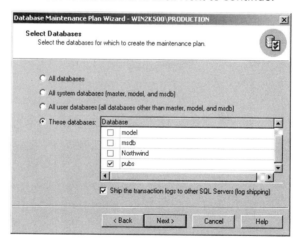

8. At the Update Data Optimization Information screen, click Next to continue.

9. At the Data Integrity Check screen, click Next to continue.

10. At the Specify Backup Plan screen, click Next to accept the defaults.

11. At the Specify Backup Disk Directory screen, click Next to accept the defaults.

12. At the Specify Transaction Log Backup Disk Directory screen, change the directory to the one you made in step 1. Click Next to continue.

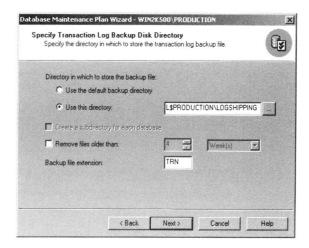

13. At the Specify the Transaction Log Share screen, enter or browse to the shared folder you created in step 1. Click Next to continue.

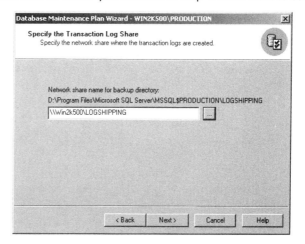

14. At the Specify Log Shipping Destinations screen, click Add to enter the information for the standby server.

15. In the Add Destination Database dialog box, choose the standby server name and the directory for incoming logs (created in step 2). Choose Create and Initialize New Database and name it pubstandby. Choose the default folders for the data and logs. Switch the database to standby mode. Click OK to save your changes.

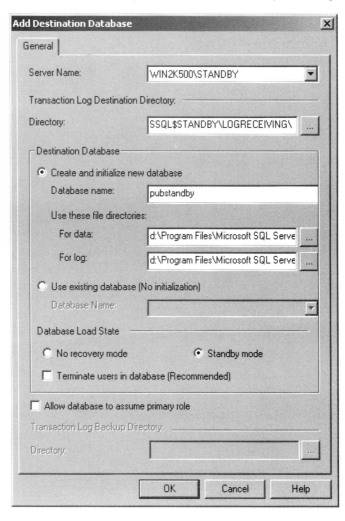

16. The Specify Log Shipping Destinations screen should list the server and database you specified in step 15. Click Next to continue.

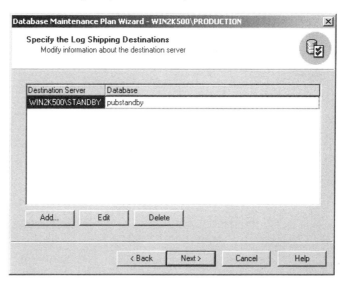

17. Choose to perform a full database backup now. Click Next to continue.

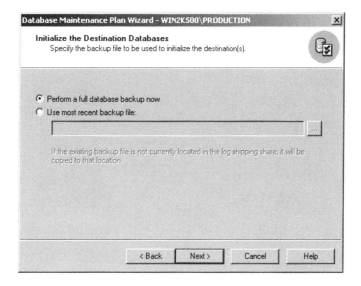

18. Choose the schedule for log shipping. To accept the default of every 15 minutes, simply click Next to continue.

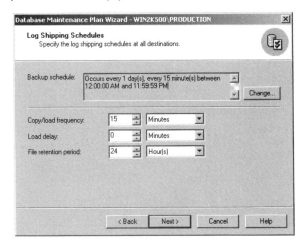

19. Leave the log shipping thresholds at their default settings and click Next to continue.

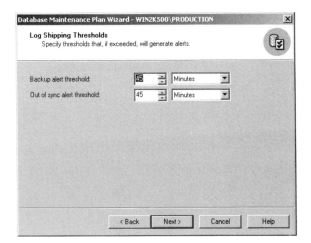

20. From the Log Monitor screen, choose the server from which you wish to monitor log shipping and the authentication model. To accept the defaults, click Next to continue.

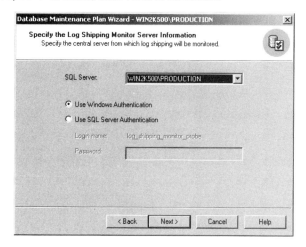

21. You can choose to generate reports from the report screen. Click Next to continue.

22. You can choose to keep a history of the plan at the next screen. Click Next to continue.

23. The summary screen shows you what the maintenance plan will do. Click Next to continue to the next screen, click Finish to save the plan, and then click OK after the plan is created.

EXERCISE 6.1 *(continued)*

24. To monitor log shipping, open Enterprise Manager and double-click the server you set up as the monitoring server in step 20. Then navigate to the Management\SQL Server Agent\Jobs folder for the monitoring server. You should see that the jobs were successfully completed (succeeded).

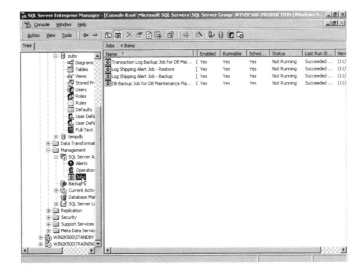

25. You can also go to the server specified as the monitoring server. You should see a new icon called Log Shipping Monitor in the Management folder. Open the monitor to see the status of log shipping

Using SQL Server to Protect Your Data

SQL Server has both automatic database recovery and support for user-initiated backups and restores. The automatic recovery feature is designed so that databases won't become corrupt if the server is unexpectedly stopped. The manual recovery features are supported to allow you to back up and restore critical databases in case of failure or user error.

Automatic recoveries happen every time SQL Server is started, and SQL Server allows you to back up your databases dynamically (while they are in use). These two features are extremely helpful because they prevent databases from getting corrupted even during unexpected outages and users can stay connected to the server during a backup.

Database Consistency Checker (DBCC)

One of the more unpleasant features of SQL Server is that the backup routines are more tolerant of errors than the restore routines. Because of this, backups may appear to work, but the backups are in fact worthless because they contain errors that cause the restore procedure to fail. There are various commands that check the database for errors.

Microsoft Exam Objective

Perform integrity checks. Methods include configuring the Database Maintenance Plan Wizard and using the Database Consistency Checker (DBCC).

These commands were already explained in Chapter 3—this is just a brief review because these commands are important for protecting your data.

These should be run on a regular basis to ensure that the database is in perfect working order:

DBCC CHECKDB Checks the database for errors. This is the command that you will probably run most often because it checks for common errors in the linkage of tables and index pages.

DBCC CHECKALLOC Checks allocation pages for errors and shows how extents have been allocated in the database.

DBCC CHECKCATALOG Checks the system tables for allocation and corruption errors.

> The Database Maintenance Plan Wizard not only allows you to run the DBCC commands, it can be set to stop the backup process if an error is found.

Transactions and Checkpoints

To help you understand backups and which part of the database is getting backed up with different commands, we must discuss transactions and checkpoints. A transaction is one or more commands that need to be processed as a whole in order to make sense. For example, withdrawing cash from an ATM is a transaction made up of two distinct parts: subtracting an amount from your account and delivering it to you as cash (see Figure 6.7). If only part of the transaction is performed, a system that is designed correctly will roll back, or throw out, the first part of the transaction.

FIGURE 6.7 A two-step transaction

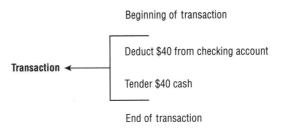

SQL Server treats each statement as a separate transaction by default, but SQL programmers can easily establish the starting and ending points of a transaction with the commands BEGIN TRANSACTION and COMMIT TRANSACTION, respectively. If the transaction is interrupted, SQL Server will roll back to the state it was in before the transaction was started. The SQL program itself can roll back the transaction by issuing a ROLLBACK TRANSACTION command at any time (such as when the user selects the Cancel button).

SQL Server doesn't write every single transaction to the database immediately; instead, transactions are cached and written to the database later. Because cached data is vulnerable to power outages, SQL Server also logs each transaction in the transaction log. In this way, SQL Server provides the best of both worlds by combining the speed of a cache with the data integrity of logged transactions. SQL Server flushes the cache to the database with a *checkpoint*; that is, it periodically writes modified data to the database. The database owner (DBO) can also issue a checkpoint at any time.

Automatic Recovery of Transactions

SQL Server incorporates a safety feature—the automatic recovery of databases—that runs whenever SQL Server is restarted. The safety feature cannot be disabled. It ensures that not only is the database brought up-to-date, but that only clean, completed transactions are put into the database.

In Exercise 6.2, you'll look at the SQL Server error log as well as the recovery interval settings.

EXERCISE 6.2

Examining the Error Log for Automatic Recovery Entries and Setting the Recovery Interval

1. Start Enterprise Manager and connect to your server.

2. Open the error log by opening the Management folder, opening the SQL Server Logs folder, and highlighting the Current log file.

3. Examine the log for transactions that were rolled forward or back. You should find transactions for the Master database, and if the server was stopped unexpectedly, you may find entries for the user databases.

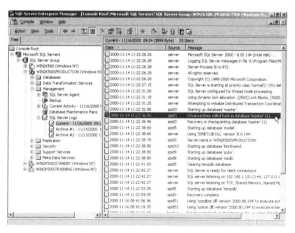

4. Close the error log.

EXERCISE 6.2 *(continued)*

5. Open the Configurations screen by highlighting and right-clicking the server and choosing Properties, or highlight the server and choose Action ≻ Properties from the main menu.

6. Choose the Database Settings tab.

7. The Recovery Interval option is near the bottom of the dialog box. Note that the default is 0, which means that SQL Server will automatically adjust the recovery interval so that restores are faster.

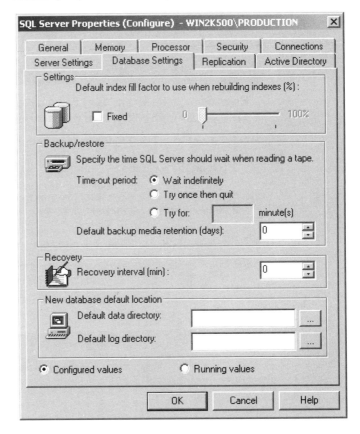

8. Close the screen by clicking Cancel or by clicking OK if you made a change.

Copying Databases with the Copy Database Wizard

There are several ways you can create a copy of your database:

- Use the Copy Database Wizard
- Do a full backup and then a restore
- Use Data Transformation Services (DTS)
- Detach a database, copy the files, and then reattach both the original and copied files
- Use SELECT INTO to copy only certain tables

Which method you use depends on whether you want the entire database or just a part, whether you need to transform the database or convert to a different sort order or character set, or whether you want to make the copy as easy as possible.

One of the neatest features of SQL Server is that it gives you the ability to easily move or copy your databases. If you want to copy your database, you can use the Copy Database Wizard or Data Transformation Services (DTS), but if you just want to move the database, you can use the sp_attach_db and sp_detach_db stored procedures.

The *sp_attach_db* and *sp_detach_db* procedures are useful if you develop a database on your laptop using SQL Personal Edition and then want to move the database to your production server. The sp_detach_db procedure closes the database and detaches the files from SQL Server so that you can move the files to another volume or server. You would then use sp_attach_db to attach the database files back into a running copy of SQL Server. Attaching and detaching databases was covered in Chapter 4.

The Copy Database Wizard is new with SQL Server 2000; it was designed to make copying databases easy. The wizard can copy only from one instance to another and cannot copy a database if one exists with the same name. To make a copy to the same instance with a different name, use DTS. (DTS is covered in Chapter 7.)

In Exercise 6.3, you'll use the Copy Database Wizard to make a copy of the database.

The Copy Database Wizard

1. Delete the Pubs database from your destination server.

2. Start the Copy Database Wizard. Choose Tools ➢ Wizards ➢ Management ➢ Copy Database Wizard or click the Wizard icon on the toolbar, and when the Select Wizard dialog box appears, choose the Copy Database Wizard from the Management category.

3. The first screen tells you what the wizard can do. Click Next to continue.

4. On the Select a Source Server screen, you can connect to the server on which the original database exists. Connect to your server and click Next to continue.

5. You can use the Select a Destination Server screen to connect to the server to which the database will get copied. Connect to your server and click Next to continue.

6. The Select the Databases to Move or Copy screen shows you which databases you can move or copy to the destination server. Select the check box in the Copy column for the Pubs database and click Next to continue.

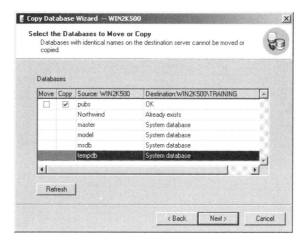

7. The Database File Location screen is where you choose the size of the new database files and the location in which they will be created. Leave the settings on the default size and location and click Next to continue.

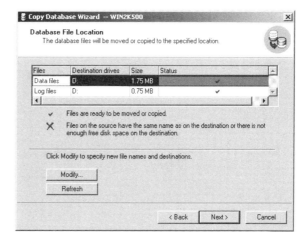

EXERCISE 6.3 *(continued)*

8. On the Select Related Objects screen, you can choose to copy objects associated with the database, such as logins, sorted procedures, jobs, and messages. Leave the defaults (which is to copy related objects) and click Next to continue.

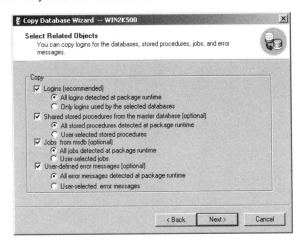

9. Use the Schedule the DTS Package screen to choose when to run the copy. Choose to run it immediately (the default) and click Next to continue.

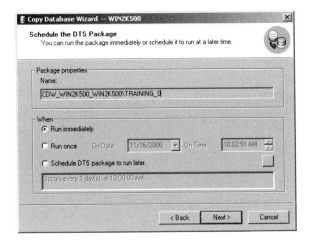

EXERCISE 6.3 *(continued)*

10. At the summary screen, click Finish to start the copy.

11. Choose OK after the package runs. You'll see a Log Detail screen, which you can examine for errors. Click Close to close the log.

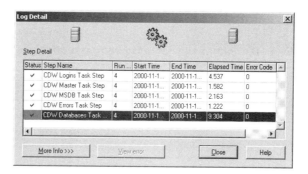

SQL Database Backup Modes

There are three backup modes your database can run in:

- Full recovery

- Bulk-Logged recovery

- Simple recovery

In *Full recovery mode*, everything gets logged in the database. Full recovery is a new option in SQL Server 2000.

Bulk-Logged recovery mode is much like it was in previous versions of SQL Server. Inserts, updates, and deletes get logged, but bulk copies, SELECT INTO statements, and index creations do not.

Simple recovery mode is basically the same as the SQL Server 7 database option of Truncate Log on Checkpoint, which means that nothing is held in the transaction log for very long. The transaction log is useful only for SQL internal recoveries in case the server is stopped unexpectedly but cannot be backed up or restored.

Simple recovery mode is the default mode for databases, but you will probably want to change it so that you can back up the transaction log separately from the database.

You can set the mode in which a database operates by using the Options tab of the database property sheet, as shown in Figure 6.8.

FIGURE 6.8 Setting the database backup mode

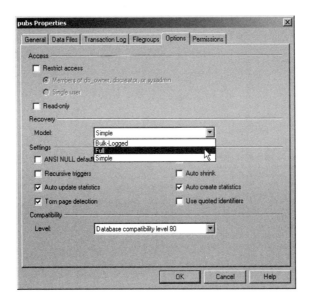

Backing Up Databases

You have several choices when backing up your data:

Full database backups   With a *full backup*, the entire database is backed up. Although they are the easiest to implement and restore from, full database backups may not be practical because of the amount of time required for very large databases.

Transaction log backups   Because the transaction log records all changes made to a database, doing a *transaction log backup* (backing up the log after performing an occasional full database backup) allows you to re-create the database without having to do a full database backup every time. You cannot back up the transaction log if you are running SQL Server in Simple recovery mode.

Differential database backups   *Differential backups* back up only data that has changed since the last full backup. This could be more efficient than transaction log backups for databases with existing data that changes often. For example, if a person's bank account changed 10 times in one day, the transaction log backup would contain all 10 changes but the differential backup would contain just the final amount.

Filegroup backups   *Filegroup backups* allow you to back up different pieces of the database, based on the various files that make up the database. Usually filegroup backups are done when the time required to perform a full database backup is prohibitive.

Microsoft
Exam
Objective

Perform disaster recovery operations.

- Perform backups.
- Recover the system state and restore data.
- Configure, maintain, and troubleshoot log shipping.

One of the best features of SQL Server database backups is that they are dynamic. That is, users do not have to disconnect from the server or even from the database while a backup is in progress. SQL Server 2000 has dramatically reduced the overhead for database backups. Various tests from Microsoft show about a 5-percent to 20-percent performance decrease during database backups.

Although databases can be backed up dynamically, various operations are not allowed during a backup:

- Creating or rebuilding indexes
- Creating or modifying tables
- Creating or modifying columns

Because SQL Server keeps the database files open while it is running, the databases are not backed up during regular Windows backups. In addition, with the default settings in SQL Server, your databases won't be backed up. You need to configure SQL Server backups for each database you want backed up. Once a backup has been made to a backup device or a file, the device (or file) is closed and will be backed up normally during Windows backups.

In Exercise 6.4, you'll attempt to rename the Master database file. The exercise demonstrates how Windows is not capable of backing up the open database file. This is an example of what can occur during a normal Windows backup when the backup program attempts to back up the database files while SQL Server is running. This exercise should help illustrate the need for some sort of organized backup program.

In Exercise 6.4, you won't be able to rename the Master.mdf file as long as SQL Server is running. If SQL Server is not running, the database files are like any other files and can be renamed. If this happens, simply change the name back to Master.mdf before restarting SQL Server.

EXERCISE 6.4

Attempting to Rename the *Master.mdf* Database File

1. Open Explorer and find the Master device—it will probably be in the \MSSQL7\Data path and be called Master.mdf.

2. Highlight the file and attempt to rename it Master.mdx. You should get an error message like the one shown here.

3. Click OK and change the name of the file back to Master.mdf.

Backing Up or Restoring to a Backup Device

SQL Server backs up databases to a *backup device* (called a *dump device* in earlier versions). SQL Server, however, has no built-in backup devices—you will need to create them yourself and configure your backups in order to have regularly backed-up databases.

You can create backup devices that point to files, or you can back up directly to tape. SQL Server 2000 uses the same tape format that various Windows backup programs use, so you can leave a single tape in the computer for both SQL Server and Windows backups.

If you use a tape drive, it should be listed on the Windows compatibility list and it should be mounted in the SQL Server computer. With some third-party backup software, the tape drive can be in a remote server, but SQL Server's native tape software doesn't allow that.

Because the majority of people back up to a file and then back the file up to tape as part of their Windows backup, we will focus primarily on backing up to files. Most of the principles for backing up to tape are the same.

Creating a Backup Device Using *Sp_addumpdevice*

Backup devices can be created with the `sp_addumpdevice` procedure. The syntax for the procedure specifies the logical name for the device and the path to the file that will be created after the backup is completed:

```
sp_addumpdevice 'type', 'logical name', 'path'
```

Follow the steps in Exercise 6.5 to make a backup device to which you can later back up the Master database.

EXERCISE 6.5

Creating a Backup Device Using T-SQL Commands

1. Create a new folder called C:\SQL2000_Backups or locate the \MSSQL7\Backup folder.

2. Open a Query Analyzer session.

3. Enter the following command:

```
sp_addumpdevice 'disk', 'master_backup',

    'c:\sql2000_backups\master.bak'
```

EXERCISE 6.5 *(continued)*

You can substitute the path to the \MSSQL7\Backup folder if you wish.

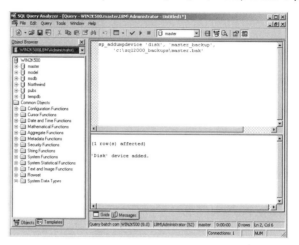

4. The results returned should say 'Disk' Device Added.

5. Verify the creation of the backup device by opening the Backup folder under the Management folder (you may have to choose Refresh to have the device appear).

Creating a Backup Device Using Enterprise Manager

Backup devices can be created quite easily using Enterprise Manager. To create a backup device, simply open the Backup folder and choose New Backup Device by clicking the right mouse button, or choose Action ➤ New Backup Device.

Follow the steps in Exercise 6.6 to create separate backup devices for the Pubs, Northwind, and Msdb databases.

EXERCISE 6.6

Creating Backup Devices Using Enterprise Manger

1. Open the Backup folder (under Management) inside Enterprise Manager.

2. Right-click (in the right pane) and choose New Backup Device or choose Action ➤ New Backup Device.

EXERCISE 6.6 *(continued)*

3. Create a device called pubs_full_backup and point it to the
   ...\Backup\Pubs_full_backup.bak file (the path will fill in automatically when you enter the name).

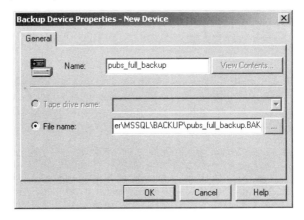

4. Click OK to make the device.

5. Create devices for the Northwind and Msdb databases using the
   same naming convention.

6. Create a device for the pubs transaction log with the name pubs_
   log_backup and with the path ...\Backup\Pubs_log_backup.bak.

7. Create a device for differential backups for the Pubs database and
   name it pubs_diff_backup with the path ...\Backup\Pubs_diff_
   backup.bak.

8. Look in the Backup folder to verify that all devices were made.

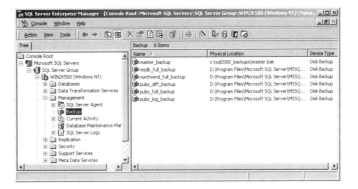

A backup device is essentially a pointer that SQL Server uses so that it knows where to put the backup file when the backup is actually done. Therefore, files are not created until the backup is actually performed.

Backing Up and Restoring Directly to or from Files

SQL Server 2000 has the capability to back up or restore directly to or from a file without requiring that a backup device be specified first.

The syntax in SQL Server to back up directly to a file is an extension of the BACKUP DATABASE command, using a TO keyword in front of the specified path and file instead of the device name. For example, to back up Pubs2 to a file, enter the following:

```
Backup Database Pubs2 to disk = 'C:\MSSQL\Dumps\Pubs2.dmp'
```

The RESTORE command works similarly, with the FROM switch added:

```
Load Database Pubs2 from disk = 'C:\MSSQL\DUMPS\Pubs2.dmp'
```

Enterprise Manager can also be used to back up to a file directly. Instead of selecting a backup device, simply enter the path of the file you wish to use, as shown in Figure 6.9.

FIGURE 6.9 Using Enterprise Manager to back up directly to a file

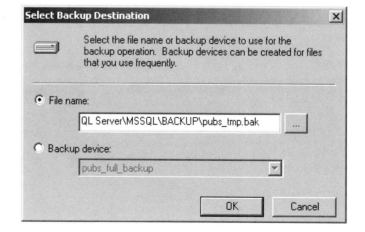

Performing Full Database Backups

The actual process of backing up the database is relatively straightforward. SQL Server allows a database to be backed up to a single backup device (or file) or to multiple devices (or files). The latter (when a database or transaction log is backed up across two or more devices) is called a *parallel striped backup*.

For example, backing up a database to tape may take an hour. If you have three tape drives in the SQL Server box and back up the database across all three devices, the backup would take approximately 20 minutes.

Another feature of striped backups is that they don't have to be restored simultaneously. A database that has been backed up on three different tape devices could be restored onto a SQL Server computer that has only one tape drive. You would restore the tapes in order: first, second, and third.

When a database backup is started, SQL Server will first do a checkpoint of the database and bring it up-to-date with all the completed transactions. SQL Server then backs up the entire database, taking note of when the backup started. If users are trying to insert or update data, they will be temporarily blocked by SQL Server while the backup process jumps ahead of the updates. SQL Server tracks all of the updates that are taking place during the backup process so they can be included in the backup as well. When the backup finishes, SQL Server will write all transactions that were completed during the backup process to the backup.

Any transactions that were not completed by the time the backup finished will not be included. Because of this, even though backups can be done during normal business hours, backing up the databases at night will help ensure that there is a clear understanding of what is in the backup as well as what didn't make it.

Backing Up the Full Database Using T-SQL Commands

Databases can be backed up by either issuing T-SQL commands or using Enterprise Manger. The syntax for the command that backs up databases is as follows:

```
Backup Database <name> to <device> (with init)
```

Earlier versions of SQL Server used the DUMP DATABASE command to back up databases. Although this older syntax is still supported in SQL Server 2000, it may be phased out in later versions and so is not recommended.

In Exercise 6.7, you'll back up the Master database using T-SQL commands (for this exercise, we assume that you have previously created the master_backup device as shown in Exercise 6.5).

EXERCISE 6.7

Backing Up Databases Using T-SQL Commands

1. Open a Query Analyzer session.

2. Enter the following command:

   Backup Database Master to master_backup with init

3. The results should look something like this.

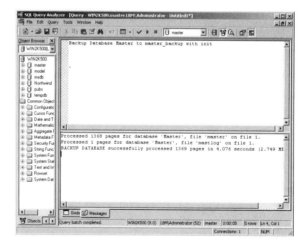

Backing Up the Full Database Using Enterprise Manager

Using Enterprise Manager to do full database backups is quite easy and intuitive, as shown in Exercise 6.8.

EXERCISE 6.8

Backing Up Databases Using Enterprise Manager

1. Highlight the Pubs database. Click the Options tab of the database's property sheet and make sure the database is not running in Simple recovery mode. If it is, switch it to Bulk-Logged mode.

2. Open the Backup dialog box by either right-clicking and choosing All Tasks ➢ Backup Database or choosing Backup Database from the Tools menu.

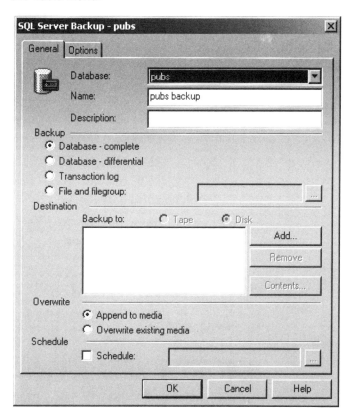

EXERCISE 6.8 *(continued)*

3. In the Destination section of the dialog box, click Add. In the Select Backup Destination dialog box, choose Backup Device, select Pubs_full_backup from the drop-down menu, and click OK to return to the Backup dialog box.

4. Select the Overwrite Existing Media option from the Overwrite portion of the screen.

Note that the default for backups is to append onto the existing backup file. You will need to select Overwrite Existing Media in order to overwrite any previous backups.

5. Click OK to start the backup. You should see blue bars go across the screen as the backup proceeds. The Pubs database should take only a few seconds to back up.

6. After the backup completes, click OK on the Confirmation screen to close the Backup dialog box.

Performing Parallel Striped Backups

Follow the steps in Exercise 6.9 to perform a parallel striped backup of the Northwind database.

EXERCISE 6.9

Performing a Parallel Striped Backup

1. Create two new backup devices—northwind_a_backup and northwind_b_backup (see Exercise 6.5 or 6.6).

EXERCISE 6.9 (continued)

2. Highlight the Northwind database and open the Backup dialog box by right-clicking and choosing All Tasks ➤ Backup Database or by choosing Backup Database from the Tools menu.

3. In the Destination area of the dialog box, click Add. In the Select Backup Destination dialog box, choose Backup Device, select the northwind_a_backup device from the drop-down menu, and click OK to return to the Backup dialog box.

4. Repeat step 3, this time selecting the northwind_b_backup device.

5. Select the Overwrite Existing Media option from the Overwrite portion of the screen.

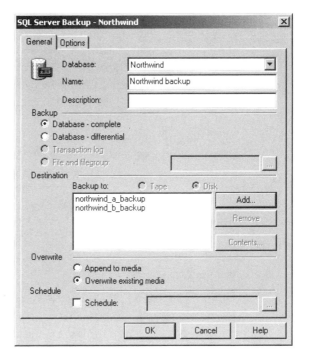

6. Click OK to perform the backup.

7. Click OK to close the Backup screen.

Performing Transaction Log Backups

If the database is not set to Simple recovery mode, the transaction log can be backed up and restored apart from the database.

The transaction log is a record of all the transactions that have occurred in a particular database. One of the features of SQL Server is that the transaction log is truncated (cleaned out) only after you issue the BACKUP TRANSACTION command. Many companies have run SQL Server for two or three months with no problems until they suddenly find that no new transactions can be recorded because the transaction log filled up.

The good news is that the transaction log will be cleaned out by SQL Server as part of a normal transaction log backup. The bad news is that SQL Server doesn't do this by default—all backups (and thus the cleaning, or truncating, of the log) must be configured by the administrator (unless you are running in Simple recovery mode, in which case the log is automatically cleaned out).

WARNING Although the Simple recovery mode option will automatically keep the log clean, it is not recommended for production environments because you cannot recover transactions that happened between database backups or do point-in-time restorations. You will also not be able to perform transaction log backups. If you do use the Simple recovery mode, make sure you perform frequent (at least nightly) database backups.

Another advantage of backing up the transaction log is that it can be restored up to a certain point in time. For example, if you had a backup of the transaction log for Wednesday and you later discovered that a major error had occurred at 4:05 P.M., you could restore the data up to 4:04 P.M., which is called point-in-time recovery.

Backing Up the Transaction Log Using SQL Syntax

Various switches can be added to the command to change the way the backup works:

TRUNCATE_ONLY This switch is used only to clean out the log. If the database is backed up in its entirety every night, maintaining a backup of the log would be redundant, yet the log still needs to be cleaned out. If this switch is used on a regular basis, you might want to set the database to Simple recovery mode.

NO_TRUNCATE This switch does the opposite of the TRUNCATE_ONLY switch—it backs up the log without cleaning it out. The main purpose of this switch is to make a new backup of the transaction log when the database itself is too damaged to work—or is completely gone.

NO_LOG   This switch does basically the same thing as TRUNCATE_ONLY, except it cleans out the log without even making a record. This switch is used for cleaning the log when it is so full the TRUNCATE_ONLY switch fails.

The log can be backed up by issuing the following command, which backs up the log and cleans it out:

```
Backup log <database> to <device>
```

Backing Up the Transaction Log Using Enterprise Manager

In Exercise 6.10, you'll add a new employee to simulate activity in the database and then back up the log.

EXERCISE 6.10

Backing Up the Transaction Log

1. In Enterprise Manager, make sure the Pubs database is set to Bulk-Logged mode and that you have made a full backup, as shown in Exercise 6.8.

2. Simulate activity in the database by issuing the following command from a Query Analyzer window in the Pubs database (the result should be that one row was affected):

```
INSERT EMPLOYEE VALUES

    ('KRM52936F', 'Katie', 'R', 'Olsen',

    DEFAULT, DEFAULT, DEFAULT, DEFAULT)
```

3. Open the Backup dialog box by highlighting the database in Enterprise Manager and selecting Backup Database from the Tools menu or by right-clicking the database and choosing All Tasks ➢ Backup Database.

4. Back up the transaction log by selecting Transaction Log in the Backup portion of the dialog box. In the Destination section, click Remove to remove any previous devices and add the pubs_log_ backup device (see step 3 in Exercise 6.9). Select Overwrite Existing Media and click OK to start the backup.

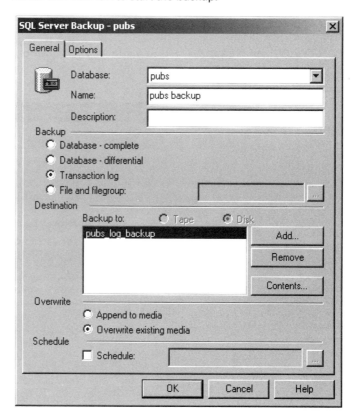

5. Click OK to close the window.

Performing Differential Backups

SQL Server 2000 gives you the ability to create a differential database backup, which records the final state of any added, edited, or deleted rows since the last full database backup. Differential backups are usually quicker to do and restore from than both full and transaction backups, but before you can do a differential backup, you have to have already done a full backup.

Differential backups, unlike transaction log backups, cannot be restored to a particular point in time because only the final state of the data is recorded. You may wish to combine differential backups with transaction log backups so you have the advantages of both types of backups.

Backing Up Using the Differential Model and T-SQL

To perform a differential backup using T-SQL syntax, simply open a Query Analyzer window and issue the following command:

```
Backup Database <database> to <device> with differential
```

Backing Up Using the Differential Model and Enterprise Manager

You can also use Enterprise Manager to perform differential backups, as demonstrated in Exercise 6.11.

EXERCISE 6.11

Performing a Differential Database Backup Using Enterprise Manager

1. Start Enterprise Manager.

2. Highlight the Pubs database and open the Backup dialog box by right-clicking and choosing All Tasks ➤ Backup Database or by choosing Backup Database from the Tools menu.

EXERCISE 6.11 *(continued)*

3. In the Backup dialog box, enter a description of the backup and select the Database - Differential radio button. In the Destination section, remove any previous devices, add the pubs_diff_backup device, and select Overwrite Existing Media. Click OK to start the backup.

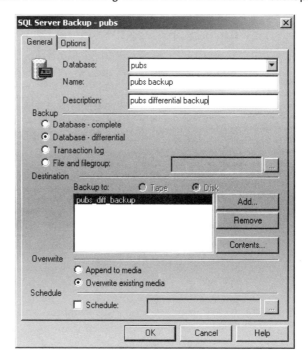

4. Click OK to close the Backup dialog box.

Performing Filegroup Backups

SQL Server 2000 also allows you to back up files and filegroups independently of the database. For example, suppose you have three data volumes (N:, O:, P:) and three filegroups (Employees, Customers, Orders), each residing on a different data volume. If the entire database took too long to back up, you could back up the Employees file on Monday, the Customers file on Tuesday, and the Orders file on Wednesday. Because the transaction log is not backed up when you back up files or filegroups, make sure you also perform a transaction log backup if you need to record the state of the database between filegroup backups.

Backing Up a Filegroup Using T-SQL Syntax

To perform the filegroup backup using T-SQL, issue the following command:

```
Backup database <database>
     file=<filename>,filegroup=<filegroup>
     to <device>
```

Backing Up a Filegroup Using Enterprise Manager

Enterprise Manager can also be used to perform a filegroup backup. In Exercise 6.12, you'll perform a filegroup backup of the Pubs database.

EXERCISE 6.12

Performing a Filegroup Backup Using Enterprise Manager

1. Start Enterprise Manager and open the Management\Backup folder.

2. Create a new device for the filegroup backup and name it pubs_ filegroup_backup.

3. Highlight the Pubs database and open the Backup dialog box by right-clicking and choosing All Tasks ➢ Backup Database or by choosing Backup Database from the Tools menu.

4. In the Backup dialog box, select the File and Filegroup radio button and click the browser button (the square button). In the Specify Filegroups and Files dialog box, select the PRIMARY filegroup (which also will select the Pubs file). Click OK to return to the Backup dialog box.

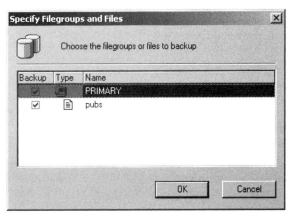

EXERCISE 6.12 *(continued)*

---

5. Enter a description for the backup. In the Destination section, remove any previous devices and select the pubs_filegroup_ backup device. Select Overwrite Existing Media and click OK to start the backup.

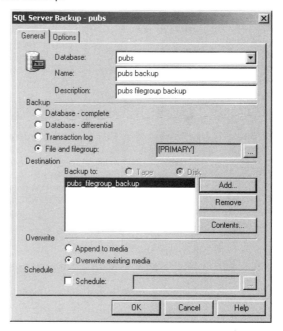

6. Click OK to close the Backup dialog box.

Scheduling Backups

SQL Server has built-in scheduling that allows you to set a recurring time for your backups. When you schedule backups, you are simply creating SQL Server jobs, which are handled by the SQL Executive service. Creating, editing, and deleting jobs is covered in detail in Chapter 8.

In Exercise 6.13, you'll schedule a backup of the Master database to occur nightly.

EXERCISE 6.13

Scheduling Backups

1. Start Enterprise Manager. Open the Databases folder. If the Master database is shown, right-click it and choose Backup Database.

If the Master database does not appear, you can change your settings to make it appear by highlighting the server and choosing Action ➢ Edit SQL Server Registration Properties or by right-clicking the server and choosing Edit SQL Server Registration Properties. Select Show System Databases and Objects and click OK. You can also leave the system databases hidden in the Databases folder and simply select the Master database from the Backup dialog box.

2. Open the Backup dialog box by highlighting the Database folder and choosing Action ➢ All Tasks ➢ Backup Database or by highlighting the Master database, right-clicking, and choosing All Tasks ➢ Backup Database.

3. Select to do a complete backup (the only possible choice for the Master database), enter a description, select the master_backup device, select Overwrite Existing Media, and check the Schedule box. Click the browser box next to Schedule to set the schedule.

4. Note that the default schedule is set for once a week on Sunday. Change the schedule by clicking the Change button to the right of the schedule.

5. In the Edit Recurring Job Schedule dialog box, you can schedule a task to start at various times and on various days. Choose Daily in the Occurs section and click OK to save your changes.

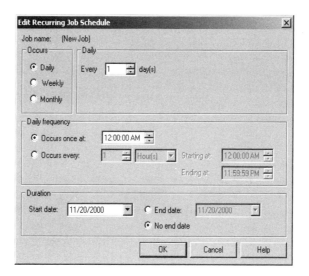

EXERCISE 6.13 *(continued)*

6. In the Edit Schedule dialog box, it should say, "Occurs every 1 day(s), at...." Click OK to save the schedule.

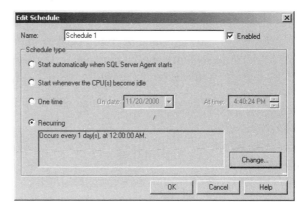

7. The Backup dialog box should look something like this. Click OK to save the scheduled backup. Note that to edit your job, you will need to go to the Management\SQL Server Agent\Jobs folder.

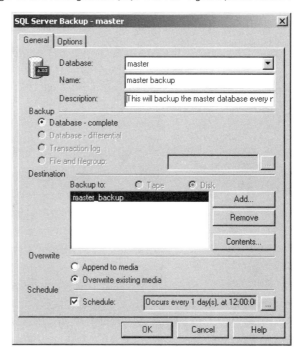

Backup Device Information

There are several different ways to get information about the backup devices and the dates and contents of the backups stored on them. The sp_helpdevice procedure can be used by itself to show all of the backup devices (as well as the system devices). You can also look at the Backup folder under Management in Enterprise Manager. And finally, you can restore just the header of a backup device to see what is in the backup.

In Exercise 6.14, you'll run the sp_helpdevice procedure and RESTORE HEADERONLY command and look at the backup (dump) devices in more detail using SQL and Query Analyzer.

EXERCISE 6.14

The *Sp_helpdevice* Procedure and *RESTORE HEADERONLY* Command

1. Start the Query Analyzer.

2. Choose Results Grid from the Query menu.

3. Enter **sp_helpdevice** in the command pane and execute the procedure.

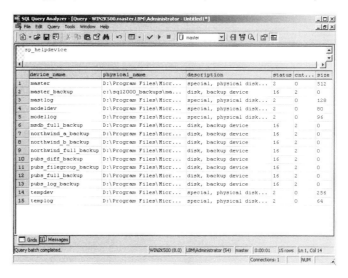

4. Enter the command **Restore headeronly from pubs_full_backup.** You should be able to see the contents of the pubs_full_backup device. You will probably have to scroll to the right to see all the fields.

5. Close the Query Analyzer.

Enterprise Manager can also be used to see the contents of backup devices. Exercise 6.15 shows how to examine backup devices.

EXERCISE 6.15

Using Enterprise Manager to Examine Backup Devices

1. Start Enterprise Manager.

2. Open the Management\Backup folder.

3. Highlight the pubs_full_backup device, right-click, and choose Properties.

4. Click the View Contents button.

5. You should see the same type of information that the RESTORE HEADERONLY command returned, including the database backed up, the type of backup, and the date of the backup, among other things. Note that you will probably have to scroll to the right to see all of the fields.

6. Click Close and Cancel to go back to Enterprise Manager.

The Database Maintenance Plan Wizard

The Database Maintenance Plan Wizard (first added to SQL Server 6.5) does a great job of scheduling backups and database maintenance.

Microsoft *Exam* *Objective*	**Perform integrity checks. Methods include configuring the Database Maintenance Plan Wizard and using the Database Consistency Checker (DBCC).**

The wizard is started from the menu or by choosing the Wizard icon. Exercise 6.16 will walk you through using the wizard to schedule regular backups of the Pubs database.

EXERCISE 6.16

The Database Maintenance Plan Wizard

1. Start the wizard by choosing Start ➢ Administer SQL Server Tasks ➢ Tools ➢ Wizards. Open the Management folder, highlight the Database Maintenance Plan Wizard, and click OK. (You can also start it by clicking the Wizard icon to open the list of wizards, highlighting it, and clicking OK.).

2. Click Next on the Introduction screen.

3. Select the databases on which you wish to run the wizard. For this exercise, you'll run it only on the Pubs database. Click Next to continue.

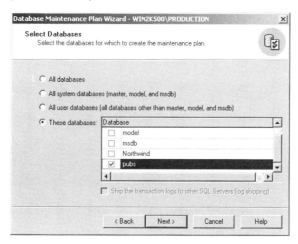

EXERCISE 6.16 *(continued)*

4. Select Reorganize Data and Index Pages to optimize the data and index pages. Click Next to continue.

If you select Remove Unused Space from Database Files, you are choosing to autoshrink the database. Note that you can change the default schedule for the reorganization by clicking the Change button.

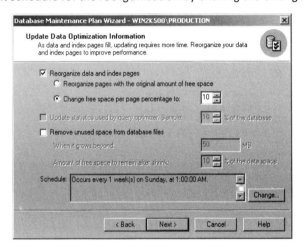

5. On the next screen, you can check the database for errors and automatically fix any errors found. Select Check Database Integrity to perform the tests. This screen offers the same functionality as the DBCC commands. Click Next to continue.

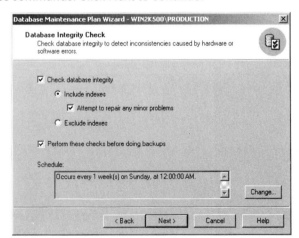

6. The choices on the next screen allow you to schedule the database backup. Note that you can uncheck the Verify option, although that is not recommended for beginning users. Click Next to continue.

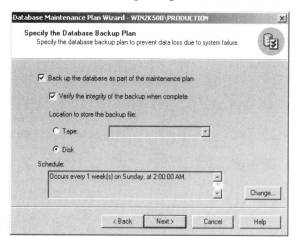

7. The next screen allows you to pick the location for the database backups. You can also set the automatic deletion of backups that are older than a specified number of weeks. Select to remove the files that are older than four weeks so that old backup files do not fill your hard drive. Note that files will be created with the *Database_type_time-stamp*.bak file-naming convention. Click Next to continue.

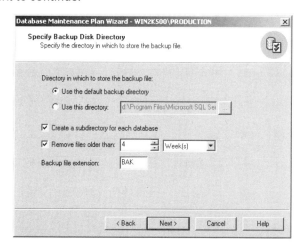

EXERCISE 6.16 *(continued)*

8. The next screen is similar to the one in step 7, except that this one pertains to the transaction logs of the database. Click Next to accept the defaults and continue.

9. Here you can generate reports and even have the maintenance report e-mailed to a specified person (providing you have e-mail support configured correctly). Click Next to continue.

10. On the Maintenance Plan History screen, you can configure how much history will be kept about the maintenance job and where the information will be stored. (You can also specify that the history be stored on a remote server.) Click Next to continue.

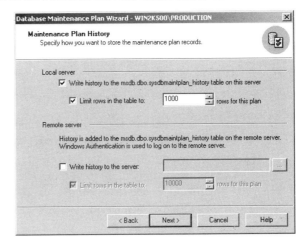

EXERCISE 6.16 *(continued)*

11. You will get a final confirmation screen about the maintenance plan. Click Finish to save the plan and OK at the Creating Confirmation screen.

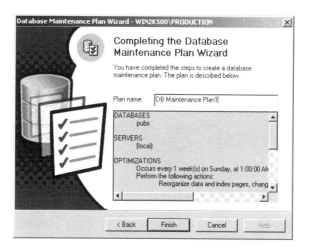

12. To monitor, edit, or delete the plan, open the Management\Database Maintenance Plan folder—your plan should be listed. To edit the plan, simply double-click it or right-click it and choose Properties.

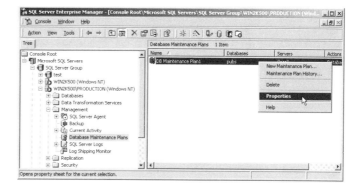

13. Click OK to save changes to the plan or Cancel to back out of any changes.

Restoring Databases

The process of restoring SQL databases can be summed up in the following steps:

- Attempt to back up the transaction log.

- Find and fix the cause of the failure.

- Drop all the affected databases.

- Restore the database from a full database backup or from a file or file-group backup.

- Restore the most recent differential database backup (if it exists).

- Restore the transaction logs from the time of the last full backup or the last differential backup (if the logs exist).

Microsoft ✓ *Exam Objective*

Perform disaster recovery operations.

- Perform backups.

- Recover the system state and restore data.

- Configure, maintain, and troubleshoot log shipping.

The older syntax of LOAD DATABASE and LOAD TRANSACTION can be used in place of the RESTORE DATABASE and RESTORE LOG commands, but they are not recommended because support for these older commands could be dropped with any newer version of SQL Server.

General Restore Steps

Although every data restoration scenario is different, there are several steps you should take when you realize the data will need to be restored.

Attempt to Back Up the Transaction Log

You should always try to create a transaction log backup after a database failure in order to capture all the transactions up to the time of the failure. You should use the no_truncate switch, which backs up the log when the database is unusable. If you successfully back up transactions to the point of the failure, simply restore this new transaction log backup set after you restore the other transaction log backups.

Find and Fix the Cause of the Failure

This step involves troubleshooting NT and/or SQL Server to determine the cause of the failure. There are two basic reasons for determining the cause—obviously, the first is to fix the problem, and the second is to take the appropriate steps to prevent it from happening in the future.

Drop the Affected Databases

Before the database can be re-created, it should first be dropped so that any references to bad hardware are deleted. You can delete it using either Enterprise Manager or the T-SQL DROP DATABASE <database> command. If hardware is not the reason you are restoring, you do not need to drop the database.

Restore the Database

Enterprise Manager can restore databases quickly. Simply highlight the database to be restored, right-click and choose All Tasks ➤ Restore Database, select the backup to restore, and click OK. If a database doesn't exist but you have a backup of it before it was deleted, you can re-create it by simply restoring the backup. Restoring a database using T-SQL syntax makes sense when restoring a database that doesn't already exist. If a database by the same name as the database in the backup set already exists, it will be overwritten. If you wish to restore a backup set to a differently named database, use the REPLACE switch (discussed later).

Although the syntax to do a restoration starts out simply, there are many options you can use to control exactly what is restored from which backup set.

The syntax to do a restoration is as follows:

```
Restore database <database> from <device> <options>.
```

Here are the most common options:

RESTRICTED_USER Only members of the db_owner, dbcreator, or sysadmin roles can access the newly restored database.

RECOVERY Recovers any transactions and allows the database to be used. This is the default if no options are specified.

NO_RECOVERY Allows additional transaction logs to be restored, and also does not allow the database to be used until the RECOVERY option is used. Basically the NO_RECOVERY switch allows you to restore multiple backups into the same database prior to bringing the database online.

If you use the NO_RECOVERY option by mistake (or end up not having any logs to restore), you can issue the command Restore Database <database> Recovery to activate the database.

REPLACE Required when the name of the database being restored is different than the one that was backed up.

STANDBY Allows the database to be read-only between log restores. This is used for standby servers or for other special purposes, such as testing the data contained in each transaction backup set.

RESTART Usually used with tape backups. RESTART allows you to restart an operation at the point of failure. For example, suppose you have five tapes and when you get to the last tape you insert the wrong one. By using the RESTART switch, you can simply insert tape 5 and quickly finish the job.

SQL Server wipes out the old database when you restore a full backup of a database—there is no merging of data.

In Exercise 6.17, you'll restore the Pubs database from a full database backup.

EXERCISE 6.17

Restoring a Full Database Using Enterprise Manager

1. Restore the Pubs database by right-clicking it and choosing All Tasks ➤ Restore Database.

2. On the list of backups, make sure that you only have the first backup (the full backup) selected (there will be a checkmark in the Restore column).

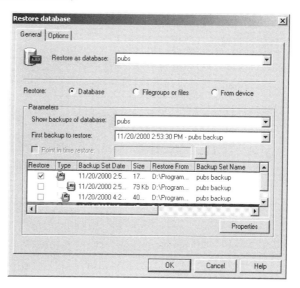

3. Go to the Options tab. Make sure that the recovery completion state is set to Leave Database Nonoperational so you can restore the transaction log later.

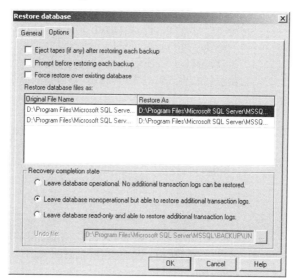

The three radio buttons at the bottom of the dialog box (in the Recovery Completion State section) correspond to the Recovery, No Recovery, and Standby options, respectively.

4. Click OK to start the restoration. Click OK at the Restoration Confirmation screen.

5. Go back to the Databases folder. The Pubs database should be grayed out and say "(Loading)" next to it.

Restoring Filegroups

You can restore filegroups by using either Enterprise Manager or T-SQL syntax. It is done in Enterprise Manager in much the same fashion as full database restorations are done.

The T-SQL syntax for restoring files and filegroups is as follows:

```
Restore Database <database> from <device>
    File=<logical filename>
    Filegroup=<logical filegroup name>
```

Restore the Most Recent Differential Backup

If you are doing differential backups, restore the most recent one. For example, you may doing full database backups on Sunday and differential backups on each weekday night. If you have a crash on Wednesday morning, you would restore the full backup from Sunday night and then restore the differential from Tuesday night.

To restore a differential backup, use the same syntax you use when restoring a full backup. Enterprise Manager screens are also similar.

Restore the Log

Enterprise Manager or the RESTORE LOG command can be used to restore transaction logs. Restoring transaction logs can be thought of as reapplying all the transactions just as they occurred.

Here is the T-SQL command to restore the log:

```
Restore Log <database> from <device> <options>
```

All the options that apply to the RESTORE DATABASE command also apply to the RESTORE LOG command, with the exception of the REPLACE option, which is not supported for log restorations.

Unlike restoring the entire database, restoring transaction logs literally reapplies all the transactions that took place between the time of the full database backup and the time of the transaction log backup, appending any changes to the database.

To restore transaction logs using Enterprise Manger, highlight the database you want restored and choose Tools ➤ All Tasks ➤ Restore Database or right-click and choose All Tasks ➤ Restore Database. Exercise 6.18 shows you how to restore the log files for the Pubs database and look at the results.

EXERCISE 6.18

Restoring Transaction Logs Using Enterprise Manager

1. Restore the Pubs database by highlighting it and selecting Restore Database from the right screen or by right-clicking and choosing All Tasks ➤ Restore Database.

2. Select From Device, then click Select Devices, and then select Add. Add just the pubs_log device to specifically restore just the transaction log. (You can also select just the log backup from the main restoration screen.)

3. Make sure you select the Restore Backup Set button and then the Transaction Log button under that.

EXERCISE 6.18 *(continued)*

If you have been appending backups to the backup devices, use the View Contents button to select the correct backup set to restore.

4. Click OK to restore the transaction log. Click OK to close the Confirmation window.

5. Test the restoration by opening a Query Analyzer window, going to the Pubs database, and entering the `select * from employee` command. The row added earlier (Katie Olsen) should appear.

Restoring to a Certain Time

SQL Server can restore transaction log backups up to a certain point in time. To do this, just choose a date and time from the Point in Time Restore dialog box, as shown in Figure 6.10.

FIGURE 6.10 Restoring to a certain point in time

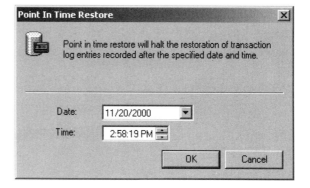

Restoring the Master Database with a Valid Backup

Because the Master database contains all the settings for SQL Server, restoring the Master database is not only more complicated, it's impossible to do accidentally. To restore the Master database, you must start SQL Server with the -m switch, which causes SQL Server to start in single-user mode.

When you rebuild the Master database, the Msdb, Model, and Distribution databases also are rebuilt (reset). You should restore these databases from your most recent backups or the scheduled jobs, alerts, operators, and ongoing replication will all disappear.

In Exercise 6.19, you'll start SQL Server in single-user mode and restore the Master database from a backup.

EXERCISE 6.19

Restoring the Master Database

1. Stop SQL Server.

2. Open a command prompt. Move to the Binn folder where SQL Server is installed.

3. Start SQL Server from a command prompt by issuing the following command:

   SQLSERVR -m

4. Minimize the command prompt.

5. Start Enterprise Manager (SQL Server will show a red stop light even though it is running).

6. Highlight the Master database.

7. Go to the Restore screen by right-clicking and choosing All Tasks ➢ Restore Database.

8. Select the master_backup device and click Restore Now.

9. After the Master database is restored, the command prompt should automatically stop SQL Server and return to a regular C:\ prompt.

10. Restart SQL Server normally.

Restoring the Master Database without a Backup

If the Master database becomes corrupt and a current backup is unavailable, there is a procedure that will allow you to re-create the Master database so that your user databases reappear. The steps are as follows:

Rebuilding the Master database does not fix the existing one; it creates a completely new Master database—just as though you reinstalled SQL Server.

- *Find and fix the cause of the failure.* Just as noted earlier, you will need to find and fix the hardware or software failure that caused the Master database to become corrupted.

- *Rebuild the Master database.* Use the `Rebuildm.exe` program to rebuild the Master database.

You will need some files from your original SQL Server CD-ROM in order to run Rebuildm.exe. Copy the \X86\DATA folder to your hard drive, change the properties of the folder to be Read-Write, and point Rebuildm.exe to that folder.

- *Attach valid database files to the Master database by running the* `sp_attach_db` *procedure for each file.* You can attach and detach databases without losing the data in the databases by using the `sp_attach_db` and `sp_detach_db` procedures. Because a newly rebuilt Master database will not know about any of your previous databases, you will need to run `sp_attach_db` for each of them.

- *Re-create the settings for SQL Server.* Because the rebuilt Master database holds all the settings for SQL Server, they will revert to the defaults. You will need to reconfigure SQL Server with its previous settings and probably stop and restart SQL Server to have them take effect. See Chapter 2 for more details on changing settings.

- *Re-create the users and security for each database.* Because the rebuilt Master database will only have the default SQL logins, you will need to re-create all of the logins. See Chapter 5 for more details.

- *Restore the Msdb, Model, and Distribution databases.* Rebuilding the Master database also rebuilds the Msdb database. Any tasks, alerts, and operators you have created will have to be re-created by hand if a current backup of the Msdb database is unavailable.

Summary

Preserving data under less than ideal situations is one of the primary responsibilities of a database administrator. There are several things to consider in protecting your data:

- Windows 2000 (and thus SQL Server) has several features that provide data protection, including disk mirroring, disk duplexing, and striped-with-parity drives (RAID 5 drives). Although a pure striped drive doesn't provide any data protection, it is the fastest way to set up your drives.

- Because SQL Server database devices are locked when SQL Server is running, data will not be backed up during normal Windows backups. The solution is to define backup devices, which are files that contain a backup of databases and transaction logs. After the backup process is complete, these devices are closed by SQL Server and can be backed up normally by Windows.

- Backups can be performed using T-SQL commands or through Enterprise Manager. Backups can also be scheduled to happen on a regular basis, in which case a SQL Executive task is created.

- When a database is restored, all the previous data and objects are deleted, but when a transaction log is restored, all the backed-up transactions are merely reapplied. Transaction logs can also be restored up to a certain date and time, making recovery from errors easier.

- Rebuilding the Master database resets it to a pristine new Master, which wipes out any users, devices, databases, and settings you may have had. The Master database can be restored only when SQL Server is run with the `-m` switch, which starts it in single-user mode. `Rebuildm.exe` is used to create a new Master database.

Exam Essentials

Know about the various RAID drive arrays.   You need to know the various advantages and disadvantages of RAID 0, RAID 1, RAID 5, and RAID 0+1 drive arrays.

Know how to perform full, differential, transactional, and filegroup backups. You need to know the T-SQL syntax and the Enterprise Manager methods of performing the various backups. You should also focus on the advantages and disadvantages of the various types of backups.

Know about the various database recovery modes. You need to know when to use Simple, Bulk-Logged, or Full recovery mode and the options and advantages and disadvantages of each.

Know how to restore a database. You need to know the SQL syntax and Enterprise Manager methods for restoring databases.

Know how to recover from a complex crash scenario. You need to know how to recover from complete crashes of SQL Server, as well as from a crashed Master database.

Key Terms

Bulk-Logged recovery mode	RAID 1
differential backups	RAID 5
filegroup backups	Rebuildm.exe
full backup	Simple recovery mode
Full recovery mode	transaction backup
RAID 0	sp_attach_db
RAID 0+1	sp_detach_db

Review Questions

1. What is the SQL Server command to back up databases?

   A. BACKUP DATABASE

   B. DUMP DATABASE

   C. BACKUP DEVICE

   D. DUMP DEVICE

2. How do you edit a recurring (scheduled) backup created with the Database Maintenance Plan Wizard? (Select all that apply.)

   A. You can't—you have to delete and re-create it.

   B. From the Database\Jobs folder within Enterprise Manager.

   C. From the SQL Agent\Jobs folder within Enterprise Manager.

   D. From the Management\Database Maintenance Plan folder within Enterprise Manager.

3. What is the SQL Server command to back up a transaction log?

   A. DUMP DATABASE /LOG

   B. DUMP LOG

   C. DUMP TRANSACTION

   D. BACKUP LOG

4. What does the NO_RECOVERY switch do?

   A. There is no such switch.

   B. It cleans out (truncates) the log without making a backup.

   C. It makes a backup of the log without cleaning it.

   D. It loads a backup of a database but leaves the database offline so you can continue restoring transaction logs.

5. When do you need to use the REPLACE switch?

    A. There is no such switch.

    B. When you are restoring into a database with data.

    C. When you are restoring into a database that is marked read-only.

    D. When the database you are restoring into has a different name than the originally backed-up database.

6. You buy a new server. Hard drive space is at a premium, but you want to use some sort of fault-tolerance. How should you install your volumes?

    A. RAID 0

    B. RAID 1

    C. RAID 5

    D. RAID 0+1

7. You have no budget for new equipment. You have a Windows 2000 server that was installed with three hard drives and two drive controllers. Which of the following can you set up with just Windows 2000? (Select all that apply.)

    A. Mirroring

    B. Duplexing

    C. Stripe

    D. Striped with parity

8. You need to create a backup job for your production server. Which program would you use?

    A. Transfer Manager

    B. Backup Manager

    C. Security Manager

    D. Enterprise Manager

9. Your database crashed. You have a recent backup. Which command would you use to get the database running again?

   A. RESTORE DATABASE

   B. RUN DATABASE RESTORE

   C. LOAD DATABASE

   D. UNDO DATABASE

10. You are a 24/7 shop. You only have one hour of maintenance opportunity every night, but your backups to tape are starting to take longer because the database is growing. Soon the backups will take longer than the one hour allocated to you. What should you do to decrease the time it takes to back up?

   A. Move the data to a RAID 5 volume.

   B. Move the data to a RAID 0+1 volume.

   C. Use replication to copy the database out to tape.

   D. Buy another tape drive and do parallel striped backups.

11. You have a recent full backup file of your database. Your hard drive that contained the database files (but none of the SQL system database files) crashed. After fixing the hard drive, which of these steps is redundant?

   A. Using the sp_attach_db procedure

   B. Creating the database

   C. Restoring the database

   D. Rebuilding the Master database

12. You wish to move a database to another SQL Server computer. You stop the first SQL Server computer and move the MDF and LDF files to the second server. What step must you take on the second server to install the database?

A. Restore the database from the MDF and LDF files.

B. Run the `sp_db_mount` procedure to bring the database online.

C. Create a new database and specify the path to the MDF and LDF files.

D. Run the `sp_attach_db` procedure.

13. You need to be able to restore your databases to any given time, but you have a very large database with many inserts and updates and it takes three hours to do a full backup. You implement the following steps: You schedule a full backup every week, with differential backups every night. You set the recovery option to Simple to keep the log small, and you schedule transaction log backups every hour. Will this solution work?

A. This solution works very well.

B. This solution will not work because you cannot combine differential backups with transaction log backups.

C. This solution will not work because you cannot schedule transaction log backups with full database backups.

D. This solution will not work because you cannot schedule transaction log backups when you have selected Simple recovery mode for a database.

14. You have three filegroups (FilesA, FilesB, FilesC). You are rotating your filegroup backups so that each filegroup gets backed up every third night. You are also doing transaction log backups. The files in FilesB get corrupted. Which of these steps would you take to restore the files? (Select all that apply and list your answers in the order the steps should be taken.)

   A. Restore the transaction log files that were created after the FilesB backup.

   B. Restore the FilesB filegroup.

   C. Back up the log with the NO_TRUNCATE switch.

   D. Restore the entire database.

15. You have an OLTP application that is mission critical, but it can survive up to 15 minutes of unscheduled downtime. You have an adequate—but not unlimited—budget. You also run daily reports on the server; they currently have to be run at night for performance reasons, but you would like to run them during the day. Which solution should you recommend?

   A. RAID 5 drives for your server

   B. A standby server with frequent transaction log backups

   C. An NT cluster server

   D. Replication to another server

16. You have a 100GB database with a 25GB transaction log. You have 10 25GB drives and 2 hard drive controllers. You want to minimize the time it takes to do backups and ensure fault-tolerance in case any drive fails. You also want to ensure maximum performance for your OLTP database. Which of these is the best solution?

    A. Create a 125GB RAID 5 set for the data and log. Create a single MDF file for the data and a single LDF file for the log. Schedule full database backups every week and transaction log backups every night.

    B. Create a 125GB RAID 0+1 set for the data and log. Create a single MDF file for the data and a single LDF file for the log. Schedule full database backups every week and transaction log backups every night.

    C. Create a 100GB RAID 5 set for the data and a 25GB RAID 0+1 set for the log. Create three filegroups for the data. Schedule a full backup every week, rotate filegroup backups during the week, and do a transaction log backup every night.

    D. Create a 100GB RAID 5 set for the data and a 25GB RAID 0+1 set for the log. Create a single MDF file for the data and a single LDF file for the log. Schedule full database backups every week and transaction log backups every night.

17. Which of these operations can you do while performing a full database backup? (Select all that apply.)

    A. Create a new index

    B. Update columns

    C. Import in a large number of rows

    D. Create a new table

18. You have a production server (called Production) that you configured using the Database Maintenance Plan Wizard to perform log shipping to two servers (called Standby1 and Standby2). Where does the Log Shipping Monitor run?

   A. On the Production server

   B. On Standby1 and Standby2

   C. On Production, Standby1, and Standby2

   D. On the server you designated in the Database Maintenance Plan Wizard

19. You have a server called Production. You are performing full backups every night at 11:00 P.M. and differential backups every hour on the hour. On Tuesday at 4:45 P.M., a user deletes all of the rows from a table. You find out after hours (the 5:00 backup was performed). What is the correct way to restore this database?

   A. Restore the full backup from Monday night. Restore the 5:00 differential backup until 4:44.

   B. Restore the full backup from Monday night. Restore each differential from Tuesday until 4:00.

   C. Restore the full backup from Monday night. Restore the differential from 4:00.

   D. Restore the full backup from Monday night. Restore the differential from 5:00.

20. What mode does a production database need to be running in to support log shipping? (Select all that apply.)

   A. Simple

   B. Transactional

   C. Full

   D. Bulk-Logged

Answers to Review Questions

1. A. You use the BACKUP DATABASE command to back up a database. There is no such command as DUMP DATABASE, although the old term for a database backup was "dump file." Also, right after the backup command, you need to specify the database you are going to back up.

2. C, D. You can edit the database maintenance plan from the SQL Agent/Jobs folder or from the Management\Database Maintenance Plan folder within Enterprise Manager. You can always edit jobs (if you have enough rights)—you don't have to delete them to fix them.

3. D. The BACKUP LOG command backs up the transaction log. The other commands will not work, although they look like they might.

4. D. NO_RECOVERY implies that more backups will be restored and does not open the database for normal use.

5. D. The REPLACE switch is used to override safety checks, such as when you restore a database to a different name.

6. C. RAID 5 (striped with parity) is the most efficient method of providing fault-tolerance. RAID 0+1 would be the fastest (it mirrors a striped array and thus loses half of the drive space), but because hard drive space is at a premium, RAID 5 is a better choice. RAID 0 is a striped array and doesn't provide any fault-tolerance, and RAID 1 is mirroring; half of the drives are used for mirroring.

7. A, B, C, D. Windows allows you to create each of these types of volumes without any extra hardware. You should note that, if you only had two hard drives, you would not be able to create a striped-with-parity drive.

8. D. Enterprise Manager is the program used to create backup jobs. DTS is used to transfer objects, and backup and security features are built into Enterprise Manager.

9. A. The RESTORE DATABASE command loads a backup. The other commands do not work, although they may look like they will.

10. D. Parallel striped backups decrease the time it takes to back up because the backup happens on two or more tape drives simultaneously. Making the hard drive array faster will not help because that is not where the bottleneck is likely to be during backups.

11. D. You need to rebuild the Master database only if it (or the drive it is on) crashes. If a single database crashes, you may need to re-create, restore, or reattach the database, depending on how it crashed.

12. D. The `sp_attach_db` procedure allows you to plug MDS and LDF files into a different SQL Server.

13. D. Transaction log backups won't work if the database is running in Simple recovery mode because the transaction log is being continually cleaned out.

14. C, B, A. You should always attempt to back up the log. Because only the FilesB filegroup is corrupt, you only have to restore the FilesB group. You restore just the transactions that took place after the last filegroup backup.

15. B. With a standby server, you can run reports as well as quickly replace the production server.

16. C. By creating RAID 0+1 drives for the log, you maximize performance. You also minimize backup and recovery time by using filegroup backups.

17. B, C. You cannot update the schema of a database, which includes changes to tables and indexes, during backups.

18. D. You can designate where you want the Log Shipping Monitor to run when you run the Database Maintenance Plan Wizard.

19. C. When you use differentials to restore, you only have to restore the most recent differential, and you cannot do point-in-time recoveries with differential backups.

20. C, D. A database needs to be running in Full or Bulk-Logged recovery mode in order to support log shipping.

Chapter

7

Managing your Data

MICROSOFT EXAM OBJECTIVES COVERED IN THIS CHAPTER:

✓ Set up Internet Information Services (IIS) virtual directories to support XML.

✓ Import and export data. Methods include the Bulk Insert task, the bulk copy program, Data Transformation Services (DTS), and heterogeneous queries.

✓ Develop and manage Data Transformation Services (DTS) packages.

✓ Manage linked servers.

  ▪ Manage OLE-DB Providers.

✓ Convert data types.

For additional coverage of the objectives in this chapter, see also Chapter 8.

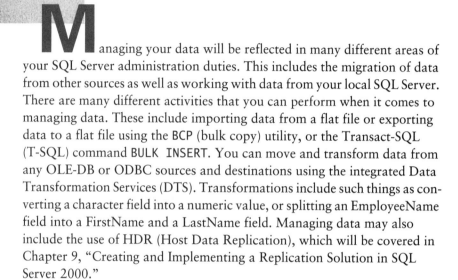

Managing your data will be reflected in many different areas of your SQL Server administration duties. This includes the migration of data from other sources as well as working with data from your local SQL Server. There are many different activities that you can perform when it comes to managing data. These include importing data from a flat file or exporting data to a flat file using the BCP (bulk copy) utility, or the Transact-SQL (T-SQL) command BULK INSERT. You can move and transform data from any OLE-DB or ODBC sources and destinations using the integrated Data Transformation Services (DTS). Transformations include such things as converting a character field into a numeric value, or splitting an EmployeeName field into a FirstName and a LastName field. Managing data may also include the use of HDR (Host Data Replication), which will be covered in Chapter 9, "Creating and Implementing a Replication Solution in SQL Server 2000."

You may also wish to move both data and database schema from one SQL Server 2000 computer to another SQL Server 2000 computer. Two other activities that involve your data are backup and restoration (addressed in Chapter 6, "Implementing Database Backups and Restorations") and replication (see Chapter 9, as noted above).

Let's look at using BCP to add data to your SQL Server.

Copying Data with BCP

Bulk copy, or BCP, is a lightning-fast command-line utility for moving data between a flat file and your SQL Server 2000 database. The upside of BCP is its speed and compatibility. If you do not have indexes created on your tables and the recovery model of the database is set to Bulk-Logged, reading an ASCII file into your server is very quick. There are several downsides, however:

- BCP has a cumbersome interface. Because it is a command-line utility, it requires you to remember a number of different switches as well as case-sensitivity.

- BCP transfers data only. It will not transfer other database objects like tables, views, and schema.

- BCP cannot do data transformations. These are such functions as converting a text string to a numeric value or vice-versa, splitting a Name field into a FirstName and a LastName field, and many other types of transformations.

With BCP, you can append data to an existing table just as you would if you were using a third-party utility like Visual Basic, but the BCP program is generally much quicker. When you export data using BCP, you will always overwrite the old flat file (if it exists).

When you use BCP to move data out of SQL Server, you should specify a name for the flat file. There are several common extensions:

BCP   Native-mode data files

csv   Comma-separated files

err   Error output files

fmt   BCP format files

txt   ASCII text files

To use BCP, you must have the appropriate permissions. When you wish to move data from a flat file into SQL Server 2000, you must have read permissions on the file itself (if using NTFS) and you must have INSERT permissions on the SQL Server table into which you would like to move the data.

To use BCP to move data from SQL Server to a flat file you must have NTFS permissions for either Change or Full Control on the directory and the file. If you are using a FAT or FAT32 partition, this is not an issue, as neither of these file systems supports permissions. Within SQL Server, you must have SELECT permissions on the table or view from which you want to pull your data.

Here is the syntax for BCP:

```
BCP{[[database_name].[owner].]{table_name | view_name} |
"query"}
{in | out | queryout | format} data_file
[-a packet_size]
[-b batch_size]
[-c]
[-C code_page]
[-e err_file]
[-E]
[-f format_file]
[-F first_row]
[-h "hint [,...n]"]
[-i input_file]
[-k]
[-L last_row]
[-m max_errors]
[-n]
[-N]
[-o output_file]
[-P password]
[-q]
[-r row_term]
[-R]
[-S server_name[\instance_name]]
[-t field_term]
[-T]
[-U login_id]
[-v]
[-V (60 | 65 | 70)] [-6]
[-w]
```

Following is an explanation of each parameter. Note that the only required parameters are `tablename`, in/out/queryout/format, `datafile`, and `login ID '/U'`.

databasename.owner.tablename or view_name or query   Specifies the name of the table you want to export from or import to. This can be a temporary table, a view, or a query. If you don't specify the *databasename* or the *owner*, these values will default to the current database and the username in the database of who is running the BCP command. For example, if you were logged in as AcctMgr in the Budget database and wanted to import into the tblBgtSummary table, you would specify `Budget.AcctMgr.tblBgtSummary` for this parameter.

in/out/queryout/format   Specifies whether you are loading data into SQL Server 2000 or extracting data out to a flat file.

datafile   Specifies the name of the flat file you wish to work with. You must specify the full file and pathname. If you do not, it will default to the local directory from which you run the BCP program. If you do not specify a filename, BCP will go into format file mode. This allows you to create a format file that can be reused later. The format file is simply a template for bulk copying data into or out of SQL Server 2000.

-a packet size   This option allows you to specify the size of the packets you are going to be transferring across the network. The default is 4096 bytes.

-b batch size   This option specifies how many records you are going to transfer in a single batch. SQL Server will treat each batch as a separate transaction. If this option is not specified, the entire file will be loaded as a single batch.

-c   This option is used to specify that the data being moved will all be converted to the character data type rather than the internal SQL Server datatypes. When used for export, it will create a tab-delimited flat file.

-C   This option (note the capital C) allows you to specify a code page for the data file. For example, you can generate a file with the code page 850, which was the default code page for SQL Server 6.

-e errfile   This option is used to create a path and filename containing the rows of data that BCP could not import or export properly. This can be very useful when you are troubleshooting your BCP operation. If you do not specify an error file, none will be generated. We suggest that you use the ERR file extension.

-E   The capital *E* specifies that identity columns in your SQL Server 2000 table should be temporarily turned off. This allows the values in the source file to replace the automatically generated identity values in the SQL Server table during the bulk copy. Identity columns are similar to the autonumber feature in Microsoft Access.

-f formatfile   This option allows you to specify the path and filename of the format file you wish to use during an insertion or extraction from SQL Server 2000. If you do not specify the *formatfile* portion of this option, BCP will prompt you for formatting information and then create a format file called BCP.fmt.

-F firstrow   The capital *F* and *firstrow* value allow you to specify a row other than the first row to begin reading into SQL Server 2000.

-h "hint"   This option allows you to specify any hints you wish to use. For example, you might create hints about check constraints or sort orders.

-i inputfile   This allows you to specify all these input parameters and store them in a file. When you run BCP again, all you need to do is specify this input file and all the stored parameters are used. As always, specify the full file and pathname.

-k   This option specifies that empty columns will retain their NULL values rather than having some default value applied to them.

-L   This option is used to specify the last row to load from the data file into SQL Server. If this is not specified, SQL Server will load all rows from the data file.

-m maxerrors   This option allows you to specify the maximum number of errors SQL Server will allow before the bulk copy process is canceled. You should specify this option if you are importing large data files. The default value is 10 errors.

-n   This option is used to specify that the data being transferred is in native format. In other words, the data being moved around retains its SQL Server 2000 datatypes. This option is especially useful when you are moving data from one SQL Server to another SQL Server.

-N   This option specifies that you will be using Unicode for character data and native format for all noncharacter data.

-o outputfile   This option specifies the name of the file that will receive any messages generated by the bulk copy. This option is useful when you run BCP from a batch file and later want to review what was processed.

-P password   This option is used to specify the password you wish to use when logging into SQL Server from BCP. If you do not specify a password, BCP will prompt you for one.

-q   This option is used to specify that quoted identifiers are being used. When this option is set, all identifiers (table name, column names, etc.) must be specified within double quotation marks.

-r row_term   This specifies the value that BCP will use to determine where one row ends and the next row begins. This is normally the \n switch, which specifies both a carriage return and line feed.

-R   This option instructs BCP to insert currency, date, and time data using the regional format for the client computer's locale setting.

-S servername   This option is used to specify the SQL Server to which you are connecting. If you don't specify a *servername*, BCP will assume the local SQL Server. Note: If you are connecting to a local server, BCP will run more quickly if you do not set this option, since setting this option forces BCP to go through the network interface rather than through an anonymous pipe.

-t field_term   This option is used to specify the field terminator. In many cases this will be the comma or a tab character.

-T   The capital *T* specifies that the bulk copy utility will connect to SQL Server over a trusted connection.

-U   This option specifies the login ID that you will use to gain access to SQL Server and is a required parameter.

-v   This option will report which DB-Library version is being used for the bulk copy process.

-V [60 | 65 | 70]   This instructs BCP to use datatypes from previous versions of SQL Server and should be used in conjunction with the -c or -n parameters.

-w   This option specifies that the data will be transferred using Unicode.

There are a few other items to keep in mind when you are using BCP. Character mode is the most flexible method of bulk copy because all data is treated as characters. This means that SQL Server and most other applications can work with the data. When you use character mode to export data, it will be stored as an ASCII text file. Native mode uses the internal SQL Server datatypes and can be faster for data transfers from one SQL Server to another SQL Server database.

When you are working with the data files, BCP needs to know where one field ends and another begins, as well as where one row of data ends and another begins. To do this, we specify a common character to be a terminator. You can use the following common characters as either field or row terminators:

\0   Specifies an ANSI NULL

\n   Specifies a new line

\r   Specifies a carriage return

\t   Specifies a tab

\\   Specifies a backslash

When you perform a bulk copy to import data, you can do it in normal mode, which means every insert is logged, or in fast mode, in which inserts are not logged. To operate in fast mode, you must set the database to Simple recovery mode and you must drop all indexes that are affected by the data transfer. Once you have done this, you can quickly add your data using bulk copy. When you do a bulk copy, you should also be aware that defaults and datatypes will always be enforced and rules, triggers, and constraints will always be ignored.

Since rules, triggers, and constraints are ignored during a fast bulk copy, you should check the validity of your data by running queries or other stored procedures. A simple way to check your constraints is to run an UPDATE statement and set a particular field equal to itself. This will force all constraints to be checked against the new data. It will also fire off any update triggers associated with the table.

Once you are happy with your data, you should re-create your indexes and then back up your database as it is now unrecoverable (because the import was not logged).

Exercise 7.1 uses BCP to create an output file. You will use this output file in the next exercise involving the BULK INSERT statement.

Creating an Output File Using BCP

1. Since BCP is a command-line utility, we will create a batch file to run our BCP command. Open the Notepad utility. Click Start ➤ Program Files ➤ Accessories ➤ Notepad.

2. From within the Notepad program, save the File as bcpOrdDet.bat in C:\Program Files\Microsoft SQL Server\MSSQL\Data.

3. Add the following code to the file. Be sure you do not add any extra characters or hit the Enter key. (While our code will span several lines on the page, yours should not.) Make sure everything is on one line. Replace the *<servername>* listed in this example with your servername.

   bcp "Northwind..Order Details" out

   "C:\Program Files\Microsoft SQL Server\MSSQL\DatabcpOrdDet.txt" -c -q -S*ServerName* -Usa -P*<password>*

4. When you are finished, save the file again and close Notepad.

5. Now it's time to run the bulk copy. Navigate to the bcpOrdDet.bat file and double-click it. It should run for a second or so and complete. It should then tell you that 2155 rows were copied.

6. If you navigate to the C:\Program Files\Microsoft SQL Server\MSSQL\Data folder, you will see the bcpOrdDet.txt file there at about 55KB. If you open the bcpOrdDet.txt file, you will see your data. It is tab-delimited. We chose the –c option, which automatically chooses the tab (\t) for a field terminator and the newline \n character for a row terminator. The –q parameter sets the quoted identifier value to on. You do this because the Order Details table has a space in it and therefore needs to be enclosed in quotation marks.

Using *BULK INSERT*

The *BULK INSERT* command treats data files like OLE-DB recordsets. Since SQL Server thinks the file is an OLE-DB recordset, it can move multiple records per step. You can move the entire file in one batch or in several batches.

One major difference between BCP and BULK INSERT is that BULK INSERT cannot move data from SQL Server to a file. Essentially, BULK INSERT gives you bulk copy capabilities through the use of T-SQL. Since BCP is a command-line utility, it can be placed into batch files; BULK INSERT cannot. You must be a member of the sysadmin or bulkadmin server roles to use the BULK INSERT command.

It is important to read through the BULK INSERT syntax and parameters at least once before the exam:

```
BULK INSERT [[database_name.][owner].]{table_name
FROM data_file}[WITH (
[BATCHSIZE = batch_size]]
[[,] CHECK_CONSTRAINTS]
[[,] CODEPAGE [= 'ACP' | 'OEM' | 'RAW' | 'code_page']]
[[,] DATAFILETYPE [= {'char' | 'native'| 'widechar' |
'widenative'}]]
[[,] FIELDTERMINATOR [= 'field_terminator']]
[[,] FIRSTROW [= first_row]]
[[,] FORMATFILE [= 'format_file_path']]
[[,] KEEPIDENTITY]
[[,] KEEPNULLS]
[[,] KILOBYTES_PER_BATCH [= kilobytes_per_batch]]
[[,] LASTROW [= last_row]]
[[,] MAXERRORS [= max_errors]]
[[,] ORDER ({column [ASC | DESC]} [, n])]
[[,] ROWS_PER_BATCH [= rows_per_batch]]
[[,] ROWTERMINATOR [= 'row_terminator']]
[[,] TABLOCK])]
```

Here are the parameters:

database_name.owner.table_name   The fully qualified table into which you BULK INSERT data.

data_file   The path and filename from which you wish to import.

CHECK_CONSTRAINTS   Specifies that constraints will be checked during the BULK INSERT.

CODEPAGE   This option specifies which *codepage* was used to generate the data file.

DATAFILETYPE   This option is used to specify in which format the data in the file has been stored. This could be character data, BCP native, Unicode character, or Unicode native.

FIELDTERMINATOR   This option specifies which character has been used as a field terminator. As with BCP, the default is a tab character (often shown as \t).

FIRSTROW   This option specifies the row with which you want to begin the BULK INSERT process. The default is the first row.

FORMATFILE   This option is used to specify the full file and pathname of a format file to be used with the BULK INSERT.

KEEPIDENTITY   This option is used to specify that IDENTITY values copied from the file will retain them rather than having SQL Server generate new values.

KEEPNULLS   This option is similar to the KEEPIDENTITY option. It specifies that NULL values in the data file will remain NULL values when loaded into the table.

KILOBYTES_PER_BATCH   This option allows you to specify the number of kilobytes to be move in each step. By default, this is the size of the entire file.

LASTROW   This option specifies which row you to want to use to end the BULK INSERT process. By default, it is the last row in the file.

ORDER   This option allows you to specify a sort order in the data file. This can improve performance in situations where the data file and SQL Server use different sort orders.

ROWS_PER_BATCH This option specifies how many rows of data to move in each step of the batch. If you use the BATCHSIZE option, you do not need to use this option. By default, all rows are moved in a single batch.

ROWTERMINATOR This option allows you to specify the end of a single row of data. The default value is the newline character \n.

TABLOCK This option specifies that a table lock, which will lock the entire table, should be used during the BULK INSERT procedure. No other users may make changes to data in the table during the upload. This can improve the BULK INSERT performance, but it will decrease performance for the other users.

In Exercise 7.2, you will use the BULK INSERT command to load your data from the bcpOrdDet.txt file you created in Exercise 7.1. To truly test the BULK INSERT command, you will first make a backup of the Order Details table using the SELECT INTO statement. You will then truncate the table, removing all data from the table in a single transaction. You will then use the BULK INSERT command to copy data from your text file back into SQL Server.

In the following exercise, you set the SELECT INTO/BULK COPY database option. This is equivalent to setting the recovery model to Simple.

EXERCISE 7.2

Loading Data Using the BULK INSERT Command

1. Open the Query Analyzer.

2. Run the following query to create a backup table of our Order Details items.

```
USE Northwind

GO

EXEC sp_dboption 'Northwind', 'select into/bulkcopy',
True

GO
```

```
SELECT * INTO tmpOrderDetails

FROM [Order Details]

GO

EXEC sp_dboption 'Northwind', 'select into/bulkcopy',
False

GO
```

3. You should be notified that 2155 rows were affected. Double-check that the rows were moved. Run the following:

```
SELECT * FROM tmpOrderDetails

GO
```

4. You should receive confirmation that there are 2155 rows in the temporary table. Now truncate the Order Details table. Run the following code and verify that there are no records left in the table by running the code sample shown after the GO keyword below.

```
TRUNCATE TABLE [Order Details]

GO

SELECT * FROM [Order Details]

GO
```

5. You should now have an empty Order Details table. Run the BULK INSERT command and move your data stored in the bcpOrdDet.txt file into the Order Details table. Run the following code:

```
BULK INSERT Northwind.dbo.[Order Details]

FROM 'C:\Program Files\Microsoft SQL
Server\MSSQL\Data\bcpOrdDet.txt'
```

6. You should see that 2155 rows were transferred. To verify, run the SQL code shown here:

```
SELECT * FROM [Order Details]

GO
```

Using Heterogeneous Queries

While importing data from text files will prove useful, it may not always meet your needs. Quite often you may need to access data from another type of database, such as Access or Oracle. Using the methods described thus far you would need to export the data from the third-party (or heterogeneous) database to a text file and then import it into your SQL Server. A better way to access heterogeneous data is to use *heterogeneous queries*.

Microsoft *Exam* *Objective*	**Manage linked servers.** • Manage OLE-DB Providers.

There are two ways to access heterogeneous data sources: ad hoc and linking servers. *Linked servers* (discussed in Chapter 3, "SQL Server Tools and Utilities") are used when you need to access you heterogeneous data on a regular basis. *Ad hoc queries* are used when you only need access to your data sources infrequently, such as for importing data. There are even two different commands for executing ad hoc queries:

- OPENROWSET can be used with any OLE-DB Provider that is capable of returning a rowset, whether or not it uses three-part notation. This is more flexible than OPENDATASOURCE but more difficult to configure.

- OPENDATASOURCE is used only with data sources that expose rowsets using the *catalog.schema.object* notation. This can be used in place of a linked server query but is not as flexible as OPENROWSET.

In Exercise 7.3 you will execute an ad hoc heterogeneous query using OPENROWSET with a SQL Server data source.

EXERCISE 7.3

Ad hoc Heterogeneous Query with OPENROWSET

1. Open Query Analyzer and log in.

2. Execute the following query view data from the pubs database using a heterogeneous query:

USE pubs

EXERCISE 7.3 *(continued)*

```
GO

SELECT hq.*

FROM OPENROWSET('SQLOLEDB','servername';'sa';'password',
    'SELECT * FROM pubs.dbo.authors ORDER BY au_lname, au_
fname') AS hq

GO
```

3. You should see a result set containing all of the data from the authors table. Close Query Analyzer.

Using Data Transformation Services

Microsoft Exam Objective

Import and export data. Methods include the Bulk Insert task, the bulk copy program, Data Transformation Services (DTS), and heterogeneous queries.

Develop and manage Data Transformation Services (DTS) packages.

Convert data types.

Most companies store their data in a variety of locations and a variety of formats. This includes Access databases, AS-400 mainframe systems, spreadsheets, and ASCII text files, among others. With *Data Transformation Services (DTS)*, you can import and export data between these sources and destinations. When you are working with data from two SQL Servers that are version 7 or higher, you can also transfer database objects and schema. This includes the stored procedures, views, permissions, table layouts, and other information and can be accomplished through the Transfer Manager.

SQL Server can move data through any OLE-DB– or ODBC-compliant data source and data destination. The DTS interface itself is a set of COM (Component Object Model)-based objects that allow you to do the following.

- Transfer data to and from Access, Excel, SQL Server, Oracle, DB2, ASCII text files, and other sources.

- Create DTS packages that are integrated with other COM-compliant third-party products.

- Schedule DTS packages.

Since COM-based objects are language independent, any computer language that supports COM can be used to interact with your DTS packages. This includes scripting languages like VBScript, JavaScript, and PerlScript. You can also use full-fledged programming languages like Visual Basic and C++ to interact with the DTS packages you create.

In the following sections, we will break down DTS into four distinct areas:

Packages   A *DTS package* encompasses all the components needed to perform an import, export, or transformation. This includes the tasks and the steps.

Import/Export Wizard   These Wizards quickly walk you through the process of creating a DTS package. Once you become more familiar with the Wizard process, you can use the dtswiz and dtsrun commands from the command line to bypass most of the Wizard's dialog boxes.

DTS Designer   This is a desktop environment similar to that found with Access or Visual Basic. You have palettes and toolboxes that allow you to visually create DTS packages.

Transfer Manager   The *Transfer Manager* is used to move data, schema, and objects (indexes, stored procedures, and so on) from one SQL Server computer to another SQL Server computer running SQL Server 7 or higher.

DTS Packages

DTS packages are a set of tasks designed into a workflow of steps. These steps and tasks are then grouped together into a package. You can create packages using the Import and Export Wizards, through a scripting language, from the command line using dtswiz and dtsrun, or visually through the DTS Designer.

Once you have created a package, it can be saved as a COM object. This means you can interact with this object through the Enterprise Manager Task Scheduler as well as the command line and COM-compliant languages. You can store your DTS packages in a number of formats and enforce several security mechanisms.

Let's first go through the components that are used to create a package. This includes:

- Task objects

- Step objects

- Connection objects

- Data pump

Task Objects

A DTS package is made up of steps that are associated with task objects. Each task defines a particular action that should be taken or some type of processing that should be done. Task objects can be used to perform the following activities:

- Move data from one OLE-DB– or ODBC-compliant data source to an OLE-DB–or ODBC-compliant data destination. This is often referred to as a Data Pump task.

- Run a T-SQL statement.

- Run a T-SQL batch.

- Execute external programs, batch files, or commands.

- Execute another DTS package.

- Execute COM-compliant scripts (VBScript, JavaScript, and PerlScript are currently supported within DTS itself).

- Gather results from other running DTS packages.

- Send e-mail using SQL Mail.

Step Objects

Step objects are used to coordinate the flow of tasks. While task objects are self-contained units, a task object that does not have an associated step object will not be executed. Essentially, you use step objects to structure your workflows.

Step objects can be executed in several different situations:

- Run step only when the prior step completes successfully.
- Run step only when the prior step fails to complete.
- Run step after prior step completes, regardless of success or failure.

This type of relationship between the different steps is known as *precedence constraints*. In other words, a later step has a precedence constraint on the prior step. Once all precedence constraints for a step are satisfied, the next step can begin execution.

Here is a quick example. Suppose you have three steps in your package. Step 1 calls a task that creates a new table. Once the new table has completed, you can run Step 2; this runs a task that runs a BCP batch to load the new table with data. Step 3 could then run a task to create new indexes on the newly created table. Step 2 has a precedence constraint on Step 1. Step 3 has a precedence constraint on Step 2.

Since task objects are separate from step objects, you can assign the same task to multiple steps.

Although task objects can be associated with multiple steps, a particular task can have only one instance of itself running at any given time.

As explained above, step objects can be executed conditionally based upon precedence constraints; another important feature of step objects is their ability to run in parallel. If a particular set of step objects has no precedence constraints, they will all run simultaneously. In Figure 7.1, you can see that steps 1 through 3 will run in parallel as none of them has a precedence constraint. Steps 4 and 5 will execute once steps 1 and 2 have completed. Steps 4 and 5 have precedence constraints. Step 6 will execute if Step 5 fails for some reason.

FIGURE 7.1 Steps can run in parallel

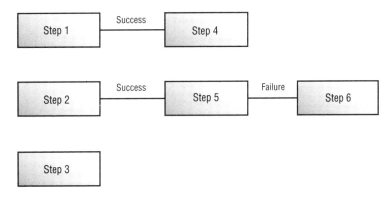

Precedence constraints are assigned by specifying that the next step will execute in one of several situations:

On success   This specifies that the next step will wait until the first step has completed successfully before beginning.

On failure   This specifies that the next step will wait until the first step issues a failure and then begin processing.

Unconditional   This option specifies that the next step will execute regardless of success or failure of the previous step.

Return codes   This option requires you to gather the return codes generated by calling a scripting language module. The scripting language allows you far more flexibility for working with your steps.

Connection Objects

In order to move data around, you must connect to both a data source and a data destination. DTS uses connection objects to accomplish this. These connection objects contain all the information necessary to make a connection, including the login IDs, passwords, filenames, locations of the data, format of the data, and so on. There are two types of connection objects:

Data file   A data file connection object specifies the location and data format of an ASCII file that will be used during the DTS process.

Data source   A data source connection object is used to specify OLE-DB– or ODBC-compliant data source and destination servers. This includes the server location, data format, login credentials, and passwords.

> **NOTE** Connections remain dormant until they are invoked. Once invoked, the connection will remain active until the DTS package has completed.

Data Pump Object

The DTS data pump object is an OLE-DB service provider that takes care of your importing, and exporting and the data transformation. It is an in-process COM server that runs in the process space of the SQL Server 2000 application. The data pump gathers data from one or more data sources and can transform the data before sending it out to one or more data destinations.

Since the DTS data pump is a COM-based object, you can greatly enhance the transformation services available by using COM-compliant scripting languages such as JavaScript, PerlScript, and VBScript. Figure 7.2 demonstrates the data flows from a data source through the data pump object and any of its transformations and then out to a data destination.

FIGURE 7.2 The DTS data flow

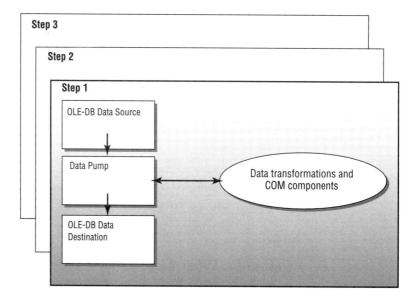

DTS Storage and Security

DTS packages can be stored in four locations. You can store them with SQL Server in the Msdb database, in the Microsoft SQL Server 2000 Meta Data Services, as a COM-based object (called a Structured Storage File), or as Visual Basic code. Each of these has advantages.

When you store packages in the Msdb database, other SQL Servers can connect to the packages and use them. This has an advantage over Meta Data Services, in that the storage requirements are lower. This in turn means that access time to the package is reduced.

Packages stored in Meta Data Services become available to other SQL Server 2000 computers. Meta Data Services can also make metadata (data about data) available to other applications. For example, it is possible to learn how many times a particular package has been run or how many packages there are. This creates a lineage, or history, of transformations that have been applied to your data. You can view the data sources and destinations as well as the transformations that have been applied. You can also see the changes to the transformations over time.

When you store packages as a Structured Storage File, they are stored as data objects and data streams. A data object is similar to a folder, while a data stream is similar to a file within that data object. These data-stream objects have an advantage in that they are easily disseminated throughout your network file servers or through e-mail. Keep in mind that any COM-compliant programming language can now manipulate your DTS package when it is stored as a COM data stream. Another advantage of a COM storage structure is the ability to encrypt your package and all its components. The only structures that are not encrypted are the VersionID, ID, Name, Description, and CreationDate.

The final method of package storage is straight Visual Basic code. This code can be opened and modified at any time and then executed just like regular VB code. This gives you a great deal of flexibility if you are a fluent VB programmer.

Two types of security are applied to your packages: DTS Owner and DTS Operator passwords. A user or application that has the DTS Operator password has the ability to execute the package but cannot modify or view the package components. A user or application with the DTS Owner password has complete access to the package. By default, when you store a package with an owner password, it will be encrypted; otherwise it is not.

Using the DTS Import and Export Wizards

In this section, we will walk through the Import Wizard process as an exercise. (Because the Export Wizard is nearly identical to the Import Wizard, it will not be covered.) In Exercise 7.4, you will import the Pubs-Authors table into the Northwind database.

The DTS Wizard has the following capabilities:

- Copies tables

- Copies query results, including the ability to create queries with the Query Builder Wizard

- Specifies data connection objects for both the source and destination

- Creates and schedules DTS packages

- Transforms data

- Runs scripting languages

- Saves packages in SQL Server, the Meta Data Services, and COM-structured storage

- Transfers database schema and objects using Transfer Manager from one SQL Server 2000 database to another SQL Server 2000 database

EXERCISE 7.4

Importing a Table Using the DTS Import Wizard

1. Open the Enterprise Manager and connect to your SQL Server.

2. Right-click the Data Transformation Services folder and choose All Tasks, then Import Data from the context menu.

3. You should now be at the Import Wizard Welcome screen. Click Next to continue.

4. You are now presented with the Choose a Data Source screen. Choose (local) for the Server. Enter **sa** as your Username, enter your sa password and choose the Pubs database for the database option. If Pubs does not show up in the drop-down listbox, click the Refresh button and try again. The Import Wizard is verifying that the data source and database really exist. If you click the Source listbox, you can see all the types of data sources and destinations currently supported in SQL Server 2000.

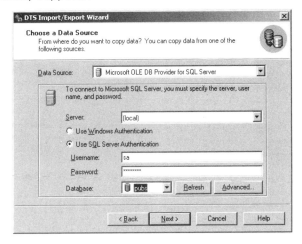

5. Click the Advanced button to display the Advanced Properties that you can work with.

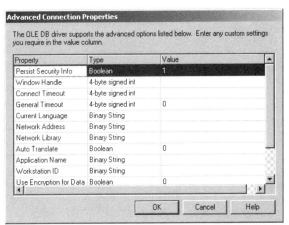

EXERCISE 7.4 *(continued)*

6. Click Cancel, then click Next to work with the Data Destination screen. Fill in the options as you did earlier, but change the database to Northwind, then click Next to continue.

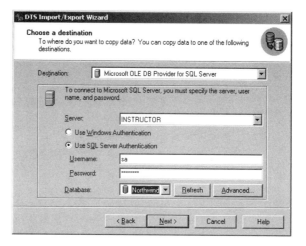

7. You are now presented with the Specify Table Copy or Query screen. If you choose Copy Table, it will move an entire table. Use a Query will allow you to specify a query and use the query builder. Since you selected a SQL Server 2000 data source and destination, you can transfer objects. This is the Transfer Manager interface. Select the Use a Query to Specify the Data to Transfer option and click Next to continue.

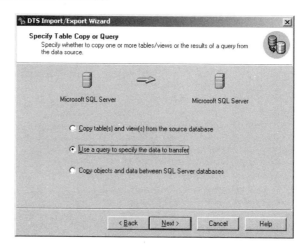

8. You are now presented with the Type SQL Statement screen as shown here. You can type in a query, use the Query Builder button, or load a query stored in a file. Once a query has been added, you can check it for syntax by clicking the Parse button. Click the Query Builder button.

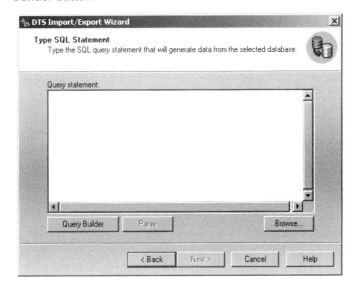

9. The Query Builder screen shows the tables in the source database. Expand the Authors table, click the au_lname field, and then click the button with the > character on it. Do the same for the au_fname and state fields. When you are finished, click Next to continue.

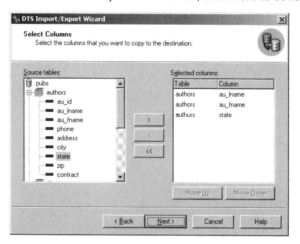

10. You are now presented with the Specify Sort Order screen. Select the au_lname field and click the right arrow again. You will be sorting this new table by the authors' last names. When you are finished, click Next to continue.

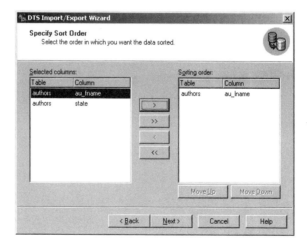

EXERCISE 7.4 *(continued)*

11. You are now presented with the Specify Query Criteria screen. Accept the defaults by clicking Next to continue.

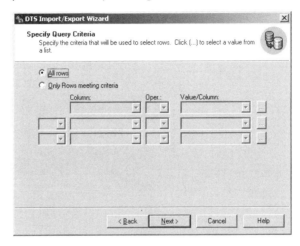

12. You should now be back at the Type SQL Statement screen, but now it has a query in it. Click Next to continue.

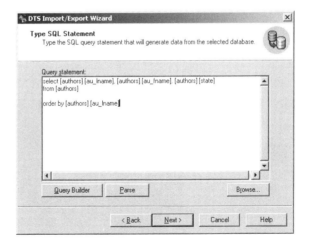

13. You should now see the Select Source Tables and Views screen. Notice that the Source table is Query and the Destination table is called Results. You can change that if you like. There is also an ellipsis (...) in the Transform field. You are going to make some minor changes here. Take a look at some of the more advanced transformations that you can work with and then make your simple change. Click the ellipsis in the Transform field.

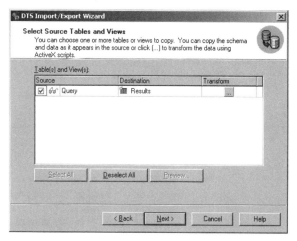

14. You are now presented with the Column Mappings and Transformations screen. Select the Create Destination Table and the Drop and Recreate Destination Table options.

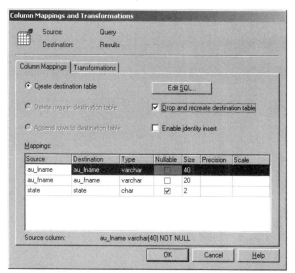

15. You are also going to edit the Create Table SQL statement. Click the Edit SQL button. Make certain that the only fields listed in the CREATE TABLE statement are the au_lname, au_fname, and state fields.

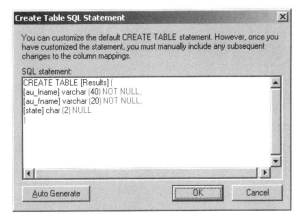

16. When you are finished, click OK. You are now back at the Column Mappings tab.

17. If you click the Transformations tab and then choose the Transform Information as it is copied to the destination option, you can specify your own custom transformations using VBScript or JavaScript.

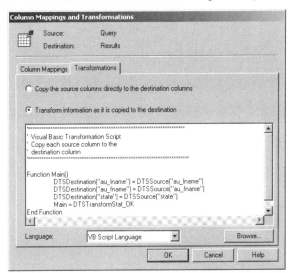

18. Click the OK button to return to the Select Source Tables screen. Click Next to continue processing.

19. You are now presented with the Save, Schedule, and Replicate Package screen shown here. The Run Immediately option will run the package as soon as it has completed. You can also choose to make the package available for replication and to set up a schedule for automatic execution. Select the Save DTS Package option to SQL Server as well. When you are finished, click Next to continue.

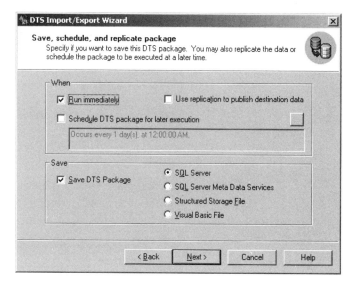

20. You are now presented with the Save DTS Package screen. Fill in the package name with **Authors**. Fill in the package description with **Authors and their home state**. Do not add a password or change any other options. Click Next to continue.

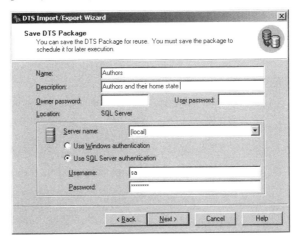

21. You are now presented with the Finish screen. Click Finish. You will see the package executing. You may be prompted with another dialog informing you that the package ran and completed successfully. Click OK and then Done to return to Enterprise Manager.

Transfer Manager

Through the Data Transformation Services Import and Export Wizards, you can transfer objects, security, and/or data from one database to another. When you use this method, the objects, data, and security in the original database are unaffected; they are copied to the receiving database, not actually moved.

In SQL Server 6.5, the Transfer Manager interface was a stand-alone component incorporated into the Enterprise Manager. In SQL Server 2000, this component has been incorporated into the DTS Import and Export Wizards.

Because new objects are being created, the user performing the transfer needs SELECT permissions in the source database and DBO permissions in the destination database.

Since this moves not only data, but schema from one SQL Server 7 or higher computer to another, this is ideal for situations when you want to transfer data from one platform to another. For example, you may wish to move both data and schema from an old SQL Server to a new system. Another nice feature of the Transfer Manager is that you can move data with one character set or sort order to another server with a different character set or sort order.

In Exercise 7.5, you will create a new database and then use the Transfer Manager to move the Pubs database to it.

EXERCISE 7.5

Copying a Database Using the Transfer Manager

1. Open the Enterprise Manager and drill down through the console tree to the Data Transformation Services icon. Right-click the icon and select All Tasks. From the All Tasks menu, select Export Data.

2. You are now at the same introduction screen that you saw for the DTS Import in Exercise 7.4. Click Next to continue.

3. Fill in the Choose a Data Source screen as shown here. Your Server should be entered as **(local)**, your Username as **sa** (don't forget the sa password), and your Database as **pubs**. If you don't see the Pubs database, click Refresh and look again.

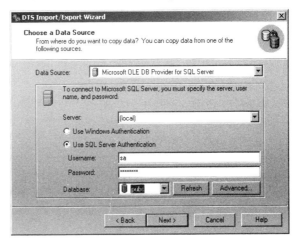

4. When you have filled in the information click Next to continue. You are now looking at the Data Destination screen. Enter **(local)** for the server again and **sa** as the login; on the Database drop-down list-box, enter **<new>**.

5. You should now see the small Create Database screen shown here. Fill in the name as **NewPubs**. The Data File Size should be 2MB and the Log File Size should be 1MB. Click OK when you are finished.

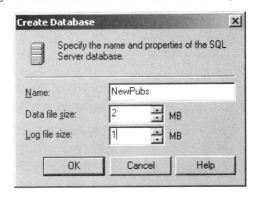

6. Your Choose a Destination screen should now have NewPubs listed in the database selection box. Click Next to continue.

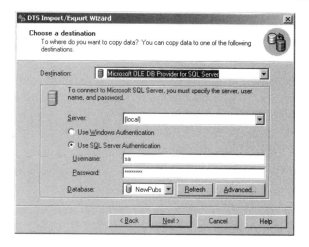

7. In the Specify Table Copy or Query screen, select the Copy Objects option and click Next.

8. You are now presented with the Select Objects to Copy screen. You can choose the following options:

Create Destination Objects This option allows you to have SQL Server generate scripts that will then create your destination objects. Optional parameters include the ability to drop those objects first if they already exist in your destination database.

Copy Data You can also have the data (rather than just the database schema) copied. When you copy the data, you need to specify whether you are going to replace the existing data or just append the copied data to it.

Use Collation This option allows you to copy data between databases that use a different collation.

Copy All Objects You can also transfer all database objects— views, stored procedures, indexes, and so on—and use the default options to do so.

EXERCISE 7.5 *(continued)*

Use Default Options Unchecking this option allows you to specify advanced copy options such as whether to copy logins, indexes, views, etc.

Script File Directory This allows you to specify the directory in which you want the scripts files generated by this transfer to reside.

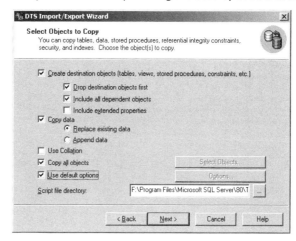

9. You should take a closer look at the default options and the transferred objects. Deselect the Transfer All Objects and Use Default Options checkboxes.

10. Click the Select Objects button. You should now see the Select Objects screen. You can choose which objects you wish to transfer, as well as which objects you wish to see in the list. As shown in the graphic, choose all the options at the top of the screen. Click the Select All button to highlight all the objects listed. Click Check, which will put a checkmark next to each object. Click OK when you are finished.

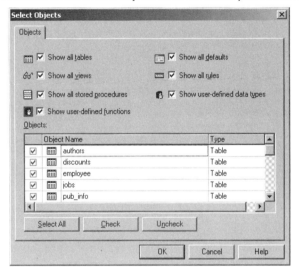

11. Click the Options button. You are now looking at the various options used for the transfer of your data.

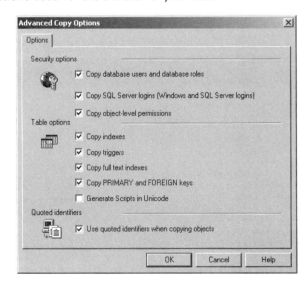

EXERCISE 7.5 *(continued)*

12. Leave all the selected options and click OK to return to the Transfer screen.

13. Click Next to continue.

14. You now have the option of deciding when you wish to run the package and whether or not you wish to save it. You are going to run the package immediately and then take a look at what it does. Click Next to continue.

15. Click Finish to complete the process. You will see the package being processed and data being moved. When it is all finished, select Close or Done to end the process.

16. You should now have a new database called NewPubs with all the data, stored procedures, views, and other items found in the original. If you don't see it in the Enterprise Manager console, right-click the Databases folder and choose Refresh.

If this exercise fails, you may need to delete the EntAppRole application role that was created in Chapter 5, "Working with SQL Server 2000 Security."

If you navigate to the C:\Program Files\Microsoft SQL Server folder, you will see a list of script files that the Transfer Manager generated. Table 7.1 lists the files and their associated properties. You should note that the naming convention for these files is *servername.databasename .extension.*

In this table, the server's name is Instructor. There are also BCP files created by the Transfer Manager to move the data from one file to the next. These have the format *dbo.table.bcp.*

TABLE 7.1 Log and Script Files Created by the Transfer Process

File Name	Purpose
Instructor.Pubs.LOG	Log of errors and warnings about the source database
Instructor.NewPubs.LOG	Log of errors and warning about the destination database

TABLE 7.1 Log and Script Files Created by the Transfer Process *(continued)*

File Name	Purpose
Instructor.Pubs.BND	Table bindings
Instructor.Pubs.DEF	Script used to create defaults
Instructor.Pubs.DP1	Script used to drop table constraints
Instructor.Pubs.DP2	Script used to drop database objects
Instructor.Pubs.DR1	Script used to add primary keys to tables
Instructor.Pubs.DR2	Script used to add defaults, rules, and other constraints
Instructor.Pubs.FKY	Script used to add foreign keys to tables
Instructor.Pubs..GRP	Script used to add roles (groups) to the database
Instructor.Pubs.ID1	Script used to create clustered indexes
Instructor.Pubs.ID2	Script used to create nonclustered indexes
Instructor.Pubs.LGN	Script used to create SQL Server logins
Instructor.Pubs.PRC	Script used to create stored procedures
Instructor.Pubs.PRV	Script used to create permissions
Instructor.Pubs.RUL	Script used to create rules
Instructor.Pubs.TAB	Script used to create tables
Instructor.Pubs.TRG	Script used to create triggers
Instructor.Pubs.UDT	Script used to create user-defined datatypes
Instructor.Pubs.USR	Script used to create user names and statement permissions
Instructor.Pubs.VIW	Script used to create views

DTS Designer

The *DTS Designer* is a GUI-based utility you can use to create and edit your DTS packages. Although the details of the GUI are beyond the scope of this book, we would like you to take a look at it. Follow the steps outlined here:

1. Open the SQL Enterprise Manager.

2. Drill down through the console tree into the Data Transformation Services folder.

3. Click the Local Packages icon. You should now see the Authors package you created earlier.

4. Right-click the Authors package and choose Design Package as shown in Figure 7.3.

FIGURE 7.3 Opening the package designer

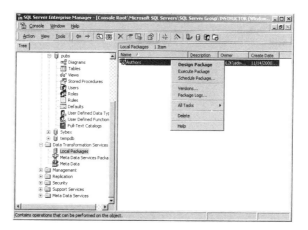

5. You should now see the DTS Designer screen with a similar layout to what is displayed in Figure 7.3.

FIGURE 7.4 DTS Designer

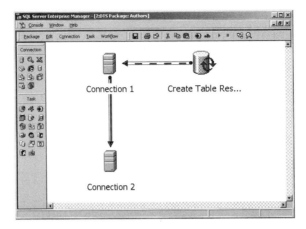

6. Right-click any of the objects or connections to view their information.

7. Close the package designer when you are finished.

Using DTSRUN

Once you have created your package, you have two choices for running it. One way is through Enterprise Manager, which works well if you have access to the program. Another way is through *DTSRUN*, a command-line utility that can be incorporated in a batch file and scheduled with other operating system commands.

There are a number of switches that can be used to modify the way DTSRUN behaves:

```
dts[/?] |
[
[
/[~]S server_name[\instance_name]
{ {/[~]U user_name [/[~]P password]} | /E }
]
{
{/[~]N package_name }
| {/[~]G package_guid_string}
| {/[~]V package_version_guid_string}
}
```

```
[/[~]M package_password]
[/[~]F filename]
[/[~]R repository_database_name]
[/A global_variable_name:typeid=value]
[/L log_file_name]
[/W NT_event_log_completion_status]
[/Z] [/!X] [/!D] [/!Y] [/!C]
]
```

~   The tilde (~) symbol specifies that following text is encrypted and in hexadecimal format.

S *server_name*   This is the name of the server to connect to.

U *user_name*   This is a valid login ID on the server specified by the S parameter.

P *password*   This is the password for the username specified by the U parameter.

E   This allows the user to connect with a trusted connection, meaning that SQL trusts Windows to verify the users password. When this is used, no password is required.

N *name*   This is the name of the DTS package to run.

G *GUID*   DTS packages are assigned a Globally Unique Identifier (GUID) at creation time that can be used instead of the name to reference the package.

V *version_id*   Each time a package is modified, it is assigned a new version ID. This option allows you to specify the version of the package to run.

M *package_password*   This is an optional password that can be assigned to a DTS package at creation time.

F *filename*   This option is used to access DTS packages that are saved as structured storage files.

R *repository_database_name*   If the package was saved in the Meta Data Services database, this option can be used to specify a repository database other than the default.

A *global_variable_name:typeid=value*   This option can be used to pass global variables to the DTS package from the command line.

L log_file_name   This keeps a package log file.

W true|false   This specifies whether or not to write the completion status of the package to the Windows Event Log.

Z   This indicates that the command line of the package has been encrypted for SQL 2000.

!X   This prevents the command from actually running and is used when you want to create an encrypted command line without actually running the package.

!D   This is used to delete packages from SQL Server.

!Y   This is used to display an encrypted command as text without actually executing it.

!C   This is used to copy the DTS command to the Windows Clipboard.

That is a lot of stuff to try to remember and enter at the command line. Fortunately there is a tool that is designed to make it easier for you: *DTSRUNUI*. This handy little tool is used to generate a DTSRUN command line for you and even encrypt it. In Exercise 7.7 you will use DTSRUNUI to make an encrypted DTSRUN command line.

EXERCISE 7.6

Using DTSRUNUI

1. Click Start and select Run.

2. In the Run dialog box, enter **DTSRUNUI** and click OK.

3. In the Location box, select SQL Server.

4. Click the ellipsis button next to the Package Name box and select the Authors package created earlier.

5. Select the proper authentication method and click the Advanced button next to Package Name.

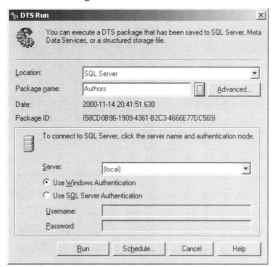

6. On the Advanced screen you can enter global variables to send to the package at execute time, write an event log, or encrypt the package for SQL Server 7 or 2000. Click the Generate button without any boxes checked to see an unencrypted command line for DTSRUN.

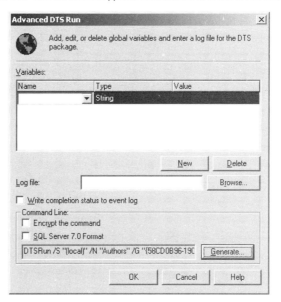

7. Now check the Encrypt the Command check box and click Generate. This generates an encrypted command line for DTSRUN that can be copied and placed in a batch file.

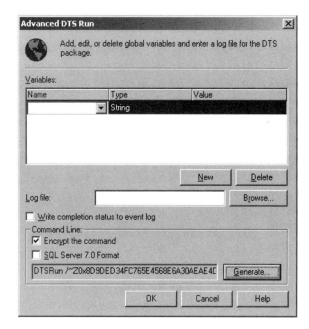

8. Click OK and click cancel so as not to run the DTS package.

Now that you know several ways to get data into your servers, let's look at a couple of ways to get that data back out, starting with XML.

Preparing IIS for XML

Microsoft **Set up Internet Information Services (IIS) virtual directories to**
Exam **support XML.**
Objective

Fully describing the Extensible Markup Language (XML) is out of the scope of this book; there are many books dedicated wholly to the subject of *XML* and its usage. Suffice to say that XML is a method of sharing data and schema on intranets or the Internet. XML uses HTML to display the information requested in an XML query.

SQL Server 2000 has XML functionality built right in, but in order to use it you must configure Internet Information Server to be able to query SQL Server for data in an XML format. To do this, you need to run the Configure SQL XML Support in IIS program to configure a Virtual Directory in IIS that points to a database in SQL Server (rather than to a directory on a hard disk as is usually the case). Once this is in place, you can simply point to the URL of the virtual directory and add an XML query in the URL to get a result set.

Once you have configured IIS to communicate with SQL Server, you can start performing XML queries by sending them as part of the URL or by using template files. Each method has pros and cons. For instance, you can send any valid query to your database directly through a URL. This gives you a great deal of flexibility, but it is not terribly secure in that anyone could send any valid query to your database over the internet. Using template files is a more secure and easier to use method. With a template file you already have the query saved as a file in a virtual directory and instead of having to type the entire query into the URL, the user only needs to enter the name of the query file. This is also more secure because the users cannot specify just any old query, they must use the queries that you design.

You can also use the FOR XML clause of the SELECT statement to access SQL using XML.

In Exercise 7.7 you will configure IIS for XML support and then query SQL Server using XML.

EXERCISE 7.7

Configuring IIS for XML Support

1. Open Configure SQL XML Support in IIS from the Start menu.

2. Expand your server and click Default Web Site.

3. From the Action menu, point to New and click Virtual Directory.

4. Enter Pubs for the Virtual Directory Name and C:\Inetpub\wwwroot for the physical path of the directory.

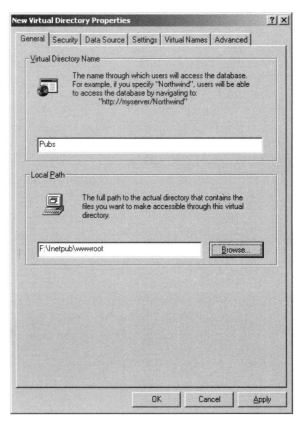

5. Switch to the Security tab. Here you can select a single login for all users of this directory, you can use Windows Integrated Authentication to allow users to access SQL with their Windows accounts, or you can use Basic Clear text, which allows users to use their Windows accounts but does not encrypt logon information (this is only used when you are configuring an IIS 4 machine behind a Proxy Server because they do not allow integrated security). For this exercise select Always Log on As and use your SA account.

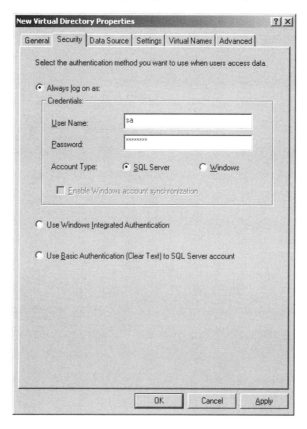

6. Switch to the Data Source tab. This is where you tell IIS which database to connect the virtual directory with. Enter your server name and select the Pubs database.

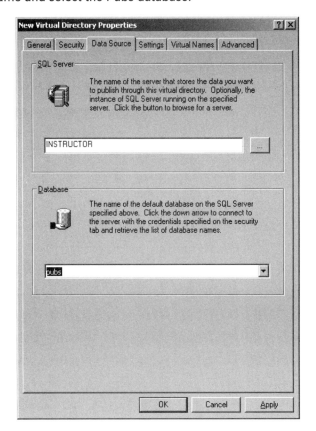

7. Switch to the Settings tab. This is where you limit the types of queries that can be processed using XML. URL queries are not generally recommended because they can be used to send any valid query to the database, which can be a security breach. Template queries are the recommended method to use because the administrator can set the query to be used. This option requires knowledge of XML programming, though. Xpath queries are for advanced users of XML; they allow users to access SQL using the Xpath language. Here you will select Allow URL Queries.

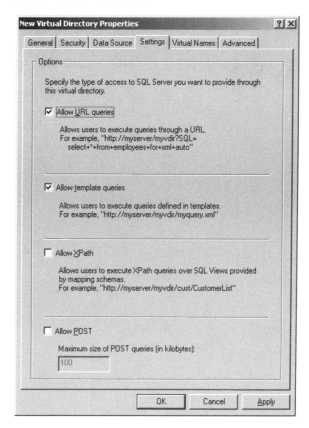

8. Switch to the Virtual Names tab. This is where you could associate a template or Xpath schema with a virtual directory to make data access easier for end users. Leave this blank because you are using URL queries.

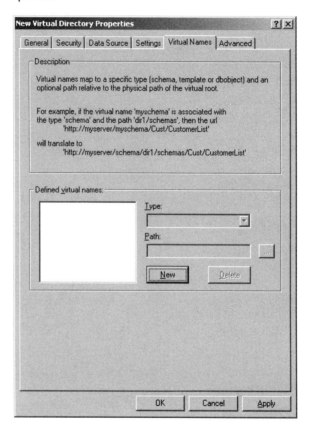

9. On the Advanced tab, leave the defaults. These settings can be used to make changes to the way IIS processes queries.

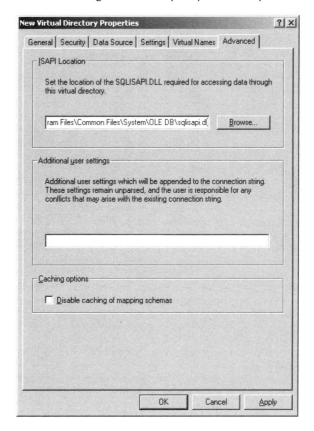

10. Click OK to create the virtual directory.

EXERCISE 7.7 *(continued)*

11. Open your Web browser and enter the following URL to perform an XML URL query:

```
http://localhost/
pubs?SQL=select+*+from+authors+for+xml+auto&root=root
```

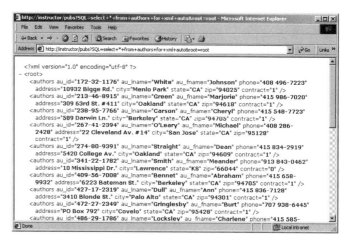

12. Close your Web browser.

Summary

In this chapter, we covered many different aspects of managing your data in SQL Server.

- We looked at migrating data from other data sources using BCP, BULK INSERT, and DTS.

- The INSERT statement is generally used to add one record at a time. When you use this statement, you must have INSERT permission on the table to which you are trying to add data and you must know something about the table's layout and design. INSERTs are logged transactions.

- The BCP (bulk copy) utility is a command-line program that can move data from a flat file (generated by any number of programs) into SQL Server or from SQL Server to a flat file very quickly. Learning how to use the BCP options is a bit painful at first, but with a little practice, this utility can become a very fast and useful tool.

- To perform a fast bulk copy, you should drop indexes on the table into which you are moving data. You should enable the Select Into/Bulk Copy database option and then run the BCP program. Keep in mind that defaults and datatypes will be enforced during the bulk copy, but triggers, rules, and default values will be ignored. You should run some type of query to check the new data for clarity and accuracy. Once you have done that, we suggest you re-create your indexes and then back up your database since a fast bulk copy is a nonlogged operation.

- One of the best new features of SQL Server 2000 is the BULK INSERT T-SQL command. The BULK INSERT statement is very similar to a T-SQL–based bulk copy command. One of the advantages of the BULK INSERT command is that it treats the flat file as an OLE-DB recordset. This allows records to be moved very quickly and efficiently into SQL Server. Note that BULK INSERT only inserts records. The quickest way to move data out of SQL Server to a flat file is to run a BCP command.

- Data Transformation Services (DTS) is an important new interface. You can create fairly complex import and export packages that can then be executed on a scheduled basis. You can move data from any OLE-DB– or ODBC-compliant source to an OLE-DB– or ODBC-compliant destination. The transformations you can perform on your data are nearly limitless. With the addition of the COM-compliant scripting languages, you can really do just about any type of data manipulation that you desire. The packages you create can be saved and scheduled for reuse. You can store your packages in the SQL Server or the Meta Data Services or as a COM-structured storage object. Each of these storage locations has some advantages. Remember that the Meta Data Services allows you to track the lineage of your data as well as the changes made to the DTS package itself. COM-structured storage makes the package simple to distribute through e-mail or a central server. Storing it in the SQL Server takes less memory, and other SQL Servers can access the package and run it.

- Accessing and running a SQL Server package brings up the security issues. By default, the packages have no security and are not encrypted. Placing a password on the package encrypts it. With an operator password in place, others who know the password can execute the package but cannot work with the package internals. When an owner password is used, others can execute the package as well as edit it.

- When you want to transfer data or schema or database objects from one SQL Server 2000 computer to another SQL Server 2000 computer, your best choice is the Transfer Manager. All the other utilities discussed in this chapter move data only. The Transfer Manager is capable of moving objects as well as data and schema, and it allows you to specify exactly which objects or data you want to move. Remember that the Transfer Manger builds script files that actually recreate the specified objects. If you use the Transfer Manager to move data as well, BCP files will also be generated for the transfer. Look at the LOG files created by the Transfer Manager. These files will store information about errors encountered during the transfer itself.

Exam Essentials

Know how to import data using the methods discussed. We discussed a variety of methods for importing data. You should be familiar with all of them and when to use each one.

Get to know DTS. DTS is a powerful tool that is capable of doing mush more than just moving data. It can change your data while it is being moved from any source to any destination. You need to know what DTS can do and how it is done.

Understand you package storage options. You have several choices of where to store your packages when you create them: the MSDB database, Meta Data Services, a Structured Storage file, or Visual Basic code. You need to know what advantages and disadvantages each of these has.

Know your options for securing packages. Because security is such a big issue in the networking world today, you will be asked how to secure your packages. You need to know what passwords to assign as well as how to encrypt the command line used to run your packages.

Key Terms

ad hoc queries	DTSRUN
BCP	DTSRUNUI
BULK INSERT	heterogeneous queries
Data Transformation Services	linked servers
DTS Designer	Transfer Manager
DTS package	XML

Review Questions

1. You need to perform regular queries against an older database that does not support three-part notation (catalog.schema.object). How should you access this data?

   A. Perform ad hoc queries using OPENROWSET.

   B. Perform ad hoc queries using OPENDATASOURCE.

   C. Use DTS to copy the data from the source server into your SQL Server and query it from there.

   D. Use BULK INSERT to copy the data from the older system into SQL Server and query the data.

2. Your users need access to one of your databases over the Internet through your IIS 5 server. They need access to the same data, and they will access the data using only one of two queries. You want to make access to the data as secure as possible; what should you do?

   A. Create a virtual directory that allows URL queries and allow Windows Integrated Authentication.

   B. Create a virtual directory that allows only Template queries and uses Basic Clear test authentication.

   C. Create a virtual directory that allows only Template queries and uses Windows Integrated Authentication.

   D. Create a virtual directory that allows only URL queries and uses Windows Integrated Authentication.

3. You need to create a DTS package, and you want to make sure it is secured so that only administrators can make changes to it. How can you do this?

   A. Assign an Operator password to the package.

   B. Assign an Owner password to the package.

   C. Use DTSRUNUI to encrypt the package.

   D. Use DTSRUN to encrypt the package.

4. Your parent company sends text files on CD-ROM on a monthly basis for you to import into your databases. Select all of the actions that you need to perform to do this as quickly as possible.

   A. Create a DTS package to import the data using a text file as the source.

   B. Use BULK INSERT to import the data.

   C. Use BCP to import the data.

   D. Drop all existing indexes on the affected table.

   E. Drop all existing data in the affected table.

   F. Set the database recovery model to Simple.

   G. Set the database recovery model to Bulk-Logged.

5. You have an XML Template query that several of your users need to access from an IIS 4 server that is protected from the Internet via a Proxy Server. Your SQL Server is not configured for Mixed Mode security. You need this to be as secure as possible. How should you configure the security settings for the virtual directory?

   A. Use Windows Integrated Authentication.

   B. Use Basic Clear Text.

   C. Set Always Log On As and assign it a Windows Login.

   D. Set Always Log On As and assign it a SQL Server Login.

6. You have created a DTS package that is run every week to make changes to your inventory database. You need to make sure that these changes are tracked so that you can verify them in case of problems. How can you keep track of the changes that the package makes to your database?

   A. Run the package with DTSRUN and specify the /T option for tracking.

   B. Save the package as a structured storage file; this will automatically track lineage.

   C. Save the package using Meta Data Services; this will automatically track lineage.

   D. Edit the package using the package designer and insert the Lineage Tracking Object to track changes to your data.

7. What happens when you run the command DTSRUN /Sproduction / Usa /Ppass /Naccounting /!X?

   A. The accounting package is deleted from the Production server.

   B. The production package is deleted from the Accounting server.

   C. If an Owner password has been assigned to the accounting package, it is removed.

   D. The package is executed but lineage is not tracked if it is saved in Meta Data Services.

8. You have just formed a partnership with another company and you need to share data with them. You need to get this new data to them every two weeks, and they use an Oracle database. You have no permanent network connection between your two offices. What is the fastest way to get your data to your new partners?

    A. Use BULK INSERT to export your data to a text file, send them the file, and have them insert the data into their database.

    B. Use the DTS Export Wizard to copy data to a text file, send your partners the file, and have them import it.

    C. Create a DTS package that exports the data to a text file, schedule it to run biweekly, send your partners the text file, and have them import it.

    D. Create a batch file that executes the BCP command to export your data to a text file, schedule it to run biweekly, send your partners the text file, and have them import it.

9. You have just configured a virtual directory to connect to your human resources database so that your Human Resources department can access the data over the Internet using XML. When they try to connect to the database, they get an error stating the page cannot be found. You verify that the query they are sending via the URL is correct. What is the problem?

    A. You forgot to set a physical path for the virtual directory when you created it.

    B. You set the security settings to Always Log on Using This Account, set the account type to Windows, and entered an account that does not have an associated SQL Server Login.

    C. You configured the wrong Virtual Name so the URL query cannot find the Virtual Directory.

    D. You did not set the server to allow Xpath queries.

10. You have just purchased a new server that has more RAM and a faster processor than your existing SQL Server 7 system. You want to install SQL Server 2000 and copy over your accounting database to the new server with all of its associated objects (including logins). What is the best way to accomplish this task?

    A. Recreate the database schema on the new server and use BULK INSERT to copy the data from the old server to the new server. Then re-create the logins for the server.

    B. Use the DTS Export Wizard and select Copy Objects from SQL Server to SQL Server. Select the default options.

    C. Use the DTS Export Wizard and select Copy Objects from SQL Server to SQL Server. Uncheck the box for Use Default options and check the box for transferring logins.

    D. Use BCP to copy the data and objects from the old server to a text file and then use BULK INSERT to import the data and recreate the database and its associated objects.

11. You have created a database application that uses Access, and you want your customers to be able to upgrade to a new version of your program that is capable of using SQL Server 2000. You want this to be as easy as possible for your customers. What should you do?

    A. Instruct your customers to export the data from Access to a text file and import the data into SQL Server using BULK INSERT.

    B. Instruct your customers to export the data from Access to a text file and import the data into SQL Server using BCP.

    C. Create a DTS package, save it as VB code, and ship the package to your customers.

    D. Create and save a DTS package as a structured storage file, create a simple application to access and run the package, and send this to your customers with instructions on how to run the application.

12. You try to import a text file into SQL Server using BCP, but you are unsuccessful. What should you check? (Select all that apply.)

    A. If you are using a FAT32 file system, check the permissions on the text file and make sure you have read permission.

    B. If you are using an NTFS file system, check the permissions on the text file and make sure you have read permission.

    C. Make sure you have INSERT permission on the destination database.

    D. Make sure you have BULK INSERT permission on the destination database.

    E. Make sure you are using Mixed Mode security because BCP is not capable of using trusted connections.

    F. Verify that you are not using a comma-separated value file because BCP only uses tab-delimited value files.

13. To use the BULK INSERT command, what is the minimum role you should be a member of?

    A. Bulkadmin

    B. Sysadmin

    C. Diskadmin

    D. Insertadmin

14. You need to use BCP to insert data from a comma-separated value file. What switches should you use to do this?

    A. /f','

    B. /r','

    C. /t','

    D. No switch is needed; commas are the default.

15. What does the command switch /Acomline:int=1 do when used with the DTSRUN utility?

    A. The package is repeatedly executed from the command line at one-hour intervals.

    B. The package is granted access to the command line when it is executed so that it may open files from hard disk.

    C. The package is granted access to comm port 1 for modem access.

    D. A global variable named comline is set to datatype integer with a value of 1 and passed to the package.

16. You need to import data into a table from a text file, and you need to make sure that none of the other database users can make changes to the table while the import is in progress. What can you do?

    A. Use the BULK INSERT statement with the /TABLOCK option to place a table lock on the table.

    B. Use BCP with the /TABLOCK option to place a table lock on the table.

    C. Use the DTS Import Wizard with the Lock Table box checked in the Advanced Options screen.

    D. Create a DTS package and execute it using the /TABLOCK option with DTSRUN.

17. You want to allow users to run a DTS package from the command line, but you want the command line switches protected so that the users cannot see sensitive passwords. How can you do this?

    A. Use DTSRUN to create an encrypted command line.

    B. Use DTSRUNUI to create an encrypted command line.

    C. Assign an Owner password to the package.

    D. Assign an Operator password to the package.

18. You need to import data into SQL Server 2000 from a data file that was exported from a SQL Server 6.5 server using the -n parameter. How can you import this data using BCP?

    A. Use the /V65 parameter.

    B. Use the /S65 parameter.

    C. BULK INSERT must be used instead of BCP.

    D. Native mode files from SQL Server 6.5 cannot be imported into SQL Server 2000. Character files must be used.

19. Which utilities can be used to extract data from a SQL Server database to a flat file? (Select all that apply.)

    A. BCP

    B. BULK INSERT

    C. DTS Export Wizard

    D. DTSRUN

    E. DTSRUNUI

    F. DTS Import Wizard

20. You need infrequent access to a database on an Oracle server. What is that best way to access this data?

    A. Ad hoc query with OPENROWSET.

    B. Ad hoc query with OPENDATASOURCE.

    C. Copy the data from Oracle to a text file and import the data into a temporary table using BULK INSERT.

    D. Copy the data from Oracle to a text file and import the data into a temporary table using DTS Import Wizard.

Answers to Review Questions

1. A . OPENROWSET is a little more difficult to configure than OPENDATASOURCE, but it will allow you to access data that does not support three-part notation. You use ad hoc queries instead of BULK INSERT or DTS because the query is being performed on a regular basis and copying the data into SQL Server every time is a slower process than using a heterogeneous query.

2. C. Allowing Basic Clear test authentication sends user names and passwords over the Internet in clear text, which allows hackers to find them easily. Allowing URL queries would allow your users to send any valid query to the database, including queries that can delete or damage your data. Allowing only Template queries limits your users to the queries you specify and using Windows Integrated Authentication encrypts login information.

3. B. An Owner password allows a user to make changes to a package, whereas an Operator password allows a user to run a package but not change it in any way. DTSRUNUI is used to encrypt the command line of a package but not the package itself, and DTSRUN is used merely to run the package, not protect it.

4. B, D, F. BULK INSERT is the fastest method for copying data into SQL Server. When you drop the indexes on the affected table, the index does not need to be updated as new data is inserted, so the operation is accelerated. You can make the operation even faster by bypassing the transaction log by setting the recovery model to Simple. Setting the recovery model to Bulk-Logged does not bypass the transaction log; it just uses it a little less.

5. C. Because your server is behind a Proxy Server and is IIS 4, you cannot use Windows Integrated Security. Basic Clear Text security sends login information in clear text and is therefore not secure. Because your server is not configured for Mixed Mode security, you cannot assign a SQL Server login to the virtual directory. The only option left is C.

6. C. Meta Data Services takes the place of the repository from SQL Server 7. It is used to track changes to the data each time the package is run.

7. A. The accounting package is deleted from the Production server. When a package is saved in Meta Data Services there is no way to disable lineage tracking.

8. C. The easiest way to do this is to create a DTS package to export the data to a text file because DTS uses BCP to export data to text files anyway.

9. B. When you configure the security settings to always use a Windows account to log in, that account must exist and have a SQL Server login mapped to it (as discussed in Chapter 5). You cannot create a virtual directory without specifying the physical directory, and allowing Xpath has no bearing on URL queries.

10. C. BULK INSERT and BCP will not copy all objects; they work only with text. Also, using the default options with the Import or Export Wizard will not copy logins. You must change the default options to copy login data to the new server.

11. D. Instructing your customers on how to export and then import is possible, but it's not easy for your customers. If you create a DTS package and save it as VB code, you cannot just run the VB code; you would need to modify it, save it, and create an application to run it. The easiest and fastest way is to save it as a structured storage file and create a simple application to access the package.

12. B, C. FAT32 file systems do not have permissions, so you need only check file permissions on NTFS drives. To use BCP, you only need INSERT permissions on the database, and BCP is fully capable of using trusted connections as well as comma-separated value files.

13. A. While sysadmin will allow you to run BULK INSERT, bulkadmin grants less authority and still allows BULK INSERT permission.

14. C. The /t switch tells BCP what to use as a field terminator, /r specifies a row terminator, /f designates a format file.

15. D. The /A switch is used to pass global variables to the package being executed.

16. A. TABLOCK is only available with BULK INSERT.

17. B. DTSTRUNUI can be used to create an encrypted command line.

18. A. Using the /V65 option tells BCP that it is using a data file from SQL Server 6.5

19. A, C. The only utilities that can export data from SQL Server are the DTS Export Wizard and BCP.

20. B. Oracle (and all other ANSI-92–compliant database systems) supports three-part notation. Therefore, OPENDATASOURCE is the fastest way to access data on an infrequent basis.

Chapter

8

Implementing Proactive Administration and IIS Support in SQL Server 2000

MICROSOFT EXAM OBJECTIVES COVERED IN THIS CHAPTER:

- ✓ Configure SQL Mail and SQLAgentMail.

- ✓ Create, manage, and troubleshoot SQL Server Agent jobs.

- ✓ Configure alerts and operators by using SQL Server Agent.

- ✓ Set up Internet Information Services (IIS) virtual directories to support XML.

Starting with SQL Server 6, Microsoft added the ability to schedule SQL Server jobs to run at predefined intervals. Another helpful administrative feature of SQL Server is its alerting capabilities. You can define alerts, which tell SQL Server what to watch for, what job to do if a particular event occurs, and whom to notify if and when the event occurs. You can also define operators, who can be e-mailed or paged to receive information about jobs and alerts.

The database that holds all of the jobs, alerts, and operators you define is the Msdb database. This database is installed by default, although there are no jobs or operators defined by default.

This chapter begins with a discussion of the Msdb database, including its system tables and information on how to back it up and restore it. It next covers the SQL Server Agent, the overall controlling service for jobs, alerts, operators, and events.

In addition, we'll explain how to create and manage alerts, operators, and jobs, showing how to set up each and how to make changes as necessary.

For complete coverage of the objectives in this chapter, please also see Chapter 7.

The Msdb Database

The *Msdb database* is a system database that is automatically created when you install SQL Server. Because the Msdb database contains all your jobs, alerts, and operators, it should be backed up on a regular basis. Once a week should be sufficient. If you make many changes to your jobs, alerts, or operators during the week, you may want to back up the database promptly after you've made the changes.

The backup process for the Msdb database is the same as for any other database. You need to define a backup device for the Msdb database, and you will probably want to schedule a backup job to back up this database on a regular basis. (See Chapter 6 for details about backing up and restoring databases as well as scheduling backup jobs.)

Backups are important because you may need to restore the Msdb database if you delete an important job, alert, or operator or if the database gets corrupted. You can restore the Msdb database in the same way that you restore other databases: In SQL Enterprise Manager, highlight the database, select Backup ➢ Restore from the Tools menu (or right-click the database and select Backup ➢ Restore from the context menu), choose a valid backup on the Restore tab, and click the Restore Now button.

Rebuilding the Msdb Database

If disaster strikes (for example, if you don't have a valid backup of the Master database, or if you wish to change the character set or sort order), you may be forced to rebuild your Master database.

When you choose to rebuild the Master database, you (without any warning or note) rebuild the Msdb database as well. Like the rebuilt Master database, the rebuilt Msdb database has all the default settings that came with SQL Server installation. This means that not a single job or operator is defined. You will need to restore all your Msdb data from a valid backup. If there is no valid backup, you will need to re-create your jobs, alerts, and operators by hand.

You can rebuild just the Msdb database by running the `Instmsdb.sql` and `Web.sql` scripts from the `MSSQL\Install` folder.

The SQL Server Agent

The *SQL Server Agent* can be thought of as an optional helper service for SQL Server. Nothing it does is technically required to make SQL Server work, but it does enough that you will probably want to enable it.

The SQL Server Agent service is in charge of finding and carrying out jobs and alerts and notifying operators on the success and/or failure of those jobs and alerts.

Configuring the SQL Server Agent

The SQL Server Agent is installed by default. This installation may not be entirely successful because it uses the account you are logged in as its service account but you may want it to use a different account. In addition, problems may be encountered when the SQL Setup program attempts to correctly configure the service for your system.

Two main settings are required for the SQL Server Agent to work properly:

- A user account, with appropriate rights, should be assigned to the service.

- The service should be configured to start automatically (if it is set to manual, you will have to start it by hand every time you reboot your server).

Although most services don't need a user account assigned to them to function correctly, services that go beyond the physical box and connect to other servers on the network (as the SQL Server Agent may do) usually do. If they don't have an account for the remote server to use to authenticate them, they connect with NULL security credentials and by default will be denied access.

Setting Up the User Account

As explained in Chapter 2, you can set up your SQL Server Agent user account before you install SQL Server and then configure the account correctly during the installation process. If you didn't do this at installation time, don't worry— you can still set up the account and configure it.

When using the Desktop version of SQL Server with Windows 9x, you cannot assign an account to the SQL Server Agent; it uses the account that is currently logged in. Not assigning an account to the agent will not affect any jobs or alerts on the local computer. The major limitation on Windows 9x computers is that they cannot be assigned as job managers for other servers.

There are three parts to setting up the SQL Server Agent user account: creating the user in Windows NT, giving the user appropriate rights, and assigning the user to the service. Here is the procedure:

- Create the user account using the Windows NT User Manager or User Manager for Domains utility or Active Directory Users and Computers in Windows 2000, just as you would for any other user. Clear the User Must Change Password at Next Logon option, and check the Password Never

Expires option. It may also be a good idea to set the User Cannot Change Password option.

- Give the user account appropriate rights. Make the user account for the SQL Server Agent a member of the Administrators group, and if you want that account to be usable on any and all SQL Server computers in the domain, make sure it's also a member of the Domain Administrators group. Assign the Log on as a Service right to this account. This right is in the Advanced Rights dialog box (choose User Rights from the Policies menu in User Manager for Domains and check the Advanced Rights box). Add the account you've created to the list of accounts that already have this right by clicking Add, then pick the appropriate account from the list.

The Services program of the Control Panel will usually assign the Log on as a Service right to a user account if it is needed and isn't already assigned.

- Assign the user to the service. The user account can be assigned to the SQL Server Agent in several different ways: during the initial installation (see Chapter 2), from the Services program of the Control Panel, from Server Manager (by selecting Services from the Computer menu), and from Enterprise Manager (by right-clicking SQL Executive and selecting Configure from the context menu).

Starting the Service Automatically

You can set SQL Server to start automatically, either by choosing the autostart option during installation (see Chapter 2) or later, through the Enterprise Manager's Server Options dialog box. If you set autostart, the MSSQLSERVER service will start when the server boots; no one needs to be logged on in order to make things happen.

It makes sense that if you have SQL Server set to start automatically, then you should also set the SQL Server Agent to start automatically. You can set this autostart option in the same way that you set autostart for the SQL Server service—during the installation of SQL Server or through the General tab of the property sheet of the SQL Server computer. However, if you don't have the SQL Server service start automatically, you shouldn't have the SQL Server Agent set to start automatically. Then you will need to manually start both services.

Changing the SQL Server Agent Password

You may occasionally want to change the password assigned to the SQL Server Agent (for example, after an employee who had access leaves). You'll need to change the password in two areas:

- In the Windows NT User Manager for Domains utility (or Active Directory Users and Computers in Windows 2000), you change the password through the user's property sheet. Replace the old password with the new one and then confirm the new password.

- Once you have changed the password, you need to tell the SQL Server Agent about it. There are several ways to reconfigure the service: through the Control Panel's Services program, by using the Server Manager's Services option on the Computer menu, or by going to the property sheet of the SQL Server Agent inside Enterprise Manager.

 Passwords, unlike usernames, are case sensitive in Windows NT.

Understanding Alerts, Jobs, and Events

The SQL Server Agent is the overall controlling service for jobs, alerts, *operators*, and events. There are separate engines for *jobs*, *alerts*, and *events*, but the SQL Server Agent is the controller for these engines.

Let's look at what happens to a common error before and after the SQL Server Agent has been configured. Suppose that the Pubs2 database log fills up and generates an 1105 error (the standard error code generated for a full log). SQL Server's own internal error generator will create the 1105 error, but without SQL Server Agent to watch for and handle the error, the problem will need to be fixed by hand. And until you resolve the problem, users will not be able to access the database. Figure 8.1 illustrates how errors are handled without jobs and alerts.

FIGURE 8.1   Flowchart of standard SQL Server error messages

With a predefined alert and job, the alert engine will be looking for the 1105 error in the Windows NT application log and will be ready to trigger a backup job that will truncate (clean out) the log, as illustrated in Figure 8.2. Now when SQL Server generates an 1105 error, the alert engine finds it and then acts on it by triggering the job. The database log is truncated, and users can resume using the database normally. If the backup failed to work, another error would be generated. At that point, the operator could be sent an e-mail message and/or paged.

FIGURE 8.2 Flowchart of SQL Server error messages, alerts, and jobs

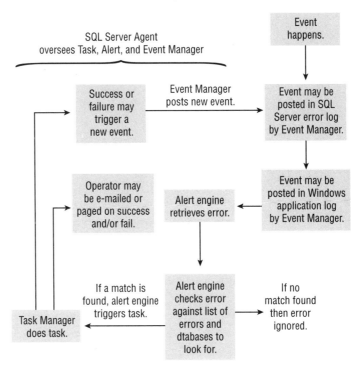

Creating and Managing Jobs

Earlier versions of SQL Server (4.21a and earlier) could schedule backups, but that was the extent of their scheduling capabilities. Beginning with version 6, SQL Server's scheduling capabilities have been greatly expanded. In SQL Server 2000, you can schedule jobs to run at regular intervals or when an alert is triggered. Replication is also supported through regularly scheduled jobs.

Microsoft ✓ *Exam Objective* **Create, manage, and troubleshoot SQL Server Agent jobs.**

Types of Jobs

SQL Server supports four general types of jobs:

TSQL jobs   These jobs are written using T-SQL commands. They are often used to back up the database, rebuild indexes, and perform other various routine database maintenance activities.

CmdExec jobs   These jobs literally open a command prompt and run some sort of batch file or executable file. Common CmdExec jobs are would include jobs to move backup files to another server or to import data using Bcp.exe.

Replication jobs   These jobs deal with replication. Normally you would use the replication wizards and prompts to help set up replication jobs, although monitoring these jobs is an important step in maintaining replication.

Active Script jobs   These jobs can run VBScript or JavaScript scripts at a regular interval.

Multiserver Jobs

SQL Server 2000 adds the ability to create jobs that run on multiple servers. To create multiple-server jobs, you must do the following:

- Ensure that all servers involved are running SQL Server 2000 on Windows NT or Windows 2000.

- Designate one server as the master server (MSX).

- Designate a master server operator (MSX Operator).

- Designate one or more servers as target servers when you create the job.

Note that a target server can report to only one master server at a time and that the SQL Server Agent needs to be set up to use a service account (not set to use the local account). You should also choose the MSX Operator carefully because that account is the only one that will be notified about multiserver jobs. Another feature of multiserver jobs is that the target server will automatically upload its job completion status to the master server.

If you want a target server to report to a different master server, you must first divorce the target server from the old master before enlisting it to the new master server.

Creating Jobs

The required elements of a job are name, schedule, and command to be executed during one or more steps. There are various ways to create and schedule jobs. The following are the most common ways:

- You can create your own jobs manually, through the `Management` folder in Enterprise Manager.

- You can use the Job Wizard to step you through the process.

- You can let Enterprise Manager create jobs for you. Enterprise Manager can create certain jobs, the most common of which is the backup job. In Chapter 6, you used the Enterprise Manager's database backup/restore dialog box to create a backup job.

- The Database Maintenance Plan Wizard can create jobs to handle routine maintenance and database backup. In Chapter 6, we explained how to create a backup job using the Database Maintenance Plan Wizard.

The Database Maintenance Plan Wizard creates one or more jobs for a given plan. For any given plan, you will probably see separate jobs for the optimizations, integrity checks, and backups.

- When you use the SQL Server Web Assistant to set up Web-page updates that happen on a regular interval, it creates a recurring job. The SQL Server Web Assistant is covered later in this chapter.

- When you install and set up replication, various jobs are created to make replication work. Replication is covered in Chapter 9.

Jobs can be scheduled in one of four ways:

When the SQL Server Agent starts   You can create a job that automatically executes whenever the SQL Server Agent starts. This would be good for an automated system of some kind.

When the CPU is idle   You can schedule a job to start after the CPU has been idle a certain amount of time, which is configurable on the property sheet of the SQL Server Agent.

One time only   A one-time-only job is usually created for a special purpose; it executes only once on its scheduled date and time.

Recurring   A recurring job happens on a regular basis. The job's frequency can be daily, weekly, or even monthly.

In Exercise 8.1, you will manually create a T-SQL job and schedule it as a recurring job. This new job will back up the Pubs database on a daily basis.

EXERCISE 8.1

Creating a Job Manually

1. In Enterprise Manager, open the Management folder and double-click Jobs. Any jobs that have previously been created (like the backup and maintenance jobs from Chapter 6) will appear in the right pane.

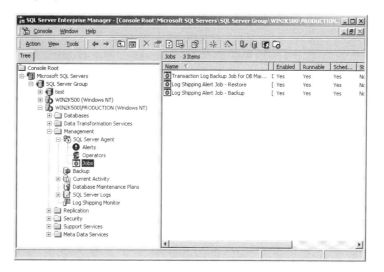

2. Click the New button (it looks like a star) on the toolbar or right-click the Jobs folder and choose New Job.

3. In the property sheet for the new job, enter a name for the job, such as **Back up Pubs database every night**.

EXERCISE 8.1 *(continued)*

Note that you can pick target servers for this job if you have enlisted this server as a master server and have designated one or more target servers from the lower-right portion of the screen.

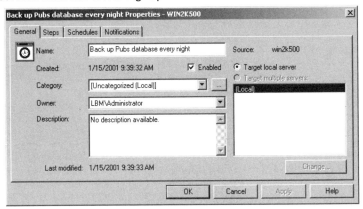

4. Click the Steps tab.

5. Create a new step by clicking the New button at the bottom of the screen.

6. Enter **Backup Pubs** for the name and **backup database pubs to pubs_backup** for the command. Make sure Transact-SQL is selected from the Type drop-down menu.

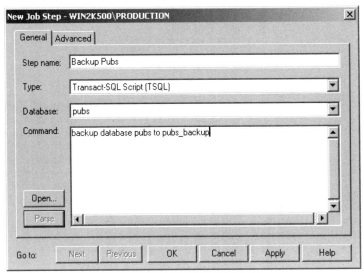

7. Click the Parse button to check the command for syntax errors. You should get an OK box. If not, fix the command until it works. Note that the Parse button will be grayed out until you make a change to the code.

8. Click the Advanced tab.

9. Change the On Success Action setting to Quit the Job Reporting Success, the number of retries to 3, and the interval to 1 minute. Click OK to save the step and return to the job's property sheet.

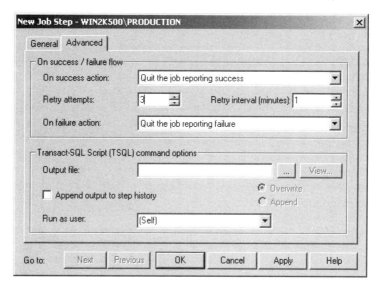

10. Click the Schedules tab. (Note that you can assign multiple schedules to a task.)

11. Click New Schedule.

12. In the New Job Schedule dialog box, enter a name for the schedule, such as **automated pubs backup on Sunday night**.

13. Change the schedule for the job by clicking the Change button.

EXERCISE 8.1 *(continued)*

14. Change the Daily Frequency setting to 11:00 P.M. Leave it set to recur weekly on Sundays. Click OK to save the changed schedule.

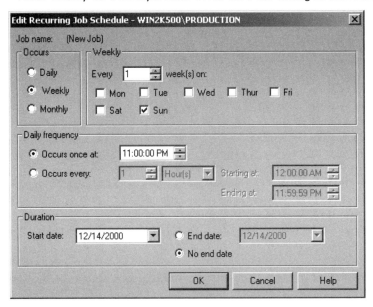

15. Back in the New Job Schedule dialog box, make sure the schedule is enabled and click OK to save it.

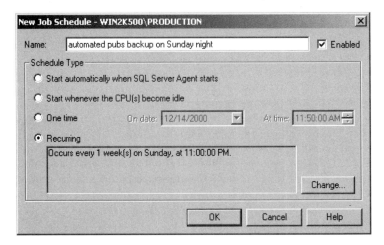

16. Click OK to save the new job. The job should now be listed in the Jobs folder.

Note that you cannot select any notifications until you have built operators (which is covered later in this chapter).

Editing Jobs

You can modify a job to change its name, type, command, or schedule. In Exercise 8.2, you will edit the job you created in Exercise 8.1 to change its schedule.

EXERCISE 8.2

Editing a Job

1. In Enterprise Manager, open the Management folder and double-click Jobs to see any jobs you have previously made.

2. Double-click the job you created in Exercise 8.1.

Note that you can add, edit, or rearrange steps for the job by selecting the Steps tab.

3. Click the Schedules tab, highlight Automated Pubs Backup, and click the Edit button.

4. Click the Change button in the lower-right corner of the dialog box.

5. In the Job Schedule dialog box, change the time of execution from 11:00 P.M. to 11:30 P.M.

6. Click OK in the Job Schedule dialog box and then click OK in the next two dialog boxes that appear to save your change.

Running Jobs Manually

Even if you have scheduled a job, you can run it manually at another time. In Exercise 8.3, you'll run the job you created in Exercise 8.1.

EXERCISE 8.3

Running a Job Manually

1. In Enterprise Manager, open the Management folder and double-click Jobs.

2. Highlight the job you created in Exercise 8.1.

3. Choose Action ➢ Start Job to start the job, or you can right-click the job and choose Start Job.

4. If you are fast enough, you can go back to the Jobs folder and see that the status of the job has changed; in the Status column, it will say "Executing Job Step 0-X." After the job has finished running, the Last Run Status column should read either "Succeeded" or "Failed," along with the date.

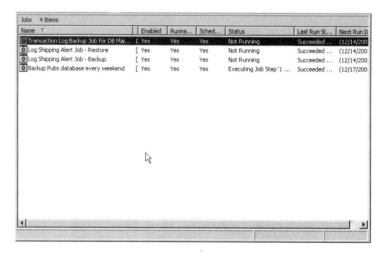

Viewing Job History

A very helpful feature of Enterprise Manager is that it keeps a record of each job's time of execution as well as whether the job was successful or not. In Exercise 8.4, you'll examine the history of the job that you ran in Exercise 8.3 to see if it was successfully completed.

EXERCISE 8.4

Examining the History of a Job

1. In Enterprise Manager, open the Management folder and double-click Jobs.

2. Highlight the job you created in Exercise 8.1.

3. Choose Action ➤ View Job History or right-click the job and choose View Job History to display the Job History screen.

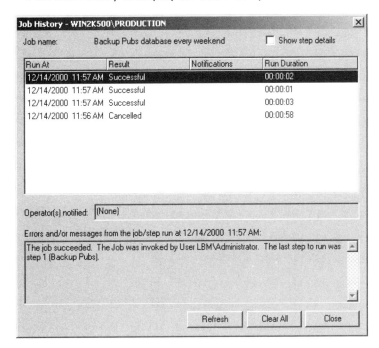

As you can see, the job is listed as Successful in the Result column. Notice also that you can refresh or clear the history by clicking the appropriate button at the bottom of the screen.

EXERCISE 8.4 *(continued)*

4. Click Close.

5. To see options for the size of the job history log, highlight the SQL Server Agent in the Management folder, right-click, and choose Properties. On the property sheet, click the Job System tab. The default settings allow a maximum of 1,000 rows of history, with a maximum of 100 rows per job. Note that you can clear the history of all jobs from here as well.

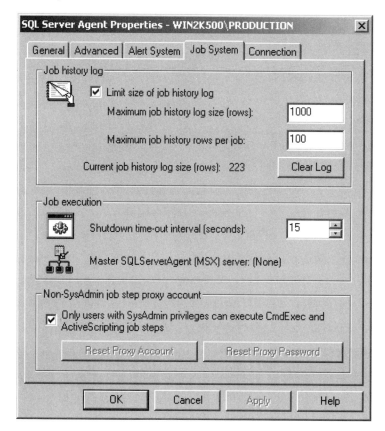

6. Click Cancel to close the dialog box.

Deleting Jobs

If you no longer need a job, you can easily delete it in Enterprise Manager. Note that if you delete a job, you also delete all its steps and history.

Rather than delete a job, you might consider disabling it temporarily. That way, you can quickly enable the job if you need it back, as opposed to having to re-create the entire job. You can enable or disable a job by double-clicking it to go to its main property sheet.

Creating and Managing Alerts

The SQL Server Agent, via the alert engine, looks in the sysalerts table to determine which errors it should be looking for. When you define an alert, you are telling SQL Server which error codes to look for in the NT application logs and what action to take if an event is found.

Microsoft Exam Objective

Configure alerts and operators by using SQL Server Agent.

Creating an Alert

Creating alerts is somewhat intuitive. There are several basic steps:

- Define the type of alert, either an alert based on a SQL Server error message or one based on a Performance Condition counter.

- If the alert is based on a SQL Server error message, define the error to look for. Alerts can be based on a generic error-message number, the error's severity, or an error happening in a specific database.

- Optionally, define the database in which the error must happen. An alert can filter error messages based on the database. For instance, an alert can be created to watch the Pubs database in case it fills up. This alert would operate only on the Pubs database; if any other database filled up, the alert wouldn't do anything.

- If the alert is based on a Performance Condition counter, define which counter to monitor and the threshold that will trigger the alert.

- Define the response of the alert. Alerts can be set up to trigger jobs automatically and/or to alert operators that the alert was activated.

- If the alert is meant to perform a job, define (or select) the job to be done. Alerts are usually created to perform a job when the alert condition is met. You can define a job that will run when the alert is triggered. Jobs can run either T-SQL statements or command-prompt programs such as Bcp.exe or Osql.exe.

- If the alert is meant to notify someone, define who will be notified and how it will be done. You can specify operators and whether they should receive an e-mail message and/or be paged when an alert is triggered. (See "Creating and Managing Operators" later in this chapter for details about setting up operators.)

- Activate the alert by selecting the Enabled box inside the Edit Alert dialog box (it is selected by default but can be deselected to temporarily disable an alert).

Follow the steps in Exercise 8.5 to create an alert. In this example, you will set up an alert to watch for the log of the Pubs database to get full and to back up the transaction log (thus clearing the log) if and when the alert is triggered.

EXERCISE 8.5

Creating an Alert Based on SQL Server Error Messages

1. In Enterprise Manager, open the Management folder and then the Alerts folder. You should see nine predefined alerts.

2. To add a new alert, click the New button on the toolbar, or choose Action ➢ New Alert, or right-click and choose New Alert.

3. You'll see the property sheet for the new alert. In the ID: New Name field, enter **Detect Full Pubs Transaction Log**.

4. In the Alert Definition section, select the Error Number radio button and enter **1105** in the associated box. From the Database Name drop-down list box, choose Pubs. Your property sheet should now look like the one here.

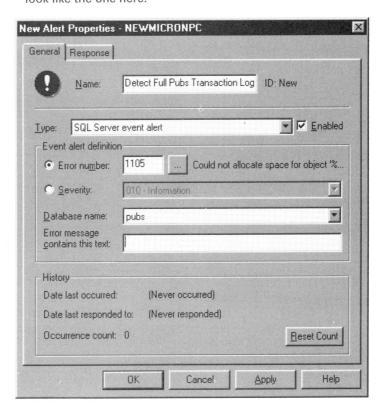

5. Click the Response tab. Select Execute Job. In the Job to Execute drop-down list box, choose New Job. This will open the New Job dialog box.

6. In the Name box, enter **Clear the Pubs log when an alert is triggered**.

7. Click the Steps tab and click New to add a new job step.

8. Enter **Clear the pubs log** for the name, and in the command box, enter the following T-SQL statement:

```
backup log pubs to pubs_log
```

EXERCISE 8.5 *(continued)*

9. Click OK to return to the Response tab, then click OK again to save the new job and return to the property sheet for the alert, which should list the job to run when the alert triggers.

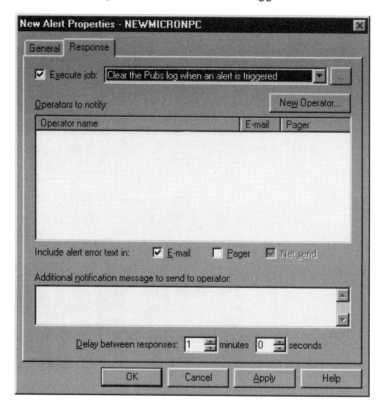

10. Click OK to save the alert. Your alert should now be listed with the default alerts.

In Exercise 8.6, you will create an alert that monitors the Performance Condition counters for SQL Server connections.

EXERCISE 8.6

Creating an Alert Based on a Performance Condition Counter

1. In Enterprise Manager, open the Management folder and then open the Alerts folder. You should see nine predefined alerts (as well as any you have made).

2. To add a new alert, click the New button on the toolbar, or choose Action ➤ New Alert, or right-click and choose New Alert.

3. You'll see the property sheet for the new alert. In the ID: New Name field, enter **Detect when Connections go over 500**.

4. Change the type to SQL Server performance condition alert. (Note that only SQL Performance Condition counters—not all counters—are visible to the agent.)

5. Change the object to SQL Server: General Statistics.

6. Change the counter to User Connections.

7. Change the Alert if Counter setting to Rises Above.

EXERCISE 8.6 *(continued)*

8. Enter **500** for the value. Your alert should look like this.

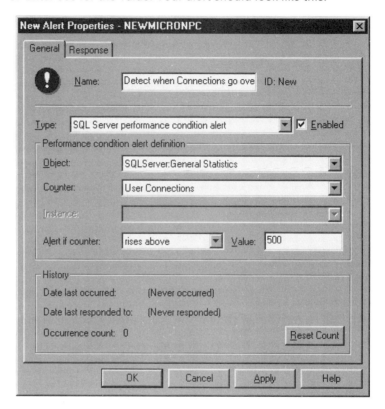

9. Click OK to save the alert.

Editing an Alert

After you've created an alert, you can easily make changes to it. Simply return to the Alerts window (located under the Management\SQL Server Agent folder), highlight the alert you want to change, and click the Edit Alert button.

Note that many of the alerts you would make based on Performance Condition counters would probably be designed to send a message to someone when the appropriate counter hit a specified number. Although the example in Exercise 8.6 is incomplete, you can edit the alert so that the appropriate person is notified. Defining operators and assigning them to alerts are covered later in this chapter.

Editing and Creating SQL Server Error Messages

One of the great features of SQL Server is the ability to add your own error messages to the basic ones provided by SQL Server. You can call the new error message from within any T-SQL script or program by using the following command:

```
Raiserror (error_number, severity, state)
```

You can then create alerts to watch for the error messages you have defined and notify you when the error is triggered.

SQL messages are stored in the sysmessages table of the Master database.server.

You can both edit the posting of existing error messages to the NT application log and create and edit new messages via the Manage SQL Server Messages menu option. In Exercise 8.7, you'll edit an existing SQL Server error message so that it won't post to the NT application log and then you'll create a new error message.

EXERCISE 8.7

Editing and Creating Error Messages

1. In SQL Enterprise Manager, highlight the server and select Action ➢ All Tasks ➢ Manage SQL Server Messages, or highlight the server, right-click, and choose All Tasks ➢ Manage SQL Server Messages.

2. Enter **1105** in the Error Number box and click the Find button on the right side of the dialog box. The 1105 message appears in the dialog box.

EXERCISE 8.7 *(continued)*

3. Double-click the message or click once on Edit to edit the message. The Edit SQL Server Message dialog box appears. Notice that the message itself cannot be edited, but you can disable (or in some cases enable) the Always Write to NT Eventlog option.

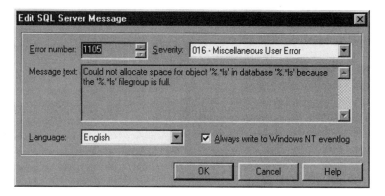

4. Click Cancel in the Edit SQL Server Message dialog box. (You should then be in the Messages tab).

5. Click New to create a new message.

6. Add a custom message to Error Number 50001 with the text **This message triggered by Custom Application. Contact the Programmers**. Check the Always Write to Windows NT Eventlog box.

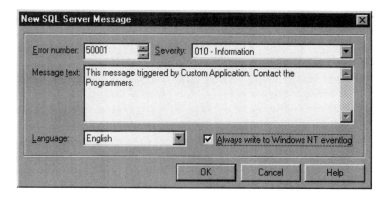

7. Click OK to go back to the Manage SQL Messages screen, then click OK to close the window.

EXERCISE 8.7 *(continued)*

8. To test the message, start the Query Analyzer.

9. Enter and execute the following query:

   ```
   raiserror (50001,10,1)
   ```

10. The error message that you just created should appear in the Results window.

11. Open the Windows NT event log (select Programs ➤ Administrative Tools ➤ NT Event Viewer) and select Log ➤ Application to display the application log. The message that you entered should appear.

12. Double-click the message for more details. You should see the Event Detail dialog box with information about the error and your message.

Forwarding Events

If you have more than one server running SQL Server, you can define a central server that will receive from other servers events for which you have (or have not) defined alerts. The server that receives these events is called an *unhandled event forwarding server*.

SQL Server 2000 also allows you to forward all events to a central server, but this could cause major traffic on a large network if many SQL Server computers were involved.

The server that is designated as the unhandled event forwarding server must be registered in Enterprise Manager.

Windows 9x cannot forward events to, or act as, an unhandled events server.

In Exercise 8.8, you will designate a server as the unhandled event forwarding server.

EXERCISE 8.8

Designating an Unhandled Event Forwarding Server

1. In Enterprise Manager, highlight the SQL Server Agent folder (found in the Management folder).

2. Open the property sheet of the Agent by right-clicking and choosing Properties or by choosing Action ➢ Properties.

3. Click the Advanced tab.

4. Check the Forward Events to a Different Server check box and choose New Forwarding Server (or you can choose a server already registered in Enterprise Manager) from the drop-down list of servers. Enter **SERVER2** if you don't have a separate server to use.

   Enterprise Manager will warn you that it can't connect to SERVER2 and ask if you still want to register it (of course, you won't see this message if you actually do have a server called SERVER2); click Yes. SERVER2 should now appear in the server to forward events to box in the SQL Server event forwarding section.

5. Select Unhandled events (the default) and select a severity of 15 and higher from the drop-down menu.

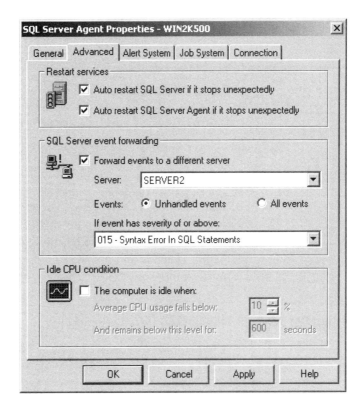

6. Because SQL Server can't connect to SERVER2, click Cancel so you don't save your changes. Of course, when you're actually designating an unhandled event forwarding server, you should click OK to save your changes. (If you click OK now, SQL Server will generate errors when it can't connect to SERVER2.)

Creating and Managing Operators

SQL Server is MAPI compliant, which means that you can use it to send and receive e-mail. Therefore, you can define operators and their e-mail addresses in SQL Server and have SQL Server notify those operators about the success and/or failure of scheduled or triggered jobs and alerts.

Microsoft *Exam* *Objectives*	**Configure alerts and operators by using SQL Server Agent.** **Configure SQL Mail and SQLAgentMail.**

SQL Server also supports many paging services and can be configured to page operators if an alert is triggered. These paging services depend on your e-mail system's capability to decode an e-mail message in order to send a page message. Operators can also be configured to be notified via the Net Send function, which is useful if the e-mail system is down or you want instant notification.

Enabling MAPI Support for E-Mail

Different versions of Windows implement *MAPI (Messaging Application Programming Interface)* for applications a bit differently. Windows NT 3.51 worked quite well with older versions of SQL Server, but to provide better security, Windows NT 4 and Windows 2000 changed the way MAPI works with services. Because of this, Service Pack 3 or later must be used with Windows NT 4 to allow MAPI to work with SQL Server and Windows Messaging (MS Mail clients), although SQL Server and Exchange work without any service packs. Of course, because SQL Server 2000 requires Service Pack 4 for Windows NT 4, installing at least Service Pack 3 is no longer an issue. Windows 2000 works fine with SQL Server for MAPI purposes without any service packs installed.

Configuring default ANSI settings is covered in Chapter 2.

Under Windows NT, you may not be able to start more than one MAPI session at a time per computer. In other words, if SQL Server has a MAPI session open and you start and stop a program such as Outlook, it may not connect—you must stop SQL Server's MAPI session, start Outlook, and then restart the SQL Server MAPI session. The easiest way to do this is to stop and start SQL Server Agent to stop and start the MAPI session. What this means in real life is that you should not use the SQL Server computer to read your e-mail if the SQL Server service is set up for e-mail operators.

There are five basic steps to installing MAPI support for Windows NT and 2000:

1. Create a user account for the SQL Server Agent and SQL Server to use.

2. Create an Exchange mailbox for the SQL user account.

3. Log in to the SQL Server computer as the SQL user account and create an Exchange profile that points to the Exchange server and mailbox created in step 2.

4. Log in to the SQL server as someone with Administration and SA rights and assign the SQL user account (created in step 1) to the MSSQLSERVER and SQL Server Agent services. Stop and restart both services.

5. Assign the profile (created in step 3) to the SQL Mail portion of SQL Server. Start the SQL Mail session.

You may need to reapply the service pack if you add any components from the original Windows NT 4 CD. You can find Service Pack 4 for Windows NT 4 on Microsoft's Web site (www.microsoft.com) or on TechNet. Use the Update command from the appropriate subdirectory (x386 for Intel-compatible computers) to install the service pack.

In Exercise 8.9, you'll install support for MAPI for Windows Active Directory and SQL Server.

EXERCISE 8.9

Installing MAPI Support in SQL Server

1. Go to Active Directory Users and Computers (or User Manager in NT 4) and make sure you have a user account created for the SQL services. Make sure Password Never Expires is checked and User Must Change Password at Next Logon is *not* checked. Make the account a member of the Domain Administrators group.

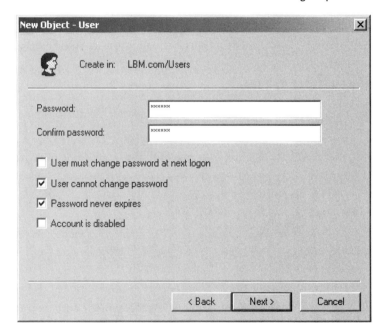

2. Start the Exchange Administrator program.

3. Create a mailbox for the SQL user account by highlighting the Recipients folder and choosing File ➤ New Mailbox. Enter the information for the SQL user account and click the Primary Windows NT Account button to assign it to the user. Click OK to save the mailbox.

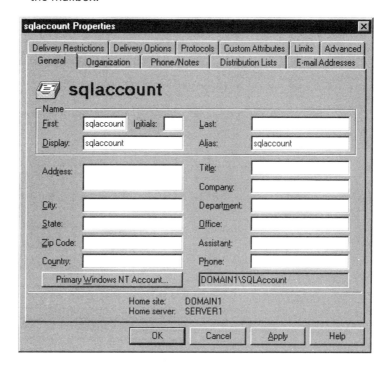

4. Create a mailbox for your personal account if one does not already exist.

5. Log in to Windows NT as the user you created for the SQL Server Agent account.

6. Open Control Panel, double-click the Mail and Fax icon, and click Add under the profile section.

7. On the first screen of the Microsoft Outlook Setup Wizard, leave Microsoft Exchange Server selected and clear all the other selections. Click Next.

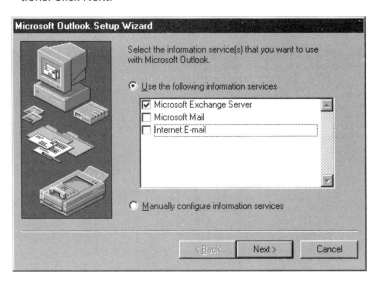

8. On the next screen, enter the name of the Exchange server and the mailbox. Click Next.

EXERCISE 8.9 *(continued)*

9. Click No when asked if you travel with the computer. Click Next.

10. Accept the default path to the address book. Click Next.

11. Do not choose to add Outlook to the startup group. Click Next.

12. Click Finish at the final screen.

13. Note the name of the profile. You will need to know this name for later steps.

14. Open Enterprise Manager.

15. Assign the SQL account to the SQL Server service by opening the property sheet for the server, clicking the Security tab, and entering the domain\username and password for the account.

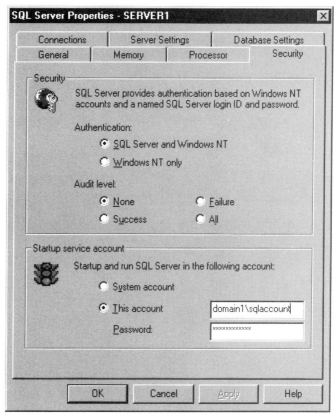

16. Assign the SQL account to the SQL Server Agent by opening the property sheet for the Agent.

17. On the General tab, enter the domain\username for the account, the password, and the name of the profile you created. Click OK.

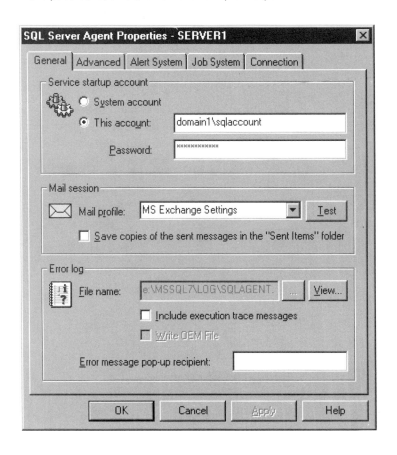

18. Start the SQL Mail session by opening the SQL Mail Configuration folder under the Support Services folder. Examine the properties of SQL Mail and make sure the profile created earlier is listed.

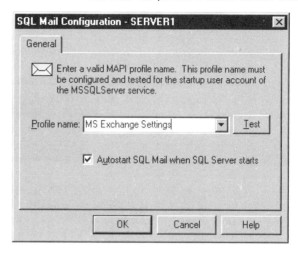

19. Click the Test button to test the profile. Select Autostart SQL Mail when SQL Server Starts. Click OK.

20. To start the SQL mail session, right-click the SQL Mail icon and choose Start. The session should start and the arrow should turn green.

Creating Operators and Testing E-Mail

To ensure that your MAPI support is configured correctly, you will want to send test messages to your operators. In Exercise 8.10, you'll create an operator and test the capability of SQL Server to send messages to that operator.

Creating an Operator and Testing E-Mail

1. Log in to Windows NT as your normal account (not the SQL Executive account).

2. In Enterprise Manager, open the Operators folder under the Management\SQL Server Agent folder.

EXERCISE 8.10 *(continued)*

3. Click the New button, or right-click and choose New Operator, or choose Action ➢ New Operator.

4. In the Edit Operator dialog box, enter an operator name, such as the NT administrator, and the e-mail name for the person you are logged in as.

5. Click the Test button to send mail to the user. SQL Server should report that the message was sent successfully.

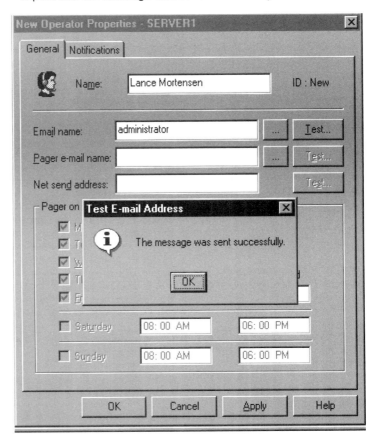

6. Click OK to save your new operator.

7. Minimize Enterprise Manager, go to your Desktop, and start your messaging client by double-clicking the Inbox. You should have received the test message.

8. Close the messaging client by selecting File ≻ Exit and Log Off.

9. Go back to Enterprise Manager and open the property sheet for the operator. Click the Notifications tab and select all the alerts you want to be sent to this operator.

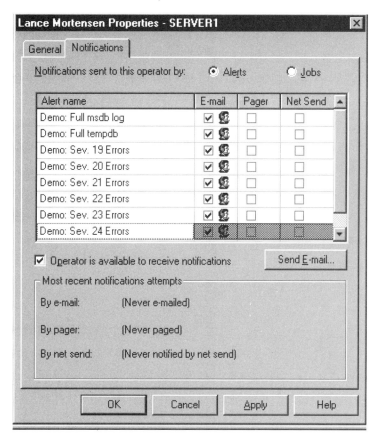

10. Click OK to save the operator.

Defining Fail-Safe Operators

After you've set up your operators (defining their working hours), you can designate a fail-safe operator in case no other operators are on duty when an alert is triggered. In Exercise 8.11, you will define a fail-safe operator.

EXERCISE 8.11

Defining a Fail-Safe Operator

1. In Enterprise Manager, highlight the SQL Server Agent folder under the Management folder.

2. Select Action ➤ Properties or right-click and choose Properties to bring up the property sheet.

3. Go to the Alert System tab. From the Fail-Safe Operator drop-down list box, select an operator you have already set up, as shown here. Check the Notify Using E-Mail box as well.

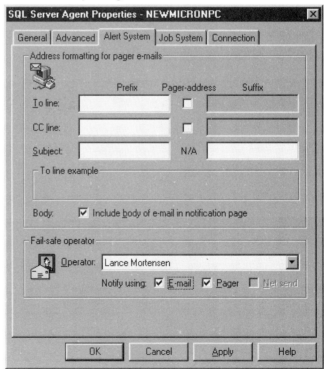

4. Click OK to save your changes.

SQL Server and the Internet

This section will introduce you to different ways of accessing data in SQL Server from Internet applications. SQL Server 2000 adds support for *eXtensible Markup Language (XML)*. SQL Server 2000 also includes a Web Assistant designed to make accessing static Web pages easier than ever before. There are also ways to access SQL data through interactive Web pages. In this section, we'll show you how to configure XML support and how to use the SQL Web Assistant. We'll also give you introductory information concerning other approaches to accessing data through the Internet.

Although this section may seem somewhat unrelated to the rest of the chapter, automating access to SQL data via Web pages is a common reason to create and manage jobs.

Static vs. Interactive Web Pages

In the early days of the Web, most pages were static in nature. They were not really designed to give the user an interface for extensive interaction. Of course, there were stunning graphics and even some animations, but the pages were still essentially static. The presentation on a static Web page consists primarily of links and text. The text and/or links might be updated periodically by the Webmaster, but the page does not accept any input from the user other than to follow a link to another static page.

Static pages have their place. If the user has no need to "drill down" to specific data and can use the contents of the page as a whole, the approach can be very valid. Properly planned links and a well-organized site can give the appearance of being fairly dynamic in response to user requests when, in reality, all the work of providing that seemingly interactive experience is being performed by the Webmaster or the individual responsible for maintaining current data on the site.

The concept of interactive pages is entirely different, as is their purpose. The key participant in an interactive Web page is the user. The user can provide input about the information retrieved, enter data into a data storage by filling out a Web-based form, and even cause events to happen halfway around the world.

One of the most recent applications for interactive Web pages is to provide merchant services. By using tools such as Microsoft Internet Information Server and Merchant Server and using SQL Server as a data store, you can build a Web site to handle merchant activities ranging from taking orders in an online bookstore to transferring funds between two financial institutions. *Internet Information Server (IIS)* handles the Web traffic, Merchant Server maintains the security of the transactions, and SQL Server provides the data storage and transactional integrity. Adding Microsoft Transaction Server to the mix adds the extra element of distributed transaction processing, allowing you to coordinate the activities of multiple SQL Server computers.

As you can see, with interactive Web pages, the only limit is the imagination of the site architect and the developer. The goal is to provide the user with a rich interactive experience. Whether you are building your Web site for internal use, as with an intranet, or planning to attract Internet customers to your site, you are building your site primarily to provide user services.

Configuring XML Support in SQL Server 2000

SQL Server 2000 supports XML by allowing you to query a SQL database using XML through an IIS Web server.

Microsoft *Exam* *Objective*	**Set up Internet Information Services (IIS) virtual directories to support XML.**

To pass XML code to SQL Server, you must first configure on the IIS server a virtual directory that points to the SQL Server computer. You must use the Configure XML Support utility (choose Start ➤ Programs ➤ SQL Administration ➤ Configure SQL XML Support in IIS) to correctly configure XML support in IIS. You can allow XML code to access tables directly, but because that would be a security risk, it is recommended that you use template files or XML path queries. You can set the security of the virtual directory by going to the property sheet of the directory (see Figure 8.3).

FIGURE 8.3 Setting the access security on a new virtual directory in IIS

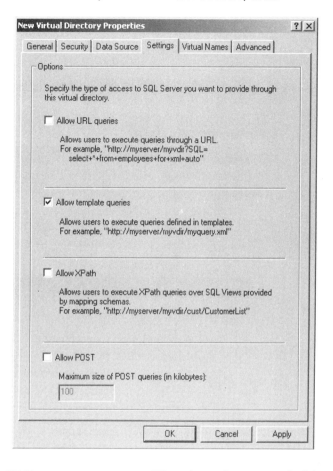

When XML requests are sent to IIS to the path you specified for SQL Server, *Sqlisapi.dll* will translate the request and send it to SQL Server.

Using the SQL Web Assistant

Although there are advantages to providing the user with an interactive experience, you may not always need to dynamically extract information from a SQL Server computer. If your requirement is for static Web pages that will be periodically updated by either the administrator or an automated service, then the SQL Web Assistant might be exactly the tool that you need. It doesn't make sense to pound a pin into the wall with a sledgehammer, and sometimes a static Web page is completely adequate.

The Web pages created by the SQL Web Assistant can be based on a stored procedure or created through a free-form query that you type as you initially run the assistant. These pages are sometimes called *push pages* because the data is pushed out of SQL Server by the queries or stored procedures that access the data. The queries or stored procedures are completely static, however. They cannot be changed by the user interacting through the browser, nor can parameters be passed to the stored procedure through the browser.

Running the Assistant

To run the SQL Web Assistant, first make sure that SQL Server is running. If it is not running, the assistant will be unable to forward the query or stored procedure call to SQL Server for processing.

You access the SQL Web Assistant through the Web Publishing folder under the Management folder in Enterprise Manager. In Exercise 8.12, you will create a new job to publish (push) Web pages.

EXERCISE 8.12

Creating a Web Publishing Job

1. First, open Enterprise Manager. To create a new Web publishing job, start the SQL Web Assistant (or Wizard) by highlighting the Web Publishing folder and selecting Action ➢ New Web Assistant Job or by right-clicking and choosing New Web Assistant Job. At the introductory screen, click Next.

2. Select the Pubs database. Click Next.

3. Notice the default name of the Web publishing job. Leave the Data from the Tables and Columns That I Select box checked and click Next.

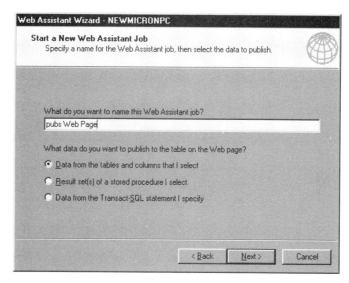

4. Select the Titles table and choose just the Title and PubDate columns. Click Next.

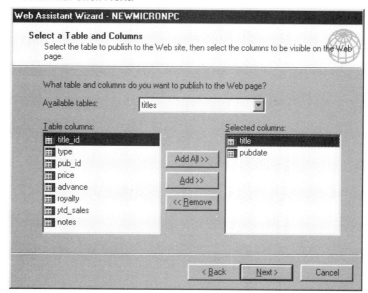

EXERCISE 8.12 *(continued)*

5. Leave All of the Rows selected. Click Next.

6. This is one of the most important screens of the wizard because it is where you schedule when the Web page will be created. To create a recurring job, select At Regularly Scheduled Intervals. Click Next.

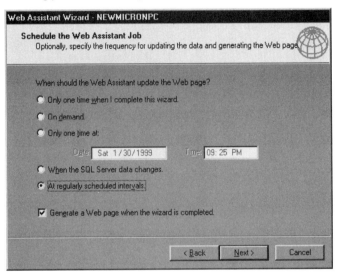

7. If you selected to update the page on a regular basis, you will be prompted to select when the job will run. Leave it at the default day and time and click Next.

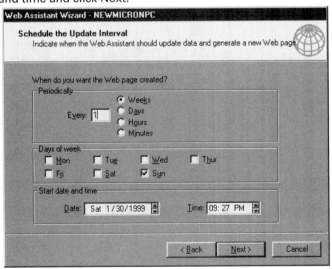

8. Enter the path to the HTML file that will be created. Note that the default path is \MSSQL\HTML. Click Next.

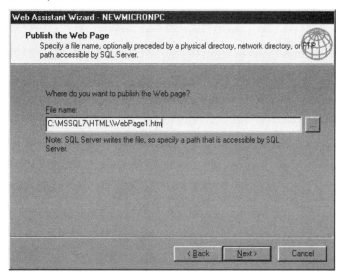

9. Leave the default settings for formatting the Web page. (You can also specify a template for more sophisticated formatting.) Click Next.

10. Change the name of the Web page and table to something more appropriate. Click Next.

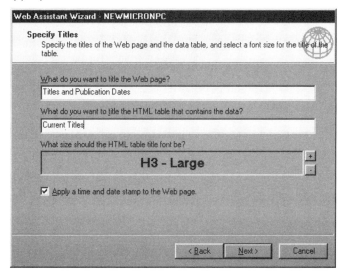

11. Leave the default settings for the data format. Click Next.

12. Note that you can add custom hyperlinks (such as back to your home page or to other supporting pages or company Web sites) from the next screen. Leave it set to No Additional Hyperlinks and click Next.

13. On the next page, you can split the results into smaller pages or limit the row count. Leave the default settings and click Next.

14. You should now see a summary page. Note that you can back up and change any item or generate the T-SQL code that the job will use. Click Finish to generate and run the recurring job.

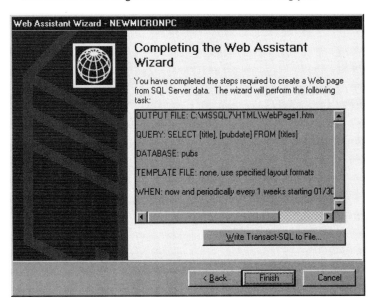

15. Click OK when the Confirmation screen comes up.

EXERCISE 8.12 *(continued)*

16. To look at your page, go to the \MSSQL\HTML folder and open the file you made (WebPage1.htm). It should look something like this.

17. Go to the Jobs folder. You should see a new job with a name similar to pubs Web Page.

18. If you examine the first step of the job, it looks something like the dialog box shown here. Note that a stored procedure is being called to read the parameters you entered when you created the Web publishing job.

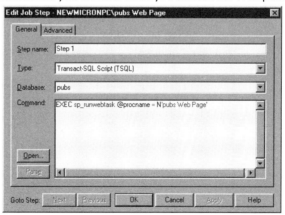

19. Close the Jobs folder.

Although you can edit the Web page directly after it has been generated, any changes that you make will be lost the next time the page is generated. If you wish to make permanent changes to the format of the page, you must either change the settings inside the Web Assistant or, for a more robust approach, use an HTML template file.

You can easily edit the schedule of a recurring Web job by going to the Schedule tab of the job's property sheet. You can also delete the Web publishing job (in case of mistakes) from the Jobs folder.

Creating Interactive Web Pages

Although static Web pages are extremely simple to produce, they may not be sophisticated enough for your Web site. For example, if you require users to enter information into a database or retrieve information based on custom parameters, you may need to use interactive Web pages. Interactive Web pages are sometimes called *pull pages* because instead of simply accessing a static page, the user provides input to pull data out of the server.

Pull pages tend to place more of a strain on your server because, rather than simply generating a Web page at certain intervals, the browser is actually calling information directly out of the database. Significant hits to your Web site can negatively affect the performance of the SQL Server computer.

When you create interactive Web pages, there are three basic ways to get at your SQL Server data (each has advantages and disadvantages):

- Internet Database Connector (IDC)
- Remote Data Services (RDS)
- ActiveX Data Objects (ADO)

Let's look at each of these three approaches in more detail. Although they are not necessarily difficult to implement, they do require programming that is beyond the scope of this book. There are numerous resources available for additional exploration of these topics.

These three methods are not the only ways to create interactive Web pages. You can also use CGI scripts and ISAPI applications, among others. Although these other approaches are just as valid, they do require significantly more programming than the methods discussed here.

Internet Database Connector

The Internet Database Connector is an ISAPI application that retrieves live data from a database through the Internet based on a user's request through hard-coded parameters or HTML input fields. Although IDC was quite effective in its time for accessing data in an ODBC data source, it does have some restrictions.

IDC is a fairly dead technology. For the most part, IDC/HTX died with the advent of ASP 2.0, although you may still find some sites that use IDC.

The most significant restriction of IDC is that it is designed to retrieve data from a database, not to input data. This means that you would have to use additional ISAPI or CGI applications to handle the data input. For this reason, pages created using IDC are often called *dynamic* (rather than *interactive) pages*. Because they cannot accept data for input into a database, they are not truly interactive.

An easier way to solve the interactivity problem with IDC is to use stored procedures on the SQL Server computer and call these stored procedures from your IDC file. Parameters can be passed to the stored procedure through HTML input fields.

Another restriction lies in the fact that IDC is an ISAPI extension. This approach is therefore valid only when using IIS as your Web server. Because this restriction is also present for the other two methods of interactive data access, you may not be able to do much about this one.

ISAPI stands for Internet Server Application Programming Interface, the programming functions for Microsoft Internet Information Server. Unlike common gateway interface (CGI) applications, ISAPI applications run in the address space of the Web server and are therefore usually faster than comparable CGI applications.

The last major restriction of IDC wasn't a restriction at all until about March 1997 when Microsoft officially introduced ADO to the world. ADO is built on the Object Linking and Embedding DataBase (OLE-DB) data access model and is Microsoft's replacement for Open Database Connectivity (ODBC). As OLE-DB matures and OLE-DB service providers become more common, ODBC will eventually be pushed out as the primary method of accessing data through a generic application programming interface (API). IDC works only through ODBC and is not an OLE-DB-compatible technology.

To use IDC in your applications, you must create two text files for every query that you wish to run. One of these files will have an extension of .idc while the other will end in .htx.

The IDC file contains all the information the Web server will need to connect to the data source and run the query. Among the information listed in the IDC file is the Data Source name of your database server, authentication information, the SQL statement that will be run against the server, and the name and location of the HTX file that will be used to format the output.

The HTX file is very similar in concept to the HTML template file mentioned earlier. The HTX file is actually an HTML template file that will determine how the output of the database request will appear in the resulting Web page. As with the HTML template used by the Web Assistant, server-side tags (<% %>) are used to indicate to the IDC application where to place the results in the HTML output.

To access the output, you can simply provide a link that points to the URL of the IDC file located in a server that has the IDC extensions installed. This IDC application can then process the query and send the results back to the calling browser by sending them through the HTX template.

Although the IDC does have some limitations in creating truly interactive pages, it is highly efficient in accessing real-time data through the Internet. Often, this can be sufficient for your requirements.

Remote Data Services (RDS)

Remote Data Services is a set of ActiveX components used to access database information through a Web browser. With the introduction of the Advanced Data Connector (later renamed the Remote Data Services of ActiveX Data Objects [ADO]), it is possible to create a disconnected recordset. Some RDS components run on the client inside the browser, whereas other components run on the Web server and interact directly with the database.

To access data through RDS, the RDS code is placed on the Web page that will receive the recordset from the database server. This control is designed to interact with a server-side component called the *RDS DataFactory* and with DHTML (Dynamic HTML). The factory is an ActiveX component that runs on the server and will accept data requests from the browser and make calls against the RDS application, an ISAPI application running on the server. The application will retrieve the results from the data source and pass the results back to the factory, which then transfers the results back to the browser.

Data updates can be made directly to the database using RDS. For maximum efficiency, however, consider isolating update transactions in temporary tables for later application to the database.

ActiveX Data Objects and Active Server Pages

The last approach that we will look at is the one that will require the greatest amount of programming but will also give you the greatest level of flexibility. That is using ActiveX Data Objects with Active Server Pages. ADO is built upon the OLE-DB standard and can access databases either through ODBC or through OLE-DB service providers.

Both ASP and RDS offer a lot of flexibility and require a good deal of programming. The biggest difference, if you want to compare and contrast, is that ASP is run server side, whereas RDS is run client side. In reality, you can use a combination of ASP and RDS to offer the greatest flexibility.

Active Server Pages are sections of tag-delimited VBScript or JavaScript code that can intermingle with normal HTML tags in an HTML style document and run on a Web server but never in a browser. If you will remember, any time that you wish to use an ActiveX component inside a Web browser, the browser must first download that component and register it on the local system. If the user has their browser security set to a level that denies the download, or if your control is not properly signed, this could cause the download to fail and the process to abort. In addition, in order for a browser to have the capacity to implement ActiveX controls, the browser must support ActiveX and be running on a 32-bit Windows operating system. This cannot always be guaranteed, unfortunately, making some applications unavailable to such users.

Active Server Pages solve this problem by forcing all ActiveX components to run on the server; the browser will receive only pure HTML, with no controls to download and no security issues to be concerned about.

Active Server Pages are controlled through some scripting language such as VBScript or JavaScript or even PERLScript (if PERLScript support is installed on the IIS server). This server-side script gives you significant flexibility while still maintaining total client-side security. A detailed discussion of implementing Active Server Pages is far beyond the scope of this book; however, there are abundant resources available to provide you with additional information.

Summary

In this chapter, you learned about creating and managing alerts, operators, and jobs to help you with your administrative duties:

- The Msdb database holds all the information for alerts, operators, jobs, and the history of jobs. Because of this, you should schedule regular backups of this database.

- The SQL Server Agent is a helper service that oversees the automation of jobs inside SQL Server. You must configure SQL Server Agent correctly before any of your alerts, operators, or jobs will work. Configuring the SQL Server Agent consists primarily of setting up a user account for it to use and assigning the account to the Agent.

- Alerts can watch the Windows NT event log, and they can cause a job to execute upon finding predefined error messages. Alerts from multiple SQL Server computers can be forwarded to a central server to make management of many servers easier.

- You can define operators so that SQL Server can e-mail and/or page the operator upon success and/or failure of jobs. SQL Server is MAPI enabled, which allows it to send and receive e-mail.

- Jobs can be defined that can run T-SQL statements, command-prompt commands, and replication jobs. Jobs can be run on a regular basis, on demand when an alert triggers, or only once.

- We finished the chapter with a look at how to automate pushing HTML Web pages from SQL data and the various methods of setting up pull pages.

Exam Essentials

Understand the process for creating and modifying jobs. Know when it is appropriate to create jobs, what they can do, and how to modify the steps and schedules of a job.

Know how to create and modify alerts. You need to know how to create alerts based on error numbers or Performance Condition counters, how to set the response of an alert, and how to modify alerts.

Know how to create and modify operators. You need to know how to enable mail support and create and modify operators to be notified by e-mail or pop-up messages.

Enable XML support for SQL Server in IIS. Know how to enable XML support for SQL Server in IIS by creating a virtual directory and know the various security settings for the virtual directory.

Be able to create a Web publishing job Know how to use the Web Publishing Wizard to create a job that will publish Web pages. You should be familiar with how to set the Web page to update when the data changes as well as how to schedule regular updates.

Key Terms

alerts	Messaging Application Programming Interface (MAPI)
events	Msdb database
eXtensible Markup Language (XML)	operators
Internet Information Server (IIS)	Sqlisapi.dll
jobs	SQL Server Agent

Review Questions

1. What rights does the SQL Server Agent service account need? (Select all that apply.)

   A. Logon as a Service right

   B. Local Administrator group membership

   C. Backup Operators membership

   D. Server Operators membership

2. What is the API set that allows SQL Server to send and receive e-mail?

   A. TAPI

   B. EAPI

   C. OLE

   D. MAPI

3. Which database holds alert and job information?

   A. The Master database.

   B. The Model database.

   C. The Msdb database.

   D. None—it is held in the Registry.

4. How can you rebuild the Msdb database?

   A. You can't; you must reinstall SQL Server.

   B. Rebuild the Master database.

   C. Rebuild just the Msdb database.

   D. Stop and restart SQL Server; the Msdb database will be rebuilt automatically.

5. Where do alerts look for errors?

   A. The Windows application log.

   B. The SQL Server event log.

   C. The Master database error log.

   D. SQL Server sends errors directly to the alert engine.

6. What kinds of jobs can be created? (Select all that apply.)

   A. T-SQL (Transact-SQL)

   B. CmdExec (command prompt)

   C. Replication

   D. Active script

7. How can you create new error messages in SQL Server?

   A. You can't.

   B. Run the Setup program and choose Custom ➢ Edit Messages.

   C. Right-click the server and choose Manage SQL Server Messages.

   D. Go to the `Messages` folder, right-click, and choose New Message.

8. What is the best way to stop an alert for a couple of hours?

   A. Disable the alert.

   B. Set the hit counter of the alert to –1.

   C. Delete the alert.

   D. Deselect any operators that were being notified.

9. What is the operator of last resort called?

   A. Weekend operator

   B. Last-chance operator

   C. Notification operator

   D. Fail-safe operator

10. What is the central server that receives alerts from other SQL Server servers called?

   A. Central alerter

   B. Standardized alerter

   C. Central control

   D. Unhandled events server

11. You have four SQL Server computers. Server1 is SQL Server 6.5 running on Windows NT Server, Server2 is SQL Server 2000 running on Windows 98, Server3 is SQL Server 2000 running on Windows NT Workstation, and Server4 is SQL Server 2000 running on Windows NT Server. Which servers can be designated as master server in a multiserver environment? (Select all that apply.)

   A. Server1

   B. Server2

   C. Server3

   D. Server4

12. You have four SQL Server computers. Server1 is SQL Server 6.5 running on Windows NT Server, Server2 is SQL Server 2000 running on Windows 98, Server3 is SQL Server 2000 running on Windows NT Workstation, and Server4 is SQL Server 2000 running on Windows NT Server. Which servers can be designated as target server in a multiserver environment? (Select all that apply.)

   A. Server1

   B. Server2

   C. Server3

   D. Server4

13. Server1 is designated as a target server for multiserver jobs. Where will the status of the jobs it gets from the master server be recorded?

    A. Only at the master server

    B. Only at the target server

    C. At both the master and target servers

    D. Nowhere

14. You want SQL Server to be able to send messages upon job completion using an Exchange operator. Which of these steps is required to create e-mail operators? (Select all that apply.)

    A. Create an Exchange account for the SQL Server Agent service account.

    B. Assign the SQL Server Agent service to use a service account.

    C. Create an operator.

    D. Assign the job to notify the appropriate operator.

15. You have created a user-defined message that says, "Please call the help desk," is numbered 50001, and is configured to post to the NT application log. Which command will display the SQL message number 50001 and post it to the Windows NT application log?

    A. PRINT 50001

    B. PRINT (50001, 10, 1)

    C. RAISERROR 50001

    D. RAISERROR (50001, 10, 1)

16. You have a master server (called production) and two target servers (sales and accounting) set for jobs. You want the sales server jobs to now be managed by a server called marketing. In what order would you complete these steps? (Select all that apply.)

    A. Enlist the sales server to the marketing server.

    B. Enlist the marketing server as a master server.

    C. Divorce the sales server from the production server.

    D. Create operator accounts for the management and sales servers.

17. You wish to allow users to connect to SQL Server via XML. Which program do you use to set up XML support?

   A. Enterprise Manager

   B. IIS Administrator

   C. Service Manager

   D. Configure XML Support utility

18. What kind of directory do you set up for IIS to support virtual SQL directories?

   A. FTP directory

   B. Root directory

   C. Virtual directory

   D. HTTP directory

19. You have created an alert that is configured to e-mail you and do a Net Send. Your MAPI server is down when the alert triggers. What will happen?

   A. You will get e-mailed and a pop-up message will occur.

   B. You will only get the e-mail.

   C. You will only get the pop-up message.

   D. You will get no notification.

20. You want SQL Server to alert you when your server CPU goes higher than 75% for more than 2 seconds. How can you do this?

   A. Create an alert based on the CPU percentage.

   B. Create a custom error. Create an alert that looks for the custom error. Use a trigger to run the RAISERROR command when the CPU is busy.

   C. Create a job that runs Performance Condition.

   D. It is not possible to create SQL alerts on counters other than SQL counters.

Answers to Review Questions

1. A, B. The service account you use for SQL Server and the SQL Server Agent needs to be at least the Local Administrators account and have the Logon as a Service right. Making the account a member of the Backup or Server Operator groups is not enough.

2. D. MAPI stands for Messaging Application Programming Interface and is the interface between SQL Server and Exchange for e-mail. TAPI is Telephony API, OLE is Object Linking and Embedding, and there is no such thing as EAPI.

3. C. The Msdb database holds alert and job information. It basically holds all of the information for the SQL Server Agent. The Master database holds information about other databases and settings, Model is a template for databases, and the Registry doesn't hold very many settings for SQL Server.

4. B. When you rebuild the Master database, you automatically rebuild the Msdb database as well. You can't choose to rebuild just the Msdb when you run `Rebuildm.exe`.

5. A. The alert engine looks in the Windows application log file for errors. Note that if the log gets full, the alert engine no longer functions correctly.

6. A, B, C, D. All of these types of jobs can be created.

7. C. You can create custom messages from the Manage SQL Server Messages option. There is no `Messages` folder, and the setup program does not allow you to create new messages.

8. A. You can disable alerts without having to delete them. You could, of course, delete the alert, but that would not be the best way because you would have to rebuild it later if you wanted to run it again.

9. D. The fail-safe operator gets notified if there is no one else. You can specify the weekend, last-chance, or notification operator by specifying the fail-safe operator.

10. D. The unhandled events server gets events from other servers.

11. C, D. Only SQL Server 2000 running on Windows NT or Windows 2000 can be master job servers.

12. C, D. Only SQL Server 2000 running on Windows NT or Windows 2000 can be job targets.

13. C. You can check the status of jobs at both the master and target servers.

14. A, B, C, D. All of these steps are required to enable e-mail notification of job completion.

15. D. The RAISERROR command needs three parameters to work. The PRINT command will not display the message and put it in the Windows log.

16. D, B, C, A. You need to create operators, create the master server, divorce the target servers from old relationships, and then enlist the targets to new master servers.

17. D. You need to use the Configure XML Support utility to set up XML to SQL support. The utility is found in the SQL 2000 program group. You can't configure XML and SQL support in Enterprise Manager, Service Manager, or IIS Administrator.

18. C. You need to create a virtual directory in IIS if you want users to access SQL Server via XML and HTTP.

19. C. The MAPI or e-mail server being down will prevent the e-mail from being sent, but the Net Send notification will create a pop-up message.

20. D. You can only build SQL Server alerts on SQL Server counters.

Creating and Implementing a Replication Solution in SQL Server 2000

MICROSOFT EXAM OBJECTIVE COVERED IN THIS CHAPTER:

✓ Configure, maintain, and troubleshoot replication services.

Replication allows for the distribution of your SQL Server 2000 data to other database engines. This includes both SQL Server 2000 databases and non-SQL Server databases such as Oracle and IBM's DB2 database. This chapter covers a great deal of ground regarding replication. We will first look at the publisher/subscriber metaphor that has been implemented in SQL Server 2000's replication strategy. This metaphor includes *publishers*, *distributors*, and *subscribers* and goes a step further by including *publications* and *articles*.

This chapter discusses the factors that affect replication—transactional consistency, latency, and site autonomy influence your distribution choice, whether it be transactional, merge, or something else. It also examines the way in which replication actually works, with the various replication agents that work in concert to move your data from a publisher through the distributor and on to the subscribers.

The administrative concerns involved with replication include security issues, data definition issues, non-SQL Server 2000 database issues, and other SQL Server configuration issues. Several replication scenarios can be implemented. These scenarios are important, since each scenario has specific advantages and disadvantages for a particular business situation that the replication strategy must address.

This chapter will detail how to install and run replication on your SQL Server 2000 computer. We will walk through the process of setting up a distributor, a publisher, and a subscriber. We will then create a publication, subscribe to it, and check whether replication is working properly.

The chapter will also look at some optimization and troubleshooting techniques specific to our replication tasks.

Overview of Replication

You use replication to put copies of the same data at different locations throughout the enterprise. The most common of the many reasons you might want to replicate your data include:

- Moving data closer to the user.

- Reducing locking conflicts when multiple sites wish to work with the same data.

- Allowing site autonomy so that each location can set up its own rules and procedures for working with its copy of the data.

- Removing the impact of read-intensive operations such as report generation and ad hoc query processing from the OLTP database.

The two basic forms of replication used in SQL Server 2000 are replication and distributed transactions. Whether you use one or the other type, copies of the data are current and consistent. You can also use both strategies in the same environment.

The main difference between replication and distributed transactions is in the timing. With distributed transactions, your data is 100 percent in synchronization, 100 percent of the time. When you use replication, there is some latency involved. It may be as little as a few seconds, or as long as several days or even weeks. Distributed transactions require that the replicated databases be connected at all times. If they are not, then the distributed transactions will fail. Replication does not have this requirement.

The Publisher/Subscriber Metaphor

SQL Server 2000 uses a publisher/subscriber metaphor to describe and implement replication. Your database can play different roles as part of the replication scenario: it can be a publisher, subscriber, distributor, or any combination of these. When you publish data, you do it in the form of an *article*, which is stored in a publication. Here is a list of key terms used as part of the publisher/subscriber metaphor.

Publisher   This is the source database where replication begins. The publisher makes data available for replication.

Subscriber   The subscriber is the destination database where replication ends and either receives a snapshot of all the published data or applies transactions that have been replicated to it.

Distributor   This is the intermediary between the publisher and subscriber. The distributor receives published transactions or snapshots and then stores and forwards these publications to the subscribers.

Publication   The publication is the storage container for different articles. A subscriber can subscribe to an individual article or an entire publication.

Article   An article is the data, transactions, or stored procedures that are stored within a publication. This is the actual information that is going to be replicated.

Two-Phase Commit   *Two-phase commit* (sometimes referred to as *2PC*) is a form of replication in which modifications made to the publishing database are made at the subscription database at exactly the same time. This is handled through the use of distributed transactions. As with any transaction, either all statements commit successfully, or all modifications are rolled back. Two-phase commit uses the Microsoft Distributed Transaction Coordinator (MS-DTC) to accomplish its tasks. The MS-DTC implements the functionality of a portion of the Microsoft Transaction Server. In this chapter, we will focus on replication as opposed to two-phase commits.

A publisher can publish data to one or more distributors. A subscriber can subscribe through one or more distributors. A distributor can have one or more publishers and subscribers.

Articles

An article is data in a table. This data can be the entire table or just a subset of the data in the table. Your articles need to be bundled into one or more publications in order for them to be distributed to the subscribers. When you want to publish a subset of data in a table, you must specify some type of partitioning, either vertical or horizontal.

With a vertical partition, you select specific columns from your table. In a horizontal partition, you select only specific rows of data from the table. Figure 9.1 shows an example of both a vertical and a horizontal partition. Here, the horizontal partition might be useful in situations where you want to make specific rows of data available to different regions. More specifically, you could create three separate articles. One article would be horizontally partitioned based on region 1. The next article would be horizontally partitioned on region 2, and the third on region 3. Each region could then subscribe to only its regional data.

FIGURE 9.1   You can create articles based on subsets of your data.

ReCode	EmpID	Q1	Q2	Q3
1	5	40.1	39.8	37.7
1	7	28.7	33.5	38.2
1	8	39.9	42.2	48.1
1	13	28.8	32.8	33.7

Horizontal partition

ReCode	EmpID	Q1	Q2	Q3
2	2		44.6	
1	5		39.8	
2	3		41.7	
3	11		28.8	
1	7		33.5	
1	8		42.2	
3	22		45.5	
1	13		32.8	

Vertical partition

Publications

Articles must be stored in a publication, which is the basis for your subscriptions. When you create a subscription, you are actually subscribing to an entire publication; however, you can read individual articles. Referential integrity is maintained within your publication because all articles in a publication are updated at the same time.

In SQL Server 2000, you can publish to non-Microsoft SQL Server computers. The replicated data does not need to be in the same sort order or data type. While it is possible to replicate to different sort orders and data types, we do not recommend it.

Replication Factors and Distribution Types

Before you can choose a distribution type, you should understand the factors that influence your decision. The three main items to consider are autonomy, latency, and transactional consistency. You must also consider the questions that must be answered in making the decision.

Autonomy   This refers to how much independence you wish to give each subscriber with regard to the replicated data. Will the replicated data be considered read-only? How long will the data at a subscriber be valid? How often do you need to connect to the distributor to download more data?

Latency   Latency refers to how often your data will be updated. Does it need to be in synchronization at all times? Is every minute enough? What if you are a salesman on the road who dials in to the office once a day? Is this good enough?

Transactional consistency   Although there are several types of replication, the most common method is to move transactions from the publisher through the distributor and onto the subscriber. Transactional consistency comes into play here. Do all the transactions that are stored need to be applied at the same time and in order? What happens if there is a delay in the processing?

Once you understand these factors, you need to start asking yourself the following questions, after which you can decide on a distribution type:

- What am I going to publish? Will it be all the data in a table, or will I partition information?

- Who has access to my publications? Are these subscribers connected or dial-up users?

- Will subscribers be able to update my data, or is their information considered read-only?

- How often should I synchronize my publishers and subscribers?

- How fast is my network? Can subscribers be connected at all times? How much traffic is there on my network?

Distribution Types

Each of the several types of distribution you can use has different levels of autonomy, transactional consistency, and latency involved. There are three basic types to choose from: snapshot replication, transactional replication, and merge replication.

When you factor in latency, autonomy, and consistency, you end up with six different distribution types:

- Distributed transactions

- Transactional replication

- Transactional replication with immediate updating subscribers

- Snapshot replication

- Snapshot replication with immediate updating subscribers

- Merge replication

As shown in Figure 9.2, distributed transactions have the least amount of latency and autonomy, but they have the highest level of consistency. Merge replication has the highest amount of latency and autonomy and a lower level of consistency.

FIGURE 9.2 Distribution types

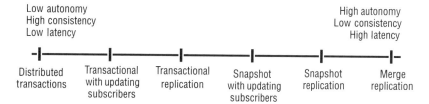

Using Distributed Transactions

When you use distributed transactions (also called two-phase commit or 2PC) to replicate your data, you have almost no autonomy or latency, but you do have guaranteed transactional consistency. With 2PC, either all changes are made at exactly the same time, or none of the changes are made. Remember that all the affected subscribers must be in contact with the publisher at all times. This type of distribution is most useful in situations where subscribers must have real-time data, as in a reservation system.

For example, think of a cruise line that has only so many rooms of a particular type available. If someone in Dallas wants the Captain's suite and someone in California also wants the Captain's suite, the first one to book the room will get it. The other booking won't be allowed, because that location will immediately show that the room is already booked.

Using Transactional Replication

When you use this distribution method, transactions are gathered from the publishers and stored in the distribution database. Subscribers then receive these transactions and must work with the data as if it were read-only. This is because any changes made to their local copy of the data might prohibit new transactions from being applied properly, which would destroy the transactional consistency.

There is, however, some limited autonomy at each site. You can introduce some latency, because the subscribers don't have to be in contact at all times. Transactional consistency can be maintained as long as the subscribed data remains unchanged by the subscribers.

The advantages to this approach include the fact that transactions are relatively small items to move through the system (unlike snapshot replication, which we will look at shortly). The main disadvantage of using transactional replication is that subscribers must treat the data as read-only.

Use this distribution method when subscribers can treat their data as read-only and need the updated information with a minimal amount of latency.

This type of replication would be useful in an order processing/distribution system with several locations where orders are taken. Each of those order locations would be a publisher, and the published orders could then be replicated to a subscription database at your central warehouse. The central warehouse could then accept the orders, fill them, and ship them out.

Using Transactional Replication with Immediate Updating Subscribers

When you use transactional replication with immediate updating subscribers, you are gaining site autonomy, minimizing latency, and keeping transactional consistency. This (in most cases) would be considered the best possible solution.

When you implement transactional replication with immediate updating subscribers, you are essentially working with all the tenets of transactional replication. The major difference is that when you change the subscription data, 2PC changes the publishing database as well. In this fashion, your local subscriber is updated at exactly the same time as the publisher. Other subscribers will have your changes downloaded to them at their next synchronization.

This scenario can be useful for a reservation system that needs to be updated frequently but does not need total synchronization. Let's use a library as an example here. You wish to reserve a book on SQL Server 2000. You go to the computer and look up the book you wish to reserve and find that one copy is currently available. When you try to reserve the book, however, you might find that your data isn't 100 percent up-to-date, and the book has already been checked out. In this example, when you try to reserve your book, the subscriber automatically runs a 2PC to the publisher. At the publisher, someone has already checked out that last copy, and therefore the update fails. At the next synchronization, your subscriber will be updated with the news that the last copy has been checked out.

Using Snapshot Replication

When you use snapshot replication as your distribution method, you are actually moving an entire copy of the published items through the distributor and on to the subscribers. This type of replication allows for a high level of both site autonomy and transactional consistency because all records are going to be copied from the publisher, and the local copy of the data will be overwritten at the next synchronization. Latency may be a bit higher as you probably will not move an entire snapshot every few minutes.

OLAP (Online Analytical Processing) servers are a prime candidate for this type of replication. The data at each subscriber is considered read-only and doesn't have to be 100 percent in synchronization all the time. This allows your MIS departments to run their reporting and ad hoc queries on reasonably fresh data without affecting the OLTP server (which is doing all of the order-processing work).

Keep in mind that administrators and MIS ad hoc queries generally don't modify the data. They are looking for historical information such as how many widgets they sold, so that data that is a few hours or even a few days old will generally not make a difference to the results returned by the queries.

Using Snapshot Replication with Immediate Updating Subscribers

The initial portion of this distribution style works just as in snapshot replication, with the added ability for the subscriber to update the publisher with new information. The updates use the 2PC protocol as described previously.

This maintains a high level of site autonomy, a high level of transactional consistency, and a moderate level of latency. The data may be downloaded to the subscriber only once a day, but any updates the subscriber tries to make to data must first be approved by the publisher.

This type of distribution is useful when you have read-only data that needs to be updated infrequently. If your data needs to be updated often, we suggest that you use transactional replication with immediate updating subscribers.

Snapshot replication might be useful when auditing your database, downloading portions of the data, and then double-checking that everything is being updated properly. The occasional mistake could then be quickly fixed and auditing could continue.

Using Merge Replication

Merge replication provides the highest amount of site autonomy, the highest latency, and the lowest level of transactional consistency. Merge replication allows each subscriber to make changes to their local copy of the data. At some point, these changes are merged with those made by other subscribers as well as changes made at the publisher. Ultimately, all sites receive the updates from all other sites. This is known as *convergence*; that is, all changes from all sites converge and are redistributed so that all sites have the same changes.

Transactional consistency is nearly nonexistent here, as different sites may all be making changes to the same data, resulting in conflicts. SQL Server 2000 will automatically choose a particular change over another change and then converge that data. To simplify: sooner or later, all sites will have the same copy of the data, but that data may not necessarily be what you want. For example, subscriber A makes changes to record 100. Subscriber B also makes changes to record 100. While this doesn't sound too bad, suppose the changes that subscriber A made to record 100 are due to changes that were made to record 50. If subscriber B doesn't have the same data in record 50, then subscriber B will make a different decision. Obviously, this can be incredibly complex.

You might wonder why anyone would want to use merge replication. There are many reasons to use it, and with some careful planning you can make merge replication work to your advantage. There are triggers you can modify to determine which record is the correct record to use. The default rule when records are changed at multiple sites is to take the changes based on a site priority, converge the results, and then send them out. The exception to this general rule is when the main database is changed as well as all of the user databases. In this case, the user changes are applied first and then the main database changes. For example, say you have a central server that you call Main, and you have 20 sales people who are using merge replication. If one of your sales people modifies record 25 and you modify record 25 at the Main server, when the records are converged, the user changes will first be placed in the Main server and then the Main server changes will overwrite them.

If you design your publishers and subscribers to minimize conflicts, merge replication can be very advantageous. Look at the highway patrol, for example. A patrol car might pull over a car and write up a ticket for speeding. At the end of the day, that data is merged with data from other officers who have also written tickets. The data is then converged back to all of the different squad car computers, and now all of the police know whom to watch for on the roads.

Replication Internals

Understanding how the transactions or snapshots are handled is essential to a full understanding of how SQL Server 2000 implements replication.

When you set up your subscribers, you can create either pull or push subscriptions. Push subscriptions help to centralize your administrative duties, since the subscription itself is stored on the distribution server. This allows the publisher to determine what data is in the subscription and when that subscription will be synchronized. In other words, the data can be pushed to the subscribers based on the publisher's schedule. Push subscriptions are most useful if a subscriber needs to be updated whenever a change occurs at the publisher. Since the publisher knows when the modification takes place, it can immediately push those changes to the subscribers.

Pull subscriptions are configured and maintained at each subscriber. The subscribers will administer the synchronization schedules and can pull changes whenever they consider it necessary. This type of subscriber also relieves some of the overhead of processing from the distribution server. Pull subscriptions are also useful in situations where security is not a primary issue. In fact, pull subscriptions can be set up to allow anonymous connections, including pull subscribers residing on the Internet.

Ordinarily, non-SQL Server databases like Oracle and Access must use push subscriptions. If you have a real need to pull with another database system, you can write your own custom program using SQL Data Management Objects (SQL-DMO).

In either a push or a pull environment, four replication agents handle the tasks of moving data from the publisher to the distributor and then on to the subscribers. The location of the particular agent is dependent upon the type of replication (push or pull) you are using.

Logreader agent Located on the distribution server, the logreader's job is to monitor the transaction logs of published databases that are using this distributor. When the logreader agent finds a transaction, it moves the transaction to the distribution database on the distributor; transactions are stored and then forwarded to the subscribers by the distribution agent for transactional and snapshot replication, or by the merge agent for merge replication.

Distribution agent The distribution agent is responsible for moving the stored transactions from the distributor to the subscribers.

Snapshot agent This agent, which is also used for snapshot replication, is responsible for copying the schema and data from the publisher to the subscriber. Before any type of replication can begin, a copy of the data must reside on each subscriber. With this baseline established, transactions can then be applied at each subscriber and transactional consistency can be maintained.

Merge agent The merge agent is responsible for converging records from multiple sites and then redistributing the converged records back to the subscribers.

We will now see how these different agents work in concert to create the different distribution types.

You do not have to choose a single type of distribution for all your subscribers. Each subscriber can implement a different type of data distribution.

Remote Agent Activation is new to SQL Server 2000. This allows you to run a distribution or merge agent on one machine and activate it from another. This can save resources on your servers in a heavy replication environment.

Merge Replication

When you use merge replication, the merge agent can be centrally located on the distributor, or it can reside on every subscriber involved in the merge replication process. When you have implemented push replication, the merge agent will reside on the distributor. In a pull scenario, the merge agent is on every subscriber.

The following steps outline the merge process and how each agent interacts with the other agents.

1. As shown in Figure 9.3, the snapshot agent that resides on the distribution server takes an initial snapshot of the data and moves it to the subscribers. This move takes place through the Distribution working folder. The folder is just a holding area for the snapshot data to wait before it is moved on to the subscriber. As stated earlier, this must be done first so that later transactions can be applied.

FIGURE 9.3 How the merge replication process works

Distribution

Publisher   Subscriber

Publishing database   Distribution database   Subscribing database

Snapshot agent

Merge agent   Merge agent
Push   Pull

Distribution
working
folder

Subscribers must have the appropriate permissions to access the Distribution working folder on the distribution server.

2. Replication can now begin.

3. The merge agent (wherever it resides) will take modifications from the publishers and apply them to the subscribers.

4. The merge agent will also take modifications from the subscribers and apply them to the publishers.

5. The merge agent will gather any merge conflicts and resolve them by using triggers. Merge information will be stored in tables at the distributor. This allows you to track data lineage.

When you use merge replication, some significant changes are made to the table schema as well as the distribution database. These changes allow the triggers to handle conflict resolution. You should keep the following in mind when implementing merge replication:

- Several system tables will be added to the databases involved.

- SQL Server creates triggers on the publishing and subscription servers used for merger replication. These triggers are automatically invoked when changes are made at either of these locations. Information about the changes is stored in the database system tables on the distribution server. With this change information, your SQL Server can track the lineage or history of changes made to a particular row of data.

- The UNIQUEIDENTIFIER column is added as a new column for each table involved in the merge replication (unless one already exists). This new column has the ROWGUID property assigned to it. A GUID is a 128-bit globally unique identifier that allows the same row of data modified in different subscribers to be uniquely identified.

Merge replication is most useful in situations where there will be few conflicts. A horizontally partitioned table based on a region code or some other ID is best suited to merge replication.

Unlike its predecessor, SQL Server 2000 allows vertical partitions for merge replication.

Conflict Resolution in Merge Replication

Performing updates to the same records at multiple locations causes conflicts. To resolve these conflicts, SQL Server 2000 adds some tables and triggers to the distribution server. The system tables on the distributor track changes made to each row. The rows are differentiated by their ROWGUID, and a history or lineage of changes is recorded for each row involved in the merge.

Using this lineage, the merge agent evaluates the current values for a record and the new values and automatically resolves conflicts using triggers. You can create your own custom conflict resolution process by customizing and prioritizing the triggers.

When you begin to customize the conflict resolution process, we suggest that you store both the record that is converged and the conflicting records that were not converged. This allows you to manually test and optimize your triggers. Note that creating and modifying triggers are beyond the scope of this book. For more information, see the SQL Server Books Online, or *MCSD: SQL Server 2000 Database Design Study Guide* (Sybex, 2000).

Snapshot Replication

When you use snapshot replication, an entire copy of the publication is moved from the publisher to the subscriber. Everything on the subscriber database is overwritten, allowing for autonomy as well as transactional consistency, as all changes are made at once. Latency can be high for this type of replication if you want it to be. You can schedule your refreshes when and as often as you wish (we have found that this normally occurs once a day, at off-peak hours). Keep in mind that snapshot replication occurs on demand. This means that no data is transferred from the publisher to the distributor until a subscriber is ready to receive it. The snapshot then moves straight through. Status information is stored in the distribution database; however, the snapshot agent and the distribution agent do all their work at the time the snapshot is initiated.

When you use snapshot replication, there is no merge agent. The distribution agent is used. If you are using a pull replication, the distribution agent is found on the subscription server. If you are doing a push replication, the agent is found on the distributor. When used in a push scenario, snapshot replication consumes a large amount of overhead on the distribution server. We suggest that most snapshot subscribers use a pull scenario at regularly scheduled intervals. The following steps (see Figure 9.4) outline the snapshot replication process:

1. The snapshot agent reads the published article and then creates the table schema and data in the Distribution working folder.

2. The distribution agent creates the schema on the subscriber.

3. The distribution agent moves the data into the newly created tables on the subscriber.

4. Any indexes that were used are re-created on the newly synchronized subscription database.

   This works in the same fashion when you are using snapshot replication with immediate updating subscribers. The only difference is that the subscriber will use a two-phase commit to update both the subscription database and the publishing database at the same time. During the next refresh, all subscribers will receive a copy of the modified data.

FIGURE 9.4 The snapshot replication process

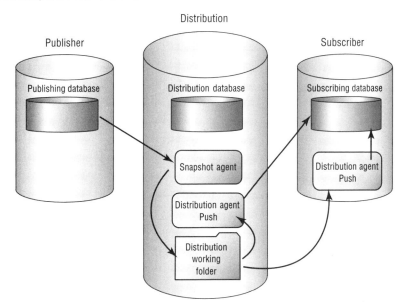

Transactional Replication

When you use transactional replication, only the changes (transactions) made to the data are moved. Before these transactions can be applied at a subscriber however, the subscriber must have a copy of the data as a base. Because of its speed and its relatively low overhead on the distribution server, transactional replication is currently the most often used form of replication. Generally, data on the subscriber is treated as read-only, unless you are implementing transactional replication with immediate updating subscribers. Because the transactions are so small, this type of replication is often set up to run continuously. Every time a change is made at the publisher, it is automatically applied to the subscriber, generally within one minute.

When you use transactional replication, there is no need for the merge agent. The snapshot agent must still run at least once; it uses the distribution agent to move the initial snapshot from the publisher to the subscriber. You also use the logreader agent when using transactional replication. The logreader agent looks for transactions in published databases and moves those transactions to the distribution database. The following steps (see Figure 9.5) outline the transactional replication process.

FIGURE 9.5 The transactional replication process

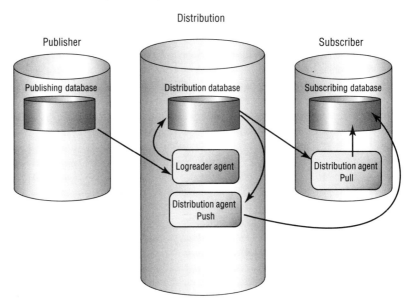

1. The snapshot agent reads the published article and then creates the schema on the subscriber and bulk-copies the snapshot over to the subscriber. (This is done only when the subscription is created or re-created.)

2. The logreader agent scans the transaction logs of databases marked for publishing. When it finds an appropriate transaction, it copies the transaction to the distribution database. The distribution database will store the transaction for a configurable length of time.

3. The distribution agent will then apply those transactions to the subscribers at the next synchronization. The subscriber then runs the `sp_repldone` system stored procedure on the distribution database. This marks the newly replicated transactions stored on the distributor in the `Msrepl_commands` table as completed.

4. When the next distribution cleanup task executes, the marked transactions are truncated from the distribution server.

Publication Considerations

Before you start your replication process, there are a few more things to consider. This includes data definition issues, IDENTITY column issues and some general rules that are involved when publishing. Keep the following data definition items in mind when you are preparing to publish data:

Timestamp datatypes   A timestamp datatype is different than a datetime datatype. Timestamps are automatically updated to the current date and time whenever the record is inserted or updated. When they are replicated, they are changed to a binary datatype to ensure that the data from the publisher matches the data at the subscriber. If it was not altered, the timestamp will automatically update itself when the transaction is applied at the subscriber. This is the opposite with merge replication, where the timestamp datatype is replicated but the data is not. This allows the timestamp to be regenerated at the subscriber and used in conflict resolution.

IDENTITY   SQL Server 2000, unlike its precursors, has the capability to replicate identity values. To do this, you must assign a range of identity values to each server involved in the replication at the time the publication is created (for example, the publisher gets 1000–2000, subscriber A gets 2001–3000, subscriber B gets 3001–4000). When each server runs out of identity values, a new range is automatically assigned.

UNIQUEIDENTIFIER   The UNIQUEIDENTIFIER will create GUIDs that are used during merge replication. If you would like to use them yourself, you can set the default value of this column to the NEWID() function. This will automatically generate a ROWGUID. This is similar to the way that IDENTITY values are automatically generated.

User-defined datatypes   If you have created your own user-defined datatypes on the publishing server, you must also create those same datatypes on the subscriptions servers if you wish to replicate that particular column of data.

You should keep the following publishing restrictions in mind as well:

- If you are not using snapshot replication, your replicated tables must have a primary key to ensure transactional integrity.

- Publications cannot span multiple databases. All articles in a publication must be derived from a single database.

- Image, text, and ntext BLOBs are not replicated when you use transactional or merge replication. Because of their size, these objects must be refreshed by running a snapshot. What will be replicated is the 16-byte pointer to their storage location within the publishing database.

- You cannot replicate from the Master, Model, Msdb, or Tempdb databases.

Replication Models

There are several different models you can use when you implement replication:

- Central publisher/central distributor

- Central publisher/remote distributor

- Central subscriber/multiple publishers

- Multiple publishers/multiple subscribers

Let's look more closely at each of these and see what business situations they most accurately represent.

Central Publisher/Central Distributor

As shown in Figure 9.6, both the Publishing database and the Distribution database are on the same SQL Server. This configuration is useful when modeling replication strategies for the following business scenarios:

- Asynchronous order processing during communication outages

- Distribution of price lists, customer lists, vendor lists, etc.

- Removal of MIS activities from the OLTP environment

- Establishment of executive information systems

One of the most important aspects of the central publisher model is the ability to move data to a separate SQL Server. This allows the publishing server to continue to handle online transaction processing duties without having to absorb the impact of the ad hoc queries generally found in MIS departments.

You can use any type of replication here—transactional, merge, or snapshot. If you do not have to update BLOB objects like text, ntext, and image datatypes, we suggest that you use transactional replication here. MIS departments generally don't need to make changes to the subscribed data.

FIGURE 9.6   The central publisher model

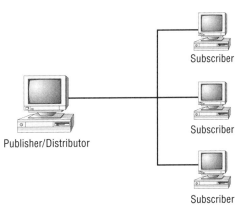

You can further reduce the impact of replication on your OLTP server by implementing pull subscriptions. This would force the distribution agent to run on each subscriber rather than on the OLTP publishing server.

Central Publisher/Remote Distributor

In this model, you remove the impact of the distribution process from your online transaction processing (OLTP) server, which gives you the best possible speed on the OLTP server. This model is useful in situations where you need the optimal performance out of your OLTP server. As discussed earlier, a single distribution server can work with multiple distributors and multiple subscribers. Figure 9.7 shows a representation of this strategy. The central publisher/remote distributor is analogous to the new remote distribution model as shown in the exam objectives.

This calls for transactional replication and minimizing the impact of replication on the publishing database. By moving just transactions, rather than moving snapshots or attempting to merge data at the publisher, you can gain the most possible speed and have the lowest impact on the publisher.

FIGURE 9.7 The central publisher/remote distributor model

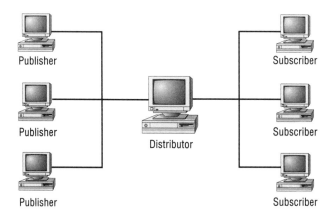

Central Subscriber/Multiple Publishers

The central subscriber model shown in Figure 9.8 is very useful in the following situations:

- Roll-up reporting
- Local warehouse inventory management
- Local customer order processing

FIGURE 9.8 The central subscriber model

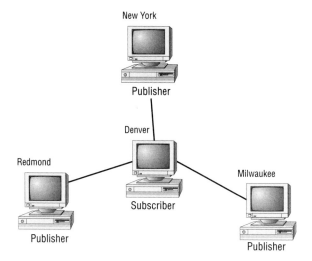

You need to keep several things in mind when you attempt to use this model. Because multiple publishers are writing to a single table in the database, you must take some precautions to ensure that referential integrity is maintained. If your New York office sent an order with a key of 1000 and your Milwaukee office also sent an order with a key of 1000, you would have two records with the same primary key. You could get bad data in your database, as the primary key is designed to guarantee the uniqueness of each record. In this situation, only one of those records would post.

To make sure that this doesn't become a problem, implement a composite primary key, using the original order ID number along with a location-specific code. You could, for example, give New York a location code of NY and the Milwaukee branch a location code of MW. This way, the new composite keys would be NY1000 and MW1000. There would be no more conflicting records and both orders would be filled from the Denver offices.

This scenario is especially suited to transactional replication, as the data at the Denver site is really read-only. Snapshot replication wouldn't work here, because that would overwrite everyone else's data. You could use merge replication if the other locations needed to be able to see all the orders placed.

Multiple Publishers/Multiple Subscribers

This model is used when a single table needs to be maintained on multiple servers. Each server subscribes to the table and also publishes the table to other servers. This model can be particularly useful in the following business situations:

- Reservations systems
- Regional order-processing systems
- Multiple warehouse implementations

Think of a regional order-processing system, as shown in Figure 9.9. Suppose you place an order on Monday, and want to check on that order on Tuesday. When you call up, you may be routed to any of several regional order processing centers. Each of these centers should have a copy of your order so that you can go over the order with a salesperson.

FIGURE 9.9 Multiple publishers of one table model

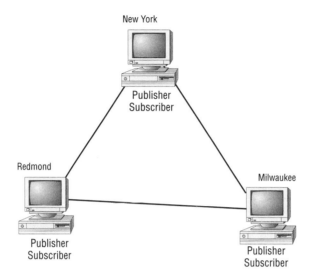

We suggest that you use transactional replication for this scenario, using some type of region code (as described in the Central Subscriber/Multiple Publishers scenario). Each order processing center should publish only its own data, but it should subscribe to data being published by the other publishers. In addition, each location should update only the data it owns. This scenario is also a good candidate for the transactional replication with an updating subscriber model. In this case, each center could update data owned by another center; however, this update would take place at both servers and therefore maintain transactional consistency.

Replicating over the Internet and to Heterogeneous Database Servers

In addition to the replication scenarios already discussed, it is possible to replicate data to non-Microsoft database servers. This is known as *heterogeneous database replication*. You can also replicate to databases across the Internet.

Heterogeneous Replication

Heterogeneous replication occurs when you publish to other databases through an ODBC or OLE-DB connection. In special cases, you can even use SQL Server 2000 to subscribe to these ODBC and OLE-DB databases. Currently, SQL Server supports replication to Access and Oracle and IBM databases that conform to the IBM DRDA (Distributed Relational Database Architecture) data protocol. To replicate to an ODBC data source, the subscriber must meet the following ODBC driver requirements:

- Must run in 32-bit mode

- Must be thread-safe

- Must allow updates

- Must support the T-SQL DDL (Data Definition Language)

- Must fully support the ODBC Level 1 Conformance standard

When you publish to these ODBC subscribers, you need to keep the following rules in mind:

- Only push subscriptions are supported.

- ODBC does not support batched statements.

- The ODBC DSN (Data Source Name) must conform to the SQL Server naming conventions.

- Snapshot data will be sent using bulk copy's character format.

- Datatypes will be mapped as closely as possible.

Before you can subscribe to ODBC publishers, the publishers need to have an HDR (Host Data Replicator) program written. The HDR will use the SQL-DMO (SQL-Distributed Management Objects) to implement the functionality of the different replication agents necessary for SQL Server 2000 to interact with the ODBC database. The SQL-DMO exposes several COM-based objects specific to replication.

Internet Replication

If you wish to enable your SQL Server to publish to the Internet, you must make some additional configuration changes to your SQL Server 2000 computer. For either a push or pull style of replication, the following must be configured:

- TCP/IP must be installed on the computers where the merge agent and distribution agents are running.

- The publishing server and the distribution server should be on the same side of the firewall.

- The publishing server and the distribution server should have a direct network connection to each other (rather than a connection across the Internet). This is for both security and latency concerns.

Some additional configuration changes need to be made if you are going to allow pull subscriptions:

- Your distribution server must have Microsoft's Internet Information Server (IIS) installed and running.

- Both the merge and distribution agents must be configured with the correct FTP address. This is done through the distribution agent or from a command prompt.

- The working folder must be available to your subscription servers.

- The FTP home folder on your IIS computer should be set to the Distribution working folder. This is normally `\\ServerName\C$\Program Files\Microsoft SQL Server\MSSQL\REPLDATA\FTP`.

For additional information on how to set up replication for the Internet, refer to the SQL Server Books Online.

Real World Scenario: Deciding on a Replication Model and Type

The company you work for has just opened up two regional branch offices in different parts of the country. You need to make sure that everyone at these offices has access to the inventory data so that they can make sales without having to call the home office to find out if the parts are in stock. They also need the capability to update their local copy of the data and have those changes reflected at the home office.

The first thing to assess is the network connections between the offices; are they reliable? If the network connections are reliable then you can use immediate updating subscribers to allow users to update local and remote data. If the network is not reliable then you may need to consider using queued immediate updating subscribers, which can handle network outage.

The next thing to consider is the type of replication. In this instance you need to know how often the data changes and how much of the data changes. If the entire database changes every day, and it is a small database, then you may be able to get away with snapshot replication. If the database is large then snapshot is not the answer because it takes too much bandwidth and you should use transactional replication.

Now you need to look at the model. In this instance you have one publisher (headquarters) and two subscribers that are quite some distance away. Because there are only two subscribers, you can use the central publisher/ multiple subscribers model. If there were more you would need to consider using a remote distributor.

Now, should the subscriptions be push or pull? Here you should consider using push subscriptions so that you have more control over when the data is replicated. If you have a large number of subscribers then you could use pull replication to remove some of the processing burden from the distributor and some of the administrative burden from yourself.

Installing and Using Replication

In this section you will learn how to configure your servers for replication. You will then walk through the process of installing a distribution database, a publishing database, and a subscription database. You will finish this section by creating and then subscribing to an article and a publication.

To successfully install and enable replication, you must install a distribution server, create your publications, and then subscribe to them. Before any of this can take place, you must first configure your SQL Server.

In order to install your replication scenario, you must be a member of the sysadmins fixed server role.

SQL Server Configuration

Before you can configure your SQL Server for replication, the computer itself must meet the following requirements:

- All servers involved with replication must be registered in Enterprise Manager.

- The SQL Server Agent account must have the Log On as a Service Advanced User right.

- If the servers are from different domains, trust relationships must be established before replication can occur.

- Any account that you use must have access rights to the Distribution working folder on the distribution server.

- You must enable access to the Distribution working folder on the distribution server. For a Windows Server, this is the \\ServerName\C$\Program Files\Microsoft SQL Server\MSSQL\REPLDATA folder. On Windows 9x/Me computers, you must create the C$ share because it only exists by default on Windows Server family operating systems.

We suggest that you use a single Windows Domain account for all of your SQL Server Agents. Do not use a LocalSystem account, as this account has no network capabilities and will therefore not allow replication. Also, you need to make the account a member of the Domain Administrators group because only administrators have access to the $ shares.

Installing a Distribution Server

Because of the great amount of information that must be presented to you about the installation process, we will not be doing an exercise here. Rather, we will walk you—step-by-step—through the installation. This will be similar to an exercise, but with extra information. Please use the walkthrough as if it were an exercise.

1. Using Enterprise Manager, connect to your SQL Server.

2. Highlight your SQL Server and choose Tools ➢ Replication ➢ Configure Publishing, Subscribers and Distribution.

3. You are now presented with a Welcome screen (see Figure 9.10). If you take a closer look at the Welcome screen, you'll see that you can create your local computer as the distributor. Note: The SQL Server's name is Instructor. Click Next to continue.

FIGURE 9.10 The Welcome screen

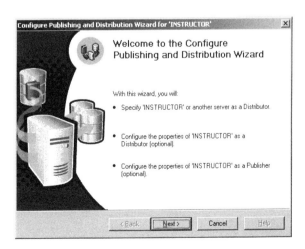

4. You are now presented with the Select Distributor screen (see Figure 9.11). Here you will decide where the distribution server is going to be installed. Only SQL Servers that are already registered in Enterprise Manager will be available from here.

FIGURE 9.11 The Select Distributor screen

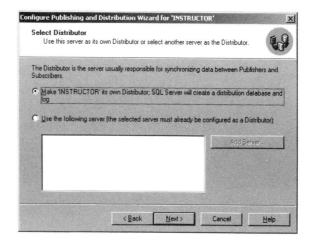

5. Keep the following in mind when you choose your distributor:

- Ensure that you have enough hard-disk space for the Distribution working folder and the distribution database.

- You must manage the distribution database's transaction log carefully. If that log fills to capacity, replication will no longer run, which can adversely affect your publishing databases as well.

- The distribution database will store all transactions from the publisher to the subscriber. It will also track when those transactions were applied.

- Snapshots and merge data are stored in the Distribution working folder.

- Be aware of the size and number of articles being published.

- Text, ntext, and image datatypes are replicated only when you use a snapshot.

- A higher degree of latency can significantly increase your storage space requirements.

- Know how many transactions per synchronization cycle there are. For example, if you modify 8000 records between synchronizations, there will be 8000 rows of data stored on the distributor.

6. Leave the defaults and click Next to continue.

7. You are now asked to specify the snapshot folder (seen in Figure 9.12). The only reason to change this is if you are replicating over the Internet and need to specify a folder that is accessible via FTP. Accept the defaults and click Next.

FIGURE 9.12 Configure a Distribution working folder

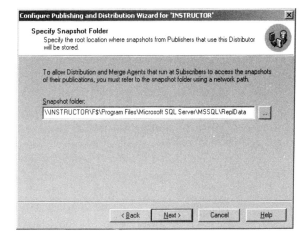

8. You now receive a warning stating that this share name can only be accessed by accounts with administrative privileges. As long as you configured the SQL Server Agent service with an administrative account, you'll be fine. Click Yes to continue.

9. You can now decide whether you want to use all the default settings for your distributor, which is recommended most of the time. Since you are seeing this for the first time, take a look at the customizable settings. Choose the Yes, Let Me Set the Distribution Database Properties option, as shown in Figure 9.13, and click Next to continue.

FIGURE 9.13 Use Default Configuration screen

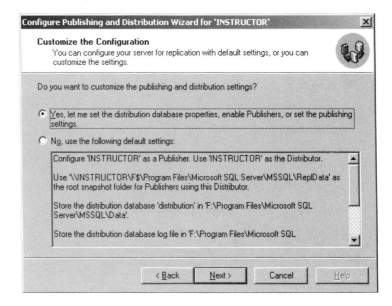

10. You are now presented with the Provide Distribution Database Information screen shown in Figure 9.14. You can supply a name for the distribution database as well as location information for its database file and transaction log. Keep the defaults and click Next to continue.

FIGURE 9.14 Provide Distribution Database Information screen

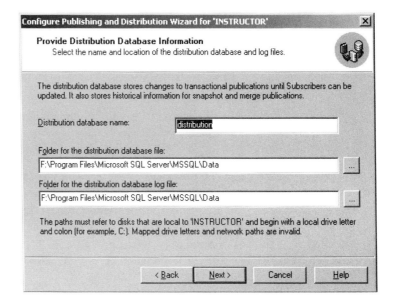

11. The Enable Publishers screen (see Figure 9.15) shows all registered SQL Servers. You can pick and choose which servers you wish to configure as publishers. The ellipsis (…) allows you to specify security credentials such as login ID and password, as well as the location of the snapshot folder. Be sure to place a checkmark next to your local SQL Server and then click Next to continue.

FIGURE 9.15 Enable Publishers screen

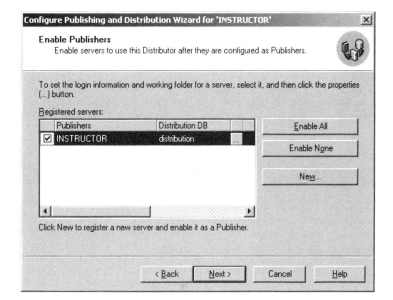

12. You are now looking at the Enable Publication Databases screen (see Figure 9.16). You can select the databases on the newly enabled publisher from which you wish to allow publishing. Select the Northwind database check box for transactional replication (the Trans column) and then click Next to continue.

 Before you can enable a publication database, you must be a member of the sysadmin fixed server role. Once you have enabled publishing, any member of that database's db_owner role can create and manage publications.

FIGURE 9.16 Enable Publication Databases screen

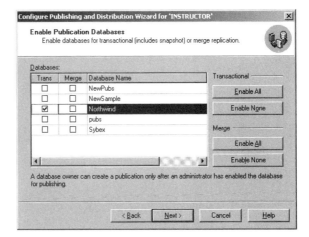

13. You are now presented with the Enable Subscribers screen shown in Figure 9.17. This is very similar to the Enable Publishers screen. For our example, we are going to use the same SQL Server for publishing, distribution, and subscribing. If you have additional SQL Servers, feel free to implement replication to them now.

FIGURE 9.17 Enable Subscribers screen

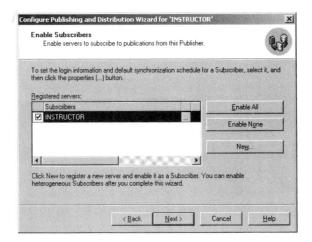

If your server isn't listed here, you can click the Register button to register another Microsoft SQL Server computer. You must set up non-Microsoft SQL Servers through the Configure Publishing and Distribution screen.

14. Click the ellipsis to modify the security credentials of the subscription server.

15. You are now looking at the General tab of the Subscriber properties sheet. Let's take a closer look at the Schedules tab shown in Figure 9.18.

FIGURE 9.18 The Schedules tab

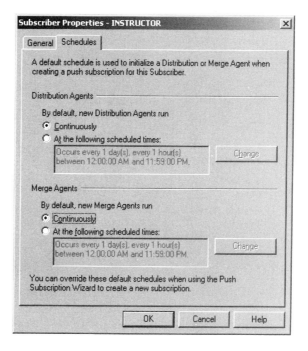

16. As shown in Figure 9.18, you can specify the replication schedule for both the merge and distribution agents. You can set the schedule to anything you like (just as when creating and scheduling SQL Server jobs). Set both options to run continuously and click OK to return to the Enable Subscribers screen.

17. Click Next to continue. You are now given a summary of the configuration options you have chosen. Click Finish to implement these configurations and enable the distribution server.

Now that you have successfully installed the distribution database and distribution server, you should see the Replication Monitor icon in the Enterprise Manager console tree, as shown in Figure 9.19.

FIGURE 9.19 The Replication Monitor icon in the console tree

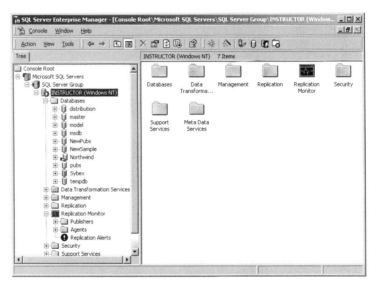

Adding a Publication

Now you can add a publication and articles to your server. When you add a new publication, you need to determine the type of replication that will be used, the snapshot requirements, and such subscriber options as updating or anonymous subscribers. You can also partition your data and decide whether you will allow push or pull subscriptions.

The Create Publication Wizard allows you to specify the following options:

- Number of articles
- Schedule for the snapshot agent
- Whether or not to maintain the snapshot on the distributor

- Tables and stored procedures you wish to publish
- Publications that will share agents
- Whether to allow updating subscribers
- Whether to allow pull subscriptions

Each publication will use a separate publishing agent by default. This option can be overridden.

In the following walkthrough, you will create a new publication based on the Categories table in the Northwind database. You will then replicate this table to the Pubs database as rtblCategories.

1. Connect to your SQL Server in Enterprise Manager. If you expand the Databases folder (shown in Figure 9.19), you will now see a hand on the Northwind database icon. This indicates that the database has been marked for replication.

2. Highlight the Northwind database and then go to Tools ➢ Replication ➢ Create and Manage Publications. You will now be presented with the Create and Manage Publications dialog box shown in Figure 9.20.

FIGURE 9.20 Create and Manage Publications window

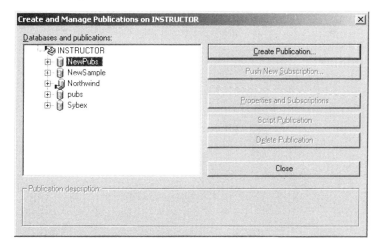

3. Highlight the Northwind database and click Create Publication.

4. The Create Publication Wizard now starts with a Welcome screen as seen in Figure 9.21. At the bottom is a check box titled Show Advanced Options in This Wizard. If this is checked and you are creating a transactional or snapshot publication, you will see screens that allow you to configure immediate updating subscribers and transform data as it is replicated. If you are configuring a merge publication, you will see these two screens anyway. Check the Show Advanced Options check box and click Next to continue.

FIGURE 9.21 Choosing to show advanced options

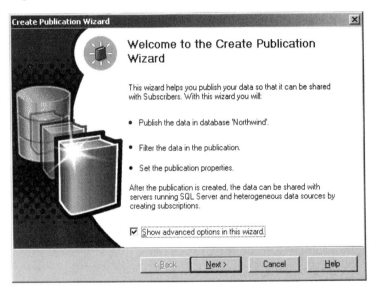

5. Now you are asked which database to publish from (as shown in Figure 9.22). Click Northwind and click Next.

FIGURE 9.22 Publishing from Northwind

FIGURE 9.22 Publishing from Northwind

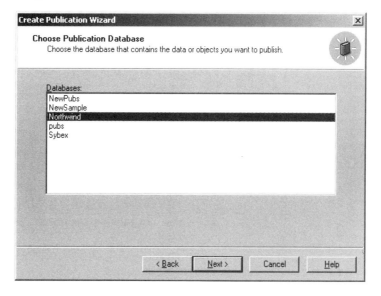

6. You can now specify what type of publication you wish to create—snapshot, transactional, or merge. For our example, select Transactional Publication, as shown in Figure 9.23, and click Next to continue.

FIGURE 9.23 Choose Publication Type screen

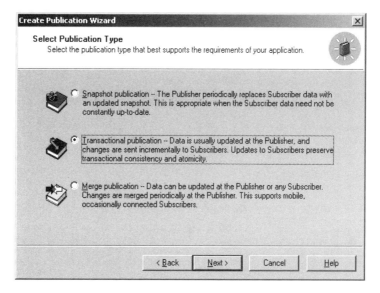

Transactional replication on the Desktop edition of SQL Server running on Windows 9x/Me is supported as subscriber only. This is because the server-side network libraries for Named Pipes are required for this type of replication and are not available on Windows 9x/Me. Windows 9x/Me Named Pipes on the client side is supported however.

7. You can now specify whether or not you wish to enable immediate updating subscribers or queued updating (see Figure 9.24). As you might recall, updating a subscriber makes changes at both the subscription server and the publishing server. Immediate updating subscribers use a two-phase commit for this process, and queued updating subscribers store the updates in a queue until they can be sent. For this example, we will leave both boxes unchecked and click Next to continue.

FIGURE 9.24 Updatable Subscriptions screen

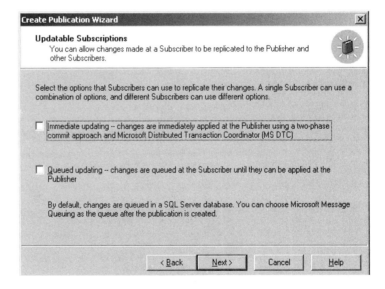

8. The next screen, depicted in Figure 9.25, asks whether you would like to transform the data as it is being replicated. This is useful if you are replicating to a database that is not an exact duplicate of the source database, perhaps to a sister company. Choose No, Subscribers Receive Data Directly and click Next to continue.

FIGURE 9.25   Transform Published Data screen

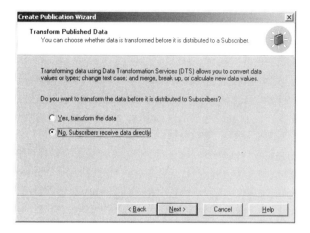

9. Figure 9.26 shows the Specify Subscriber Types screen. When you were working on the distribution database installation, you learned that you could specify only Microsoft SQL Servers as subscribers. Although you can enable non-Microsoft SQL Servers as subscribers from here, we are not going to do that in this walkthrough. Leave the default Servers Running SQL Server 2000 checked and click Next to continue.

FIGURE 9.26   Specify Subscriber Types screen

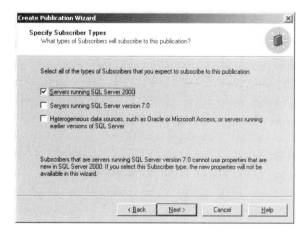

10. Here you can determine which tables you wish to publish from. In essence, you are creating your articles. Click the check box next to the Categories table, as shown in Figure 9.27.

FIGURE 9.27 Specify Articles screen

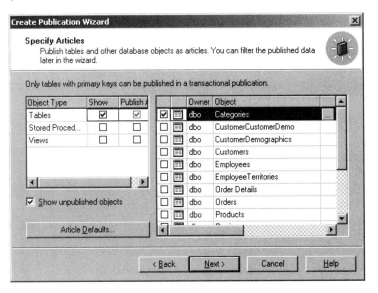

11. As you can see in Figure 9.27, selecting an article creates the ellipsis button. Click the ellipsis.

12. You are now presented with the Categories properties sheet. The General tab (see Figure 9.28) allows you to specify the article name, a description, the destination table name, and destination table owner. Change Destination Table Name to rtblCategories and be sure to specify the owner as dbo, as shown in Figure 9.28.

FIGURE 9.28 Categories properties sheet

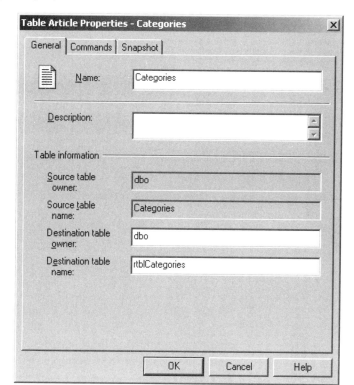

13. The Snapshot tab allows you to specify what will happen during the snapshot process. Will you drop the existing table? Will you truncate the data in it? Leave the default options and click OK to return to the Specify Articles screen. Once back at the Specify Articles screen, click Next to continue.

14. You are now presented with a warning that identity values for this table will not be replicated. This is fine for our example, so click Next to continue.

15. You are now presented with the Select Publication Name and Description screen. Note that the publication name has been changed to Northwind_Categories. When you are finished, you should have something similar to Figure 9.29. Click Next to continue.

FIGURE 9.29 Select Publication Name and Description screen

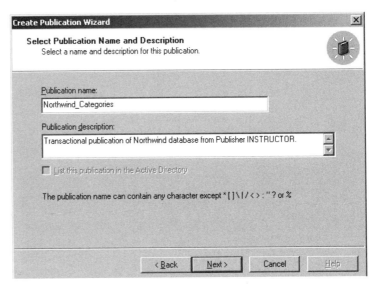

16. You now see the Customize the Properties of the Publication screen, as shown in Figure 9.30. From here you can accept the default filtering and partitioning options or you can customize them. Although we will not make changes to these options, let's take a look at them. Click the Yes, I Will Define option and then click Next to continue.

FIGURE 9.30 Customize the Properties of the Publication screen

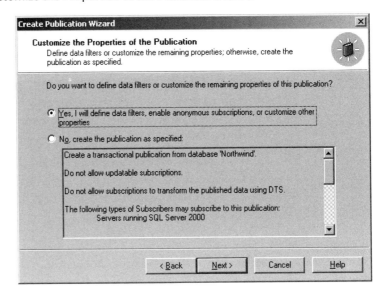

17. As seen in Figure 9.31, you are now asked which type of filtering to perform: vertical or horizontal. Check both boxes and click Next.

FIGURE 9.31 Choosing partitioning types

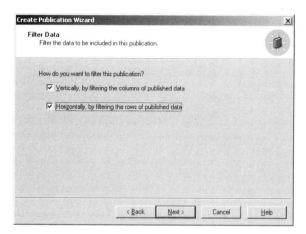

18. From the Filter Table Columns screen shown in Figure 9.32, you can select which columns you wish to exclude from your replication. Click Next to continue.

FIGURE 9.32 Filter Table Columns screen

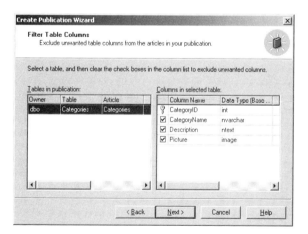

19. You can now filter the rows, as shown in Figure 9.33. If you click the ellipsis, you can create a new filter by filling in a Where clause, as shown in Figure 9.34. Since we are just looking at these options, click Cancel and click Next to continue.

FIGURE 9.33 Filter Table Rows screen

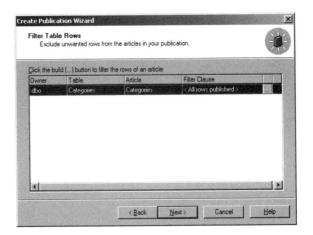

FIGURE 9.34 Specify Filter window

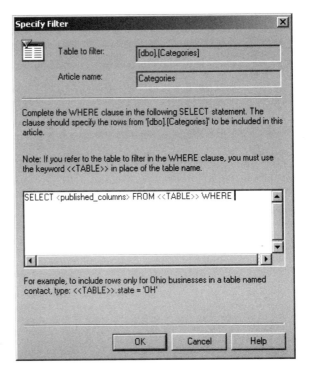

20. You are now asked whether or not you wish to allow anonymous subscribers. If you have many subscribers, or if you are allowing subscriptions across the Internet, you may wish to allow anonymous subscribers. Anonymous subscribers reduce some of the administration of your replication. Note, however, that this choice may compromise security. Leave the default No, Only Allow Named Subscriptions and click Next to continue.

21. You are now presented with the Set Snapshot Agent Schedule screen (see Figure 9.35). Remember that before replication can begin, a snapshot of your data must be moved to the subscriber to set a baseline for all future replication. Click the Change button to set up your snapshot schedule. A snapshot schedule is useful when you have nonlogged operations running on the publisher. If an operation is not logged it won't be replicated. This can come in handy if you are replicating text, ntext, or image datatypes. Click Next to continue.

FIGURE 9.35 Set Snapshot Agent Schedule screen

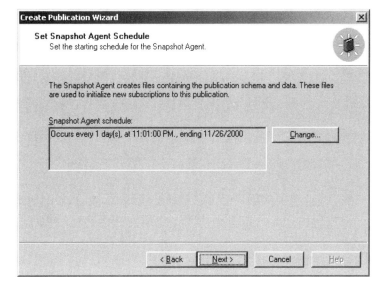

22. You are now at the Finish screen. You can review the options you have chosen; when you are ready, click Finish to complete the creation of your publication. After some processing takes place, you will return to the Create and Manage Publications screen shown in Figure 9.20 but with a change: your new publication, Northwind_Categories, should be listed.

23. From here, you can push this publication to subscribers or you can look over its properties and subscriptions by clicking the Properties and Subscriptions button. When you do this, you will see much of the information you entered displayed in a set of pages, as shown in Figure 9.32. When you are finished, click OK to return to the Create and Manage Publications screen.

FIGURE 9.36 Northwind_Categories properties sheet

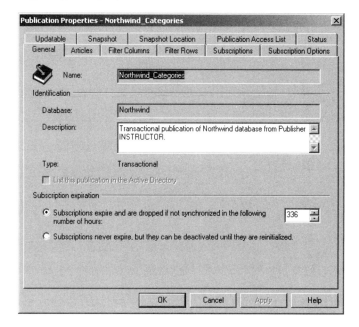

24. From the Create and Manage Publications screen, you can also delete your publications. Click Close to finish.

Creating a Subscription

As part of the process of creating a subscription, you will be able to specify the publishers you wish to subscribe to and a destination database to receive the published data, verify your security credentials, and set up a default schedule. We are going to create a pull subscription in this example.

1. Connect to your SQL Server, highlight the Server, and choose Tools ➤ Replication ➤ Pull Subscription to Your ServerName.

2. You are now looking at the Pull Subscription to *server name* window, as shown in Figure 9.37. In the rest of the examples, the Server Name is Instructor and this will be reflected in the figures and steps.

FIGURE 9.37   Pull Subscription to Instructor screen

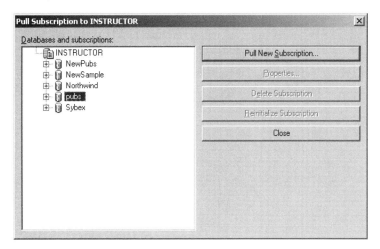

3. Click the Pubs database and then click Pull New Subscription.

4. As always, you are presented with a Welcome screen. Check the Show Advanced Options check box at the bottom of the screen. This will present you with the option to configure immediate updating and queued subscribers. Click Next to continue.

5. As seen in Figure 9.38, you are now asked where you would like to start looking for publications. You can check with registered servers (the traditional method) or you can look in Active Directory (new to SQL Server 2000). We will look in registered servers, so click the appropriate radio button and click Next.

FIGURE 9.38 Specifying where to look for a publication

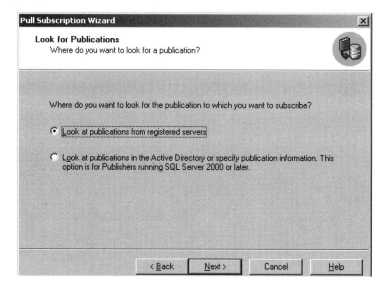

6. You can now see a list of publishers. By expanding the publishers, you can see the publications that they have made available. If you do not see your publishing server here, you can click the Register Server button to register another server. Expand your server and then click the Northwind_ Categories publication, as shown in Figure 9.39. Click Next to continue.

FIGURE 9.39 Choose Publication screen

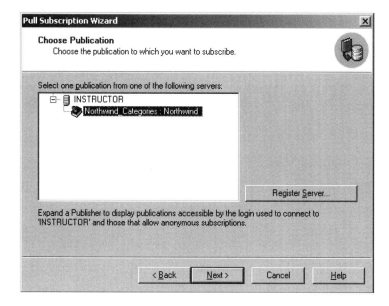

7. You must now choose your destination database. Since we clicked on the Pubs database at the beginning of this walkthrough, it should default there. If it doesn't, select it now, as shown in Figure 9.40. Click Next to continue.

FIGURE 9.40   Choose Destination Database screen

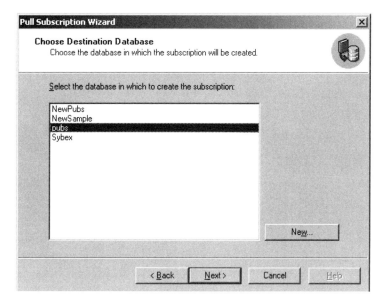

8. If the schema and tables don't already exist at the subscriber, they must be initialized there. Take the default value, as shown in Figure 9.41, and click Next to continue.

FIGURE 9.41 Initialize Subscription screen

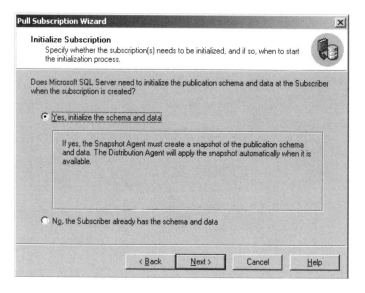

9. You are now asked where the subscriber should retrieve the snapshot files from. This is new in SQL Server 2000. You can specify a network folder, a CD-ROM, or any other media that suits your needs. Accept the defaults shown in Figure 9.42 and click Next to continue.

FIGURE 9.42 Setting the snapshot file location

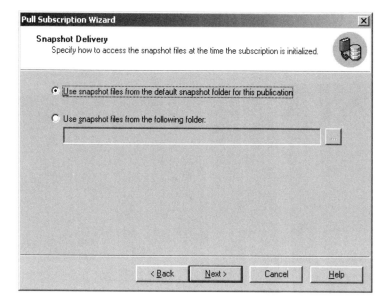

10. You can now set the synchronization schedule. For snapshots, it might be wise to set up some type of regular schedule. For merge replication, you will most likely use a manual form of synchronization called *on demand*. Since you are using transactional replication, select Continuously, as shown in Figure 9.43. Click Next to continue.

FIGURE 9.43   Set Distribution Agent Schedule screen

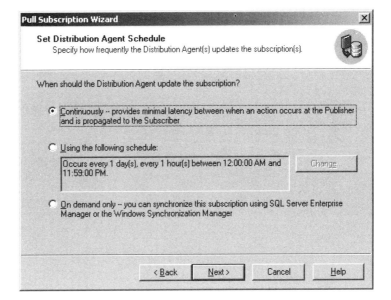

11. You are now looking at the Start Required Services screen. Because all your agents use the SQL Server Agent service to interact with the various servers, the SQL Server Agent must be running. If it is not, click the check box to force the service to start (see Figure 9.44). Once you have it running, click Next to continue.

FIGURE 9.44 Start Required Services screen

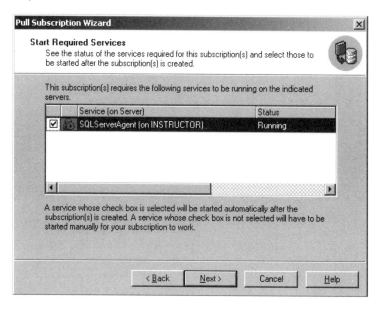

12. You are now at the Finish screen again. As with other screens of this type, you can review your subscription. When you are satisfied, click Finish to create the subscription.

13. You should now be back at the Pull Subscription to Instructor screen, but this time your subscription should be displayed, as shown in Figure 9.45. Here too, you can choose your subscription and look at its properties sheet, as shown in Figure 9.46. You can also delete the subscription or reinitialize it. When you are finished, click Close.

FIGURE 9.45 Pull Subscription to Instructor screen

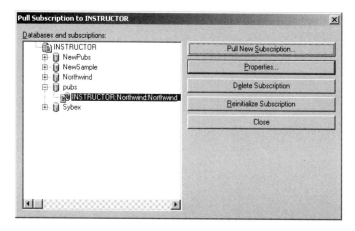

FIGURE 9.46 Pull Subscription properties sheet

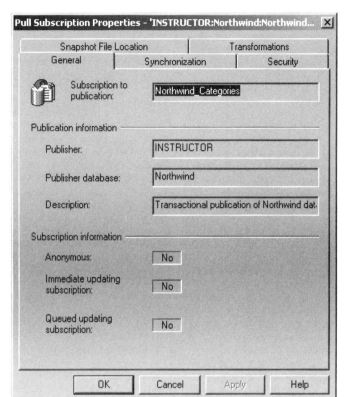

14. If you expand your Pubs database folder, you will notice that there is now a Pull Subscriptions folder in it. There is also a Publications folder under the Northwind database, as shown in Figure 9.47. You can highlight these items and then double-click the publication or subscription in the right pane for additional information about them.

FIGURE 9.47 Publications and Subscriptions are shown in their own folders under the appropriate database.

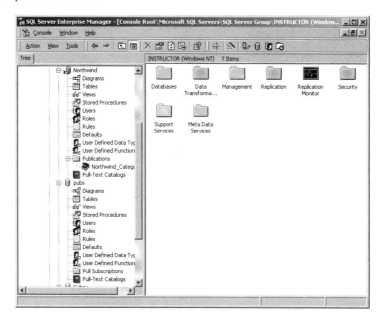

Testing Replication

You can now verify that replication is running properly. In the following steps, you will check for the initial snapshot synchronization. You will then add some data to the Categories table and review the data in the rtblCategories table to make sure that it was replicated. Follow these steps to test replication.

1. Connect to your database and expand the Databases folder and then the Pubs database. Click the Tables icon. You should see the rtbl Categories table in the details pane, as shown in Figure 9.48. If you do not, you may need to refresh the tables. To do this, right-click the Tables icon and choose Refresh from the context menu.

FIGURE 9.48   The rtblCategories table is now in the Pubs database.

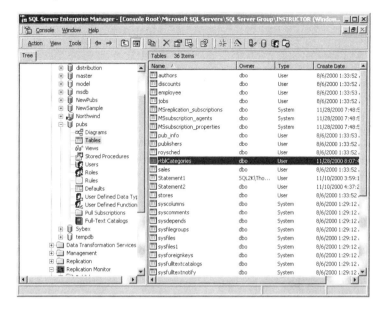

2. Now check your data. Open the Query Analyzer and specify the Pubs database. Run the following query to verify that there is data in the rtblCategories table:

```
SELECT * FROM rtblCategories
GO
```

3. You should have eight records returned to you. Now add a new record to the Categories table in the Northwind database and verify that the record has been replicated properly. Run the following code to add a new record.

```
USE Northwind
GO
INSERT INTO Categories
VALUES('Beer', 'Beers of the World', '')
GO
```

4. You should get the message that one row was added. Give the server about a minute to catch up and move and apply the transaction; then run the following query:

USE pubs
GO
SELECT * FROM rtblCategories
GO

5. You should get nine records back. The last record should be the Beers of the World record, as shown in Figure 9.49.

FIGURE 9.49 Successful replication

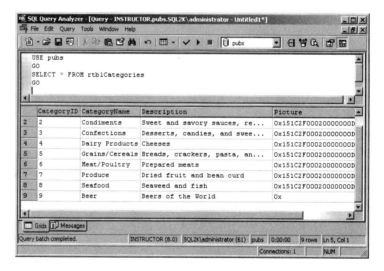

Managing Replication

Managing and maintaining replication can be very intensive work for an administrator. Microsoft SQL Server 2000 has included many tools in the Replication Monitor to make this job a lot easier. Before we look at the various tools and methodologies, let's look at some of the administrative issues you should consider.

Administrative Considerations

This section provides some tips for optimizing your replication as well as some tips to minimize your administrative duties:

- Use a remote distributor to minimize the impact of replication on your publishing servers.

- Use pull subscriptions to off-load the work from the distributors to each subscriber.

- Use immediate updating subscribers rather than merge replication if possible.

- Replicate only the data you need. Use filters to partition your data.

- Keep in mind that replication increases network traffic. Make sure your network can handle it.

- Use primary keys on replicated tables to ensure entity integrity.

- Using the same SQL Server Agent Domain account for all servers involved in replication will minimize the impact of administering security issues.

- Ensure that replication jobs and their agents are running smoothly. Check the agent histories and logs periodically.

- Create and monitor replication alerts.

- Ensure that the distribution database and the Distribution working folder have enough space and that they have the appropriate permissions assigned to them.

- Develop a recovery and resynchronization plan. You can use replication scripts for version control as well as a huge part of the recovery process.

- Keep a valid backup of the distribution database and make sure that the database and log do not fill to capacity.

It is essential that the distribution database and log do not fill to capacity. When this database or log fills to capacity, it can no longer receive publication information. When this occurs, the logged transactions at the publisher cannot be removed from the log (unless you disable publishing). Over time, your Publishing database's transaction log will also fill to capacity, and you will no longer be able to make data modifications.

Replication Backup Considerations

When you perform backups of your replication scenario, you can make backups of just the publisher, the publisher and distributor, the publisher and subscriber, or all three. Each of the strategies has its own advantages and disadvantages. The following list highlights these distinctions:

Publisher only   This strategy requires the least amount of resources and computing time, since the backup of the publisher does not have to be coordinated with any other server backups to stay synchronized. The disadvantage is that restoration of a publisher or distributor is a slow and time-consuming process.

Publisher and distributor   This strategy accurately preserves the publication as well as the errors, history, and replication agent information from the distributor. You can recover quickly as there is no need to reestablish replication. The disadvantages of this strategy are the coordination of the backups and the amount of storage and computing time necessary to perform a simultaneous backup.

Publisher and subscriber(s)   This strategy significantly reduces the recovery time by removing the initialization process (running a snapshot). The main disadvantages of this strategy manifest themselves when you have multiple subscribers. Every subscriber will have to be backed up and restored.

Publisher, distributor, and subscriber(s)   This strategy preserves all of the complexity of your replication model. The disadvantages are storage space and computing time. This scenario also requires the most time for recovery.

Using the Replication Monitor

You can administer your publishers, subscribers, and publications as well as the different replication agents through the Replication Monitor utility. You can also look at agent properties and histories and even set replication alerts with this utility.

The Replication Monitor resides on the computer where the distribution server has been installed and gathers replication information about the different replication agents. This includes the agent history with information about inserts, updates, deletes, and any other transactions that were processed. Through the Replication Monitor you can also edit the various schedules and properties of the replication agents.

Follow these steps to work with the various agents:

1. Open the Enterprise Manager on the SQL Server where the distribution server was installed.

2. Expand the Replication Monitor icon, then the Agents folder and finally, highlight the Snapshot Agents, as shown in Figure 9.50.

FIGURE 9.50 The Snapshot Agents in the Replication Monitor

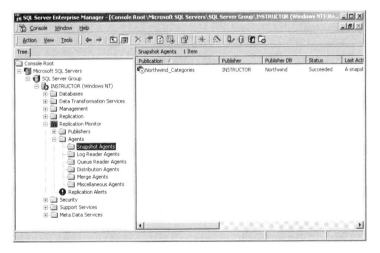

3. If you right-click Northwind_Categories in the details pane, you will see that you can view the Agent history, properties, and profile. You can also start or stop the agent. There are options to modify the refresh rate and choose the columns to view. Right-click and choose Agent History.

4. You are now presented with the Snapshot Agent History, as shown in Figure 9.51. You can filter the list to show information based on all sessions; sessions in the last 7 days, the last 2 days, the last 24 hours, the last 100 sessions, or sessions with errors. You can also look at the Agent Profile and its settings as well as the Monitor Settings. The Monitor Settings allow you to specify how often the items in the Replication Monitor will be refreshed.

FIGURE 9.51 Snapshot Agent History screen

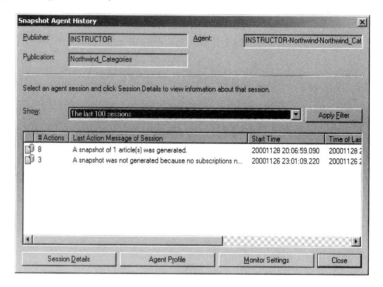

You can look at the details of a particular session, as shown in Figure 9.47. Session details include information about all the different processes that took place during the session.

FIGURE 9.52 Session details

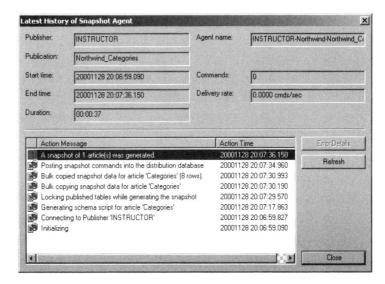

1. Close the Agent History. Right-click Northwind_Categories and choose Agent Properties. You are now looking at the properties sheets (see Figure 9.53). These operate in the same fashion as the scheduled jobs that you have already worked with. When you are finished browsing, close the Agent History.

FIGURE 9.53 Northwind_Categories agent job properties

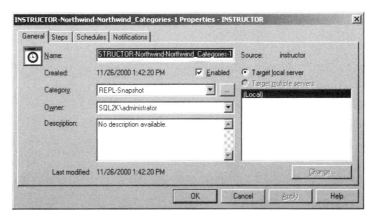

The other agents provide similar information. The history keeps track of everything that has happened during the replication. After a successful log is read and moved to the distributor and the subscriber pulls the transaction, the distribution server needs to be cleaned up. Once a transfer has been successfully completed, a cleanup job will run.

There is at least one cleanup job for every subscriber. In other words, if you have 20 subscribers to your database, you will have at least 20 cleanup jobs on the distributor. If you click the Miscellaneous Agents folder in the console tree, you will see some of the cleanup jobs that have been created (shown in Figure 9.54). These are explained below.

FIGURE 9.54   Miscellaneous Agents' clean up jobs

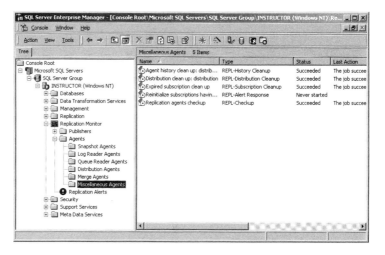

Agent History Clean Up: Distribution   This job cleans up the historical information in the Distribution Agents History tables after they have aged out.

Distribution Clean Up: Distribution   This job cleans up the distributor by removing transactions from the distribution database after they have aged out.

Expired Subscription Clean Up   This job removes expired subscription information from the Subscription database.

Reinitialize Subscriptions Having Data Validation Failures   This job reinitializes all subscriptions that failed because of problems with data validation.

Replication Agents Checkup   This job watches for replication agents that are not actively adding information to their history logs.

Working with Replication Scripts

Now that you have replication set up and working properly, you may wish to save all your hard work in the form of a replication script. Scripting your replication scenario has the following advantages:

- You can use the scripts to track different versions of your replication implementation.

- You can use the scripts (with some minor tweaking) to create additional subscribers and publishers with the same basic options.

- You can quickly customize your environment by making modifications to the script and then rerunning it.

- Scripts can be used as part of your database recovery process.

Let's do another walkthrough and create some replication scripts for your current setup.

1. Highlight your server in the console tree and then choose Tools ➤ Replication ➤ Generate SQLScript.

2. You are now presented with the Generate SQL Script pages, as shown in Figure 9.55. You can script the distributor and the publications for the various replication items stored with this distribution server. The File Options tab allows you to save your script to several different file types. The default storage location for your scripts is `C:\Program files\Microsoft SQL Server\MSSQL\Install`. This particular folder holds many other scripts that are used to create and install your SQL Server and several databases.

FIGURE 9.55 Generate SQL Script pages

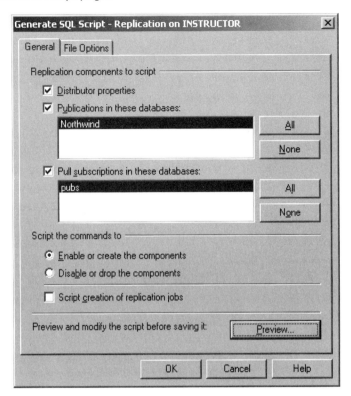

3. The Preview button allows you to view the scripts themselves, as shown in Figure 9.56.

FIGURE 9.56   Replication Component Script Preview screen

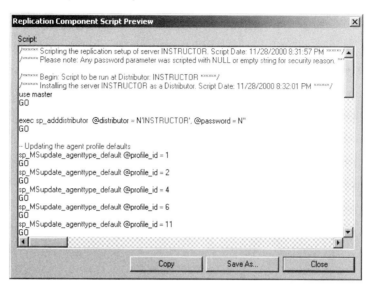

4. When you are finished viewing the scripts, click Close. You can now close the replication scripting property sheets.

Replication of Stored Procedures

There are many stored procedures that are used to create and install replication on your computer. Here is a short list of stored procedures that you will most likely use to gather administrative information about your SQL Server replication configuration:

sp_helpdistributor   This gathers information about the distribution database, the distributor, the working directory, and the SQL Server Agent user account.

sp_helpdistributiondb   This gathers information about the distribution database, its files, and their location, as well as information regarding the distribution history and log.

sp_helppublication   This gathers publication information and configuration options.

sp_helpsubscription   This gathers information associated with a particular article, publication, subscriber, or set of subscriptions.

sp_helpsubscriberinfo   This gathers information about the configuration setting of a subscriber, including information regarding frequency of the subscription, retry delays, and much more.

Replication and Performance Counters

Replication also exposes many new and useful performance counters that can be used in your optimization efforts. As you recall, performance counters are grouped into performance objects and are used in the SQL Server Performance Monitor. With all of these new performance counters, you can track how effective your replication strategies are and then fine-tune your scenario.

Summary

In this chapter, you learned the following:

- Replication is used to distribute data to other database engines in your enterprise. This can be used for a variety of reasons.

- Microsoft SQL Server uses a publisher/subscriber metaphor.

- When implementing replication, three primary factors determine whether you will distribute data using distributed transactions, transactional replication with or without updating subscribers, snapshot replication with or without updating subscribers, or merge replication:

  - Autonomy

  - Latency

  - Transactional consistency

- Merge replication allows for great autonomy and latency; however, your transactional consistency is in question until records are converged and conflicts resolved.

- When you decide to publish, bear some things in mind about your data:

  - Replication treats user-defined datatypes, IDENTITY and UNIQUEIDENTIFIER, and timestamp columns a bit differently than you might expect. In general, these columns will be converted when they are replicated.

- Nonlogged operations are not replicated except through a snapshot. This means that if you make changes to text, ntext, or image columns, these columns will be replicated only when you schedule a snapshot to refresh your tables.

- There are several different replication models you can choose from in order to optimize and suit your business needs:
  - Central publisher/central distributor
  - Central publisher/remote distributor
  - Central subscriber/multiple publishers
  - Multiple publishers/multiple subscribers
  - Heterogeneous environments

- When you replicate to the Internet, you need to use TCP/IP, and you should keep both the publisher and the distributor directly connected on the same side of your firewall.

- Most of your replication administration can be handled through the Replication Monitor on the distribution server.

- You can generate replication scripts that you can use to create additional subscribers or re-create your entire replication scenario.

- To do all of the moving and management of your data, Microsoft has created several agents. These include:
  - The logreader agent
  - The distribution agent
  - The snapshot agent
  - The merge agent

- These agents reside on different servers, depending on whether you are using a pull or a push subscription.

Exam Essentials

Know the publisher/subscriber metaphor.   Publishers contain the original copy of the data where changes are made. Subscribers receive copies of the data from the publishers. The data is disseminated to the subscribers through the distributor.

Know the types of replication.   There are three basic types of replication: snapshot, transactional, and merge. These can be used in different ways, such as immediate or queued updating. You should be familiar with the basic types.

Know the models.   You also need to be familiar with the various models; that is, who publishes, who subscribes, and who distributes.

Understand how articles work.   Remember that an article is just a table that is published as part of a publication. Articles can be vertically partitioned or horizontally partitioned.

Key Terms

article	publisher
convergence	replication
distributor	subscriber
publication	two-phase commit

Review Questions

1. Your users need a local copy of your sales database, which is stored in your New York office, in your satellite offices located in Berlin, London, and Moscow. Changes are made to the sales database throughout the day, but your users do not need to see these changes immediately. You want to use as little bandwidth as possible because you have slow, expensive network connections. Which type of replication should you use?

   A. Merge

   B. Transactional

   C. Snapshot

   D. Transactional with updating subscribers

   E. Snapshot with updating subscribers

2. Your users need a local copy of your sales database, which is stored in your New York office, in your satellite offices located in Berlin, London, and Moscow. Changes are made to the sales database throughout the day but your users do not need to see these changes immediately. You want to use as little bandwidth as possible because you have slow, expensive network connections. Which replication model should you use?

   A. Central subscriber/multiple publishers

   B. Multiple publishers/multiple subscribers

   C. Central publisher/central distributor

   D. Central publisher/remote distributor

3. You are using a replication scenario with a single publisher and several subscribers. The subscribers need to update the data that they subscribe to so you decide to use transactional replication with updating subscribers. This works fine for some time until replication starts failing on one of the servers in a remote office. What is the most likely cause of this problem?

   A. The SQL Server Agent has stopped.

   B. The Distributed Transaction Coordinator has stopped.

   C. The network connection is down intermittently.

   D. The distribution database transaction log is full.

4. Which component in a replication scenario contains the original copy of the data to be replicated?

   A. Publisher

   B. Subscriber

   C. Distributor

   D. Agent

5. You work for a multinational company where each branch office has its own accounting department. The network connections between the branch offices are reliable but they are consistently at 80 percent usage during the day. Each of your branch office accounting departments needs a copy of the accounting database that they can update locally, and they need it to be as current as possible. Which replication type best suits your needs?

   A. Merge

   B. Transactional

   C. Snapshot

   D. Transactional with updating subscribers

   E. Snapshot with updating subscribers

6. After successfully installing replication, you notice that the snapshot agent is failing because it cannot access the distribution working folder. How can you fix this?

   A. Stop and restart the snapshot agent.

   B. Use transactional replication instead of snapshot.

   C. Assign the SQL Server Agent service account to the Domain Administrators group.

   D. Free up disk space on the distributor.

7. You have a company with several sales offices located throughout the country. Headquarters needs an up-to-date copy of the sales offices databases. When headquarters sends new inventory to the sales office, they want to update the database at headquarters and have the new data replicated to the respective sales offices. How could you make sure that the sales offices are only getting the data that pertains to their particular office?

   A. Create multiple horizontally partitioned articles at headquarters.

   B. Create multiple vertically partitioned articles at headquarters.

   C. Create a single horizontally partitioned article at headquarters.

   D. Create a single vertically partitioned article at headquarters.

8. You have a company with several sales offices located throughout the country. Headquarters needs an up-to-date copy of the sales offices databases. When headquarters sends new inventory to the sales office, they want to update the database at headquarters and have the new data replicated to the respective sales offices. Which replication type should you use?

   A. Merge

   B. Transactional

   C. Snapshot

   D. Transactional with updating subscribers

   E. Snapshot with updating subscribers

9. You have a company with several sales offices located throughout the country. Headquarters needs an up-to-date copy of the sales offices databases. When headquarters sends new inventory to the sales office, they want to update the database at headquarters and have the new data replicated to the respective sales offices. Which replication model should you use?

A. Central subscriber/multiple publishers

B. Multiple publishers/multiple subscribers

C. Central publisher/central distributor

D. Central publisher/remote distributor

10. A small automotive parts company has four shops, each with its own inventory database to maintain. The owner wants the shops to be able to share inventory so that they can pick up a part from another nearby store rather than waiting for a shipment from the manufacturer. To do this, they want to be able to update their local copy of the inventory database, decrement the other store's inventory, and then go pick up the part. This way, the other store won't sell their part because it will have already been taken out of stock. Which replication type should you use to accomplish this?

A. Merge

B. Transactional

C. Snapshot

D. Transactional with updating subscribers

E. Snapshot with updating subscribers

11. A small automotive parts company has four shops, each with its own inventory database to maintain. The owner wants the shops to be able to share inventory so that way they can pick up a part from another nearby store rather than waiting for a shipment from the manufacturer. To do this, they want to be able to update their local copy of the inventory database, decrement the other store's inventory, and then go pick up the part. This way, the other store won't sell their part because it will have already been taken out of stock. Which replication model should you use to accomplish this?

    A. Central subscriber/multiple publishers

    B. Multiple publishers/multiple subscribers

    C. Central publisher/central distributor

    D. Central publisher/remote distributor

12. A small automotive parts company has four shops, each with its own inventory database to maintain. The owner wants the shops to be able to share inventory so that they can pick up a part from another nearby store rather than waiting for a shipment from the manufacturer. To do this, they want to be able to update their local copy of the inventory database, decrement the other store's inventory, and then go pick up the part. This way, the other store won't sell their part because it will have already been taken out of stock. What can you do to ensure that each store does not overwrite the records of the other stores accidentally?

    A. Create a field that contains a UNIQUEIDENTIFIER datatype to differentiate the records.

    B. Create a field with the NEWID() function to differentiate the records.

    C. Create a composite primary key that uses a location code and a store code to differentiate the records.

    D. Create a constraint that does not allow the stores to update the data of the other stores.

13. You have a single publisher/multiple subscribers replication scenario and you want to configure replication on all of the subscribers as quickly as possible. What is the fastest method to configure replication on your subscribers?

    A. Run the Pull Subscription Wizard on each subscriber.

    B. Push the subscription from the publisher to each subscriber.

    C. Run the Pull Subscription Wizard on one subscriber, generate replication scripts on that subscriber, and modify and run the scripts on the remaining subscribers.

    D. Run the Pull Subscription Wizard on one subscriber and use DTS to copy the database to the remaining subscribers.

14. When checking the subscriber database in a transactional replication scenario, you notice that updates are no longer happening. When you check the publisher you notice that the database is working properly but the transaction log seems to be filling up even though you are performing regular backups. What is the most likely cause?

    A. The subscriber database does not have access to the distribution working folder.

    B. The distribution database transaction log has filled to capacity.

    C. The publisher has lost its network connection to the distributor.

    D. The logreader agent has been stopped on the distributor.

15. You are configuring a snapshot replication scenario with a single publisher and almost 100 subscribers. You want to remove as much burden from the distributor as possible. What should you do?

    A. Create push subscriptions so that the snapshot agent runs on the distributor.

    B. Create pull subscriptions so that the snapshot agent runs on the subscriber.

    C. Create push subscriptions so that the distribution agent runs on the distributor.

    D. Create pull subscriptions so that the distribution agent runs on the subscriber.

16. When using snapshot replication, where is the replicated data stored before it is sent to the subscriber?

   A. In the distribution database

   B. In the distribution database transaction log

   C. In the Distribution working folder

   D. In the Publisher database transaction log

17. What is the distribution database used for in snapshot replication?

   A. It is not used.

   B. It is used to store historical information.

   C. It is used to store text, ntext, and image data.

   D. It is used to store replicated data.

18. You are using a transactional replication scenario and you notice that your text fields are not being updated regularly. Changes are made to the text fields on a weekly basis, but the changes to the text fields are showing up at the subscribers only once a month. Why is this?

   A. The text fields were created with the Not for Replication option.

   B. The publication schedule was set to replicate the text fields only on a monthly basis.

   C. The subscribers are refreshed with a snapshot on a monthly basis.

   D. The subscribers are configured to pull the text fields only once a month.

19. You are using a multiple publishers/multiple subscribers scenario with transactional replication in which you do not want users to be able to modify data that has come from another database. To do this, you create a constraint that does not allow users to modify data that does not use their own location code. If this constraint gets replicated, it would prevent users from modifying their own local data. How do you prevent the constraint from being replicated?

A. Create the constraint with the Not for Replication option.

B. Use snapshot instead of transactional replication because it does not replicate constraints, triggers, or stored procedures.

C. Configure the publisher to drop and re-create the constraints when replicating data.

D. Do nothing; constraints are not replicated.

20. In order to use the Replication Monitor to check the status of replication, which server would you connect to?

A. The publisher

B. The subscriber

C. The distributor

D. Any of the above

Answers to Review Questions

1. B. Because the entire database does not change every day, you do not need to use snapshot. Also, snapshot would use a great deal more bandwidth than transactional. Because the subscribers do not need to update their copy of the data, you do not need the added complexity of merge or updating subscribers.

2. D. The models that involve multiple publishers obviously won't work here because you only have one publisher. The remote distributor option can save long distance charges because instead of making several long distance calls from New York to the satellites you can place a distributor in London and let the distributor make less expensive calls to the remaining satellites.

3. C. Answers A and B would certainly stop an immediate updating subscriber from replicating, but they are not the most likely cause here. Remember that the DTC needs a reliable network connection to do its job.

4. A. The publisher contains the original copy of the data.

5. D. Because the network is running very close to capacity most of the time, it would not support snapshot replication. Because the users would only be updating their own data, merge replication would be overkill. Transactional with updating subscribers fits your needs because the network usage is lower than snapshot and still allows users to update local copies of the data.

6. C. The $ share that replication uses as the distribution working folder is only accessible by administrators.

7. A. Horizontally partitioning the data means that you would only be replicating a subset of records to the sales offices. In this example, you could replicate only the records where the store ID is equal to the store that is subscribing to the publication. You need to create an article for each sales office because they each need to subscribe to a specific subset of the data.

8. D. Because each office needs to be able to update their own inventory databases each time they make a sale, and headquarters needs to be able to update the main database, you need to give them the capability to update. Merge replication would be overkill here since each sales office does not need to update other sales offices data.

9. C. Because you are using transactional replication with updating subscribers, you can use a central publisher at headquarters with each sales office being a subscriber.

10. A. In this scenario you do not have a central "main" database that each subscriber will update. All of the stores must be able to update data for the other stores' data. The best way to accomplish this is through merge replication.

11. B. Each store will publish its inventory database and subscribe to the other stores' inventory databases.

12. C. Each store needs to be identified with its own code so that the records of one store do not overwrite the records of other stores. For example, you do not want the alternators record from one store to overwrite the alternators record of another store because the inventory count would be off. Creating a primary key will accomplish this. Creating a constraint will not work because each store needs to update the other stores' data, and merge replication automatically creates a UNIQUEIDENTIFIER column using the NEWID() function.

13. C. Answers A and B would work, but they are slower than generating replication scripts. Answer D would not work because DTS does not copy subscription information.

14. B. The most likely cause here is that the distribution database log has been filled to capacity. That stops transactional replication in its tracks. The best thing to do to prevent this is to set up a maintenance plan for the distribution database.

15. D. If you pull the subscription to each of the subscribers, the distribution agent will run on the subscribers and remove some of the processing burden from the distributor.

16. C. Snapshot files are stored in the Distribution working folder by default. That can be changed when the publication is first set up if you prefer.

17. B. In snapshot replication, the distribution database stores historical information about the replication; the actual data is stored in the distribution working folder.

18. C. Text, ntext, and image data are only replicated when the snapshot is refreshed. The only thing that is replicated through transactions is the pointer record that tells SQL Server where the data is located in the database.

19. A. In order to keep a constraint from being replicated you need to specify the Not for Replication option when creating it.

20. C. The Replication Monitor runs on the distributor, where most of the replication process takes place.

Chapter 10

Monitoring and Optimizing SQL Server 2000

MICROSOFT EXAM OBJECTIVES COVERED IN THIS CHAPTER:

✓ **Optimize database performance. Considerations include indexing, locking, and recompiling.**

✓ **Optimize data storage.**

- Optimize files and filegroups.
- Manage database fragmentation.

✓ **Troubleshoot transactions and locking by using SQL Profiler, SQL Server Enterprise Manager, or Transact-SQL.**

✓ **Optimize hardware resource usage. Resources include CPU, disk I/O, and memory.**

- Monitor hardware resource usage by using the Windows System Monitor.
- Resolve system bottlenecks by using the Windows System Monitor.

✓ **Optimize and troubleshoot SQL Server system activity. Activities include cache hits, connections, locks, memory allocation, recompilation, and transactional throughput.**

- Monitor SQL Server system activity by using traces.
- Monitor SQL Server system activity by using the Windows System Monitor.

Imagine for a moment that you are the chief operating officer of a rather sizable company. It is your job to make sure that the company runs smoothly and that everything gets done efficiently. How will you do this? You could just guess at it, randomly assigning tasks and then just assuming that they are going to be done. Imagine the chaos that would ensue if you were to use this approach. Nothing would get done. Some departments would have too much to do, others would have nothing to do, and your company would go bankrupt.

A better approach would be to ask for reports from the various department managers and base your decisions on those reports. You might discover, for instance, that the accounting department has too much work and could use some help. Based on this report, you could hire more accountants. You might find that the production department has very little to do because the sales department has not been doing a good job, and based on this report, you could motivate the salespeople to get to work so that production would have something to do.

Now, instead of being in charge of the entire company's operations, you are actually in charge of your SQL Server. Here too, you need to make certain that everything is getting done efficiently. Again, you could just guess at this and randomly assign tasks, but that is both defeatist and an invitation to disaster. You need to get reports from your "department managers": the CPU, the disk subsystem, the database engine, etc. Once you have these reports, you can assign tasks and resources accordingly.

Most systems administrators don't perform monitoring and optimization functions because they believe they don't have the time. Most of their time is spent on fire fighting—that is, troubleshooting problems that have cropped up. It's safe to say that if they had taken the time to monitor and optimize the systems, those problems might never have arisen in the first place. That makes monitoring and optimization *proactive* troubleshooting, not *reactive*, as is the norm.

In this chapter, we will discuss the various methods and tools for getting the reports you need from your SQL Server. As is best with monitoring and tuning, we'll start at the bottom and work our way up; we'll discuss the tools (Windows System Monitor, SQL Profiler, and Query Governor) and then move into repairs.

Using Windows System Monitor

In order to get your company to function properly, you need to make certain that the very foundation of the company is doing its job. You need a management group that works well together and gets things done, a group where each will pull their own share of the load.

Microsoft Exam Objective

Optimize hardware resource usage. Resources include CPU, disk I/O, and memory.

- Monitor hardware resource usage by using the Windows System Monitor.
- Resolve system bottlenecks by using the Windows System Monitor.

Optimize and troubleshoot SQL Server system activity. Activities include cache hits, connections, locks, memory allocation, recompilation, and transactional throughput.

- Monitor SQL Server system activity by using the Windows System Monitor.

With SQL Server, this management group is the computer system itself. SQL cannot function properly if it does not have available system resources such as memory, processor power, fast disks, and a reliable network subsystem. If these systems do not work together, the system will not function properly. For example, if the memory is being overused, the disk subsystem will slow down because the memory will have to write to the pagefile (which is on the disk) far too often. To keep such things from happening, you will need to get reports from the subsystems; you can do this by using the *Windows System Monitor*.

Windows System Monitor, which comes with Windows, is located in the Administrative Tools folder on the Start menu and is labeled Performance. There are three sections of the program to consider:

System Monitor This view displays a graph of system performance. As values change, the graph will spike or dip accordingly. It is also used to read performance information recorded in log files.

Counter logs Counter logs record information about performance over time. They are useful for trend tracking.

Trace logs Unlike counter logs, this type of log is event driven, so it is not always running. An event that might start a trace log would be disk I/O or network access.

Alerts With alert view you can tell Windows System Monitor to warn you when something bad is looming on the horizon, perhaps when CPU use is almost—but not quite yet—too high. This type of warning gives you time to fix potential problems before they become actual problems.

With each of these views, you monitor *objects* and *counters*. An *object* is a part of the system, like the processor or the physical memory. A *counter* displays the number that tells you how much that object is being used. For example, the % Processor Time counter under the Processor Object will tell you how much time your processor spends working. Table 10.1 lists common counters and their recommended values. Exercise 10.1 discusses how to use Windows System Monitor for real-time data, and Exercise 10.2 describes logging data with Windows System Monitor.

TABLE 10.1 Common Counters and Values in Windows System Monitor

Object	Counter	Recommended Value	Use
Processor	% Processor Time	Less than 75%	The amount of time the processor spends working.
Memory	Pages/Sec	Fewer than 5	The number of times per second that data had to be moved from RAM to disk and vice versa.

TABLE 10.1 Common Counters and Values in Windows System Monitor *(continued)*

Object	Counter	Recommended Value	Use
Memory	Available Bytes	More than 4MB	The amount of physical RAM available. This number should be low since it uses as much RAM as it can grab for file cache.
Memory	Committed Bytes	Less than physical RAM	The amount of RAM committed to use.
Physical Disk	Average Disk Queue	Less than 2	This is the number of requests waiting to be written to disk.
Disk	% Disk Time	Less than 50%	The amount of time that the disk is busy reading or writing.
Network Segment	% Network Utilization	Less than 30%	The amount of network bandwidth being used.

In order to see the Network Segment: % Network Utilization, you must install the Network Monitor Agent in the Add/Remove Programs applet in Control Panel.

WARNING   If you don't enable the logical disk counters by executing diskperf -yv, all logical disk counters will read zero. Physical disk counters are turned on by default in Windows 2000.

EXERCISE 10.1

Monitoring with Windows System Monitor

1. Log in to Windows as Administrator.

2. From the Start menu, select Programs ➢ Administrative Tools ➢ Performance.

3. Click the + icon on the toolbar to start adding counters to the chart.

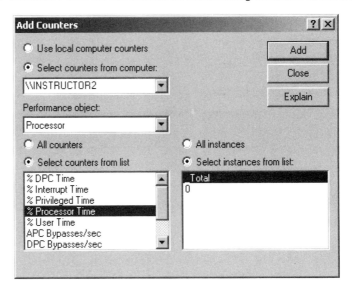

4. In the Object box, select Processor (not Process).

5. In the Counter box, select % Processor Time and click Add.

6. In the Object box, select Memory.

7. In the Counter box, select Pages/Sec and click Add.

8. Click Close and notice the graph being created on the screen.

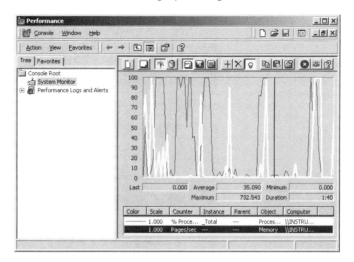

9. Press Ctrl+H and notice the current counter turn white. This makes the chart easier to read.

10. In the left pane, under Performance Logs and Alerts, select Alerts.

11. On the Action menu, select New Alert Settings.

12. Enter **Test Alert** in the name box.

13. In the Comment box type **Processor Alert**.

14. Click Add, select Processor in the Object box and % Processor Time in the Counter box, and click Add, then Close.

15. Select Alert When the Value Is Under and set the value to 100. This will generate an alert if the processor is not busy 100 percent of the time. In the real world, this would be set to Over 70 percent, thus warning you just before it becomes a serious problem.

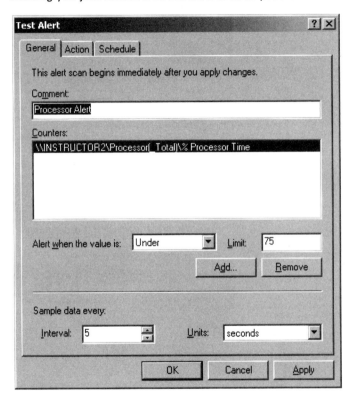

EXERCISE 10.1 *(continued)*

16. On the Action tab, check the Send a Network Message To box and enter your machine name in the text box below.

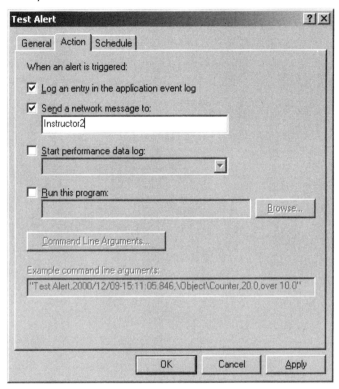

17. Click OK to start the alert and watch the alerts generated for a short time. Then right-click the alert and select Stop to stop the alert from firing.

18. Exit Windows System Monitor.

EXERCISE 10.2

Logging with Windows System Monitor

1. Open Windows System Monitor in the Administrative Tools menu.

2. In the left pane, select Counter Logs.

3. On the Actions menu, select New Log Settings and name it Test Log.

4. Under the Counters box, click Add.

5. In the Object box, select Processor (not Process).

6. In the Counter box, select % Processor Time and click Add.

7. In the Object box, select Memory.

8. In the Counters box, select Pages/Sec and click Add.

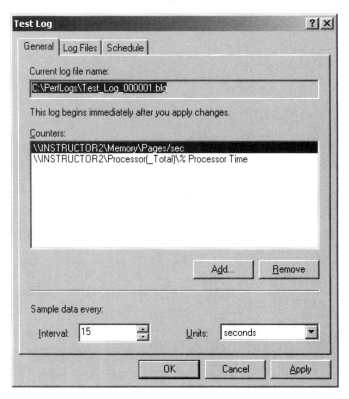

9. Click Close to return to the previous dialog box.

10. On the Log Files tab, notice the location and name of the files that will be created and click OK to start the log.

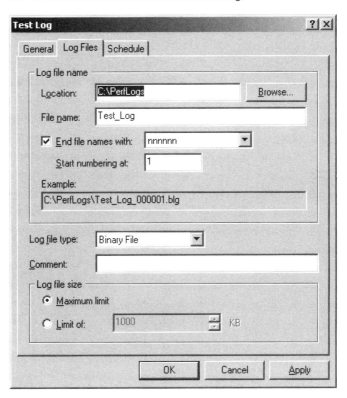

11. Allow the log to run for about five minutes to gather some data.

12. Right-click the Test Log and select Stop to stop the log so that you can read from it.

13. In the left pane, click System Monitor.

14. Now right-click in the gray area of the chart and select Properties.

15. On the Source tab, click Log File.

16. Click Browse, select the log file created in step 9, and click OK.

17. Click the + icon on the toolbar to add objects to the graph.

18. In the Object box, select Processor (not Process).

EXERCISE 10.2 *(continued)*

19. In the Counter box, select % Processor Time and click Add.

20. In the Object box, select Memory.

21. In the Counter box, select Pages/Sec and click Add.

22. Click close and notice that the recorded data now appears in the graph.

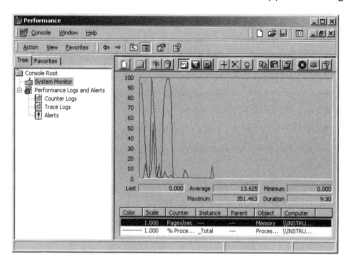

23. Close Windows System Monitor.

You can monitor SQL Server as well as Windows using Windows System Monitor, since SQL provides its own objects and counters. Table 10.2 describes some of the more common SQL Server counters and objects to monitor.

TABLE 10.2 Common SQL Windows System Monitor Counters

Object	Counter	Use
SqlServer:Buffer Manager	Buffer Cache Hit Ratio	How much data is being retrieved from cache instead of disk.

TABLE 10.2   Common SQL Windows System Monitor Counters *(continued)*

Object	Counter	Use
SqlServer:Buffer Manager	Page Reads/Sec	Number of data pages that are read from disk each second.
SqlServer:Buffer Manager	Page Writes/Sec	Number of data pages that are written to disk each second.
SqlServer:General Statistics	User Connections	Number of user connections. Each of these will take some RAM.
SQLServer:Memory Manager	Total Server Memory (KB)	Total amount of memory that SQL has been dynamically assigned.
SQLServer:SQL Statistics	SQL Compilations/ Sec	Number of compiles per second.

Now that you have the system resources working together, you can start creating queries. Rather than randomly creating queries and hoping they work quickly, let's see how you can create queries and start the optimization process at the same time using Query Analyzer.

Using Query Analyzer

Up to this point, you have been using *Query Analyzer* to enter queries and see results, but it can do more. One clue as to its enhanced capabilities comes from its name: Query *Analyzer*. It is used not only to enter queries, but also to analyze them, to see how many resources they consume, and to see how fast they run. As you will see in Exercise 10.3, it accomplishes this feat by timing each step of the execution; this includes parsing the command you typed in and checking for errors, loading the data into memory, performing the query on the data, and more. If you would like to see a graphic representation of everything SQL Server is doing with your query, you can tell it to display an execution plan (also shown in Exercise 10.3). This will display a series of icons that lead you through the execution process.

EXERCISE 10.3

Using Query Analyzer

1. On the Start menu go to Programs ➢ Microsoft SQL Server, and click Query Analyzer.

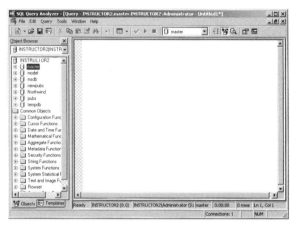

2. When asked to log in, use Windows Authentication. You will see the Query window.

3. On the Query menu, select Current Connection Properties.

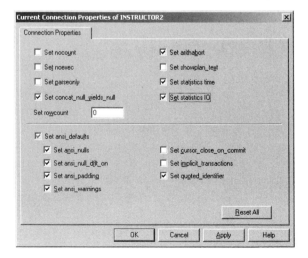

4. In the Properties sheet, check Set Statistics Time and Set Statistics IO. Set Statistics Time displays CPU time used, while Set Statistics IO displays disk time.

5. On the Query menu, select Show Execution Plan to see a graphic representation of how SQL Server executes your query.

6. On the Query window toolbar, select Northwind in the DB list box to set Northwind as the default database.

7. In the Query window, type the following query:

   SELECT * FROM employees

8. Click the Messages tab (at the bottom of the screen) and notice the Execution, Parse, and Compile times, then click the Execution Plan tab.

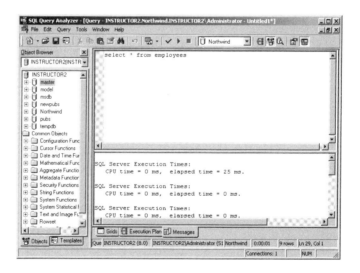

9. In the Execution Plan pane, hold your mouse pointer over each icon in turn; notice that they come with tool tips to help you better understand each step of execution.

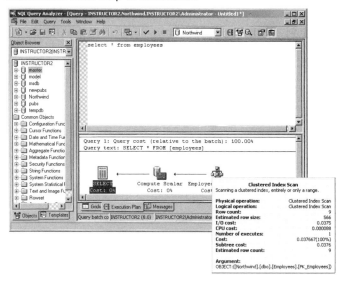

10. Close Query Analyzer.

Once the analysis is complete, you will have a better idea of how to build your queries and optimize them for speed, but you will not yet have the full picture. To get a full understanding of how your queries respond to everyday use, you need to monitor them under stress—that is why we have SQL Profiler.

Monitoring with SQL Profiler

When running a company, once you have the management team working in harmony, you can focus your attention on the rest of the workforce. In this analogy, Query Analyzer would be like interviewing prospective employees: you want to be sure they have the appropriate qualifications, can fit in with the rest of the team, and will do their fair share of the work before you hire them. Like new employees, new queries need to be monitored regularly (with queries, on a day-to-day basis).

Microsoft ***Exam*** ***Objective***	**Optimize and troubleshoot SQL Server system activity.** **Activities include cache hits, connections, locks, memory** **allocation, recompilation, and transactional throughput.** ▪ Monitor SQL Server system activity by using traces.

Profiler allows you to monitor and record what is happening inside the database engine. This is accomplished by performing a *trace*, which is a record of data that has been captured about *events*. These can be stored in a table, a trace log file, or both for future reference.

The actions you will be monitoring are called *events* and are logically grouped into *event classes*. Some of these events are useful for maintaining security, and some are useful for troubleshooting problems, but most of these events are used for monitoring and optimization (as described in Exercise 10.4).

EXERCISE 10.4

Monitoring with SQL Profiler

1. From the Start menu, go to Programs ➢ SQL Server and click Profiler.

2. On the File menu, select New, then click Trace to bring up the Trace properties sheet. You will be asked to log in at this point; do so with either form of authentication.

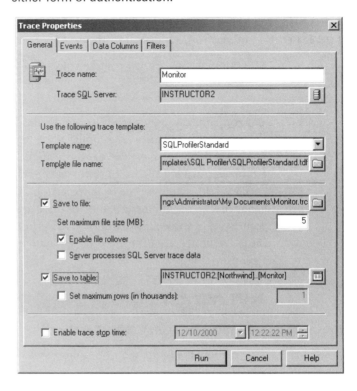

3. In the Trace Name box, type **Monitor**.

4. There are several templates to choose from in the templates drop-down list box. Each of them gives you a preset trace definition to work with. Leave the template name as SQLProfilerStandard.

5. Check the Save to File check box and click Save to accept the default name and location.

6. Check the Save to Table check box, log in to the server again, and fill in the following:

Database: Northwind

Table: Monitor

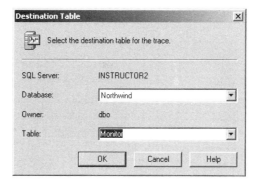

7. Click the Events tab.

8. Under Available Event Classes, select Objects and click Add. This will monitor the opening and closing of objects such as tables.

9. Click the Data Columns tab to change the data you see in the trace.

10. Under Unselected Data, select End Time and click Add.

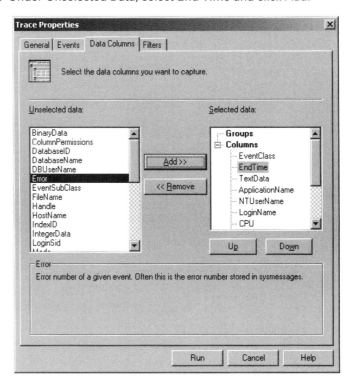

11. Click Run to start the trace.

12. Leave Profiler running and open Query Analyzer; log in using Windows Authentication.

13. Execute the following query:

   `USE Northwind`

   `SELECT * FROM products`

EXERCISE 10.4 *(continued)*

14. Switch back to Profiler and click the Pause button (double blue lines). Notice the data that was collected by the trace.

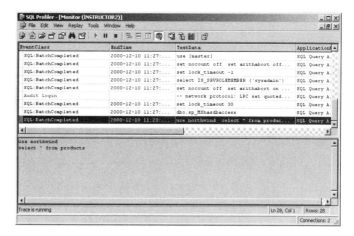

15. Close Profiler and Query Analyzer.

You may have found the amount of data collected by the trace overwhelming. That data was for only one user executing one query. Imagine trying to sort through a trace of hundreds of users with dozens of queries—a daunting task, to say the least. Fortunately, you will not be subjected to such tortures, since you can filter your trace data.

Filtering the Trace Data

Filtering is a simple process to grasp, much like making coffee. Because in most cases you do not want the grounds saturating the finished product, you place a filter in the coffeepot to separate the grounds and the finished coffee. In this way, you get only what you want, and the rest is discarded.

The principle is the same with Profiler. When you create and execute a trace, it returns a great deal of data that you don't necessarily want or need to see. For example, a great deal of information about system objects is returned, and every application you use to access SQL (for example, Enterprise Manager) will be recorded in the trace. To continue our coffee analogy, if you don't want the "coffee grounds" of extraneous data, you need to put a *filter* on the trace, as shown in Exercise 10.5.

Filtering Traces

1. Open Profiler and select File ➤ New ➤ Trace to bring up the Trace properties sheet (you will be asked to log in again).

2. In the Trace Name box, type **Filter**.

3. Check the Save to File check box and accept the default filename in the subsequent Save As dialog box.

4. Click the Events tab.

5. Under Available Events, select Objects and click Add.

6. Click Run to start the trace.

7. Open Query Analyzer and log in using Windows Authentication.

8. Execute the following query:

   ```
   USE northwind

   SELECT customerid, od.orderid, productname, quantity

   FROM [order details] od inner join products p

   ON od.productid = p.productid

   INNER JOIN orders o

   ON o.orderid = od.orderid

   WHERE customerid = 'hanar'
   ```

9. Close Query Analyzer, switch back to Profiler and click the Pause button. Notice the how much of the data in the trace is system data (for example, sysdatabases).

10. On the File menu, select Properties.

11. Click the Filters tab. You will notice that the only information filtered out is that which comes from Profiler.

12. Check the Exclude System IDs check box and click Run.

13. Click OK on the subsequent warning that you will need to stop and restart the trace.

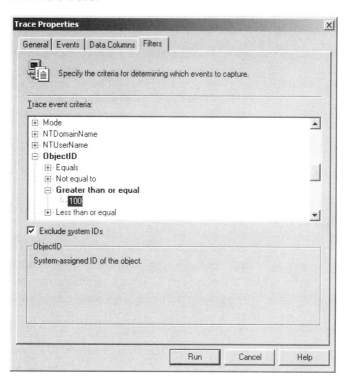

14. On the toolbar, click the Stop button.

15. On the toolbar, click the Start button.

16. Switch back to Query Analyzer and execute the same query as before with one change in the last line, as noted here:

UASE northwind

SELECT customerid, od.orderid, productname, quantity

FROM [order details] od inner join products p

```
ON od.productid = p.productid

INNER JOIN orders o

ON o.orderid = od.orderid

WHERE customerid = 'quick'
```

17. Switch back to Profiler and click the Pause button. Notice that no system data was captured this time.

18. Close Profiler and Query Analyzer.

It is highly unlikely that you will be able—or want—to watch Profiler constantly to see whether anything important happens. This is not a problem, since you can always replay the traces.

Replaying a Trace File

When solving a problem or dealing with an untoward event, one of the first things to do is to try to re-create the circumstances and chain of events that led up to the event. As an administrator, you are going to be called in all the time to try to deal with such problems as slow response time and even server crashes.

You can re-create the problem-causing events by replaying a trace. Loading your saved traces into Profiler will allow you to replay them against the server and to figure out exactly where the problem occurred. An especially nice touch is that you don't have to play the whole trace all at once; you can take it step-by-step to see exactly where the problem lies. Exercise 10.6 walks you through replaying a trace.

Replaying a Trace in Profiler

1. Open Profiler; select File ➤ Open ➤ Trace File.

2. In the Open dialog box, select Monitor and click OK.

3. On the toolbar in the Trace window, click the Execute Single Step button (double braces {} with an arrow over the top). This will execute a single step at a time.

4. After you log in, on the Replay SQL Server dialog box, select all the defaults and click start.

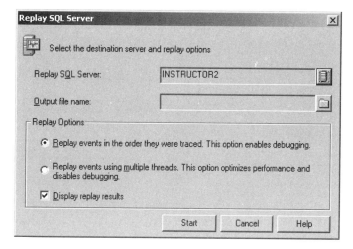

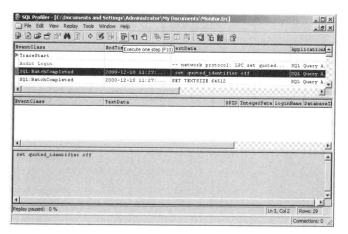

5. Scroll down and select the first line you find that contains SQL:BatchCompleted.

EXERCISE 10.6 *(continued)*

6. On the toolbar, click the Run to Cursor button (an arrow pointing to double braces {}). This will execute all steps between the current position and the event you have selected.

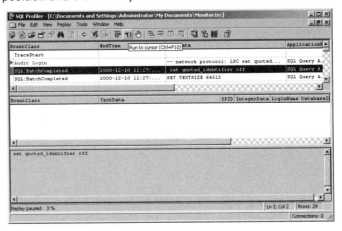

7. Click the Start Execution button (a yellow arrow) to finish replaying the trace.

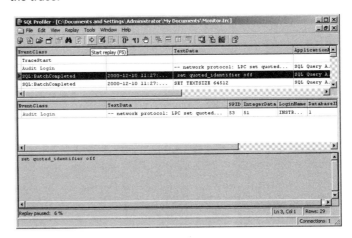

8. Close Profiler.

The Profiler is a wonderful tool for monitoring database activity and reporting problems, but that is not all it can do. Profiler comes with yet another Wizard that will help you even further to improve the performance of your queries: the Index Tuning Wizard.

Using the Index Tuning Wizard

Systems, like automobiles or musical instruments, must be properly tuned to function properly. If even one SQL Server index were out of tune, it could slow down the entire system. Perhaps the wrong columns were indexed from the beginning, or maybe users started querying different data over time, which would require the creation of new indexes. If any of this is true, your indexes need tuning.

The one thing you need before you can run the *Index Tuning Wizard* is a workload. You get this by running and saving a trace in Profiler. It is best to get this workload during times of peak database activity to make sure that you give the Wizard an accurate load. (If you aren't sure about which events to trace, you can base your trace on the Sample 1 Trace SQL definition, which defines a standard set of events to capture.) Exercise 10.7 shows you how to use the Index Tuning Wizard.

EXERCISE 10.7

The Index Tuning Wizard

1. Open Profiler.

2. On the Tools menu, select Index Tuning Wizard. This will open the Welcome screen.

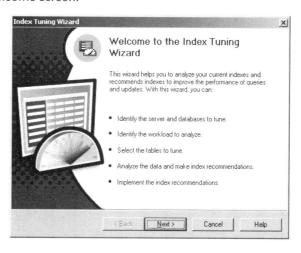

3. Click Next and log in.

4. Select Northwind as the database to tune.

EXERCISE 10.7 *(continued)*

5. Check Keep All Existing Indexes.

6. Check Thorough as the analysis type.

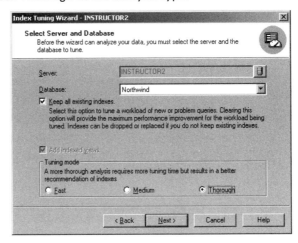

7. Click Next.

8. Click the My Workload File button.

9. In the File Open dialog box, select the Monitor trace (created earlier) and click OK to return to the Specify Workload screen, where you will see the Monitor file listed under My Workload File.

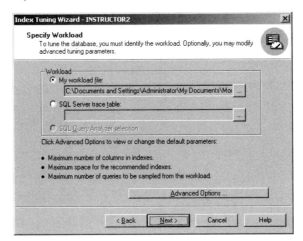

10. When returned to the Specify Workload screen, click the Advanced Options button, note the defaults, and click OK.

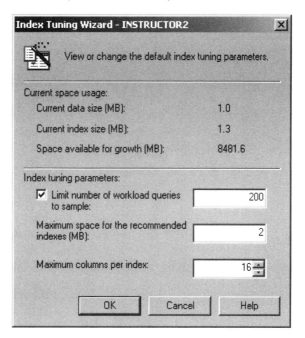

11. Click Next.

12. In the Select Tables to Tune screen, click Select All Tables.

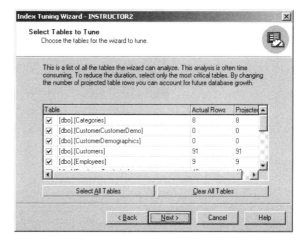

13. Click Next, and the Wizard will start tuning your indexes.

14. You should now see a series of recommendations; click Next.

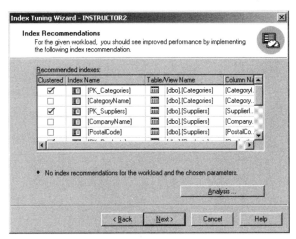

15. On the final screen, click Finish to end the Wizard.

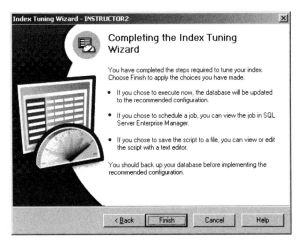

16. When you receive a message stating that the Wizard has completed, click OK.

17. Exit Profiler.

Tips and Techniques

If you want the best results from SQL Server's monitoring tools, you need to know and use the proper techniques. If you don't, the end result will not be what you are hoping for—or what you need.

Setting a Measurement Baseline

You will never know if your system is running slower than normal unless you know what normal is. That is what a *measurement baseline* does: it shows you the resources (memory, CPU, etc.) SQL consumes under normal circumstances. You create it before putting your system into production so that you have something to compare your readings to later on.

The first thing you need to create an accurate measurement baseline is a test network with just your SQL Server and one or two client machines. You limit the number of machines involved because all networks have broadcast traffic, which is processed by all the machines on the network. This broadcast traffic can throw your counts off, sometimes a little, sometimes quite a bit. You may instead want to consider shutting down as many machines as possible and generating your baseline during off-hours.

You can then start your baseline. The Windows counters mentioned at the outset as well as the preset SQL counters should provide an accurate baseline with which you can compare future readings. Then you can move to the next technique.

Data Archiving and Trend Tracking

While the consequences of throwing away your SQL monitoring records are not quite as severe as facing an IRS auditor without records and receipts, you still need to save, or *archive*, them. One of the primary reasons to do so is to back up requests for additional equipment. For example, if you ask for funds to buy more memory for the SQL Server but don't bring any proof that the system needs the RAM, you are probably not going to get the money. If you bring a few months worth of reports, however, and say, "After tracking SQL for a time we've found this…" management may be far more willing to give you the money you need. Using archived data in such fashion is known as *trend tracking*.

One of the most valuable functions of using your archived data for trend tracking is proactive troubleshooting; that is, anticipating—and avoiding—problems before they arise. Suppose you had added 50 new users to your network about three months ago and were about to do it again. If you had archived your data from that period, you would be able to recall what those 50 users had done to the performance of the SQL Server, and you could compensate for it. On the other hand, if you had thrown that data away, you might be in for a nasty surprise when your system unexpectedly slows to a crawl.

Optimizing Techniques

SQL Server has the ability to dynamically adjust most of its settings to compensate for problems. It can adjust memory use, threads spawned, and a host of other settings. In some cases, unfortunately, those dynamic adjustments may not be enough and you may need to make some manual changes.

Microsoft
Exam
Objective

Optimize and troubleshoot SQL Server system activity. Activities include cache hits, connections, locks, memory allocation, recompilation, and transactional throughput.

Optimize database performance. Considerations include indexing, locking, and recompiling.

Optimize data storage.

- Optimize files and filegroups.

- Manage database fragmentation.

Troubleshoot transactions and locking by using SQL Profiler, SQL Server Enterprise Manager, or Transact-SQL.

We'll look at a few specific areas that may require your personal attention.

Queries and Stored Procedures

The first thing to ask yourself when you are getting slow response times is whether you could be using a stored procedure here instead of a local query. Stored procedures are different from local code in two ways: they are stored on the SQL Server, so they do not need to be transmitted over the network and thus cause congestion. In addition, stored procedures are precompiled on the server; this saves on system resources, since local code must be compiled once it gets to the system.

Overall, stored procedures are the way to go, but if you need to use local queries, you should consider how they are written, since poorly constructed queries can wreak havoc on your system. If, for example, you have a query that is returning every row of a table when only half of that is required, you should consider rewriting it.

Tempdb

Is your Tempdb big enough to handle the load that your queries put on it? Think of Tempdb as a scratchpad for SQL; when queries are performed, SQL uses this scratchpad to make notes about the result set. If it runs out of room to make these notes, system response time can slow down. Tempdb should be between 25 and 40 percent of the size of your largest database (for example, if your largest database is 100MB, Tempdb should be 25 to 40MB).

Query Governor

Right out of the box, SQL will run any query you tell it to, even if that query is poorly written. You can change that by using the *Query Governor*. This is not a separate tool but part of the database engine, and it is controlled by the Query Governor Cost Limit. This setting tells SQL not to run queries longer than x (where x is a value higher than zero). If, for example, the Query Governor Cost Limit is set to 2, any query that is estimated to take longer than two seconds would not be allowed to run. SQL is able to estimate the running time of a query because it keeps statistics about the number and composition of records in tables and indexes. The Query Governor Cost Limit can be set by using the command `sp_configure 'query governor cost limit', '1'` (the 1 in this code can be higher). It can also be set on the Server Settings tab of the Server properties sheet in Enterprise Manager.

If the Query Governor Cost Limit is set to zero (the default), all queries will be allowed to run.

Max Async I/O

It goes without saying that SQL needs to be able to write to disk since that's where the database files are stored, but is it writing to disk fast enough? If you have multiple hard disks connected to a single controller, multiple hard disks connected to multiple controllers, or a RAID system involving striping, the answer is probably no. The maximum number of asynchronous input/output (*Max Async I/O*) threads by default in SQL is 32. That means that SQL can have 32 outstanding read and 32 outstanding write requests at a time. Thus, if SQL needs to write some data to disk, it can send up to 32 small chunks of that data to disk at a time. If you have a powerful disk subsystem, you will want to increase the Max Async I/O setting.

The setting to which you increase it depends on your hardware, so if you increase the setting, you must then monitor the server. Specifically, you will need to monitor the Physical Disk: Average Disk Queue Windows System Monitor counter, which should be less than 2 (note that any queue should be less than 2). If you adjust Max Async I/O and the Average Disk Queue counter goes above 2, you have set it too high and will need to decrease it.

You will need to divide the Average Disk Queue counter by the number of physical drives to get an accurate count. That is, if you have three hard disks and a counter value of 6, you would divide 6 by 3—which tells you that the counter value for each disk is 2.

LazyWriter

LazyWriter is a SQL process that moves information from the data cache in memory to a file on disk. If LazyWriter can't keep enough free space in the data cache for new requests, performance slows down. To make sure this does not happen, monitor the SQL Server: Buffer Manager—Free Buffers Windows System Monitor counter. LazyWriter tries to keep this counter level above zero; if it dips or hits zero, you have a problem, probably with your disk subsystem. To verify this, you need to check the Physical Disk: Average Disk Queue Windows System Monitor Counter and verify that it is not more than 2 per physical disk (see the previous section). If the queue is too high, LazyWriter will not be able to move data efficiently from memory to disk, and the free buffers will drop.

RAID

RAID (Redundant Array of Inexpensive Disks) is used to protect your data and speed up your system. In a system without RAID, data that is written to disk is written to that one disk. In a system with RAID, that same data is written across multiple disks, providing fault-tolerance and improved I/O. Some forms of RAID can be implemented inexpensively in Windows, but this uses such system resources as processor and memory. If you have the budget for it, you might consider getting a separate RAID controller that will take the processing burden off Windows. RAID is discussed in detail in Chapter 4, but here is a quick refresher:

RAID 0 stripe set   This provides I/O improvement but not fault-tolerance.

RAID 1 mirroring   This provides fault-tolerance and read-time improvement. This can also be implemented as duplexing, which is a mirror that has separate controllers for each disk. This is the best place to put your transaction logs because it gives the fastest sequential write speed while still offering fault-tolerance.

RAID 0+1 mirrored stripe set   This is a stripe set without parity that is duplicated on another set of disks. This requires a third-party controller since Windows does not support it natively. If you have this in place, data or log files can be placed here. (You probably won't see this as an option on the exam, but it is good to know for the real world.)

RAID 5 stripe set with parity   This provides fault-tolerance and improved I/O. This is where data files should be placed because of the read speed that it offers.

Adding Memory

SQL Server, like most BackOffice products, needs significant amounts of RAM. The more you put in, the happier SQL will be. If your Buffer Cache Hit Ratio counter is less than 90 you definitely need more RAM.

Manually Configuring Memory Use

While SQL is capable of dynamically assigning itself memory, it is not always best to let it do so. A good example of this is when you need to run another BackOffice program, like Exchange, on the same system as SQL Server. If SQL is not constrained, it will take so much memory that there will be none left for Exchange. This constraint is the *max server memory* setting; by adjusting it you can stop SQL Server from taking too much RAM. You could also set *min server memory*, which tells SQL never to use less than the set amount; this should be used in conjunction with *set working size*. Windows uses virtual memory, which means that data that is in memory and has not been accessed for a while can be stored on disk. The set working size option stops Windows from moving SQL data from RAM to disk, even if it is idle. This can improve SQL Server's performance since data will never need to be retrieved from disk (which is about 100 times slower than RAM). If you decide to use this option, you should set min server memory and max server memory to the same size and then change the set working size option to 1.

Optimizing Stored Procedures

When a user executes a query, SQL Server creates an execution plan to return a result set. Among other things, this execution plan tells SQL Server which indexes to use against which columns to get results in the least amount of time. Stored procedures are precompiled on the server, which means that their execution plans remain in memory after they are run for the first time after SQL Server is started. This is good because it speeds up stored procedure execution, but it has a drawback. If an index changes on the underlying table, the stored procedure will not use the new index until it is recompiled (meaning that a new execution plan is created). There are three ways to force SQL Server to create a new execution plan for stored procedures:

- Stop and restart the SQL Server service. This will force SQL Server to recompile the stored procedure the first time it is run. This is not the generally recommended way to accomplish this task because it forces all users to disconnect from the server.

- Create the stored procedure using the `WITH RECOMPILE` clause in the definition. This forces SQL Server to create a new execution plan for the stored procedure every time it is executed. This is useful for stored procedures that have a large number of variables and parameters that change each time the procedure is executed.

- Use the `sp_recompile` system stored procedure to force SQL Server to recompile a stored procedure the next time it is executed. This is the best way to recompile a stored procedure that has few variables and just needs access to a new index.

Stored procedures will be automatically recompiled when the underlying table changes but not when an index is added.

Proper Indexing

If you want SQL Server queries to run as fast as possible, you must create the proper indexes. As we discussed earlier in this book, there are two types of indexes to choose from: clustered and nonclustered.

Clustered indexes are a lot like a dictionary: they change the physical structure of the data to match the constraints of the index. That means that if you index on last name, for example, Adams would be placed physically in front of Barnes in the data file.

A *nonclustered index* is more like the appendix at the back of a book: it is topically arranged and contains pointers to where the data resides in the data file.

Clustered indexes are great for searching on ranges of data (e.g. Jones–Thompson) because all SQL Server has to do is find the first value in the range; the rest of the values will come immediately after because the data has been physically arranged that way. Nonclustered indexes are useful for single value searches. If you were to perform range searches against a nonclustered index, SQL Server would need to constantly return to the index to locate the next record in the search, and the index would slow the query down.

Optimizing Locks

It goes without saying that you do not want other users to be able to make changes to data while you are reading or modifying it yourself. This would cause confusion and inaccuracies in your database, and your system would soon go from being a database server to being a large, beige paperweight. To keep this from happening, SQL Server automatically places locks on the data that is being accessed to limit what other users can do with that data. There are several types of locks in SQL Server, but you are only concerned with two of them here:

- Shared locks are placed on data that is being accessed for read purposes. In other words, when a user executes a SELECT statement, SQL Server places a shared lock on the data requested. Shared locks allow other users to access the locked data for reading, but not modification.

- Exclusive locks are placed on data that is being modified. This means that when a user executes an INSERT, UPDATE, or DELETE statement, SQL Server uses an exclusive lock to protect the data. Exclusive locks do not allow other users to access the locked data for any purpose; the data is exclusively available to the user that placed the lock.

SQL Server does a great job of dynamically setting these locks, so you do not need to be concerned with setting these locks yourself. What you do need to be concerned with is making sure that your queries are properly written so that SQL Server does not place locks that get in the users' way. The primary cause of this are deadlocks.

Deadlocks occur when users try to place exclusive locks on each other's objects. For example: User1 places an exclusive lock on Table1 then tries to place an exclusive lock on Table2. User2 already has an exclusive lock on Table2, and User2 tries to put an exclusive lock on Table1. This condition could cause SQL Server to enter an endless loop of waiting for the locks to be released, but fortunately there is an algorithm built right into SQL Server that looks for and rectifies this problem. SQL Server picks one of the users (called the *victim* in SQL Server terminology) and kills their query. The user whose query was killed will receive an error message stating that they are the victim of a deadlock and should try their query again later.

This can cause aggravation among the users because it slows their work. The way to avoid this is by monitoring SQL Server using one of three methods:

- Use Profiler to monitor the Lock:Deadlock and Lock:Deadlock Chain events in the Locks event class.

- Check the Current Activity folders under Management in Enterprise Manager.

- Use the `sp_lock` stored procedure to find out what locks are in place.

When you find the cause of the deadlock, you can have your developers rewrite the offending queries.

Defragmentation

SQL Server stores objects in the database in 8KB chunks called pages. When an object requires more space in the database file, SQL Server allocates eight contiguous pages (called an extent) to the object rather than just a single page at a time. This is done in an effort to keep the object's pages as close together as possible so that data access is faster. Over time, however, the object's pages will be scattered throughout the data file, a condition called *fragmentation*. This fragmentation can slow the server down and therefore needs to be detected and corrected.

You can detect fragmentation on a table or index in a database by using the DBCC SHOWCONTIG (*Objectname*) command. This is designed specifically to find fragmentation in a database. For example, here is what the command would look like when run against the Employees table in the Northwind database:

```
USE Northwind
DBCC SHOWCONTIG (Employees)

DBCC SHOWCONTIG scanning 'Employees' table...
Table: 'Employees' (1977058079); index ID: 1, database ID: 6
TABLE level scan performed.
- Pages Scanned................................: 1
- Extents Scanned.............................: 1
- Extent Switches.............................: 0
- Avg. Pages per Extent.......................: 1.0
- Scan Density [Best Count:Actual Count].......: 100.00%
[1:1]
- Logical Scan Fragmentation ..................: 0.00%
- Extent Scan Fragmentation ...................: 0.00%
- Avg. Bytes Free per Page....................: 4945.0
- Avg. Page Density (full)....................: 38.91%
DBCC execution completed. If DBCC printed error messages,
contact your system administrator.
```

Here is what all of that means:

Pages scanned   The number of pages used by the object.

Extents scanned   The number of extents used by the object.

Extent switches   The number of times that DBCC had to switch to another extent when checking each page of the object. This should be one less than the total number of extents.

Avg. pages per extent   The number of pages used per extent.

Scan density   Should be 100; if it is less, there is some fragmentation.

[Best count:Actual count]   Best count is the ideal number of extent changes that should be made. Actual count is the actual number of extent changes that occurred. If actual is higher than best, there is some fragmentation in the database.

Logical scan fragmentation   The number of pages that are out of order in the leaf levels of an index. If this is more than 0, there is fragmentation in the index.

Extent scan fragmentation   The number of extents that are out of order in an index. If this is higher than 0, there is fragmentation in the index.

Avg. bytes free per page   The amount of free space on the pages of the object. The higher this number is, the less full the pages are. Lower numbers are best.

Avg. page density (full)   Tells you how full your pages are on average.

If you find that one of your tables is fragmented, you can drop and recreate the clustered index on the table to defragment it. Another option is to use the DBCC DBREINDEX command to rebuild the index. The difference between these two options is that DBCC DBREINDEX will allow users to access the database while it is running, but it is not as accurate as dropping and recreating the clustered index on a table.

Real World Scenario: Optimizing a Server

You have just bought a new server and you want to be certain that it is always running at optimum efficiency. The first thing you need to do is create a measurement baseline because you do not know what slow is unless you know what normal is. You realize the best way to do this is to place the server and one or two clients on a test network so that your counts are not thrown off by broadcast traffic.

Once you have the baseline you are ready to start creating queries to run against the server. You know that most of the users will be accessing common queries to retrieve data, so you make many of your queries into stored procedures because they reside on the server, are easier to manage, and are faster because they are precompiled. All of the queries are run through Query Analyzer first to make sure that they are not too slow to be put into production.

Once the queries are placed in production, you regularly run Profiler against the server to make sure that the server is not slowing down due to more-than-expected usage and perhaps unexpected queries that require new indexes to be created.

You also regularly run Windows System Monitor to verify that your hard disks and processor are not being overburdened and that you have enough RAM to support all of your users.

You can use this data in the future for trend tracking. That way you will know what to expect from a major change on the system if you have performed similar changes before. You can also use this data for proof that you need new hardware when the time comes—financial departments are not given to handing out money just because the computer department says it needs it.

Summary

This chapter has stressed the importance of monitoring and optimization. Monitoring allows you to find potential problems before your users find them; without it, you have no way of knowing how well your system is performing.

- Windows System Monitor can be used to monitor both Windows and SQL Server.

- Query Analyzer can be used to see how a query will affect your server before you allow users access to it.

- Profiler is used to monitor the system on a day-to-day basis to make sure the server is running as expected.

- The Index Tuning Wizard can be used to create and maintain indexes to keep your server running as quickly as possible.

- Don't forget to archive your data for trend tracking and reporting purposes—you will need it later.

- Some performance issues that you need to keep in mind:

  - Max Async IO

  - LazyWriter

  - Query Governor

  - Make sure you have enough RAM

  - Create the proper indexes

  - Use the proper RAID

Exam Essentials

Know your counters.   Know your counters and the acceptable values for each of them.

Get to know RAID.   RAID can affect the performance of your system, so you need to understand how to use it. RAID 1 is for T-logs, and RAID 5 is for data files. Use hardware RAID over software RAID whenever possible.

Familiarize yourself with Profiler.   Profiler is going to prove very useful in your career as a database administrator because you can use it to find out what is going on behind the scenes. Because of its usefulness, you can expect to see it on the exam.

Key Terms

archive	measurement baseline
clustered index	nonclustered index
counter	objects
event class	Query Analyzer
events	Query Governor
filter	RAID
Index Tuning Wizard	set working size
LazyWriter	SQL Profiler
Max Async I/O	trace
max server memory	trend tracking

Review Questions

1. You have a database that has been in production for some time and you have just created some new queries to run against the database. The queries are designed to search for individual Employee ID numbers and return values about sick leave and vacation time. The problem is that the query runs fairly slow and the users are complaining that the entire server seems slower with the new query in place. What can you do to speed it up?

   A. Create a clustered index on the Employee ID column.

   B. Create a nonclustered index on the Employee ID column.

   C. Add more RAM to the system.

   D. Add a new disk to the system and configure it for RAID 5.

2. Your users have been complaining that, ever since the new employees came on board, the SQL Server has slowed down. When monitoring your system, you notice that the Pages/Sec counter is at 6 consistently and the Buffer Cache Hit Ratio is about 75 sustained. What should you do?

   A. Add another SQL Server to the network and replicate the database to the new server.

   B. Add another hard disk to the server and implement RAID 5.

   C. Add more RAM to the server.

   D. Set the Query Governor to 2.

3. You have just created a 500GB database to hold inventory data. After placing the database into production, you notice that the response time of the server has slowed. What can you do to improve performance?

   A. Increase the size of the Tempdb database to 125GB.

   B. Increase the size of the Tempdb database to 500GB.

   C. Set the Query Governor to 0.

   D. Increase the Max Async I/O parameter.

4. You want to improve disk performance without adding any load to the processor. How can you do this?

   A. Increase the Max Async I/O parameter.

   B. Increase the LazyWriter parameter.

   C. Implement RAID 5.

   D. Implement RAID 0+1

5. When performing routine maintenance on your server, you notice that the % Processor Time counter has been at 82 percent consistently since you added about 50 new users to the system. What should you do to remedy this without impacting the users?

   A. Nothing. 82 percent is an acceptable range for this counter.

   B. Purchase a faster processor.

   C. Move some of the users' databases to another SQL Server.

   D. Replace the current SQL Server with a faster server.

6. You have been diligently monitoring your system and have noticed that the Average Disk Queue Length counter is consistently running at 12. You have a RAID 5 system with seven disks in the array. You are concerned that this may be too slow. What should you do?

   A. Nothing. Twelve is an acceptable range for this counter.

   B. Add another disk to the array.

   C. Switch to RAID 1.

   D. Switch to RAID 0+1.

7. You have been running a trace against your SQL Server for some time and you notice that there is far too much data in the trace. You are only interested in seeing the user data. What should you do?

   A. Configure a filter to remove any reference to Profiler from the trace.

   B. Remove the system Event class from the trace.

   C. Exclude the system IDs from the trace.

   D. There is nothing you can do—the system data must be displayed in every trace.

8. One of your users is complaining that whenever she runs a certain query, she loses her connection to the SQL Server and does not receive the results of the query. She is forced to reconnect to the server when this happens and it is slowing her down in her work. What can you do to find the problem?

   A. Run the query yourself on your own machine to see if it crashes your system.

   B. Run the query in Query Analyzer with the Set Statistics IO option set.

   C. Run a trace while the user is performing the query and replay the trace against a test server to find the exact step that is causing the problem.

   D. Run a trace while the user is performing the query and replay the trace against the production server to find the exact step that is causing the problem.

9. After adding about 100 new users to your server, you notice that the Average Disk Queue counter is at about 3 on a consistent basis. You need to fix this so you decide to add more disks to the subsystem, but the counters are still too high. What should you do?

   A. Add more RAM.

   B. BAdd more disks to the array.

   C. Purchase a faster processor.

   D. Remove the users form the system and add them to another SQL Server.

10. You have several users that all use the same query to return data from a human resources table. What can you do to get the results to the users as fast as possible?

    A. Integrate the query into the front-end code so that it resides at each of the users machines.

    B. Use stored procedures so that the query can be accessed from the server.

    C. Integrate the query into the front-end code and set the Query Governor option to 0.

    D. Integrate the query into the front-end code and increase the Max Async I/O parameter.

11. You want to prevent users from running queries that take longer than three seconds to complete. What code should you run?

    A. `sp_configure 'query governor', '3'`

    B. `sp_querygov '3'`

    C. `sp_cost_limit '3'`

    D. D. `sp_configure 'query governor cost limit', '3'`

12. In order to get an accurate measurement baseline, where is the best place perform your measurements?

    A. On the production network at peak hours.

    B. On the production network during off-peak hours.

    C. On a test network with just the server and one or two clients.

    D. Using just the server, not attached to a network.

13. You have just created a query that involves several complex joins and mathematical calculations. How can you be certain that this query will not adversely affect system performance before you put it into production?

A. Run the query in Query Analyzer against the production server with the Set Statistics IO and Set Statistics Time options on.

B. Run the query in Query Analyzer against a test server with the Set Statistics IO and Set Statistics Time options on.

C. Run the query against a test server and use Profiler to trace the system activity.

D. Run the query against the production server and use Profiler to trace the system activity.

14. You have just created a customer information table in which you store addresses. You need geographic information for marketing on a weekly basis so you perform queries to find all of the customers in a given zip code ordered by last name. How can you make this query as fast as possible?

A. Create a clustered index on the zip code column of the table.

B. Create a nonclustered on the zip code column of the table.

C. Create a clustered index on the last name column of the table.

D. Create a nonclustered on the last name column of the table.

15. You want to monitor the percent of network utilization because your users have been complaining about slow response times, but you cannot find the proper counter to do this. What do you need to do?

A. Run the command `netperf -yv` at the command prompt to start the network counters.

B. Start the Windows System Monitor in network monitor mode.

C. Install the Network Monitor Agent.

D. Install the TCP/IP protocol; the counter will be installed automatically.

16. When monitoring the network usage, you notice that it is at about 35 on a sustained basis. What should you do?

    A. Remove the TCP/IP protocol and use NetBEUI instead.

    B. Remove the TCP/IP protocol and use NWLink instead.

    C. Segment the network with a router or bridge.

    D. Nothing. 35 is an acceptable range for this counter.

17. You are working for a small company that does not have the budget for more than one server, but you still need to run SQL Server and Exchange (for e-mail). How can you get both products to work on the same server?

    A. Set the Max Async I/O on SQL Server to be lower than Exchange.

    B. Set the LazyWriter parameter on SQL Server to be lower than Exchange.

    C. Set the max server memory setting to leave enough RAM for Exchange.

    D. Set the min server memory setting to leave enough RAM for exchange.

18. After using a trace in Profiler to monitor database activity, what should you do with the trace file?

    A. Delete it; it is useless.

    B. Save it on disk so you can use it later for trend tracking.

    C. Archive it to tape (or another backup medium) and keep it for trend tracking.

    D. Print out the trace summary, put it in a binder, and then delete the trace file.

19. You have had a database in production for several months and people are starting to complain about slow system response time. You suspect that some new queries that people are using do not use the indexes on the system properly. What can you do to optimize the system?

    A. Drop and re-create your indexes.

    B. Create a trace during peak hours and run the Index Tuning Wizard to create new indexes based on that trace.

    C. Create a trace during off-peak hours and run the Index Tuning Wizard to create new indexes based on that trace.

    D. Turn the queries into stored procedures.

20. You want to be warned when the processor reaches 70 percent utilization so that you can monitor the system closely and make sure that this does not develop into a more serious problem. What should you do?

    A. Create an alert that sends you a message whenever the % Processor Time is over 70.

    B. Create an alert that sends you a message whenever the % Processor Time is under 100.

    C. Create a Trace Log that fires whenever the % Processor Time is over 70.

    D. Create a Counter Log that fires whenever the % Processor Time is over 70.

Answers to Review Questions

1. B. Adding more RAM and RAID 5 will give you better performance, but if you do not have the proper indexes in place, the enhancements are for naught. When you are searching for single values (as in this example), you should create a nonclustered index on the affected column.

2. C. The values of the counters indicate that there is not enough RAM to support the new users.

3. A. The size of Tempdb should be 25 to 40 percent of the size of the largest database on the system so the SQL Server has enough room to perform necessary functions during query processing.

4. D. The only answer here that will improve disk performance without adding load to the processor is RAID 0+1 because you must buy a separate RAID controller to handle it. This controller will have its own processor to handle the extra processing burden.

5. B. The acceptable range for the % Processor Time counter is 75 percent. To fix this without affecting the users, you can purchase a faster processor and upgrade the current system after-hours.

6. A. When you divide the value of the counter (12) by the number of disks in the array (7), the actual value of the counter per disk is 1.7. The acceptable value of this counter is less than 2, so you do not need to do anything to fix this; it is fine the way it is.

7. C. You can easily exclude the system data from the trace by checking the Exclude System IDs check box on the Filters tab.

8. C. If you know that a query is going to crash the client, it will definitely cause some problems at the server as well. You should run the replay against a test server to avoid affecting other users.

9. A. If you do not have enough RAM on your system, it must write to the page file excessively. This will cause the disk queue to exceed acceptable limits even though you have added more disks to the array. The way to stop this excessive paging is by adding more RAM.

10. B. Stored procedures are queries that reside on the SQL Server. They are precompiled and remain in RAM so that they run faster than local code.

11. D. The correct code is `sp_configure 'query governor cost limit', '3'`.

12. C. The best place to perform the measurements is on a test network. That way your counts are not thrown off by the broadcast traffic that exists on all networks. If you cannot afford to set up a test network, use the production network off-hours with most of the machines shut off.

13. B. You should run the query against the production server with the Set Statistics options turned on so that you can see the effect the query will have on the CPU and hard disks.

14. A. Because you are regularly searching for ranges of zip codes, you should create a clustered index on the zip code column.

15. C. You need to install the Network Monitor Agent to see the % Network Utilization counter.

16. C. When the network utilization gets above 30 on a sustained basis, you need to segment the network to get rid of some of the broadcast traffic that is affecting the network. Changing to one of the other available protocols would only make the problem worse because they add more broadcast traffic than TCP/IP.

17. C. The max server memory setting will stop SQL Server from taking more RAM than you specify. This will force SQL Server to leave enough RAM for Exchange.

18. C. You need to keep this data on hand for trend tracking, but you do not want to waste disk space, so you should back it up to tape.

19. B. Create a trace during peak hours and use that trace as the workload file for the Index Tuning Wizard; it will then create the proper indexes for you.

20. A. An alert will send you a message; trace and counter logs do not.

Glossary

Active Directory   Windows 2000 directory services. Active Directory is an X.500 database that can be used to store objects such as users, printer, file shares, etc. Users can then search this database for objects so that they can log on to the network, print, access file shares, and so on.

ActiveX Data Objects (ADO)   A COM (Component Object Model) object set created by Microsoft intended to replace all other database access object models in future releases of Microsoft products. ADO is a very robust object model in that it defines a core set of functions and allows extensions to be built into the model to support the individual features of certain types of databases. It is specifically designed to access OLE-DB data sources.

ad hoc queries   Queries that are designed and executed by users on an infrequent basis.

alert   A mechanism that tells SQL Server which error codes to look for in the Windows NT Application log, and what action to take if an event is found. Alerts can be based on a severity level, an error code, and the database in which the error occurred. An alert can notify an operator and/or perform a task. Alerts are stored in the Msdb database.

alias   A mechanism that allows a login to access a database under the username assigned to another login. The alias is stored in the sysalternates system table of the database. Each login can have either a username in a database or an alias, but not both. An alias can be used to consolidate permissions under special user accounts, such as DBO. These have been kept in SQL Server 7 for backward compatibility. SQL 7 uses the concept of roles, which replaces the need for an alias.

application role   A special role type in SQL Server that allows users to access databases only when they are using the proper application.

archive   Data that is kept for future reporting and research purposes. This is usually stored on a removable media such as magnetic tape or CD-ROM.

article   The basic unit of replication. An article is one or more columns and rows of a table.

authentication mode   Defines how users access SQL Server. Specifically, it defines whether or not users are allowed to access SQL Server using nontrusted connections. The two authentication modes are Windows Authentication mode and Mixed Mode.

automatic recovery   A feature built into SQL Server that ensures that a database is brought up to date when the server is first started. Transactions completed since the last checkpoint process are rolled forward and put into the database, while partially completed transactions are rolled back or removed from the database. Every time SQL Server is restarted, SQL Server runs its automatic recovery feature.

B-Tree format   The format used for indexes in SQL Server. B-Tree is short for *balanced tree*. It is called this because every page of the index is exactly the same distance from the root as is every other page at the same level. A B-Tree resembles a pyramid.

BackOffice   Microsoft's line of client/server support applications that run on Windows NT Server. Some components of BackOffice are Microsoft SQL Server, Systems Management Server (SMS), Internet Information Server (IIS), Exchange Server, SNA Server, and Proxy Server.

backup device   A file or tape to which SQL Server backs up a database. Also called a *dump device*. SQL has no built-in backup devices that point to files or tapes. You will need to create all your backup devices that point to files or tapes.

backup domain controller (BDC)   A server that keeps a copy of the Authentication database from the Primary Domain Controller (PDC). Users can log on to either the PDC or any of the BDCs. Domain controllers are used for network login validation.

BCP (Bulk Copy Program)   A command-line utility used for transferring information into and out of SQL Server.

broken ownership chain   See *ownership chain*.

browser   See *Web browser*.

BULK INSERT   A Transact-SQL command that is used to import data from text files into tables.

Bulk-Logged recovery mode   Bulk-Logged recovery mode works much like the Bulk Copy option worked in earlier versions of SQL Server. Inserts, updates, and deletes get logged, but bulk copies, Select Into statements, and index creations do not.

caching   A speed optimization technique that keeps a copy of the most recently used data in a fast, high-cost, low-capacity storage device rather than in the device upon which the actual data resides. Caching assumes that recently used data is likely to be used again. Fetching data from the cache is faster than fetching data from the larger, slower storage device. Most caching algorithms also copy next-most-likely-to-be-used data and perform write-caching to further increase speed gains.

character set   The set of characters that SQL Server will recognize and therefore store. Of the 256 characters contained in each character set, the first 128 are the same throughout the various code pages. The last 128 characters, also known as extended characters, differ according to the set.

checkpoint   The mechanism by which SQL Server periodically writes modified data to a hard disk. The DBO of a database may also issue a checkpoint at any time by running the Checkpoint command in the appropriate database. By default, the checkpoint process wakes up once a minute and checks every transaction log for five minutes' worth of changes to the data pages in cache. If five minutes of changes or more are found, the data pages are written to disk. This establishes a known point of consistency between the data pages on hard disk and the transactions stored on hard disk. The five-minute period is known as the recovery interval and can be modified.

client   A computer on a network that subscribes to the services provided by a server.

Client Network utility   A utility used to configure SQL Server client net libraries. It also reports on the DB-Libraries that are in use for a particular client.

client/server   A network architecture that dedicates certain computers, called *servers*, to act as service providers to computers called *clients*, on which users perform work. Servers can be dedicated to providing one or more network services, such as file storage, shared printing, communications, e-mail, and Web response.

client/server application   An application that is split into two components: computer-intensive processes that run on application servers and user interfaces that run on clients. Client/server applications communicate over the network through interprocess communication mechanisms (IPCs).

clustered index   An index type in SQL Server that physically arranges the data in the table based on the constraints of the index.

collation   A set of rules determining how data is sorted, compared, and presented to the user.

column   The component of a table that holds individual pieces of data. In a database, a row in a table is often referred to as an entity. The column is an attribute of the entity and describes an aspect of the row. For example, a row of data might describe an individual. A column describes the name of the individual or the eye color, etc.

commit   The process whereby completed transactions are put into the database. SQL Server will automatically commit the data at regular intervals, or a manual commit can be initialized by the DBO or SA.

Component Object Model (COM)   COM is an object-oriented architecture for building reusable application components. COM provides a specification, or model, for what an object is, and it provides services for both the creation of objects and the communication between a client and the server objects. COM replaces OLE (Object Linking and Embedding) and has other advantages. COM's most notable advances are its binary compatibility and cross-platform development capabilities, code reusability, and version control.

computer name   A 1-to-15-character NetBIOS name used to uniquely identify a computer on the network.

concurrency   The ability of SQL Server to support multiple users at the same time, even if those users want the same data.

constraint   A property that can be placed on a column to reject invalid data.

convergence   The point in time when all tables involved in merge replication hold the exact same data.

counter   A statistic used for reporting in Performance Monitor and Windows System Monitor.

Control Panel   A collection of programs in Windows that control the function of specific operating-system services by allowing users to change default settings for the service to match their preferences. The Windows Registry contains the Control Panel settings on a system and/or per-user basis.

cross join A cross join is also know as a Cartesian product, where every row of one table is matched with every row of a second table. Cross joins almost never produce data of interest, unless you need to generate large amounts of test data.

Data Access Objects (DAO) A set of programmable objects that Microsoft Access developers use to manipulate data through Jet, the data-access engine for Access and other Microsoft Desktop products.

data cache SQL Server does its own caching of data to speed up access to databases. The size of the data cache can be indirectly manipulated by allocating more or less RAM to SQL Server.

data control language A subset of the Transact-SQL language that is used to modify the permissions on databases and objects.

Data Definition Language (DDL) A subset of the Transact-SQL language that is used to create and modify the schema of a database.

data files The database files that hold data and indexes in a SQL Server database. These files have an MDF or NDF extension.

data mart A database system concerned with live updates and new data, such as an online ordering system. See also *OLTP* or *online transaction processing*.

Data Source Name (DSN) A user-created identifier used by ODBC to negotiate connections to any ODBC-compliant data source. A DSN consists of a server location and a driver name and can optionally contain a database name and authentication information. See also *ODBC*.

Data Transformation Services A tool in SQL Server that is used to transfer data from one data source to another; it is also capable of changing the data as it is being moved.

data warehousing Storage and querying of historical data, also referred to as *decision-support systems*. The main focus of data warehousing is the ability to quickly query existing data and perform complex analyses, usually looking for patterns or other relationships that are difficult to locate during the day-to-day operations of a company.

database file   In SQL Server 2000, databases are stored on two types of database files. One file stores the actual data and indexes while the other file stores the transaction log. By default, the first data file has an MDF extension. Additional data files have an NDF extension. The transaction log files always have a default extension of LDF.

database management system (DBMS)   An environment created specifically for the purpose of working with databases. The term *database management system* usually refers to an electronic system or a computer program designed to work with databases. Microsoft Access and FoxPro are both examples of database management systems.

Database Maintenance Plan Wizard   A Wizard (step-by-step utility) provided with SQL Server 2000 that helps you schedule backups and perform database optimizations and consistency checking. This Wizard can also automate and schedule these routine database maintenance tasks.

database user   A SQL Server login ID that has been mapped into a particular database. Without a valid mapping, a login will not have access to a database.

datatype   A component of a SQL Server database that determines what kinds of data, such as character data, numeric data, or date/time data, can be stored in a column. A column can hold data of only a single datatype.

DB-Library   A set of functions and connectivity programs that allow clients to communicate programmatically with database engines. A database engine is responsible for processing queries, maintaining data, ensuring data consistency, and providing a mechanism for backup and restoration.

DBCC (database consistency checker)   SQL Server commands used to check the consistency of databases. These commands are generally used to gather information about the status of a database rather than to make changes to it.

DBO (Database Owner)   In SQL Server, a user who has full permissions in a particular database. This includes the ability to back up and restore the database and transaction log. The SA is also considered the DBO of every database. The DBO is specified through the sp_changedbowner stored procedure.

DBOO (Database Object Owner)   In SQL Server, a user who creates a particular database object. The DBOO has all rights on that object, including the right to allow other database users to use the object.

decision support system   A system that is designed to analyze existing data to discover trends and to help perform business analyses.

default   A SQL Server object assigned to a column or user-defined datatype in a table. If no data is entered, the default value will be used. This can also refer to the default database that is assigned to a SQL Server login ID. If the login attempts to run a query without specifying a database, the query will be applied to the default database.

default instance   With a default instance, only the computer name serves as the name of the SQL Server instance. Only one default instance at a time can be run on a single computer. SQL Server 6.*x* and 7 could be installed only as default instances.

Desktop   A directory represented by the background of the Windows Explorer shell. By default, the Desktop holds objects that contain the local storage devices and available network shares. Also a key operating part of the Windows GUI.

differential backups   Backups that include only data that has changed since the last full backup. This could be more efficient than transaction log backups for databases with existing data that changes often. For example, if a person's bank account changed 10 times in one day, the transaction log backup would contain all 10 changes whereas the differential backup would contain just the final amount.

distributed query   A query that is executed against more than one server at a time.

Distributed Transaction Coordinator (DTC)   The DTC helps coordinate queries that are run between two or more SQL Servers. The DTC ensures that the transaction is performed simultaneously on both servers, or not at all.

distributor   For replication in SQL Server, the server that keeps track of replication. It copies the data from the publishing server, stores it, and then forwards it to all subscribing servers. If you designate the SQL Server machine on which you are installing publishing as the one that holds the Distribution database, you are installing a *local distribution server*. Designating a remote server rather than a local one as your distribution server may make better use of a WAN.

domain   In Microsoft networks, an arrangement of client and server computers, referenced by a specific name, that share a single security permissions database. On the Internet, a domain is a named collection of hosts and sub-domains, registered with a unique name by the InterNIC (the agency responsible for assigning IP addresses).

domain controller   A server that authenticates workstation network login requests by comparing a username and password against account information stored in the user accounts database. A user cannot access a domain without authentication from a domain controller. Windows NT employs a single primary domain controller (PDC) per domain. To help off-load some of the workload, backup domain controllers (BDCs) can be created and enabled within a domain.

DTS Designer   A tool used to graphically design Data Transformation Services packages.

DTS package   An object in SQL Server that contains all of the tasks and constraints that are needed to transfer and transform data with DTS.

DTSRUN   A program that can be used to execute DTS packages from the command line.

DTSRUNUI   The graphic version of DTSRUN. This program can also be used to encrypt the command that is used to execute a DTS package from the command line.

dump device   See *backup device*.

dynamic backup   A type of backup that allows you to back up your SQL Server databases while they are in use. Users can stay connected to the server and run most queries while a dynamic backup is in progress.

dynamic link library (DLL)   A set of modular functions that can be used by many programs simultaneously. There are hundreds of functions stored within DLLs.

electronic mail (e-mail)   A type of client/server application that provides a routed, stored-message service between any two user e-mail accounts. E-mail accounts are not the same as user accounts, but a one-to-one relationship usually exists between them. Because all modern computers can attach to the Internet, users can send e-mail over the Internet to any location that has telephone or wireless digital service.

Enterprise Manager   The main SQL Server administration program provided with SQL Server 2000. Multiple servers can be monitored and maintained by SQL Enterprise Manager. Enterprise Manager works with SQL Server through the SQL-DMO.

enterprise network   A complex network consisting of multiple servers and multiple domains; it can be contained within one or two buildings or encompass a wide geographic area.

event class   A logical grouping of events in Profiler.

events   A statistic used for reporting in Profiler.

Exchange   See *Microsoft Exchange*.

Explorer   The default shell for Windows operating systems. Explorer implements the more flexible Desktop object paradigm rather than the Program Manager paradigm used in earlier versions of Windows. See also *Desktop*.

extent   In SQL Server, the unit of allocation for tables and indexes. All SQL Server objects and data are stored in tables. Tables and indexes are organized into extents. Each extent consists of eight 8KB pages. When a table or an index requires additional storage space, a new extent is allocated.

extended stored procedure   See *stored procedure*.

eXtensible Markup Language (XML)   A special markup language that is designed to share both data and schema over the Internet. For example, you could share a catalog table via XML and search engines would be able to tell which part was the description, price, quantity in stock, etc.

extranet   A network between two or more companies that takes advantage of the low-cost Internet connection rather than privately held dedicated communication lines.

Fast BCP A form of importing data with the BCP utility that takes place when there are no indexes on the table being imported to and when the Select Into/Bulk Copy database option is set.

field In a table, a field contains all of the data of a single type, such as all of the last names in the table or all of the addresses. This can be thought of as vertical.

file allocation table (FAT) The file system used by MS-DOS and available to other operating systems, such as Windows (all variations), OS/2, and Windows NT. FAT has become something of a mass-storage compatibility standard because of its simplicity and wide availability. FAT has few fault-tolerance features and can become corrupted through normal use over time. In the new 32-bit Windows 95/98/Me platforms, FAT32 is also available. FAT32 has many new features, including the ability to address more than 2GB of hard disk space.

filegroup A logical grouping of data files in a database. This can be used to optimize databases and simplify backups of very large databases.

filegroup backups Filegroup backups allow you to back up different pieces of the database based on the various files that make up the database. Usually filegroup backups are done when the time required to perform a full database backup is prohibitive.

fill factor The amount of space that is filled in a data or index page. For example, a fill factor of 70 would leave 30 percent of a page empty for any new data that needs to be inserted.

filter Used to exclude unwanted data from a trace in Profiler.

fixed database role A special role in a database that has predefined permissions.

fixed server role A special role on the server with predefined permissions.

flat-file database A database whose information is stored in files and is accessed sequentially. Examples of flat-file database programs include dBASE, Access, FoxPro, and other personal computer databases.

full backup In full backups, the entire database is backed up. Although they are the easiest to implement and restore from, full database backups may not be practical because of the amount of time required for very large databases.

Full recovery mode   Full recovery means that everything gets logged in the database. Full recovery is a new option in SQL Server 2000.

group   A security entity to which users can be assigned membership for the purpose of granting a broad set of permissions. By managing permissions for groups and assigning users to groups, rather than assigning permissions to users, security administrators can more easily manage large security environments. SQL Server 6.5 differs from most network applications in that it allows a user to be a member of only one other group besides the Public group. SQL Server 2000 allows users to be a member of as many groups as they please. Groups have also been renamed in SQL 2000 to *database roles*.

guest user   If a specific user doesn't exist in the database permissions list but a user called *guest* does, then users in SQL Server will have the rights of the guest user in that particular database.

heterogeneous queries   Queries that are executed against a third-party database server or a SQL Server that does not recognize the security of the local server.

horizontal partitioning   In SQL Server replication, a method by which you can publish only certain rows of a table. This is often referred to as *horizontal filtering*. See also *vertical partitioning*.

HTML   See *Hypertext Markup Language*.

HTTP   See *Hypertext Transfer Protocol*.

hyperlink   A link in text or graphics files that has a Web address embedded within it. By clicking on the link, you jump to another Web address. You can identify a hyperlink because it is a different color from the rest of the Web page.

Hypertext Markup Language (HTML)   A textual data format that identifies sections of a document as headers, lists, hypertext links, and so on. HTML is the data format used on the World Wide Web for the publication of Web pages.

Hypertext Transfer Protocol (HTTP)   An Internet protocol that transfers HTML documents over the Internet and responds to context changes that happen when a user clicks on a hyperlink.

IDE   A simple mass-storage-device interconnection bus that operates at 5Mbps and can handle no more than two attached devices. IDE devices are similar to but less expensive than SCSI devices.

IIS   See *Internet Information Server*.

index   A data structure that provides a mechanism for resolving queries more efficiently by working through a subset of the data rather than all of it. A full table scan can be avoided by using an index. In SQL Server, each table is allowed one *clustered* index. This index is the actual sort order for the data in the table. *Nonclustered* indexes consist of a list of ordered keys that contain pointers to the data in the data pages. Up to 249 nonclustered indexes can be created per table, but these occupy more space than clustered indexes do.

Indexed Sequential Access Method (ISAM)   A method of data access that uses file I/O routines with indexing and a few enhanced features. This type of data access is normally found when using flat-file databases like dBASE, FoxPro, and Access or DB2.

Index Tuning Wizard   A Wizard in Profiler that is used to define and optimize indexes.

Industry Standard Architecture (ISA)   The design standard for 16-bit Intel-compatible motherboards and peripheral buses. The 32/64-bit PCI bus standard is replacing the ISA standard. Adapters and interface cards must conform to the bus standard(s) used by the motherboard in order to be used with a computer.

inner join   An inner join is when the rows of one table are matched with rows of another table on columns they have in common.

Internet   A voluntarily interconnected global network of computers based on the TCP/IP protocol suite. TCP/IP was originally developed by the U.S. Department of Defense's Advanced Research Projects Agency to facilitate the interconnection of military networks and was provided free to universities. The obvious utility of worldwide digital network connectivity and the availability of free complex networking software developed at universities doing military research attracted other universities, research institutions, private organizations, businesses, and finally the individual home user. The Internet is now available to all current commercial computing platforms.

Internet Explorer   A World Wide Web browser produced by Microsoft and included free with Windows 95/98/Me and Windows NT 4/2000.

Internet Information Server (IIS)   A server produced by Microsoft that serves Internet higher-level protocols like HTTP and FTP (file transfer protocol) to clients using Web browsers.

Internet Protocol (IP)   The network-layer protocol upon which the Internet is based. IP provides a simple, connectionless packet exchange. Other protocols such as UDP or TCP use IP to perform their connection-oriented or guaranteed delivery services.

Internet Service Provider (ISP)   A company that provides dial-up or direct connections to the Internet.

Internetwork Packet eXchange (IPX)   The network protocol developed by Novell for its NetWare product. IPX is a routable protocol similar to IP but much easier to manage and with lower communication overhead. The term IPX can also refer to the family of protocols that includes the Synchronous Packet eXchange (SPX) transport layer protocol, a connection-oriented protocol that guarantees delivery in order, similar to the service provided by TCP.

interprocess communication channel (IPC)   A generic term describing any manner of client/server communication protocols, specifically those operating in the session, presentation, and application layers. Interprocess communication mechanisms provide a method for the client and server to trade information.

intranet   A privately owned network based on the TCP/IP protocol suite.

I/O (input/output)   The process of reading and writing data back and forth from cache to disk. The smallest unit of I/O in SQL Server is the 8KB page. All I/O happens in page increments. *Logical I/O* is defined as a data read or write operation that is made to cache or disk. *Physical I/O* is subclassified as a data read or write that is made to disk only.

IP   See *Internet Protocol*.

IP address   A four-byte (32-bit) number that uniquely identifies a computer on an IP internetwork. InterNIC assigns the first bytes of Internet IP addresses and administers them in hierarchies. Huge organizations like the government or top-level ISPs have class A addresses, large organizations and most ISPs have class B addresses, and small companies have class C addresses. In a class A address, InterNIC assigns the first byte, and the owning organization assigns the remaining three bytes. In a class B address, InterNIC or the higher-level ISP assigns the first two bytes, and the organization assigns the remaining two bytes. In a class C address, InterNIC or the higher-level ISP assigns the first three bytes, and the organization assigns the remaining byte. Organizations not attached to the Internet are free to assign IP addresses as they please.

IPC   See *interprocess communication channel*.

IPX   See *Internetwork Packet eXchange*.

ISA   See *Industry Standard Architecture*.

ISP   See *Internet Service Provider*.

Jet   The data engine for Microsoft Access and other Microsoft Desktop products. Microsoft Access ships with Jet. Microsoft Visual Basic also uses Jet as its native database. Jet can also be accessed by Excel, Word, Project, SQL Server 2000, and PowerPoint through VBA (Visual Basic for Applications).

job   A task, such as a backup procedure, performed by a system. In SQL Server, you can schedule jobs to run at regular intervals or when an alert is triggered. In SQL Server 7 and higher a job can run a Transact-SQL command, a command-prompt utility, a Visual Basic or JavaScript script, or replication procedures.

kernel   The core process of a preemptive operating system, consisting of a multitasking scheduler and the basic services that provide security. Depending on the operating system, other services such as virtual memory drivers may be built into the kernel. The kernel is responsible for managing the scheduling of threads and processes.

LazyWriter   A system process responsible for physical I/O. The role of the LazyWriter is to flush pages from cache to disk as free buffers are needed by the system. The LazyWriter differs from the checkpoint in how it performs its work. The checkpoint process executes its work in spikes and then goes back to sleep. The LazyWriter may be continuously active, writing out pages from cache to disk as needed.

linked servers   A remote SQL Server to which security access has been granted for the purpose of querying the remote server.

local group   A group that exists in a Windows NT/2000 computer's local security database. Local groups can reside on NT Workstation or NT Server computers and can contain users or global groups.

lock   A mechanism by which SQL Server manages concurrency. SQL Server places locks on data when it is being accessed by a client application. SQL Server locks are primarily *page* locks. This means that when a client accesses a single record on an 8KB page, SQL Server will lock the entire page until it is appropriate to release the lock. SQL Server also supports *table* locks for times when it would make more sense to lock the entire table rather than individual pages. Row-level locking is also supported automatically with SQL Server 2000.

lock escalation   The SQL Server process of increasing a lock from the page to the table level. When a transaction acquires a configured number of page locks, a table lock is set and the page locks are released. This behavior is configured through lock-escalation thresholds.

logging   The process of recording information about activities and errors in the operating system.

logical I/O   See *I/O*.

login   A name that, when combined with a password, allows access to SQL Server resources. Logins are stored in the sysxlogins system table. (For easier queries, use the syslogins view.) This table is located in the Master database only, and there is only one per server.

long filename (LFN)   A filename longer than the eight characters plus three-character extension allowed by MS-DOS. In Windows NT/2000 and Windows 95/98/Me, filenames can contain up to 255 characters.

Makepipe   A command-line utility that can be used in conjunction with the Readpipe utility to verify that the Named Pipes protocol is working properly.

MAPI   See *Messaging Application Programming Interface*.

Master database   The system database that contains all the settings for the SQL Server engine, including configurations, user accounts, and links to user databases. This information is known collectively as the system catalog.

Max Async I/O   A setting in SQL Server that can be used to control the way SQL Server writes to hard disk.

max server memory   A setting in SQL Server that controls the maximum amount of memory that SQL Server allocates for itself.

measurement baseline   A performance measurement that is taken on a test network and used for comparison against future readings.

Messaging Application Programming Interface (MAPI)   Messaging application standard developed to allow for interaction between an application and various message service providers. It is essentially a set of ANSI-standard DLLs. SQL Server 2000 has the ability to generate e-mail to any MAPI-compliant message service provider (post office).

Microsoft Exchange   Microsoft's messaging application. Exchange implements MAPI as well as other messaging protocols such as POP, SNMP, and fax services to provide a flexible message composition and reception service.

Microsoft Query   A utility used to graphically create SQL statements for any ODBC-compliant data source. Microsoft Query (also called *MS Query*) can link to Microsoft Office applications (such as Word and Excel), and other ODBC-compliant applications and databases.

Mixed Mode   An authentication mode in SQL Server that allows both trusted and nontrusted connections.

mixed security   A SQL Server security mode that combines the functionality of integrated security with the flexibility of having SQL Server manage its own login accounts. In mixed mode, Windows NT accounts can be linked into SQL Server (using trusted connections), but unique SQL Server login accounts can also be created and used if a trusted connection is not possible. This is sometimes referred to as SQL Authentication in SQL Server 2000.

MMC (Microsoft Management Console) The MMC is Microsoft's new framework utility for managing the various Windows NT services and functions. All Microsoft's new BackOffice applications use MMC, including SQL Server, SMS, and IIS. One of the advantages of the MMC is that different management *snap-ins* can be added to the utility at the same time, which means that management of servers is more standardized and can be done from one application.

Model database The template database for SQL Server that is used when new databases are created. All users, groups, and security existing in this database are automatically part of any new databases, but changes made to the Model database will not affect existing databases.

MS Query See *Microsoft Query*.

Msdb database A SQL Server database that stores information about the alerts, tasks, events, and replication tasks created on that server by the SQL Server Agent service. The Msdb database also includes information about system operators.

multiprocessing Using two or more processors simultaneously to perform a computing task. Depending on the operating system, processing may be done asymmetrically, wherein certain processors are assigned certain threads independent of the load they create; or symmetrically, wherein threads are dynamically assigned to processors according to an equitable scheduling scheme. The term usually describes a multiprocessing capacity built into the computer at a hardware level in that the computer itself supports more than one processor. However, *multiprocessing* can also be applied to network computing applications achieved through interprocess communication mechanisms. Client/server applications are examples of multiprocessing.

Multiprotocol A network library available with SQL Server. Multiprotocol allows SQL Server to communicate over any open interprocess communication (IPC) mechanism. It also provides support for integrated security and encryption. Multiprotocol takes advantage of remote procedure calls (RPCs) to pass information between the client and server.

multitasking The capacity of an operating system to switch rapidly among threads of execution. Multitasking allows processor time to be divided among threads as though each thread ran on its own slower processor. Multitasking operating systems allow two or more applications to run at the same time and can provide a greater degree of service to applications than single-tasking operating systems like MS-DOS can.

multithreaded Multithreaded programs have more than one chain of execution, thus relying on the services of a multitasking or multiprocessing operating system to operate. Multiple chains of execution allow programs to simultaneously perform more than one task. In multitasking computers, multithreading is merely a convenience used to make programs run more smoothly and to free the program from the burden of switching between tasks itself. When multithreaded applications run on a computer with multiple processors, the computing burden of the program can be spread across many processors. Programs that are not multithreaded cannot take advantage of multiple processors in a computer.

named instance SQL Server 2000 adds the ability to install a completely separate copy of SQL Server (in a different folder) that can run at the same time as other copies of SQL Server on the same computer. This second, third (and so on) copy of SQL Server is called a named instance. While there can only be a single default instance, there can be many named instances, as long as you have enough hardware to run them. A named instance is known by the name of the computer combined with the name of the instance. For example, Server1/test would be the name of a named instance. Older clients cannot connect to named instances.

Named Pipes An interprocess communication (IPC) mechanism that is implemented as a file system service, allowing programs to be modified to run on it without using a proprietary API. Named Pipes was developed to support more robust client/server communications than those allowed by the simpler NetBIOS. Named Pipes is the default SQL Server protocol and is required for installation.

native API The methods of data access that are specific to a certain database management system. Also called the *proprietary interface*. (API stands for *application programming interface*.) These are generally implemented as a set of DLLs or COM-based objects.

nesting role   The process of adding a database role as a member of another database role.

network operating system   A computer operating system specifically designed to optimize a computer's ability to respond to service requests. Servers run network operating systems. Windows NT Server is a network operating system.

nonclustered   See *nonclustered index*.

nonclustered index   A type of index in SQL Server in which the index is a separate object in the database and therefore does not rearrange the data in the tables.

nontrusted connection   A connection in SQL Server where SQL does not trust Windows to verify the user's passwords.

normalizing   The process of organizing data into tables, in a consistent and complete format, in order to create a relational database.

NT Event Viewer   A Windows NT utility used to view Windows NT events and errors. The Application log records SQL Server events and errors as well as events from other applications running under Windows NT.

NTFS   A secure, transaction-oriented file system developed for Windows NT that incorporates the Windows NT security model for assigning permissions and shares. NTFS is optimized for hard drives larger than 500MB and requires too much overhead to be used on hard disk drives smaller than 50MB.

object permissions   SQL Server permissions that generally allow users to manipulate data controlled by a database object. For example, to view the information in a table, you must first have the SELECT permission on that table. If you want to run a stored procedure, you must first have the EXECUTE permission on that stored procedure. Object permissions can be granted by the SA, DBO, or DBOO.

objects   Anything created in SQL Server is referred to as an object.

ODBC (Open Database Connectivity)   An API set that defines a method of common database access. Client applications can be written to the ODBC API. ODBC uses a Data Source Name (DSN) to make a connection to a database and to load an appropriate ODBC driver. This driver will translate client calls made to the ODBC API into calls to the native interface of the database. The goal of ODBC is to provide interoperability between client applications and data resources.

OLE-DB (Object Linking and Embedding DataBase)   A method of common database access which defines an interface based on the COM (Component Object Model) rather than a traditional API interface like ODBC. The goal is similar to ODBC, which is to provide interoperability between client applications and data resources.

OLTP   See *Online Transaction Processing*.

Online Transaction Processing (OLTP)   A type of database activity that involves frequent changes to the data stored in your database. This is the opposite of online analytical processing (OLAP) that rarely changes data, but runs frequent ad hoc–type queries to generate MIS reports.

operator   A user who is notified about certain network events. In SQL Server, operators can be defined by name, along with their e-mail and pager addresses. Operator information is stored in the Msdb database. Operators are notified about the success and/or failure of scheduled jobs and alerts.

optimization   Any effort to reduce the workload on a hardware or software component by eliminating, obviating, or reducing the amount of work required of the component through any means. For instance, file caching is an optimization that reduces the workload of a hard disk drive.

OSQL   A command-line utility that uses ODBC and provides a query interface to the SQL Server. You can run Transact-SQL statements as well as stored procedures and DBCC commands from OSQL; ISQL (which uses DB-Library) is also supported in SQL 2000 for backward compatibility.

outer join   An outer join is when all rows from the first table are reported, as well as any rows from the second table that have a column in common with the first table.

ownership chain   In SQL Server, the result of a user who owns an object creating another object based on the original one, such as when a user creates a view based on a table. This ownership chain has only one object owner. If another user creates an object based on the original owner's object, this now becomes a *broken ownership chain*, because different users own objects within the permission chain. If a person who owns objects that are dependent on each other grants another person rights to the final object, the ownership chain is unbroken. However, if the second person then grants rights to a third person, the ownership chain becomes broken, as the third person needs rights from the first person, not the second person.

page   The smallest unit of data storage in SQL Server. Every page is 8KB in size with a 96-byte header. Data rows are written to data pages, index rows to index pages, and so on.

parallel striped backup   A SQL Server backup created across two or more backup devices.

PCI   See *Peripheral Connection Interface*.

PDC   See *primary domain controller*.

per-seat license   A type of SQL Server license that allows you to pay once for each seat (person) in your company and then use any number of connections to any number of SQL servers.

per-server license   A type of SQL Server license that allows you to pay for only a connection to a single server.

Performance Monitor   A Windows NT utility that tracks statistics on individual data items, called *counters*. You can get information about the performance of SQL Server through Performance Monitor. For example, you can monitor the log space used, the number of current connections, and memory use. See also *Windows System Monitor*.

Peripheral Connection Interface (PCI)   A high-speed 32/64-bit bus interface developed by Intel and widely accepted as the successor to the 16-bit ISA interface. PCI devices support I/O throughput about 40 times faster than the ISA bus.

permissions   SQL Server security constructs that regulate access to resources by username or role affiliation. Administrators can assign permissions to allow any level of access, such as read-only, read/write, or delete, by controlling the ability of users to initiate object services. Security is implemented by checking the user's security identifier against each object's access control list.

physical I/O   See *I/O*.

preemptive multitasking   A multitasking implementation in which an interrupt routine in the kernel manages the scheduling of processor time among running threads. The threads themselves do not need to support multitasking in any way because the microprocessor will preempt the thread with an interrupt, save its state, update all thread priorities according to the operating system's scheduling algorithm, and pass control to the highest-priority thread awaiting execution. Because of the preemptive feature, a thread that crashes will not affect the operation of other executing threads.

primary domain controller (PDC)   In a Microsoft network, the domain server that contains the master copy of the security, computer, and user accounts databases (often referred to as the SAM database) and that can authenticate workstations or users. The PDC can replicate its databases to one or more backup domain controllers (BDCs). The PDC is usually also the master browser for the domain.

procedure cache   After SQL Server fulfills its requirements for RAM from the RAM assigned to it, the rest is assigned to cache. The cache is divided into a data cache and a procedure cache. The procedure cache contains stored procedures that have been run by users or the system. The ratio of procedure cache to data cache is now set automatically by SQL Server 2000.

process   A running program containing one or more threads. A process encapsulates the protected memory and environment for its threads.

Program Developers' Kit (PDK)   Extra SQL Server documentation and programming examples useful to developers who wish to know which DLL (dynamic link library) functions are available and how they work in SQL Server.

Public role   A role that exists in every SQL Server database. Any rights granted to the Public role automatically apply to all users in the database, including the guest user (if present).

publication   In SQL Server replication, a collection of *articles*. Subscribing servers can subscribe to an entire publication only. In earlier versions of SQL Server, it was possible to subscribe to an individual article in a publication.

publisher   In SQL Server replication, the server that has the original data and that makes that data available to other replication servers.

pull page   A model of Web-page creation in which a server-side process requests data dynamically from the database when the Web browser makes the request. No static page is created. The HTML response to the request is created dynamically by the server-side process.

push page   A model of Web-page creation in which static Web pages are created by executing queries on a SQL Server and formatting the output in HTML. This HTML page is placed on a Web server and can be accessed by a Web browser. Although the pages can be updated frequently, they are still static pages.

query   A request sent to SQL Server to manipulate or retrieve data. Queries can have many formats, but the most common are known as SELECT queries.

Query Analyzer   An interactive SQL interface for Windows, this utility allows you to run all the same commands that the OSQL command-line utility does. It has an added advantage of being a Windows interface. This allows you to run multiple queries and view the results of such queries in their own separate windows.

Query Governor   A setting in SQL Server that can be used to prohibit SQL Server from executing long-running queries.

query optimizer   In SQL Server, a mechanism that determines which index (or no index) will result in the lowest amount of logical I/O. This is done by evaluating the data and the restrictions that the query is requesting. With this information, the query optimizer estimates how many pages will be read for each possible scenario and chooses the scenario with the lowest estimated page I/O.

RAID (Redundant Array of Inexpensive Disks)   RAID is a grouping of disks that is viewed by the operating system as a single disk for the purpose of fault-tolerance and speed enhancement.

RAID 0   RAID 0 writes data across multiple hard-disk partitions in what is called a *stripe set*. This can greatly improve speed as multiple hard disks are working at the same time. RAID 0 can be implemented through the use of Windows NT software or on third-party hardware.

RAID 0+1   See *RAID 10*.

RAID 1   RAID 1 uses disk mirroring, which writes information to disk twice—once to the primary file, and once to the mirror.

RAID 5   RAID 5 (*striped with parity*) writes data to hard disk in stripe sets. Parity checksums will be written across all disks in the stripe set; they can be used to recreate information lost if a single disk in the stripe set fails.

RAID 10   RAID 10 (often referred to as *RAID 0+1*) implements striping as in RAID 1 and then mirrors the stripe sets.

Rebuildm.exe   This program copies a clean version of the Master and other system databases to SQL Server. It is most commonly used when the Master database is corrupt and SQL Server won't start.

Remote Data Objects (RDO)   A COM (Component Object Model) encapsulation of the ODBC API. RDO is a very thin layer of software that provides an object model for calling the ODBC API.

read-ahead   A SQL Server mechanism for retrieving data from disk into cache before the data is actually needed. Separate read-ahead threads pull the data into cache, thus freeing the query thread to process the data that it finds in cache.

READPIPE   A command-line utility that can be used in conjunction with the MAKEPIPE utility to verify that the Named Pipes protocol is working properly.

record   An object in a table that contains all of the data related to a single entity. This can be thought of as horizontal.

Registry   A database of settings required and maintained by Windows and its components. The Registry contains all the configuration information used by the computer. It is stored as a hierarchical structure and is made up of keys, hives, and value entries. You can use the Registry Editor (REGEDT32 or REGEDIT) to change these settings.

relational database   A database composed of tables that contain related data and other objects, such as views, stored procedures, rules, and defaults. Also, a database of related information that supports the SQL query language. SQL Server databases are stored on database devices.

relational database management system (RDBMS)   A database management system that supports true data, transactional integrity, and a server-side relational database engine. SQL Server is an RDBMS.

Remote Procedure Calls (RPC)   A network interprocess communication mechanism that allows an application to be distributed among many computers on the same network.

removable media database   A SQL Server database created on a removable medium, such as a CD-ROM or floppy disk. Removable media databases can be sent to another location and used from that location.

replication   For SQL Server systems, the ability to automatically copy data and changes made to data from one server to another server. The data may not be copied immediately, so replication is used when "real-enough-time" data replication is needed. In replication, the change is made to one server and then sent out to one or more servers. There is another type of replication called two-phase commit, which is used in conjunction with the MS-DTC to provide 100 percent synchronization 100 percent of the time.

roll back   To cancel an entire transaction if any part of the transaction fails and undo any changes made to data.

row   In a SQL Server database, a complete set of columns within a single table; it represents a single entity in a table.

RPC   See *Remote Procedure Calls*.

rule   In a SQL Server database, an object that is assigned to a column so that data being entered must conform to standards you set. Rules can enforce domain integrity (a valid range of values). You can create rules to enable pattern matching, enable a range of values, or force a selection from a list of values.

SA, sa (System Administrator)   The default login ID for SQL Server; the global administrator of the SQL Server system. This ID has no restrictions on what it can do within the SQL Server environment. By default, anyone who has logged in to SQL Server will be able to use the SA account unless you change this.

SAM   See *Security Accounts Manager*.

SELECT command   The SELECT statement can be used to retrieve specific rows and columns of information from one or more tables in one or more databases. There are three basic components to every SELECT statement: SELECT, FROM, and WHERE.

scheduling   The automation of tasks in SQL Server. Tasks that can be automated include backups, transfers, index creation and reorganization, and other maintenance procedures.

script   A saved query that has an .SQL extension by default. Scripts can be loaded, edited, and run from Query Analyzer or OSQL. Scripts can also be created by Enterprise Manager for existing databases and objects. Scripts are saved as ASCII text and generally have an .SQL extension.

SCSI   See *Small Computer Systems Interface*.

security   Measures taken to secure a system against accidental or intentional loss of data, usually in the form of accountability procedures and use restriction. SQL Server security is based on the server, database, and database objects.

Security Accounts Manager (SAM)   The module of the Windows NT Executive that authenticates a username and password against a database of accounts, generating an access token that includes the user's permissions. Also known as the *Directory database*. In Windows 2000, the SAM has been replaced with Active Directory.

security identifier (SID)   A unique code that identifies a specific user or group to the Windows NT security system. Security identifiers contain a complete set of permissions for that user or group.

server   A computer dedicated to servicing requests for resources from other computers on a network. Servers typically run network operating systems, such as Windows NT Server. The basic functionality of a server can be added to by installed programs such as SQL Server.

service   A process dedicated to implementing a specific function for other processes. Most Windows NT components are services. SQL Server is composed of two main services, MSSQLSERVER, which is the main database engine, and SQL Server Agent, which is the helper service. Additional services that make up the SQL Server include the MS-DTC

(Microsoft Distributed Transaction Coordinator), used for two-phase commits, and the Index server, which can allow SQL Server to run queries that use Web page indexes.

service accounts   A special account used by server applications (like SQL Server) to log on with. This allows the server applications to have special security access to the operating system and network.

Service Pack   A group of bug fixes and enhancements offered by Microsoft on a (semi) regular basis. There are various Service Packs for different applications. As of this writing, the current Service Packs include NT 4 Service Pack 6 and Windows 2000 Service Pack 1.

set working size   A setting in SQL Server that can be used to tell the operating system to leave all of SQL Server's information in RAM at all times and never move it to disk.

severity level   For a system error, a component of the error message that provides information about the error. Levels from 0 to 10 are informational, 11 to 16 are user errors, 17 and 18 are resource problems, and 19 to 25 are fatal errors.

SID   See *security identifier*.

Simple recovery mode   This recovery mode automatically cleans out the transaction log. This mode corresponds to the SQL Server 7 Truncate Log on Checkpoint option.

Small Computer Systems Interface (SCSI)   A high-speed, parallel-bus interface that connects hard disk drives, CD-ROM drives, tape drives, and many other peripherals to a computer.

sort order   In SQL Server, an option that determines how the system will collate, store, and present data. The sort order options available depend on the character set chosen. The most important sort order descriptions include dictionary order, binary order, case-sensitive, and case-insensitive.

Sp_attach_db   This stored procedure allows you to take MDF and LDF database files and attach them into an existing SQL Server so that the database can be made live again.

Sp_detach_db This stored procedure allows you to take a database offline and detach the database files from SQL Server so the database files (and thus the database) can be moved to a different server.

spid (server process ID) In SQL Server, the number that identifies a connection currently accessing the SQL Server machine. It is most often found in Enterprise Manager in the Activity window, or by running the sp_who stored procedure.

Sqlisapi.dll The DLL that provides the interface between SQL and IIS for XML integration.

SQL-DMO (SQL Server Distributed Management Objects) An interface that exposes COM-based objects that other programs can take advantage of to manipulate the SQL Server Engine and the SQL Server Agent utilities.

SQL login See *login*.

SQL Server administrator The individual usually responsible for the day-to-day administration of SQL Server databases. The administrator takes over where the programmer stops.

SQL Server Agent A SQL Server service that can take care of automating tasks on your server. The service includes managers that can handle alert processing, tasking, event processing, and replication. It works for local automation with the local system account, but for many activities that occur over the network, it will need to be assigned a separate logon account that has administrative rights to the computer, as well as the Log on as a Service right.

SQL Server Books Online All the books that normally ship with Microsoft SQL Server, in an electronic format.

SQL Server developer The individual responsible for designing, programming, and populating SQL Server databases.

SQL Server Engine The core service (MSSQLSERVER) that performs all query-related activities of SQL Server as well as the data storage and management.

SQL Server Web Wizard A SQL Server utility that facilitates the creation of push Web pages. It can use the SQL Executive service to schedule the creation of the static Web pages in order to keep them more current.

SQL Trace   A part of the database engine that is used to gather and report information requested by SQL Profiler.

SQLMaint   A SQL Server utility that can be used to create tasks that will take care of day-to-day administration of SQL Server. This includes automating backups, updating statistics, and rebuilding indexes. SQLMaint is configured by the Database Maintenance Plan Wizard.

SQL Profiler   A SQL Server utility that can be used to create trace files. Trace files can track all connections to SQL Server and what those connections are doing. These are often used for security and for optimization.

statement permissions   SQL Server permissions that allow database users and groups to perform tasks that are not specific to objects. These permissions are generally related to the creation of certain database objects.

stored procedure   In SQL Server, a set of Transact-SQL statements combined together to perform a single task or set of tasks. This object is like a macro, in that SQL code can be written and stored under a name. Invoking the name actually runs the code. Because stored procedures are precompiled, they run much more quickly and efficiently than regular queries do. There are three types of stored procedures: system, user-defined, and extended. *System stored procedures* are shipped with SQL Server and are denoted with an sp_ prefix. These are typically found in the Master database. *User-defined stored procedures* can be registered with the system by the SA. *Extended stored procedures* work outside the context of SQL Server and generally have an xp_ prefix. These are actually calls to DLLs.

stripe set   The Windows implementation of RAID 0.

striping with parity   The Windows implementation of RAID 5.

subscriber   In SQL Server replication, the server that gets data originating on the publishing server and updates one or more tables with both new and changed data.

system stored procedure   See *stored procedure.*

system table   Tables in relational databases that are used for administrative purposes by SQL Server. For example, in the Master database, the sysxlogins table, which holds SQL logins and passwords, is a system table. The Master database has two sets of system tables. The first set, known as the system catalog, tracks information about the configuration of SQL Server as a whole. Every database also has a database catalog made up of system tables that track configuration information about that particular database. This would include the objects in the database as well as the permissions granted on those objects. System tables generally begin with the *sys* prefix.

suspect database   A database that SQL Server believes to be corrupt or otherwise unavailable. A database can be marked suspect for a number of reasons, such as when a database device is offline or has been removed or renamed.

table   In a SQL Server database, the object that contains rows and columns of data.

Taskbar   The gray bar at the bottom of the screen; it replaces the Task Manager in previous versions of Windows. The Taskbar holds the Start menu button and buttons that represent running programs It is used to switch between running programs and to choose the Start menu.

Task Manager   An application that manually views and can close running processes in Windows NT and 2000. In Windows 95/98/Me, the Task Manager is called the Close Program window. Task Manager can also be used to view CPU and memory statistics. Press Ctrl+Alt+Del to launch the Task Manager.

TCP   See *Transmission Control Protocol.*

TCP/IP   See *Transmission Control Protocol/Internet Protocol.*

TechNet   Microsoft's monthly CD-ROM set that contains patches to existing programs, technical notes about issues (bugs), and white papers describing technologies in more detail. Most of the information in TechNet can also be found on Microsoft's Web site.

Tempdb database   A SQL Server database reserved for storing temporary objects. These may be tables or stored procedures and can be created implicitly by SQL Server or explicitly by the user. The Tempdb database is also used to store server-side cursors.

thread   A list of instructions running on a computer to perform a certain task. Each thread runs in the context of a process, which embodies the protected memory space and the environment of the threads. Multithreaded processes can perform more than one task at the same time.

trace   In Profiler, the process of tracking events and reporting them to the user.

trend tracking   The process of researching archived data to find out what happens when certain activities take place, such as adding new users or creating new databases.

T-SQL   See *Transact-SQL*.

Transact-SQL (T-SQL)   SQL is a database language originally designed by IBM that can be used for queries as well as to build databases and manage security of the database engine. Microsoft SQL Server uses Transact-SQL (T-SQL), an enhanced version of the SQL language, as its native database language.

transaction   A logical set of one or more commands that need to be processed as a whole in order to make a complete unit of work.

transaction backup   A transaction backup allows you to back up just the changes since the last backup instead of the entire database. The database cannot be running in Simple recovery mode if you want to perform transaction backups. Transaction backups can be restored to a particular point in time.

Transaction SQL   See *Transact-SQL*.

transaction log   In SQL Server, a reserved area in the database that stores all changes made to the database. All modifications are written to the transaction log before writing to the database. The transaction log provides a durable record of database activity and can be used for recovery purposes.

Transfer Manager   In Data Transformation Services, the object that is used to copy objects from one SQL Server to another. This only functions with SQL Server 7 or higher.

Transmission Control Protocol (TCP)   A transport layer protocol that implements guaranteed packet delivery using the Internet Protocol (IP). See also *TCP/IP* and *Internet Protocol*.

Transmission Control Protocol/Internet Protocol (TCP/IP)   A suite of network protocols upon which the global Internet is based. TCP/IP is a general term that can refer either to the TCP and IP protocols used together or to the complete set of Internet protocols. TCP/IP is the default protocol for Windows NT and 2000.

trigger   A SQL Server object that is a stored procedure. A trigger activates when data is added, updated, or deleted from a table. Triggers are used to ensure that tables linked by keys stay internally consistent with each other.

trusted connection   A connection made by a user in which SQL Server trusts Windows to verify the users password.

two-phase commit   A type of data replication for SQL Server. With two-phase commit, two or more SQL Server computers either complete a transaction simultaneously or not at all. The Distributed Transaction Coordinator (MS-DTC service) is designed to help manage these types of transactions.

UNC   See *Universal Naming Convention*.

Unicode   Unicode characters are represented by 16 bits (2 bytes), which means that you can choose from approximately 64,000 characters. The disadvantage of Unicode characters (and thus columns) is that they take twice as much room to store as regular (8-bit) characters.

Uniform Resource Locator (URL)   An Internet standard naming convention for identifying resources available via various TCP/IP application protocols. For example, `http://www.microsoft.com` is the URL for Microsoft's World Wide Web server site, while `ftp://ftp.microsoft.com` is a popular FTP site. A URL allows easy hypertext references to a particular resource from within a document or mail message.

Universal Naming Convention (UNC)   A multivendor, multiplatform convention for identifying shared resources on a network. The convention is *servername\sharename*.

user   In SQL Server, a database-specific identifier that maps to a login and allows access to database resources. If a user is mapped to a login entry in the sysxlogins system table of the server, that login is allowed access to the database and database objects. Users are stored in the sysusers system table of each database.

username   A user's account name in a login-authenticated system (such as Windows NT and SQL Server).

VBSQL   One of the interfaces provided with the native API of SQL Server. VBSQL is designed for use from Visual Basic and Visual Basic for Applications (VBA) applications.

vertical partitioning In SQL Server replication, a method by which you can publish only certain columns of a table. This is often referred to as a vertical filter. See also *horizontal partitioning*.

view In SQL Server, an object that is usually created to exclude certain columns from a table or to link two or more tables together. A view appears very much like a table to most users.

Web browser An application that makes HTTP requests and formats the resultant HTML documents for the users.

Web page Any HTML document on an HTTP server.

Win16 The set of application services provided by the 16-bit versions of Microsoft Windows: Windows 3.1 and Windows for Workgroups 3.11.

Win32 The set of application services provided by the 32-bit versions of Microsoft Windows: Windows 95/98/Me/NT/2000.

Windows 2000 Microsoft's latest 32-bit operating system. It includes all of the services necessary to create a peer-to-peer or domain-based network. Windows 2000 uses Active Directory as its directory service. Windows 2000 Server family systems are capable of supporting thousands of users at a time and allow for such things as load balancing, clustering, terminal services, and so on.

Windows 95/98/Me The current 32-bit version of Microsoft Windows for medium-range, Intel-based personal computers; this system includes peer-networking services, Internet support, and strong support for older DOS applications and peripherals. SQL Server 2000 (Desktop version) can run on Windows 95/98/Me.

Windows Authentication mode An authentication mode in SQL Server that allows only trusted connections.

Windows for Workgroups 3.11 The current 16-bit version of Windows for less powerful, Intel-based personal computers; this system includes peer-networking services.

Windows NT A 32-bit version of Microsoft Windows for powerful Intel-based computers. The system includes peer-networking services, server-networking services, Internet client and server services, and a broad range of utilities. Windows NT Workstation is a version of Windows NT that is primarily used on desktop and laptop computers, but can act as a server for up to 10 simultaneous connections.

Windows NT Server is a version of Windows NT that is primarily used as a file/application server that can theoretically have thousands of simultaneous users connected to it. Windows NT Server Enterprise Edition is designed for large corporations and supports more powerful hardware.

SQL Server (Desktop or regular version) runs on either version of Windows NT. SQL Server Enterprise Edition requires Windows NT Enterprise Edition.

Windows System Monitor   The next iteration of Performance Monitor, this is a Windows 2000 utility that tracks statistics on individual data items, called *counters*. You can get information about the performance of SQL Server through Windows System Monitor. For example, you can monitor the log space used, the number of current connections, and memory use. See also *Performance Monitor*.

workgroup   In Microsoft networks, a collection of related computers, such as a department, that don't require the uniform security and coordination of a domain. Workgroups are characterized by decentralized management as opposed to the centralized management that domains use. See also *domain*.

World Wide Web (WWW)   A collection of Internet servers providing hypertext-formatted documents for Internet clients running Web browsers. The World Wide Web provided the first easy-to-use graphical interface for the Internet and is largely responsible for the Internet's explosive growth.

WWW   See *World Wide Web*.

XML   See *eXtensible Markup Language (XML)*.

Index

Note to the reader: Throughout this index **boldfaced** page numbers indicate primary discussions of a topic. *Italicized* page numbers indicate illustrations.

Symbols and Numbers

* operator in SELECT statement, 128–129
2PC (two-phase commit), 516

A

Access
    fully qualified name for linking to, 112
    linking to database, **118–120**
    replication to, 537
    security configuration, 125–126, 128
account delegation, 276
Action menu (Enterprise Manager), **95**
    ◄ New SQL Server Group, 90
    ◄ New SQL Server Registration, 91
    ◄ New Web Assistant Job, 492
Active Directory, 648
Active Directory Users and Computers, 480
Active Script jobs, 457
Active Server Pages, **501–502**
ActiveX Data Objects (ADO), 500, **501–502**, 648
ad hoc queries, 396–397, 648
Add Counters dialog box, 600, *600*
Add Destination Database dialog box, *320*
Administrative Tools menu, ◄ Data Sources
    (ODBC), 71
administrator tasks in SQL Server, **15–16**

Advanced Connection Properties dialog box, *405*
Advanced Data Connector, *501*
Advanced DTS Run dialog box, *425*, *426*
Advanced Server version of Windows 2000, 10
Agent History Clean Up: Distribution job, *576*
alerts, **467–477**, 648
    creation, **467–472**
        based on performance condition counter,
        471–472
        based on SQL Server error messages, 468–470
    editing, **472**
    fail-safe operator for, 488
    operator notification about, 478
    in Windows System Monitor, 598
aliases, 648
    for database tables, 112
    to Oracle database, 121
ALTER DATABASE statement, 168
    to create filegroup, **197–199**
    to expand database, 184–185
    MODIFY NAME parameter, 191
    to remove filegroup, **199–202**
    syntax, 180–181
anonymous subscribers, 559
ANSI NULL Default option for database, 177
ANSI settings, configuration, **67–69**
AppleTalk, SQL Server support, 32
application role, **264–266**, 648
archive, **625–626**, 648
articles in replication, 516, **516–517**, 648

D

E

O

S

X

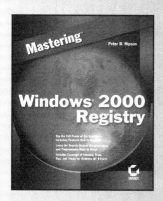

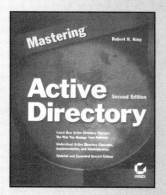
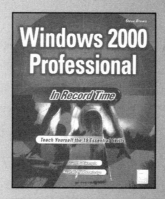

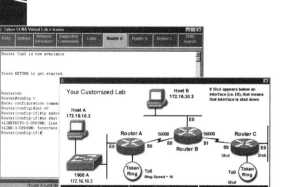

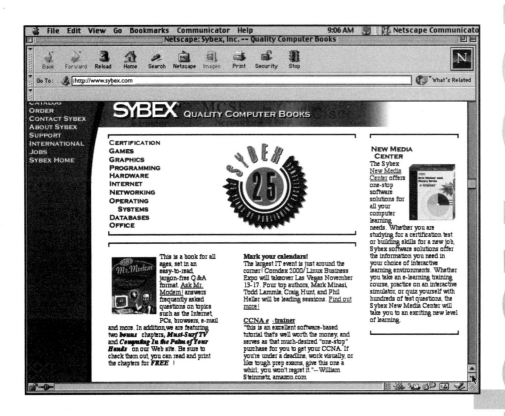

The Complete MCSE Solution

SYBEX®

Microsoft's® new exam track for the Windows 2000 MCSE requires four core and three elective exams. The core, design, and additional elective exams for the Windows 2000 MCSE are listed in the table below.

For more information, visit **www.microsoft.com/trainingandservices**.

Exam #	Exam Title	Product Title	ISBN
Required Core Exams			
70-210	Installing, Configuring, and Administering Microsoft Windows 2000 Professional	MCSE: Windows 2000 Professional Study Guide	ISBN: 0-7821-2751-7
		MCSE: Windows 2000 Professional Exam Notes	ISBN: 0-7821-2753-3
		MCSE: Windows 2000 Professional e-trainer	ISBN: 0-7821-5008-X
		MCSE: Windows 2000 Professional Virtual Test Center	ISBN: 0-7821-3000-3
70-215	Installing, Configuring, and Administering Microsoft Windows 2000 Server	MCSE: Windows 2000 Server Study Guide	ISBN: 0-7821-2752-5
		MCSE: Windows 2000 Server Exam Notes	ISBN: 0-7821-2754-1
		MCSE: Windows 2000 Server e-trainer	ISBN: 0-7821-5009-8
		MCSE: Windows 2000 Server Virtual Test Center	ISBN: 0-7821-3001-1
70-216	Implementing and Administering a Microsoft Windows 2000 Network Infrastructure	MCSE: Windows 2000 Network Infrastructure Administration Study Guide	ISBN: 0-7821-2755-X
		MCSE: Windows 2000 Network Infrastructure Administration Exam Notes	ISBN: 0-7821-2761-4
		MCSE: Windows 2000 Network Infrastructure Administration e-trainer	ISBN: 0-7821-5007-1
		MCSE: Windows 2000 Network Infrastructure Administration Virtual Test Center	ISBN: 0-7821-3002-X
70-217	Implementing and Administering a Microsoft Windows 2000 Directory Services Infrastructure	MCSE: Windows 2000 Directory Services Administration Study Guide	ISBN: 0-7821-2756-8
		MCSE: Windows 2000 Directory Services Administration Exam Notes	ISBN: 0-7821-2762-2
		MCSE: Windows 2000 Directory Services Administration e-trainer	ISBN: 0-7821-5010-1
		MCSE: Windows 2000 Directory Services Administration Virtual Test Center	ISBN: 0-7821-3003-8

(Already have your MCSE for NT 4 or taken the three core "NT" exams? If so, then you qualify to take the Accelerated Windows 2000 Exam in lieu of the four new core exams in the Windows 2000 MCSE track. The MCSE: Accelerated Windows 2000 Study Guide covers all objectives sets from the four core exams in a more consise manner on the assumption that you already have a pretty good sense of what the technology is about.)

Exam #	Exam Title	Product Title	ISBN
70-240	Microsoft Windows 2000 Accelerated Exam for MCPs Certified on Microsoft Windows NT 4.0.	MCSE: Accelerated Windows 2000 Study Guide	ISBN: 0-7821-2760-6
		MCSE: Accelerated Windows 2000 Exam Notes	ISBN: 0-7821-2770-3
Choose 1 More Core Exam			
70-219	Designing a Microsoft Windows 2000 Directory Services Infrastructure	MCSE: Windows 2000 Directory Services Design Study Guide	ISBN: 0-7821-2757-6
		MCSE: Windows 2000 Directory Services Design Exam Notes	ISBN: 0-7821-2765-7
or			
70-220	Designing Security for a Microsoft Windows 2000 Network	MCSE: Windows 2000 Network Security Design Study Guide	ISBN: 0-7821-2758-4
		MCSE: Windows 2000 Network Security Design Exam Notes	ISBN: 0-7821-2766-5
or			
70-221	Designing a Microsoft Windows 2000 Network Infrastructure	MCSE: Windows 2000 Network Infrastructure Design Study Guide	ISBN: 0-7821-2759-2
		MCSE: Windows 2000 Network Infrastructure Design Exam Notes	ISBN: 0-7821-2767-3
Choose 2 Electives			
70-222	Migrating from Microsoft Windows NT 4.0 to Microsoft Windows 2000	MCSE: Windows 2000 Migration Study Guide	ISBN: 0-7821-2768-1
		MCSE: Windows 2000 Migration Exam Notes	ISBN: 0-7821-2769-X
70-224	Installing, Configuring, and Administering Microsoft Exchange 2000 Server	MCSE: Exchange 2000 Server Administration Study Guide	ISBN: 0-7821-2898-X
		MCSE: Exchange 2000 Server Administration e-trainer	ISBN: 0-7821-5012-8
		MCSE: Exchange 2000 Server Aministration Virtual Test Center	ISBN: 0-7821-3017-8
70-225	Designing and Deploying a Messaging Infrastructure with Microsoft Exchange 2000 Server	MCSE: Exchange 2000 Design Study Guide	ISBN: 0-7821-2897-1
70-227	Installing, Configuring, and Administering Microsoft Internet Security and Acceleration (ISA) Server 2000	MCSE: ISA Server 2000 Administration Study Guide	ISBN: 0-7821-2933-1
70-228	Installing, Configuring, and Administering Microsoft SQL Server 2000 Enterprise Edition	MCSE: SQL Server 2000 Administration Study Guide	ISBN: 0-7821-2921-8
		MCSE: SQL Server 2000 Administration Virtual Test Center	ISBN: 0-7821-3016-X
70-229	Designing and Implementing Databases with Microsoft SQL Server™ 2000 Enterprise Edition	MCSE: SQL Server 2000 Design Study Guide	ISBN: 0-7821-2942-0